Master Dogen's

Shobogenzo

Gudo Nishijima was born in Yokohama, Japan in November 1919, and graduated from the Law Department of Tokyo University in September 1946.

In October 1940 he first met Master Kodo Sawaki, whose teaching he received until Master Kodo's death in December 1965. During this time, he combined the daily practice of Zazen and study of Shobogenzo with a career at the Japanese Ministry of Finance and at a securities financing company. In December 1973 he became a priest under the late Master Renpo Niwa, and in December 1977 he received the transmission of Dharma from the same Master (who subsequently became the abbot of Eihei-ji temple). Shortly thereafter he became a consultant to the Ida Ryogokudo company, and in 1987 established the Ida Ryogokudo Zazen Dojo in Ichikawa City near Tokyo. Now in his seventies, he continues to give instruction in Zazen, and lectures on Master Dogen's works, in Japanese and in English, at various locations in Tokyo and Osaka and at Tokei-in temple in Shizuoka prefecture.

Gudo Nishijima's other publications in English include "How to Practice Zazen" (with Joe Langdon) and "To Meet the Real Dragon" (with Jeffrey Bailey). He has recently published a Japanese translation of Master Nāgārjuna's Mūlamadhyamakakārikā, and is presently at work on an English translation.

Chodo Cross was born in Birmingham, England in December 1959. He went to Japan in January 1982, following graduation from Sheffield University, met Nishijima Roshi in June 1982, and received the Buddhist precepts in May of the following year. In December 1994 he returned to England in order to train to be a teacher of the F. M. Alexander Technique. He is presently a student at the Alexander Re-education Centre in Aylesbury.

R. Kusman

Master Dogen's

Shobogenzo

Book 3

Translated

by

Gudo Wafu Nishijima

Chodo Cross

Windbell
PUBLICATIONS

Windbell Publications Ltd.
London

4-505 Kamishakujii 3-19
Nerima-ku
Tokyo 177, Japan

Distributed in Europe by Wisdom Books,
402 Hoe Street, London E17 9AA
Tel: 081-520-5588. Fax: 081-520-0932

Distributed in the USA by Windbell Publications,
PO Box 578, Woods Hole, MA 02543-0578

Printed and bound by Biddles Limited,
Guildford, Surrey.

ISBN 0 9523002 3 0

Contents

Preface *ix*

Notes on the Translation *xi*

42 TSUKI 都機 *1*

43 KUGE 空華 *9*

44 KOBUSSHIN 古仏心 *23*

45 BODAISATTA-SHISHOBO 菩提薩摩埵四摂法 *29*

46 KATTO 葛藤 *35*

47 SANGAI-YUISHIN 三界唯心 *43*

48 SESSHIN-SESSHO 説心説性 *51*

49 BUTSUDO 仏道 *61*

50 SHOHO-JISSO 諸法実相 *79*

51 MITSUGO 密語 *93*

52 BUKKYO 仏経 *101*

53 MUJO-SEPPO 無情説法 *113*

54 HOSSHO 法性 *125*

55 DARANI 陀羅尼 *131*

56 SENMEN 洗面 *139*

57 MENJU 面授 *155*

58 ZAZENGI 167
坐禅儀

59 BAIKE 171
梅華

60 JUPPO 185
十方

61 KENBUTSU 191
見仏

62 HENSAN 207
偏参

63 GANZEI 215
眼睛

64 KAJO 221
家常

65 RYUGIN 227
龍吟

66 SHUNJU 233
春秋

67 SOSHI-SAIRAI-NO-I 241
祖師西来意

68 UDONGE 247
優曇華

69 HOTSU-MUJOSHIN 253
発無上心

70 HOTSU-BODAISHIN 265
発菩提心

71 NYORAI-ZENSHIN 277
如来全身

72 ZANMAI-O-ZANMAI 281
三昧王三昧

APPENDICES

Chinese Masters 287

Sanskrit Glossary 289

Bibliographies 299

Acknowledgments

This translation and its publication have been made possible by the benevolence of the following sponsors:

The Japan Foundation

Mr. Hideo Ida, President of Ida Ryogokudo Co., Ltd.

Mr. Tadashi Nakamae,
President of Nakamae International Economic Research

We should like to thank Michael Luetchford and Jeremy Pearson for their efforts in publishing this book. Our thanks also go to Yoko Luetchford for her work on checking the kanji, and to Emma Gibson for her invaluable help with proofreading.

Preface

Shobogenzo was written by Master Dogen in the thirteenth century. I think that reading Shobogenzo is the best way to come to an exact understanding of Buddhist theory, because Master Dogen was outstanding in his ability to understand and explain Buddhism rationally.

Of course, Master Dogen did not depart from traditional Buddhist thought. But at the same time, his thought as expressed in Shobogenzo follows his own unique method of presentation. If we understand what this method is, Shobogenzo is not so difficult to read. But unless we understand his method of thinking, it is completely impossible for us to understand what Master Dogen is trying to say in Shobogenzo.

Buddhists revere Buddha, Dharma and Samgha. Buddha means Gautama Buddha. Samgha means those people who pursue Gautama Buddha's truth. Dharma means reality. Master Dogen's unique method of thought is his way to explain what Dharma is.

Basically, he looks at a problem from two sides, and then tries to synthesize the two viewpoints into a middle way. This method has similarities with dialectic method in western philosophy, particularly as used by Hegel and Marx.

Hegel's dialectic, however, is based on belief in spirit, and Marx's dialectic is based on belief in matter. Master Dogen, through the Buddhist dialectic, wants to lead us away from thoughts based on belief in spirit and matter.

Master Dogen recognized the existence of something which is different from thought; that is, reality in action. Action is completely different from intellectual thought and completely different from the perceptions of our senses. So Master Dogen's method of thinking is based on action, and because of that, it has some unique characteristics.

First, Master Dogen recognized that things we usually separate in our minds are, in action, one reality. To express this oneness of subject and object Master Dogen says, for example, *"If a human being, even for a single moment, manifests the Buddha's posture in the three forms of conduct, while [that person] sits up straight in samādhi, the entire world of Dharma assumes the Buddha's posture and the whole of space becomes the state of realization."* This sentence, taken from the chapter *Bendowa*, is not illogical, but it reflects a new kind of logic.

Secondly, Master Dogen recognized that in action, the only time that really exists is the moment of the present, and the only place that really exists is this place. So the present moment and this place—the here and now—are very important concepts in Master Dogen's philosophy of action.

The philosophy of action is not unique to Master Dogen; this idea was also the center of Gautama Buddha's thought. All the Buddhist patriarchs of ancient India and China relied upon this theory and realized Buddhism itself. They also recognized the oneness of reality, the importance of the present moment, and the importance of this place.

But explanations of reality are only explanations. In Shobogenzo, after he had explained a problem on the basis of action, Master Dogen wanted to point the reader into the realm of action itself. To do this, he sometimes used poems, he sometimes used old Buddhist stories that suggest reality, and he sometimes used symbolic expressions.

So the chapters of Shobogenzo usually follow a four-phased pattern. First Master Dogen picks up and outlines a Buddhist idea. In the second phase, he examines the idea very objectively or concretely, in order to defeat idealistic or intellectual interpretations of it. In the third phase, Master Dogen's expression becomes even more concrete, practical and realistic, relying on the philosophy of action. And in the fourth phase, Master Dogen tries to suggest reality with words. Ultimately, these trials are only trials. But we can feel something that can be called reality in his sincere trials, when we reach the end of each chapter.

I think this four-phased pattern is related with the *Four Noble Truths* preached by Gautama Buddha in his first lecture. By realizing Master Dogen's method of thinking, we can come to realize the true meaning of Gautama Buddha's *Four Noble Truths.* This is why we persevere in studying Shobogenzo.

Gudo Wafu Nishijima

Ida Zazen Dojo
Tokyo
February 1994

Notes on the Translation

Aim

In this book, as in Books 1 and 2, the primary aim of the translation has been to stay faithful to the original Japanese text and let Master Dogen speak for himself, confining interpretation and explanation as far as possible to the footnotes.

Source text

The source text for chapters 42 to 72 is contained in volumes 7 to 9 of Nishijima Roshi's 12-volume *Gendaigo-yaku-shobogenzo (Shobogenzo in Modern Japanese). Gendaigo-yaku-shobogenzo* contains Master Dogen's original text, notes on the text, and the text rendered into modern Japanese. Reference numbers enclosed in brackets in the left margin of this translation refer to corresponding page numbers in *Gendaigo-yaku-shobogenzo,* and much of the material reproduced in the footnotes comes from *Gendaigo-yaku-shobogenzo.*

Gendaigo-yaku-shobogenzo is based upon the 95-chapter edition of Shobogenzo, which was arranged in chronological order by Master Hangyo Kozen, sometime between 1688 and 1703. The 95-chapter edition is the most comprehensive single edition, including important chapters such as *Bendowa* and *Hokke-ten-hokke* which do not appear in other editions. Furthermore, it was the first edition to be printed with woodblocks, in the Bunka era (1804–1818), and so the content was fixed at that time. The original woodblocks are still preserved at Eihei-ji, the temple in Fukui prefecture which Master Dogen founded.

Sanskrit terms

As a rule, Sanskrit words such as *samādhi* (the balanced state), *prajñā* (real wisdom), and *bhikṣu* (monk), which Master Dogen reproduces phonetically with Chinese characters, 三昧 (ZANMAI), 般若 (HANNYA), and 比丘 (BIKU), have been retained in Sanskrit form.

In addition, some Chinese characters representing the meaning of Sanskrit terms which will already be familiar to readers (or which will become familiar in the course of reading Shobogenzo) have been returned to Sanskrit. Examples are 法 (HO; "reality," "law," "method," "things and phenomena"), usually translated as "Dharma" or "dharmas"; 如来 (NYORAI; "Thus-Come"), always translated as *"Tathāgata"*; and 声聞 (SHOMON; "voice-hearer"), usually translated as *"śrāvaka."*

The glossary provided in the appendix contains all Sanskrit terms appearing in this book not included in the Sanskrit glossary in Books 1 and 2.

Chinese proper nouns

In general Chinese proper nouns have been romanized according to their Japanese pronunciation—as Master Dogen would have pronounced them for a Japanese audience. Thus, we have let the romanization of all names of Chinese masters follow the Japanese pronunciation, while also adding an appendix showing the Chinese romanization of Chinese masters' names.

Chinese text

Master Dogen wrote Shobogenzo in Japanese, that is to say, using a combination of Chinese characters (squared ideograms usually consisting of many strokes) and the Japanese phonetic alphabet which is more abbreviated. Chinese of course is written in Chinese characters only. Therefore when Master Dogen quotes a passage, or borrows a phrase, from a Chinese text—as he very often does—it is readily apparent to the eye as a string of Chinese ideograms uninterrupted by Japanese squiggles. We have attempted to mirror this effect, to some degree, by using italics for such passages and phrases.

Meaning of 正法眼蔵 (SHOBOGENZO), "The Right-Dharma-Eye Treasury"

正 (SHO) means "right" or "true."

法 (HO), "Law," represents the Sanskrit *"Dharma,"* which means reality.

眼 (GEN) "eye," represents direct experience.

正法眼 (SHOBOGEN), "the right-Dharma-eye," therefore describes the right or true experience of reality.

蔵 (ZO), "storehouse" or "treasury," suggests something that contains and preserves the right experience of reality. Thus, Nishijima Roshi has interpreted the words 正法眼蔵 (SHOBOGENZO), "the right-Dharma-eye treasury," as an expression of the practice of just sitting in Zazen.

Nishijima Roshi's right-Dharma-eye is, for me, evidenced nowhere more clearly than in his introduction to one of the chapters of this book, chapter 50, Shoho-jisso. Any virtue that this translation has stems entirely from the profoundly philosophical mind, the imperturbable balance, and the irrepressible optimism and energy of Nishijima Roshi.

Chodo Cross
5, Chiltern Close,
Aylesbury, England
February 1997

Shobogenzo

Chapters 42 to 72

開経偈

無上甚深微妙法

百千萬劫難遭遇

我今見聞得受持

願解如来真実義

KAIKYOGE

MUJO-JINSHIN-MIMYO-HO

HYAKU-SEN-MAN-GO-NAN-SOGU

GA-KON-KENMON-TOKU-JUJI

GAN-GE-NYORAI-SHINJITSU-GI

Verse for Opening the Sutras

The supreme, profound, subtle and fine Dharma,

In hundred thousand myriad kalpas is hard to meet.

Now that I see and hear it and am able to receive and retain it,

I desire to understand the real meaning of the Tathāgata's teaching.

[42]

都機 [1]

TSUKI

The Moon

***Tsuki** means "the moon"; in this chapter Master Dogen uses the moon as a symbol to explain the relationship between an abstract concept and a concrete entity. The moon existed yesterday, it exists today, and it will exist tomorrow. We can say that at one moment in time the moon is a unique and independent entity. At the same time, there is the abstract concept "the moon." The concept "the moon" is an abstraction of the concrete moon which exists at one moment; that is the moon yesterday, the moon today, the moon tomorrow. Although the unique, concrete moon is the origin of the abstract concept "the moon," we are prone to discuss philosophical problems only in terms of abstract concepts, forgetting concrete facts, and creating a division between thinking and perception. Buddhist philosophy synthesizes the two factors, and here Master Dogen explains the mutual relationship between thinking and sensory perception comparing the abstract concept "the moon," with the concrete moon. Secondly, Master Dogen uses the relationship between moon and cloud to explain the relationship between subject and object. Buddhist theory says that reality is oneness between subject and object here and now. Master Dogen explains this using the example of the moon and a cloud that surrounds the moon.*

[3] **The round realization of moons** is not only three and three before and not only three and three after.[2] The state in which moons are round realiza-

---

1. All chapters of Shobogenzo have at least two Chinese characters in the title. Thus, in the chapter title, for the sake of conformity, Master Dogen represents the Japanese word *tsuki*, "moon," phonetically with two Chinese characters 都 (TSU) and 機 (KI). In the chapter itself, Master Dogen uses the usual character for moon; 月 (GETSU, *tsuki).*

2. 前三三、後三三 (ZEN SANSAN, GO SANSAN), "three and three before, three and three after," suggests random concrete facts as opposed to general abstractions. See, for example, *Shinji-shobogenzo*, pt. 2, no. 27: *Monju asks Mujaku: Where have you come from? Mujaku says: The south. Monju says: How is the Buddha-Dharma of the south dwelt in and maintained? Mujaku says: Few bhikṣus in the age of the latter Dharma observe the precepts. Monju says: How big are the saṃgha? Mujaku says: In some cases three hundred, in some cases five hundred. Mujaku asks Monju: How is the Buddha-Dharma here dwelt in and maintained? Monju says: The common and the sacred live together, and dragons and snakes mix in confusion. Mujaku says: How big are the saṃgha? Monju says: Three and three before, three and three after.*

tion is not only three and three before and not only three and three after.[3] Therefore...

Śākyamuni Buddha says,

> *The Buddha's true Dharma-body*[4]
> *Is just like space.*
> *Manifesting its form according to things,*
> *It is like the moon in water.*[5,6]

The *reality as it is*[7] in this *"is like the moon in water"* may be the [oneness of] *water-and-moon*, or it may be *the water's reality*,[8] or *the moon's reality*,[9] or *being in reality*,[10] or *the reality of being in*.[11] *"Being like"* does not express resemblance; being like is concrete existence.[12] *The Buddha's true Dharma-body"* is *the reality itself*[13] of *space*. This *space* is the *Buddha's true Dharma-body* of *reality itself*. Because [space] is the Buddha's true Dharma-body, the whole earth, the whole world, the whole Dharma, and the whole of *manifestation*, are themselves naturally space. The *reality itself* of the manifest hundred things and myriad phenomena is totally the true Dharma-body of Buddha, and it *is like the moon in water*. The time of the moon is not always night, and night is not always dark. Do not limit yourself to narrow human consideration. There may be day and night even where there is no sun or moon. The sun and the moon are not for day and night. The sun and the moon each are reality as it is, there-

---

3. The opening sentences suggest the oneness of realization and moons, denying that the scientific or materialist viewpoint of the moon is the only viewpoint.

4. 法身 (HOSSHIN) represents the Sanskrit *dharmakāya*.

5. 如水中月 (NYO-SUI-CHU-GETSU, or *suichu no tsuki no gotoshi*). On the surface 如 (NYO, *gotoshi*) means "like," and 中 (CHU) means "in," but in his commentary Master Dogen explores the meaning of these two characters more deeply.

6. *Kon-komyo-kyo (Golden Light Sutra)* vol. 24. The verse is also quoted in *Shinji-shobogenzo*, pt. 2, no. 25 and in Shobogenzo, chap. 10, *Shoaku-makusa*.

7. 如如 (NYO-NYO). 如 (NYO) means "like." At the same time, as a suffix, 如 (NYO) affirms the thing itself or the thing as it is. Further, the character sometimes represents the state of reality as it is, as in the word 如来 (NYORAI), "the thus-come," or "the one who has arrived at reality" (from the Sanskrit *Tathāgata*). Therefore 如如 (NYO-NYO) means reality itself or reality affirmed as it is.

8. 水如 (SUINYO).

9. 月如 (GETSUNYO).

10. 如中 (NYOCHU).

11. 中如 (CHUNYO). 中 (CHU) as a preposition means "in" and as a noun means "the middle" or "the center." Master Dogen often uses the character 中 (CHU) to represent the concrete state of being in reality. For other examples of this usage see notes to chap. 14, *Sansui-gyo*, chap. 22, *Bussho*, and chap. 38, *Muchu-setsumu*.

12. 如は是なり (NYO *wa* ZE *nari*). The various meanings of 是 (ZE) are discussed at length in chap. 6, *Soku-shin-ze-butsu*.

13. The characters 猶若 are read in the poem as *nao...gotoshi*, "just like," or "indeed similar to." In Master Dogen's commentary the characters 猶若 (read as YU-NYAKU), mean "reality itself."

fore [the moon] is not one moon or two moons and not a thousand moons or ten thousand moons. Even if the moon maintains and relies upon a view of itself as one moon or two moons, that is the view of the moon, but it is not necessarily an expression of the Buddha's truth or the wisdom of the Buddha's truth. So although the moon was there last night, tonight's moon is not yesterday's moon. We should master in practice that the moon tonight, at the beginning, middle, and end, is the moon tonight. Because the moon succeeds the moon, the moon exists and yet is not new or old.[14]

[6] Zen Master Banzan Hoshaku says:[15]

Mind-moon, alone and round.
Light swallows myriad phenomena.
Light does not illuminate objects,
Neither do objects exist.
Light and objects both vanish,
This is what?

What has now been expressed is that the Buddhist patriarchs and the Buddha's disciples always have the state of *mind-moon*. Because we see the moon as the mind, it is not the mind unless it is the moon, and there is no moon which is not the mind. *Alone and round* means lacking nothing. That which is beyond two and three is called *myriad phenomena. Myriad phenomena,* being moonlight itself, are beyond "myriad phenomena"; therefore *light swallows myriad phenomena*. Myriad phenomena have naturally swallowed moonlight, and so he expresses light swallowing light as *"light swallows myriad phenomena."* It may be, for another example, that the moon swallows the moon, or that light swallows the moon. This being so, he says, *"Light does not illuminate objects, Neither do objects exist."* Because [buddhas][16] have got the state like this, when *people must be saved through the body of a buddha, they manifest at once the body of a buddha and preach for them the Dharma*.[17] When people must be saved through a common[18] physical body, they manifest at once a common physical body and preach for them the Dharma. There is no such instance which is not the turning of the Dharma-wheel in the moon. Even though the illumina-

14. Because the moon is as it is at every moment, even though the moon exists as an ongoing entity, it is never new or old.

15. *Keitoku-dento-roku*, chap. 7.

16. The subject may be understood as 仏祖仏子 (BUSSO BUSSHI), "the Buddhist patriarchs and the Buddha's disciples," from the opening sentence of the commentary.

17. Alludes to the 25th chapter of the Lotus Sutra, *"The Universal Gate of the Bodhisattva Regarder of the Sounds of the World."* See LS 3.252.

18. "Common" is 普現 (FUGEN), lit. "universally manifest." Universally manifest physical bodies means bodies which can be seen everywhere, such as those listed in the Lotus Sutra—bodies of generals, kings, monks and lay people, boys and girls, gods, dragons, et cetera.

tion of phenomena by yin-energy and by yang-energy[19] is produced by the fire-pearl and the water-pearl,[20] at the same time it is just the direct manifestation of reality. This mind is the moon itself, and this moon is naturally the mind. The Buddhist patriarchs and the Buddha's disciples master the principles of the mind and master the facts of the mind like this.

[8] An eternal Buddha says, *"One mind is the whole Dharma, and the whole Dharma is one mind."*[21] So the mind is the whole Dharma, and the whole Dharma is the mind. And, because the mind is the moon, it may be that the moon is the moon. Because the whole Dharma as the mind is totally the moon, the whole world is the whole moon, and the *thoroughly realized body*[22] is in its entirety the thoroughly realized moon. Even among the *three and three before and after*—which belong directly to eternity—is any not the moon? The sun-faced buddhas and moon-faced buddhas which are the present body-mind or object-subject may all be *in the moon*. Living-and-dying, coming-and-going, are both *in the moon*. The whole Universe in ten directions may be the top, bottom, left, and right of *in the moon*.[23] Daily functions[24] now are the hundred things being utterly clear *in the moon*, and are the mind of the ancestral masters being utterly clear *in the moon*.[25]

[10] Great Master Jisai[26] of Tosu-zan mountain in Joshu district, the story goes, is asked by a monk, *"How is the moon when not yet round?"*

The Master says, *"Swallowing three or four [concrete moons]."*

---

19. 陰精陽精 (ONSHO YOSHO), "*yin*-energy and *yang*-energy." In general, *yin* is associated with the moon, and *yang* is associated with the sun.

20. Chap. 7 of *Daichido-ron* (the Chinese translation of the Mahā-prajñā-pāramitopadeśa) says: *"There are two kinds of brightness: The first is fire-energy. The second is water-energy. The pearl of the sun is fire-energy and the pearl of the moon is water-energy."* The fire-pearl thus suggests the sun, and the water-pearl suggests the moon.

21. The quotation can be found, for example, in *Maka-shikan*, a text which Master Dogen would have studied from the age of twelve when he began monastic life on Mt. Hiei, the head temple of the Tendai Sect in Japan. *Maka-shikan* (摩訶止観) which means "The Great [Practice of] Stopping and Reflecting" is a twenty-fascicle record of the lectures of Master Tendai Chigi (538–597), who is generally regarded as the founder of the Tendai Sect in China.

22. 通身 (TSUSHIN). See chap. 33, *Kannon*.

23. 月中 (GETSUCHU), "in the moon," means "in the presence of the moon" and at the same time "the reality of the moon." See note 11.

24. 日用 (NICHIYO). 日 (NICHI) means both "daily" and "the sun."

25. Alludes to the saying 明明百艸頭、明明仏祖 (MEI-MEI *[taru]* HYAKU-SO-TO, MEIMEI *[taru]* BUSSO *[no]* I). *"Clear, clear are the hundred things; clear, clear is the will of the Buddhist patriarchs."* The saying is attributed to the Happy Buddha, *Hotei*. See *Shinji-shobogenzo*, pt. 1, no. 8; also Shobogenzo, chap. 22, *Bussho*, chap. 23, *Gyobutsu-yuigi*, chap. 36, *Komyo*, et cetera.

26. Master Tosu Daido (819–914), successor of Master Suibi Mugaku (a third-generation descendant of Master Seigen Gyoshi). Before becoming the disciple of Master Suibi, he was a student of the Garland Sutra. In his later years, Master Tosu returned to Tosu-zan mountain in his home district and built a hut there where he lived for 30 years, receiving many visitors.

The monk says, *"And after it has been round?"*

The Master says, *"Vomiting seven or eight."*[27]

The states under investigation now are *not yet being round* and *having been round.* Both are moments of the moon. Among three or four [concrete moons] in the moon, there is one [conceptual moon] which is not yet round.[28] Among seven or eight [concrete moons] in the moon, there is one [conceptual moon] which has been round. Swallowing is [a concrete matter of] three or four; this moment is the realization of *the time when the moon is not yet round.* Vomiting is [a concrete matter of] seven or eight; this moment is the realization of *having been round.* When the moon swallows the moon,[29] it is [a concrete matter of] three or four. In the act of swallowing, the moon exists and is realized. The moon is the realization of swallowing. When the moon vomits the moon, it is [a concrete matter of] seven or eight. In the act of vomiting, the moon exists and is realized. The moon is the realization of vomiting. Therefore it is swallowing wholly and it is vomiting wholly. The whole earth and the whole heavens are the act of vomiting, and the entire heavens and the entire earth are the act of swallowing. We should swallow the self and should swallow the external world. We should vomit the self and should vomit the external world.

[12] *Śākyamuni Buddha addresses Bodhisattva Diamond-Treasury:*[30] *"Just as, for example, moving eyes are able to stir calm waters and still eyes make fire seem to swirl, so too it is that [when] a cloud flies the moon moves and [when] a boat sails the shore drifts."*[31]

We must clarify and master in practice the present preaching of the Buddha that *[when] a cloud flies the moon moves and [when] a boat sails the shore drifts.* We must not understand it hastily and must not compare it with the sentiments of the common man. Still, those who see and hear this preaching of the Buddha in accordance with the preaching of the Buddha are few. When we are able to learn in accordance with the preaching of the Buddha, round realization[32] is not always "the body-mind" and not always "bodhi" or

27. *Rento-eyo,* chap. 21, and *Hekigan-roku,* no. 79.

28. "Three or four [concrete moons]" is 三個四個 (SANKO SHIKO). "One [conceptual moon]" is 一枚 (ICHIMAI). Chinese and Japanese use different counters for different objects. The counter 個 (KO) is used for small inanimate objects like potatoes or pebbles. The counter 枚 (MAI) is for thin flat objects such as sheets of paper, photos and paintings. In the story the counter 個 (KO) is used. Master Dogen uses both counters in his commentary; 個 for concrete moons, and 枚 for the moon as an abstract concept or picture.

29. When the moon realizes itself in action.

30. Called *Vajragarbha* in Sanskrit.

31. *Dai-hoko-engaku-shutara-ryogi-kyo (The Mahāvaipulya Round Realization Sutra).*

32. 円覚 (ENGAKU), "round realization," suggests the concrete experience of wholeness in Zazen.

"nirvāṇa." Bodhi, and nirvāṇa, are not always "round realization" and not always "the body-mind." The words now spoken by the Tathāgata that *"[when] a cloud flies the moon moves and [when] a boat sails the shore drifts"* mean that at the time of the cloud's flying the moon is moving, and at the time of the boat's sailing the shore is drifting. The point is that the moving together of the cloud and the moon, in the same step, at the same time, in the same Way, is beyond beginning and end and is beyond before and after. The moving together of the boat and the shore, in the same step, at the same time, in the same Way, is beyond starting and stopping and is not a cycle. Similarly, when we learn human action, a person's action is beyond starting and stopping, and the action of stopping and starting is beyond the person. Do not think of human action in the relative terms of starting and stopping. The flying of a cloud, the moving of the moon, the sailing of a boat, and the drifting of a shore, are all like this. Do not stupidly think limited thoughts according to the small view. Do not forget the principle that the flying of a cloud is beyond east, west, north, and south, and the moving of the moon is ceaseless day and night, past and present. The sailing of a boat and the drifting of a shore, both being beyond the three times, are able to utilize the three times. For this reason, *"Having arrived directly at the present, we are full up and not hungry."*[33]

[15] Still, stupid people have understood that the unmoving moon appears to move because of the flying of a cloud, and that the motionless shore seems to drift because of the sailing of a boat. If it were as stupid people say, how could it be the teaching of the Tathāgata? The fundamental principle of the Buddha-Dharma is never the small thoughts of human beings and gods: although it is unthinkable, it is that there is only practice at every opportunity. Who could fail to sift through the boat and the shore over and over again? Who could fail to put on their eyes at once and look at the cloud and the moon?

[16] Remember, the teaching of the Tathāgata does not liken a cloud to something else, does not liken the moon to something else, does not liken a boat to something else, and does not liken a shore to something else. We should consider this truth quietly and master it in practice. A step of the moon is the round realization of the Tathāgata, and the round realization of the Tathāgata is the action of the moon, which is beyond movement and stillness and beyond progress and retreat. Because the moon's moving is never a metaphor, its essence and form are *alone and round*. Remember, the gait of the moon—even if it is a gallop—is beyond beginning, middle, and end. For this

---

33. Master Reiun Shigon said, *"Having arrived directly at the present, I have no further doubts."* See chap. 9, *Keisei-sanshiki*.

reason, the first moon and the second moon exist.[34] The first and the second are both the moon itself. What is *truly lovely for practice* is the moon; what is *truly lovely for serving offerings* is the moon; and what *swings the sleeves and goes at once* is the moon.[35] Its roundness and sharpness are beyond waxing and waning. Using and not using the cycle of waxing and waning, letting go and holding back, it gives free play to the elegant ways,[36] and so it exists like this in many moons.

Shobogenzo Tsuki

Written at Kannon-dori-kosho-horin-ji temple on the 6th day of the 1st lunar month in [the 4th year of] Ninji.[37]

Śramaṇa Dogen

34. 第一月、第二月 (DAI-ICHI-GETSU, DAI-NI-GETSU), lit. "moon number one and moon number two," or "the primary moon and the secondary moon," means the first month and the second month, or the moon and its reflection, or concentrated mind and divided mind. The words 第二月 (DAI-NI-GETSU) appear in *Shinji-shobogenzo*, pt. 1, no. 83.

35. One night Seido, Hyakujo, and Nansen happen to be enjoying the moon. The Master [Baso] asks, *"How is it just at this moment?"* Seido says, *"It is truly lovely for serving offerings."* Hyakujo says, *"It is truly lovely for practice."* Nansen swings his sleeves and goes [to the Zazen Hall] at once (*Go-to-egen*, chap. 3).

36. Alludes to the words of Master Tendo Nyojo quoted in chap. 38, *Muchu-setsumu*, para. [175]: *"Dreams going awry and dreams coming true, / Holding back and letting go, / We give free play to the elegant ways."*

37. 1243. The year is identified, using the Chinese dating system, by the characters 癸卯 (KIBO). 癸 is the tenth calendar sign (the younger brother of water) and 卯 is the fourth horary sign (the rabbit). These signs identify the year as 1243, which, in the Japanese system, was both the 4th and final year of the Ninji era and the 1st year of the Kangen era. See also chap. 16, *Shisho*, note 74.

[43]

空華

KUGE

Flowers in Space

***Ku** means "the sky," or "space," and **ge** means "flowers." What are flowers in space? Master Dogen uses the words "flowers in space" to express all phenomena in this world. According to the ideas of the German philosopher Immanuel Kant, we cannot be sure whether things really exist in this world, but we can be sure that there are phenomena which we can perceive with our senses. Therefore, for him, phenomena are not necessarily identified with reality although they do actually appear in this world. He refused to discuss the metaphysical problem of "real existence" and based his philosophy on human reason. The same idea was present in ancient Buddhism. Master Dogen thought that this skeptical attitude was important in considering the meaning of our life, and so in this chapter he explains the meaning of "flowers in space," which in Buddhism expresses real phenomena.*

19] **The founding Patriarch says:**

> *A flower is five petals opening,*
> *Effects naturally are realized.*[1]

We should learn in practice this moment of a flower opening, and its brightness, color, and form. The composition of a flower is five petals, and the opening of five petals is a flower. Penetration of the truth of a flower is *"I originally came to this land, to transmit the Dharma and to save deluded emotional beings."*[2] The state that is visited by brightness and by color may be present in this learning in practice. *"I entrust effects to effects themselves"*: this expresses *natural realization.*[3] *"Natural realization"* means enacting causes and accepting effects. The world has causes, and the world has effects. We enact the cause-and-effect that is this world, and we accept the cause-and-effect that is the

---

1. 一華開五葉、結果自然成 (IKKE-KAI-GO-YO, KEKKA-JINEN-JO) are the third and fourth lines of a four line poem by Master Bodhidharma, quoted in *Keitoku-dento-roku,* chap. 3. 結果 (KEKKA) can be translated as 1) "effects," and 2) "the bearing of fruit." The fourth line can be read, "The bearing of fruit is naturally realized."

2. 吾本来此土、伝法救迷情 (*Ware moto shido ni kitari, Ho o tsutaemeijo o sukuu).* The first and second lines of Master Bodhidharma's poem.

3. 自然成 (JINEN-JO). As a compound, 自然 (JINEN) means "naturally," but in his commentary Master Dogen considers the meaning of the characters 自 (JI) and 然 (NEN) separately.

world. *The [natural] self*[4] is *itself*,[5] and the self is inevitably just you, in other words, the four elements and five aggregates. Because we are *utilizing a true human being without rank*,[6] the state is not I and not anyone else, and so we call what is indefinite *"the self."*[7] *"The state of being [natural]"*[8] means *agreement*.[9] *"Natural realization"* is the very moment of opening flowers and bearing fruit,[10] and the very moment of transmitting the Dharma and saving the deluded. For example, the time and place that blue lotus[11] flowers open and spread are in the midst of fire and in the time of fire.[12] And all sparks and flames exist at the place and at the time that blue lotus flowers open and spread. Beyond the time and the place of blue lotus flowers, not a single spark is born, and not a single spark has vivid life. Remember, in a single spark there are hundreds and thousands of clusters of blue lotus flowers, and they open and spread in space, they open and spread on the ground, they open and spread in the past, and they open and spread in the present. To experience the actual time and the actual place of fire is to experience blue lotus flowers. We should not pass by the time and the place of blue lotus flowers, but should experience them.

[22] An ancestor says:

> *Blue lotus flowers open inside fire.*[13]

So *blue lotus flowers* inevitably open and spread *inside fire*.[14] If we want to know *the inside of fire*, it is the place where blue lotus flowers open and spread.

---

4. 自 (JI). As a noun, 自 (JI), means "self." As an adverb it means "by itself," "spontaneously," or "naturally."

5. 己 (KO) means self, and in normal usage it only appears in compounds—most commonly the compound 自己 (JIKO), "self." Here however, Master Dogen uses the character independently. He says 自は己なり (JI *wa* KO *nari*), lit. "self is itself."

6. 使得無位真人 (SHITOKU MU-I SHINJIN), words of Master Rinzai. See *Shinji-shobogenzo*, pt. 2, no. 47.

7. 自 (JI). See note 4.

8. 然 (NEN) means "as is," "being so," or "in such and such a state." Used as a suffix, 然 (NEN) makes 自 (JI), "self," into an adjective, "natural," or into an adverb, "naturally." 然 (NEN) cannot ordinarily be used as a noun, but here Master Dogen uses it as a noun —"the state of being so."

9. 聴許 (CHOKO), "permission," "approval," or "agreement," here suggests acceptance of things as they are.

10. 結果 (KEKKA), translated in Master Bodhidharma's poem as "effects." See note 1.

11. 優鉢羅 (UBARA) is a transliteration of the Sanskrit *utpala*, which means the blossom of the blue lotus. See Book 1, Glossary.

12. Blue lotus flowers, which bloom on pools in hot weather during the summer, are a symbol of coolness. Fire symbolizes heat.

13. This is the second line of an eight-line verse by Master Do-an Josatsu (dates unknown), successor of Master Kyuho Dogen. The verse is quoted in *Keitoku-dento-roku*, chap. 29.

14. 火裏 (KARI). 裏 (RI) means 1) the back side of something, 2) the inside of something, and, by extension, the concrete place of something—as in 這裏 (SHARI), "this concrete place."

We should not, out of attachment to human views and views of gods, neglect to research *the inside of fire*. If we are to doubt, we might doubt that lotus flowers have grown in water, or we might doubt that other flowers are present on branches and twigs. Again, if we are to doubt, we might doubt that the objective world[15] is stably established, but this we do not doubt. None other than Buddhist patriarchs knows that *the opening of flowers is the occurrence of the world.*[16] *Flowers opening* are *three and three before, and three and three after.*[17] In order to make up these numbers, they have accumulated material particles and exalted them. Letting this truth come to us, we should consider spring and autumn: Not only in spring and in autumn do flowers and fruit exist; existence-time always has flowers and fruit. Every flower and fruit has maintained and relied upon a moment of time, and every moment of time has maintained and relied upon flowers and fruit. For this reason, all miscellaneous things have flowers and fruit: trees all have flowers and fruit; trees of gold, silver, copper, iron, coral, crystal, and so forth, all have flowers and fruit; and trees of earth, wind, fire, water, and space, all have flowers and fruit. Flowers are present in human trees, flowers are present in human flowers, and flowers are present in withered trees. In such circumstances there are the flowers in space[18] of which the World-honored One speaks. Yet people of small knowledge and small experience do not know of the colors, brightness, petals, and flowers of flowers in space, and they can scarcely even hear the words "flowers in space." Remember, in Buddhism there is talk of flowers in space. In non-Buddhism they do not even know, much less understand, talk of flowers in space. Only the buddhas and the patriarchs know the blooming and falling of flowers in space and flowers on the ground, only they know the blooming and falling of flowers in the world, and so on; only they know that flowers in space, flowers on the ground, flowers in the world, and so on, are sutras. This is the standard for learning the state of buddha. Because flowers in space are the vehicle upon which Buddhist patriarchs ride, the Buddhist world and all the buddhas' teachings are just flowers in space.

[26] Nevertheless, when the common and the stupid hear the Tathāgata's words that *"What is seen by clouded eyes is flowers in space,"* they imagine that *"clouded eyes"* means the upset eyes of ordinary beings. They imagine that sick

15. 器世間 (KISEKEN), lit. "vessel world." Traditionally, 器世間 (KISEKEN) is opposed to 有情世間 (UJO-SEKEN), "the world of the sentient."

16. These are the words of Master Prajñātara, Master Bodhidharma's master.

17. 前三三、後三三 (ZENSANSAN, GOSANSAN) suggests random concrete facts as opposed to neat general abstractions. See notes to the opening paragraph of chap. 42, *Tsuki*.

18. 虚空華 (KOKUGE). 虚空 (KOKU) suggests concrete three-dimensional space (see chap. 77, *Koku*). By using this expression at this point, Master Dogen indicates that the expression 空華 (KUGE), which appears henceforward, means flowers (that is, real phenomena) in concrete space.

eyes, because they are upset, perceive *flowers in space* in a pure void. Because [stupid people] attach to this theory, they have concluded that the triple world, the six states, the existence of the Buddha-nature, and the non-existence of the Buddha-nature all do not exist, but are deludedly seen to exist. They excitedly consider that if we could stop this deluded cloudedness of the eyes, we would not see this floweriness in space, and this is why we say that *space is originally without flowers*. It is pitiful that people like this do not know the time of, or the beginning and end of, the flowers in space of which the Tathāgata speaks. The truth that buddhas speak of clouded eyes and flowers in space is never seen by the common man and non-Buddhists. By practicing this flower of space,[19] the buddha-tathāgatas receive the robes, the seat [of preaching], and the [master's] room, and they attain the truth and get the effect. Picking up a flower and winking an eye are all the Universe, which is realized by clouded eyes and flowers in space. The right-Dharma-eye treasury and the fine mind of nirvāṇa, which have been authentically transmitted to the present without interruption, are called clouded eyes and flowers in space. Bodhi, nirvāṇa, the Dharma-body, selfhood, and so on, are two or three petals of five petals opened by a flower in space.

[29] Śākyamuni Buddha says,

> *It is like a person who has clouded eyes*
> *Seeing flowers in space;*
> *If the sickness of clouded eyes is cured,*
> *Flowers vanish in space.*[20]

No scholars have clearly understood this statement. Because they do not know space,[21] they do not know flowers in space. Because they do not know flowers in space, they do not know a person who has clouded eyes, do not see a person who has clouded eyes, do not meet a person who has clouded eyes, and do not become a person who has clouded eyes. Through meeting a person who has clouded eyes, we should know flowers in space and should see flowers in space. When we have seen flowers in space we can also see *flowers vanish in space*. The idea that once flowers in space vanish they can never reappear is the view and opinion of the small vehicle. At a time when

---

19. 空華 (KUGE). In general 空華 (KUGE) suggests images, or phenomena, and has been translated as plural. In this case it is preceded by 此 *(kono)*, "this," and so it is singular. "The flower of space," or "the flower of the state of śūnyatā," suggests the system of Buddhist philosophy.

20. *Shuryogon-kyo (Śūraṃgama-sūtra)* vol. 4.

21. 空 (KU). As a noun, 空 (KU, *sora*) means "the sky" or "space." As an adjective it means "bare," "empty" *(kara)*, or "void," "meaningless" *(muna[shii])*. At the same time, in Buddhist sutras, 空 (KU) sometimes means "the immaterial," as opposed to matter, and it sometimes represents the Sanskrit *śūnyatā*, "emptiness"; that is, the state of detachment in which things are seen as they are—see Book 1, Glossary. See also chap. 2, *Maka-hannya-haramitsu* and chap. 22, *Bussho*.

flowers in space could not be seen, what could exist? Only knowing that flowers in space can become an object to get rid of, [scholars] do not know the great matter that follows from flowers in space, and do not know the seeding, maturation, and falling free of flowers in space. Among scholars today who are common men, most think that the place where yang-energy resides may be space, or that the place where the sun, moon, and stars are suspended may be space, and so for example they believe that *flowers in space* might describe the appearance of colorful forms which are like floating clouds in clear sky and like flying blossoms being blown east and west and up and down by the wind. They do not know that the four elements as creator and creation, together with the real dharmas[22] of the objective world, on the one hand, and original realization,[23] original nature and so forth, on the other hand, are all called *flowers in space*. Furthermore, they do not know that the four elements and so on which are the agents of creation exist because of real dharmas, and they do not know that the objective world abides in its place in the Universe because of real dharmas; they see only that real dharmas exist because of the objective world. They understand only that flowers in space exist because of cloudedness in the eyes; they do not understand the truth that cloudedness in the eyes is caused to exist by virtue of flowers in space. Remember, in Buddhism a person of clouded eyes is a person of original realization, a person of subtle realization, a person of the buddhas, a person of the triple world, and a person in the ascendant state of buddha.[24] Do not stupidly see cloudedness as delusion and learn that true reality exists elsewhere. To do so would be the small view. If cloudedness and flowers were delusion, that which attaches to the wrong view that they are delusion, and the attachment itself, must all be delusion. If both [subject and object] were delusion, there would be no possibility of establishing any truth. There being no truth to establish, [to assert] that cloudedness and flowers are delusion would be impossible.

33] When realization is clouded, each of the many dharmas in realization is a dharma adorned with cloudedness. When delusion is clouded, each of the many dharmas in delusion is a dharma adorned with cloudedness. For the present, we can say that when clouded eyes are balanced, flowers in space

---

22. 諸法 (SHOHO), "real dharmas," means real things and phenomena—not only objects of perception and not only subjective concepts, but things and phenomena which are realized in action here and now.

23. 本覚 (HONGAKU). In the Tendai Sect, which Master Dogen entered at the age of twelve, there are two contradictory theories—that human beings have the Buddha-nature originally, and that the Buddha-nature can be attained through efforts in our life. The idea of original realization comes from the former theory.

24. 仏向上人 (BUTSU-KOJO-NIN). See chap. 28, *Butsu-kojo-no-ji*.

are balanced; when clouded eyes are non-arising,[25] flowers in space are non-arising; and when all dharmas are real form, clouded-flowers are real form. We should neither discuss this as past, present, or future, nor relate it to beginning, middle, and end. Because it is not hindered by arising and passing, it can cause arising and passing to arise and pass—arising in space[26] and passing in space, arising in clouded eyes[27] and passing in clouded eyes, arising in flowers[28] and passing in flowers, and so on for all other times and places. Learning of flowers in space may take many forms: there is what is seen by clouded eyes, what is seen by clear eyes, what is seen by the Buddha's eyes, what is seen by the patriarchs' eyes, what is seen by the eyes of the truth, what is seen by blind eyes, what is seen by three thousand years, what is seen by eight hundred years, what is seen by hundreds of kalpas, and what is seen by countless kalpas. All these see flowers in space, but space itself is multifarious, and flowers also are diverse. Remember that space is a thing.[29] This space unfailingly yields flowers as all the hundred things[30] yield flowers. To express this truth, the Tathāgata says, *"Space is originally without flowers."*[31] Although there are originally no flowers, now there are flowers—a fact which is true for peach and plum trees and true for apricot and willow trees.[32] [The Tathāgata's expression] is like saying *"the apricot yesterday was without flowers but the apricot in spring has flowers."* Still, when the season arrives and just then flowers bloom, this may be the flowers' time or it may be the flowers arriving.[33] This exact moment of flowers arriving is never a random

25. 無生 (MUSHO) expresses the state at the moment of the present. At the same time, 無生 (MUSHO) is sometimes used as a synonym for *nirvāṇa,* the state which is not disturbed by arising and passing conditions.

26. 空中に (KUCHU *ni*) means "in space," "in the midst of space," or "in the concrete reality of space." 中 (CHU) lit. means "the middle" (as in beginning, middle, and end). As a suffix it means the midst of something and by extension—in Master Dogen's usage—the concrete reality of something.

27. 翳中に (EICHU *ni*).

28. 華中に (KECHU *ni*).

29. 一艸 (ISSO), lit. "one weed." Space is a thing in the sense, for example, that it is one of the six elements: earth, water, fire, wind, space, and consciousness.

30. 百艸 (HYAKUSO), lit. "the hundred weeds," means miscellaneous concrete things. Whereas phenomenologists only affirm that flowers bloom, i.e., phenomena exist, Master Dogen insists that things also exist—phenomena are things and things are phenomena.

31. 空本無華 (KU-HON-MUGE). Source not traced. For explanation of the meaning of 無 (MU), "being without," see chap. 22, *Bussho.*

32. "Plum" is 李 (RI, *sumomo),* and "apricot" is 梅 (BAI, *ume).* In Japan the tree referred to as *ume* is accurately translated as a Japanese apricot *(Prunus mume).* At the same time it is included in trees of the genus *Prunus,* which can be classified as plum trees. In this chapter, the two varieties are distinguished, but where no distinction is necessary the translation of 梅 (BAI, *ume)* as "plum" rather than "apricot" has been preferred. See chap. 59, *Baike.*

33. The words describe spring directly as a simple fact, but that fact can be interpreted from two sides—flowers wait to bloom in spring, and spring waits for flowers to bloom.

event. Apricot and willow flowers inevitably bloom on apricot and willow trees; looking at [apricot and willow] flowers we can identify apricot and willow trees, and looking at apricot and willow trees we can distinguish [apricot and willow] flowers. Peach and plum flowers never bloom on apricot or willow trees. Apricot and willow flowers bloom on apricot and willow trees, and peach and plum flowers bloom on peach and plum trees. Flowers in space blooming in space are also like this; they never bloom on other things and never bloom on other trees. Looking at the various colors of space flowers, one imagines the limitlessness of space fruits. Watching flowers in space open and fall, we should learn of the spring and autumn of flowers in space. Spring for flowers in space and spring for other flowers may be alike. As flowers in space are miscellaneous, so must spring seasons be of many kinds. Thus do springs and autumns of the past and present exist. People who understand that flowers in space are not real but other flowers are real are people who have not seen or heard the Buddha's teaching. To understand, on hearing the preaching that *space is originally without flowers,* that there now exist flowers in space which originally did not exist, is the near-sighted and small view. We should step ahead and take the broad view. An ancestral Master[34] says, *"Flowers have never appeared."* The realization of this principle is, for example, the truth that flowers have never appeared,[35] that flowers have never disappeared, that flowers have never been "flowers" and that space has never been "space." We should not engage in idle discussion of existence and non-existence, confusing the before and after of flower-time. Flowers always seem to be imbued with all colors. [But] colors are not always limited to flowers: other seasons also have blues, yellows, reds, whites, and other colors. Spring brings in flowers, and flowers bring in spring.

[38] The mandarin Cho Setsu[36] is a lay disciple of Sekiso.[37] The poem he makes on realizing the truth is as follows:

> *Brightness is serenely illuminating the whole sands-of-the-Ganges world.*

This *brightness* has clearly realized the Monks' Hall, the Buddha Hall, the Kitchen Hall, and the Temple Gate.[38] The *whole sands-of-the-Ganges world* is realized by brightness, and is brightness realized.

---

34. Master Taiso Eka. See *Keitoku-dento-roku,* chap. 3.

35. Because real phenomena exist at the moment of the present.

36. Apart from the fact that he became the disciple of Master Sekiso at the recommendation of Great Master Zengetsu, his life history is not known. The poem is recorded in *Goto-egen,* chap. 6.

37. Master Sekiso Keisho (807–888), successor of Master Dogo Enchi.

38. Alludes to the words of Master Unmon Bun-en quoted in chap. 36, *Komyo:* Unmon asks, *"Just what is this brightness that is present in all people?"* The assembled monks make no reply. [Unmon] himself says in their place, *"The Monks' Hall, the Buddha Hall, the Kitchen, and the Three Gates."* See also *Shinji-shobogenzo,* pt. 1, no. 81.

[39] *All souls, common and sacred, are my family.*

It is not that there are no common men and saints. [But] do not insult common men and saints by this [discrimination].

[40] *When not one image appears*[39] *the total body manifests itself.*

Image and *image* are *one* by *one.*[40] This state is inevitably *not appearance,*[41] and it is the *total manifestation* of *the total body*. For this reason he says that *one image is not appearance.*[42]

[40] *If the six sense organs are slightly moved [the mind] is covered with clouds.*

Although *the six sense organs* are the eyes, ears, nose, tongue, body, and sense-center, they are not always two times three; they may be *three and three before and after.*[43] *Moving* is as Mt. Sumeru,[44] as the Earth, as the six sense organs, and as *slight moving* itself. Because moving is as Mt. Sumeru, not moving is also as Mt. Sumeru. For example, it forms clouds and produces water.[45]

[42] *By eliminating disturbances*[46] *we redouble the disease.*

We have not been free of disease hitherto; we have had the Buddha bug and the patriarch bug. Intellectual excluding now adds to the disease and

---

39. 一念不生 (ICHI-NEN-FUSHO). 一 (ICHI) means "one." 念 (NEN) means "image" or "thought." 不 (FU) expresses negation. 生 (SHO) means "to appear" or "to arise." In the poem, read as ICHI-NEN *sho[ze] za[reba]*, or "when an image does not arise," these four characters suggest the desirable state in which no isolated thought emerges in Zazen, so that the body-mind is free to reflect the whole.

40. 念念一一なり (NEN-NEN ICHI-ICHI *nari*), "image-image is one-one." Whereas the poem seems to describe an ideal situation, Master Dogen's comment is a stark description of concrete facts: he simply notices the existence of an image at a moment. This is reminiscent of Master Dogen's instruction for Zazen in *Fukan-zazengi Shinpitsu-bon*: 念起即覚 (NEN *oko[ra ba] suna[wachi] kaku[se yo]*). "When an image arises, just be aware of it."

41. 不生 (FUSHO), "not appearance," here suggests the state at the moment of the present in which time stands still. See note 25. Master Dogen explains this usage in chap. 3, *Genjo-koan*.

42. 一念不生 (ICHI-NEN-FUSHO) can be interpreted as a description of momentary reality: *"The one image [of reality] is beyond appearance, and the total body [of reality] manifests itself."*

43. We should not always understand "sense organs" as an abstract, inclusive concept.

44. Mt. Sumeru, standing at the center of the universe, is generally understood to be a symbol of stability, or non-movement. But Master Dogen's view of movement transcends the ordinary idea of movement relative to non-movement.

45. Movement is reality itself, symbolized by clouds and water.

46. 煩悩 (BONNO) in modern Japanese usage, as defined by the *Kenkyusha* dictionary, means "earthly passions" or "carnal desires." Here 煩悩 (BONNO) represents the Sanskrit *kleśa* which is defined by MW as follows: *pain, affliction, distress, pain from disease, anguish; wrath, anger; worldly occupation, care, trouble. Kleśa* are emotional imbalances that hinder a Buddhist practitioner from harmonizing with the truth—just as interference hinders the reception of a radio signal. Traditional examples of *kleśa* are greed, anger, ignorance, arrogance, doubt, and false views.

augments the disease. The very moment itself of *eliminating* is inevitably *disturbance*. They are simultaneous and are beyond simultaneousness. Disturbances always include the fact of [trying to] eliminate them.

[43] *To approach the Truth intentionally is also wrong.*

To turn one's back on the Truth is wrong, and to approach the Truth is also wrong. The Truth is the approaching and the turning away, which, in each instance of approaching or turning away, are the Truth itself. Is there anyone who knows that this *wrong is also the Truth?*

[43] *In following worldly circumstances there are no hindrances.*

Worldly circumstance and *worldly circumstance follow* each other, and *following* and *following* is *worldly circumstances*. This state is called *without hindrances*. We should learn the state beyond hindrance and no hindrance as that which is obstructed by the eyes.[47]

[44] *Nirvāṇa, and living-and-dying, are just flowers in space.*

"Nirvāṇa" means the state of anuttara-samyak-saṃbodhi. The abode of Buddhist patriarchs and the disciples of Buddhist patriarchs is just this state. *Living-and-dying* is *the real human body.*[48] This *nirvāṇa and living-and-dying* are this reality, and at the same time they are just *flowers in space*. The roots and stalks, twigs and leaves, flowers and fruit, and brightness and colors of flowers in space, are each the blooming of flowers in space. Space-flowers inevitably bear space-fruit and drop space-seeds. Because the triple world which we are experiencing now is the *five petals opening* of flowers in space, *It is best to see the triple world as the triple world.*[49] [The triple world] is this *real form* of *all dharmas.*[50] It is this *flower form* of *all dharmas;* and all dharmas, from these to others beyond imagination, are flowers in space and fruit in space. We should learn by experience that they are identical to those in apricot, willow, peach, and plum trees.

---

47. 被眼碍 (HI-GAN-GE, or *me [ni] saera[ru]*), "being obstructed by the eyes," suggests the state in which eyes inevitably see all things as they are.

48. Master Engo Kokugon said, *"Living-and-dying, coming-and-going, are the real human body."* See chap. 50, *Shoho-jisso.*

49. 不如三界見於三界 (SANGAI *no* SANGAI *o genzuru ni shika zu*), from the *Nyorai-juryo (Tathāgata's Lifetime)* chapter of the Lotus Sutra (LS 3.18). The characters 不如 can be read in two ways: 1) *shika zu* ("be best"), and 2) *gotoku nara zu* ("not like"). This gave rise to three traditional interpretations of the words. The interpretation of the *Hokke-ron (Flower of Dharma Commentary)* is that [the Tathāgata sees the triple world] *"not like [people of] the triple world seeing the triple world."* The interpretation of the *Dana-ryu (Dāna School)* is similar, suggesting that the triple world which the Buddha sees is different from the triple world which the common man sees. Master Dogen favored the interpretation of the *Enshin-ryu (Blessed Mind School)* that *"It is best to see the triple world as the triple world,"* i.e., there is no triple world seen by the Buddha other than the triple world seen by the common man. See chap. 47, *Sangai-yuishin.*

50. 諸法実相 (SHOHO-JISSO). See chap. 50, *Shoho-jisso.*

[46] Zen Master Reikun[51] of Fuyo-zan mountain in the Fuchou district of the great kingdom of Sung, when first entering the order of Zen Master Shishin[52] of Kisu-ji temple, asks, *"What is buddha?"*

Kisu says, *"If I tell you, will you believe me or not?"*

Master [Reikun] says, *"How could I not believe the Master's honest words?"*

Kisu says, *"You yourself are just it."*

Master [Reikun] says, *"How should I maintain it?"*

Kisu says, *"When an instance of cloudedness is there in the eyes, flowers in space tumble down."*[53]

[47] The words that Kisu now speaks, *"When an instance of cloudedness is there in the eyes, flowers in space tumble down,"*[54] express maintenance of buddha. So remember, the tumbling down of clouded-flowers is what buddhas realize, and the flowers and fruit of eyes-and-space are what buddhas maintain. With cloudedness they make eyes real. Flowers in space are realized in eyes, and eyes are realized in flowers in space. It may be that *When flowers in space are there in the eyes, a single instance of cloudedness tumbles down,*[55] and *When an eye is there in space, all instances of cloudedness tumble down.*[56] This being so, cloudedness is *the manifestation of all functions,*[57] eyes are *the manifestation of all functions,* space is *the manifestation of all functions,* and flowers are *the manifestation of all functions. Tumbling down* is the *thousand eyes* and is the *thoroughly-realized-body* as an eye.[58] In sum, at the time and place an eye exists, there are inevitably flowers in space and flowers in eyes. We call flowers in eyes flowers in space. And an expression of eyes-and-flowers is always open and clear.

---

51. Master Fuyo Reikun (dates unknown), successor of Master Kisu Shishin. His posthumous title is Great Master Kosho.

52. Master Kisu Chijo (dates unknown), successor of Master Baso Do-itsu. Zen Master Shishin is his posthumous title.

53. *Keitoku-dento-roku*, chap. 10.

54. 一瞖在眼空華乱墜 (ICHI-EI-ZAI-GEN-KUGE-RANTSUI), lit. "one cloudedness being present in eyes, space-flowers tumble." In other words, at a moment when we realize our own delusion, phenomena become real.

55. 空華在眼一瞖乱墜 (KUGE-ZAI-GEN-ICHI-EI-RANTSUI), lit. "space-flowers being present in eyes, one cloudedness tumbles." In other words, when we are looking at real phenomena, we transcend our delusion at that moment.

56. 一眼在空衆瞖乱墜 (ICHI-GEN-ZAI-KU-SHU-EI-RANTSUI), lit. "one eye being present in space, all kinds of cloudedness tumble." In other words, when our whole body-mind is existing in concrete space [e.g. in Zazen], we are transcending all kinds of delusion.

57. 全機の現 (ZENKI *no* GEN), the words of Master Engo Kokugon. See chap. 41, *Zenki*.

58. In other words, transcendence of subjective delusion and objective images is the vigorous state of reality symbolized by Bodhisattva Avalokiteśvara. See chap. 33, *Kannon*.

[149] For this reason, Great Master Kosho[59] of Roya-san mountain says:

How wondrous are the buddhas in the ten directions!
They are originally just the flowers in our eyes.
And if we want to know the flowers in our eyes,
They are originally just the buddhas in the ten directions.
If we want to know buddhas in ten directions,
They are other than the flowers in our eyes.
If we want to know flowers in eyes,
They are other than the buddhas in the ten directions;
And when we understand this situation clearly,
The fault is with buddhas in ten directions.
Not understanding this situation clearly,
Voice-hearers might dance
And the independently-awakened might put on make-up.[60]

[150] Remember, *the buddhas in the ten directions* are not unreal; they are originally just *the flowers in our eyes*. The place where the buddhas of the ten directions abide is *in the eyes*, and anywhere other than *in the eyes* is not the abode of buddhas. *The flowers in our eyes* are neither non-existence nor existence, they are neither immaterial nor real; they are naturally just *the buddhas in the ten directions*. Now if we want to know only the buddhas of the ten directions, one-sidedly, they are other than the flowers in our eyes; and if we want to know only flowers in eyes, one-sidedly, they seem to be other than the buddhas of the ten directions. Both *clear understanding* and *unclear understanding*, because they are like this, are flowers in the eyes and buddhas in the ten directions. *Wanting to know* and *it not being so*[61] are the very realization of *wondrousness;* they are great wonders. The fundamental meaning of the flowers in space, and the flowers on the ground, of which the buddhas and the patriarchs speak, is such *giving of free play to the elegant ways*.[62] Even teachers of sutras and teachers of commentaries are able to hear the name of flowers in space, but none other than a Buddhist patriarch has the means or the circum-

---

59. Master Roya Ekaku (dates unknown), successor of Master Fun-yo Zensho. While Master Roya was a layman his father, who was the local governor, died, so Master Roya set off to return to his family's home. But on the way back he stopped at Yakusan mountain and decided to become a monk. He was praised in his day, along with Master Seccho Myokaku, as one of *the two gates of sweet dew*. Great Master Kosho is his posthumous title.

60. *Śrāvakas* (voice-hearers) and *pratyeka-buddhas* (the independently-awakened) might rejoice in having understood what they have not really understood. The verse is quoted in *Goto-egen*, chap. 12.

61. 不是 (FUZE), translated in the poem as "are other than..."

62. Alludes to words of Master Tendo Nyojo quoted in chap. 38, *Muchu-setsumu*, para. [175]: *"Dreams going awry and dreams coming true, / Holding back and letting go, / We give free play to the elegant ways."* See also the final paragraph of chap. 42, *Tsuki*.

stances to experience the lifeblood of flowers on the ground. One who has apprehended the lifeblood of flowers on the ground speaks the state of a Buddhist patriarch.

[52] Zen Master Etetsu[63] of Sekimon-zan mountain in the great kingdom of Sung is a venerable patriarch in the order on Ryozan mountain.[64] In the story, a monk asks him, *"What is the jewel in the mountain?"* The point of this question is, for example, the same as in asking *"What is buddha?"* It is like asking *"What is the truth?"* The Master says, *"Flowers in space unfold on the ground. Even if we buy throughout the country, there is no gate."*[65] This expression should never be compared with other expressions. Ordinary teachers in many districts, when discussing flowers in space as "flowers of emptiness,"[66] speak only of arising in emptiness and passing in emptiness.[67] None has understood *reliance on space;*[68] how much less could any understand *reliance on the ground.*[69] Only Sekimon has understood. The meaning of *relying on the ground* is that beginning, middle, and end are, ultimately, *relying on the ground. "To unfold"* is to open.[70] Just at this moment, there is unfolding *from the whole Earth,* and there is opening *from the whole Earth.*[71] *"Even if we buy throughout the country, there is no gate":* it is not that there is no *buying throughout the country;* it is

---

63. Master Sekimon Etetsu (dates unknown), successor of Master Sekimon Ken-un.

64. 梁山 (RYOZAN) generally refers to Master Ryozan Enkan. However, the exact relationship between Master Sekimon and Master Ryozan Enkan is unclear.

65. *Tensho-koto-roku,* chap. 24.

66. "Flowers in space" and "flowers of emptiness" are originally the same characters, 空華 (KUGE). "Flowers of emptiness" suggests the interpretation of *śūnyatā* which Master Dogen has opposed in this chapter—the interpretation that phenomena are devoid of reality.

67. 於空 (O-KU), "in emptiness," suggests intellectual effort to relate phenomena to the concept *śūnyatā.* 於 (O, or *[ni] oi[te]*) means "at," "in," "on," or "in regard to." This expression is distinct from the more concrete expression used earlier, 空中 (KUCHU), "in space," which means "inside space," or "in the concrete reality of space." See note 26.

68. 従空 (JUKU), "from space," "relying on space," or "on the basis of space," suggests a more concrete state than 於空 (O-KU), "in emptiness." 従 (JU, or *[ni] yori[te]*) means "following from," "relying on," or "on the basis of."

69. 従地 (JUCHI), "from the ground," "on the ground," "relying on the ground," or "on the basis of the ground," is Master Sekimon's expression. It suggests a still more concrete state.

70. Master Dogen explains the character 発 (HOTSU) in Master Sekimon's words with the character 開 (KAI). 発 (HOTSU) means "to shoot out," "to emit," or "to open up." It is used, for example, to describe the establishment of the will to the truth. See chap. 70, *Hotsu-bodaishin.* 開 (KAI) means "to open"; at the same time, it also sometimes means "to disclose" or "to reveal." See chap. 17, *Hokke-ten-hokke.*

71. 従尽大地 (JUJINDAICHI), "from the whole Earth," or "on the basis of the whole Earth," is Master Dogen's expression. Thus, four expressions may be contrasted in this part: 1) 於空 (O-KU), "in emptiness"; 2) 従空 (JUKU), "on the basis of space"; 3) 従地 (JUCHI), "on the basis of the ground"; and 4) Master Dogen's suggestion of Zazen which is 従尽大地 (JUJINDAICHI), "from the whole Earth."

buying the gateless.[72] Flowers in space exist on the basis of unfolding from the ground, and the whole ground exists on the basis of the opening of flowers. So remember, there is a principle that flowers in space cause both the ground and space to unfold.

Shobogenzo Kuge

Preached to the assembly at Kannon-dori-kosho-horin-ji temple on the 10th day of the 3rd lunar month in the 1st year of Kangen.[73]

---

72. "The gateless" is 無門 (MUMON), translated in Master Sekimon's words as "there is no gate." Master Dogen does not deny the effort to get something, and at the same time he suggests that we get reality (in which there is no concept "gate") just in action (buying) itself.

73. 1243.

[44]

古仏心

KOBUSSHIN

The Mind of Eternal Buddhas

Ko means "old" or "eternal," ***butsu*** *means "buddha" and* ***shin*** *means "mind." So* ***kobusshin*** *means "the mind of eternal buddhas." In this chapter, Master Dogen cites examples of the mind of eternal Buddhas, quoting Master Tendo Nyojo, Master Engo Kokugon, Master Sozan Konin, and Master Seppo Gison. Then he explains a story about National Master Daisho (Master Nan-yo Echu) and his disciple that suggests the oneness of the mind of eternal Buddhas and miscellaneous concrete things. At the end of the chapter he quotes Master Zengen Chuko's words on the matter.*

[55] **The succession of the Dharma** by ancestral patriarchs is forty patriarchs from the Seven Buddhas to Sokei[1] and forty buddhas from Sokei to the Seven Buddhas. Because each of the Seven Buddhas has the virtue of ascending and of descending,[2] they extend to Sokei and extend to the Seven Buddhas. Because Sokei has the virtue of ascending and of descending, he receives the authentic transmission from the Seven Buddhas, he receives the authentic transmission from Sokei, and he passes the authentic transmission to later buddhas. But it is beyond only former and later. At the time of Śākyamuni Buddha, all the buddhas of the ten directions are present; at the time of Seigen, Nangaku is present;[3] at the time of Nangaku, Seigen is present; and so on—at the time of Sekito, Kozei is present.[4] Their not hindering each other may be different from having no connection. We should investigate the presence of such virtue. Each of the forty Buddhist patriarchs mentioned above is an eternal buddha. At the same time, each has a mind, a body, a state of brightness, and a national land. Each has passed away long

1. Master Daikan Eno, the 33rd patriarch. See chap. 15, *Busso.*

2. 向上向下 (KOJO-KOGE). The virtue of 向上 (KOJO), "ascending," or "the ascendant state," is discussed in chap. 28, *Butsu-kojo-no-ji,* and in the chapter of the same title in the 28-chapter edition of Shobogenzo. See Book 4, Appendix.

3. Master Seigen Gyoshi (died 740) and Master Nangaku Ejo (677–744) were both disciples of Master Daikan Eno. Master Dogen's lineage is through Master Seigen Gyoshi. The Rinzai lineage is through Master Nangaku Ejo.

4. Master Sekito Kisen (700–790) was the successor of Master Seigen. Kozei (Ch: Kiangsi) refers to Master Baso Do-itsu (709–788), successor of Master Nangaku.

ago and has never passed away at all. It may be that both never having passed away, and having passed away long ago, are equally the virtue of an eternal buddha. Those who learn in practice the truth of eternal buddhas realize in experience the truth of eternal buddhas; they are the eternal buddhas of each age. Although the "eternal"[5] of "eternal buddhas" is exactly the same as the "old"[4] in "new and old," [eternal buddhas] have completely transcended past and present;[6] they belong directly in eternity.[5]

[58] My late Master says, *"I have met with the eternal Buddha Wanshi."*[7]

Clearly, an eternal buddha is present in the house of Tendo, and Tendo is present in the house of an eternal buddha.

[58] Zen Master Engo[8] says, *"I bow to the ground[9] before the true eternal Buddha Sokei."*

Remember, we should bow down to the thirty-third patriarch from Śākyamuni Buddha, bowing to him as an eternal buddha. Because Zen Master Engo has the resplendent brightness of an eternal buddha, in the state of having met with an eternal buddha, he is able to prostrate himself like this. This being so, mindful of the state of Sokei which is right from beginning to end, we should remember that eternal buddhas are the grasping of a nose-ring[10] like this. One who has this ability to grasp a nose-ring is just an eternal buddha.

[59] Sozan[11] says, *"On the peak of Daiyu-rei mountain[12] an eternal buddha is present, and he is radiating brightness that shines on this place."*[13]

---

5. 古 (KO) lit. means "old" or "ancient," but in this sentence Master Dogen indicates that in the phrase 古仏 (KOBUTSU) the character means not only "old" but also "eternal."

6. 古今 (KOKON), lit. "ancient-present," means not only "past and present" or "ancient and modern times," but also "all ages" or "eternity."

7. Master Wanshi Shokaku (1091–1157), successor of Master Tanka Shijun. In around 1130 Master Wanshi became the Master of Keitoku-ji temple on Mt. Tendo, where—almost 100 years later—Master Dogen finally met Master Tendo Nyojo.

8. Master Engo Kokugon (1063–1135), successor of Master Goso Ho-en.

9. 稽首 (KEISHU) means a prostration in which the head touches the ground.

10. 巴鼻 (HABI), lit. "grasping of the nose" refers to the ring used to lead a water-buffalo by the nose. It suggests humility and self-control.

11. Master Sozan Konin (837–909), a successor of Master Tozan Ryokai.

12. The name of a mountain in Kiangsi province in southeast China.

13. The full story is: Master Sozan asks a monk how much the monk intends to pay a craftsman for building a monument—three coins, two coins, or one coin. The monk goes to see Master Razan Dokan who resides in a hut on Daiyu mountain. Master Razan recommends the monk to take the middle way. Hearing of this, Master Sozan prostrates himself towards Daiyu-rei mountain and says, *"I had thought there was no-one, but on the peak of Daiyu-rei mountain an eternal buddha is present, and he is radiating brightness that shines on this place."* See *Shinji-shobogenzo*, pt. 1, no. 97, and *Rento-eyo*, chap. 22.

Remember, Sozan has already met with an eternal buddha. We need not search elsewhere; the place where an eternal buddha exists is the peak of Daiyu-rei mountain. Those who themselves are not eternal buddhas cannot know the place where eternal buddhas appear. One who knows the concrete place where an eternal buddha exists may be an eternal buddha.

[60] Seppo[14] says, *"The eternal Buddha Joshu!"*[15]

Remember, even though Joshu is an eternal buddha, if Seppo had not been endowed with his own share of an eternal buddha's power, it might be hard for him to realize the secret of how to pay homage to an eternal buddha. In his action now, as he relies on the influence of an eternal buddha and learns from an eternal buddha, there is effort *beyond conversing,*[16] which is, in other words, Old Man Seppo, the great stout fellow, himself. The everyday customs of eternal buddhas, and the dignified behavior of eternal buddhas, are not similar to and never the same as those of people who are not eternal buddhas. This being so, by learning in practice the state of Joshu which is *good in the beginning, middle, and end,*[17] we should learn in practice *the lifetime*[18] of an eternal buddha.

[62] National Master Daisho,[19] of Kotaku-ji temple in the Western Capital,[20] is a Dharma-successor of Sokei, revered and venerated by human emperors and celestial emperors alike, and one who is rarely seen and heard [even] in China. Not only is he the teacher of four generations of emperors, but the emperors themselves lead his carriage into the imperial court. Still more, invited to the palace of the God Indra, he ascends far into the heavens and, for Indra among celestial multitudes, he preaches the Dharma.

[63] The National Master is once asked by a monk, *"What is the mind of eternal buddhas?"*

The Master says, *"Fences, walls, tiles, and pebbles."*

---

14. Master Seppo Gison (822–907), successor of Master Tokuzan Senkan.

15. *Goto-egen*, chap. 7 relates that on hearing the words of Master Joshu Jushin (778–897), Seppo says, *"The eternal Buddha Joshu!"* He just does prostrations towards Joshu, and subsequently does not converse. See also *Shinji-shobogenzo*, pt. 3, no. 84, and *Rento-eyo*, chap. 21.

16. 不答話 (FUTOWA), "not conversing," appears in the story in *Goto-egen* and in *Shinji-shobogenzo.*

17. 初中後善 (SHOCHUGO-ZEN), "good in the beginning, middle, and end," alludes to a phrase in the Lotus Sutra. See LS 1.42 and Shobogenzo, chap. 17, *Hokke-ten-hokke.*

18. 寿量 (JURYO), "lifetime," alludes to 如来寿量 (NYORAI-JURYO), "The Tathāgata's Lifetime" as described in the 16th chapter of the Lotus Sutra, *Nyorai-juryo.*

19. Master Nan-yo Echu (died 775), successor of Master Daikan Eno. National Master Daisho is his posthumous title.

20. 西京 (SEIKYO), "Western Capital," in this case refers to the area of China now called Luoyang. There were five areas of Tang China called 西京 (SEIKYO), "Western Capital."

The question says *"this has got it"* and says *"that has got it."* [The monk] has taken this expression of the truth and made it into a question. And this question far and wide has become an eternal expression of the truth. Thus, myriad trees and hundreds of weeds, which are *flowers opening,* are eternal buddhas' expressions of the truth and eternal buddhas' questions. The nine mountains and eight oceans, which are *the occurrence of the world,*[21] are eternal buddhas' sun-faces and moon-faces and eternal buddhas' skin, flesh, bones, and marrow. Furthermore, there may be instances of the eternal mind practicing buddha,[22] there may be instances of the eternal mind experiencing buddha,[23] there may be instances of the eternal mind making buddha,[24] and there may be instances of the eternity of buddha making up a mind.[25] The reason we speak of "the eternal mind" is that the mind is eternal. Because [the unity of] the mind and buddha is inevitably eternal, the eternal mind is *a chair of bamboo and wood,* is *not being able to find a person who understands the Buddha-Dharma even if we search the whole Earth,* and is *the Master calling this what?*[26] The moment and causes-and-conditions of the present, and the lands-of-dust and space of the present, are both nothing other than the eternal mind. They maintain and rely upon the eternal mind, and they maintain and rely upon the eternal state of buddha—it is maintenance and reliance upon two heads with one face, two things in a picture.

[65] The Master says, *"Fences, walls, tiles, and pebbles."* The point here is that there is a line of attack whereby, facing fences, walls, tiles, and pebbles, we express them: *Fences, walls, tiles, and pebbles.* And there is another mode of expression: there is a line of retreat whereby, inside the concrete place of fences, walls, tiles, and pebbles, *Fences, walls, tiles, and pebbles* speak. In the state of round realization and perfect realization in which these expressions are realized, there are walls standing a thousand feet or ten thousand feet high, there are fences standing around the earth and around the heavens, there is the covering of a tile or half a tile, and there are sharp edges of pebbles, big ones and small ones. What exists like this is not only the mind but also the body itself, and even object-and-subject. This being so, we should ask, and we should say, *"What are fences, walls, tiles, and pebbles?"* And if we

---

21. Master Prajñātara said, *"The opening of flowers is the occurrence of the world."* See chap. 43, *Kuge.*

22. 行仏 (GYOBUTSU), "practicing buddha," or "acting buddha," is discussed in detail in chap. 23, *Gyobutsu-yuigi.*

23. 証仏 (SHOBUTSU), "experiencing buddha" also appears in chap. 23, *Gyobutsu-yuigi.* See also, for example, chap. 36, *Komyo,* para. [126].

24. 作仏 (SABUTSU), "making buddha" or "becoming buddha," is discussed in chap. 20, *Kokyo,* from para [175].

25. 仏古の為心なる (BUKKO *no* ISHIN *naru*), or "buddha-eternity becoming the content of a mind," suggests the decision to be a Buddhist.

26. Alludes to a conversation between Master Gensa Shibi and Master Rakan Keichin, recorded in chap. 47, *Sangai-yuishin.* See also *Shinji-shobogenzo,* pt. 2, no. 12.

want to converse, we should answer, *"The mind of eternal buddhas."* Maintaining and relying upon the state like this, we should investigate further: Just what are *fences and walls*? What do we call *"fences and walls"*? With what forms and stages are they furnished at this moment? We should investigate them like this, in detail. Are fences and walls caused to appear through a process of production,[27] or is production caused to appear on the basis of fences and walls? Are they products or are they beyond production? Should we see them as sentient or as insentient? Are they appearing before us now, or are they beyond appearance in the present? In the state like this of mental effort, and of learning in practice, whether it is in the heavens above or in the human world, and whether it appears in this land or in other worlds, the mind of eternal buddhas is fences, walls, tiles, and pebbles. No additional speck of dust has ever protruded to taint it.

[68] Great Master Zengen Chuko,[28] the story goes, is asked by a monk, *"What is the mind of eternal buddhas?"*

The Master says, *"The world is shattered."*

The monk says, *"Why is the world shattered?"*

The Master says, *"How is it possible to be without our own body?"*[29]

As regards this *world*, its ten directions are totally the world of Buddha, and there has never been any world that is not the world of Buddha. As regards the form and stages of *being shattered,* we should learn them in practice in this whole world in ten directions, never learning them as self. Because we do not learn them as self, the very moment of *shatteredness* is one thing, two things, three, four, and five things, and therefore limitless things. Each thing is its *own body* in *the undecided state of being without.*[30] *Our own body* is *the undecided state of being without*. Do not selfishly begrudge the moment of the present and thus fail to make your own body into the mind of eternal buddhas. Truly, prior to the Seven Buddhas the mind of eternal buddhas stands as a wall, and after the Seven Buddhas the mind of eternal buddhas sprouts. Prior to

27. 造作 (ZOSA), lit. "made by building," has the connotation of human intentionality or enforcement. It represents the Sanskrit *saṃskṛta* (put together) and is opposed to the term 無作 (MUSA), "without being made," which represents the Sanskrit *asaṃskṛta* (unadorned, without elaboration). See Book 1, Glossary.

28. Master Zengen Chuko (dates unknown), successor of Master Dogo Enchi (769–835). He was the *tenzo* (cook) in the order on Dogo-zan mountain, where he realized the Dharma one day on hearing a child reciting the *Kannon-kyo.* After that he lived and taught at Zengen.

29. *Keitoku-dento-roku,* chap. 11.

30. 寧無 (NEIMU). In the story, these characters (read as *Nanzo… nakara n ya)* mean "How is it possible for… not to exist?" At the same time 寧 (NEI, or *mushiro)* means "A rather than B" or "preferably"; it suggests the existence of two possibilities and therefore openness or undecidedness. Moreover, Master Dogen frequently uses 無 (MU) to mean "the state of being without [anything superfluous or lacking]." See, for example, chap. 22, *Bussho.*

all the buddhas the mind of eternal buddhas flowers, and after all the buddhas the mind of eternal buddhas bears fruit. Prior to "the mind of eternal buddhas" the mind of eternal buddhas is liberated.

Shobogenzo Kobusshin

Preached to the assembly at Rokuharamitsu-ji temple[31] on the 29th day of the 4th lunar month in the 1st year of Kangen.[32]

31. Rokuharamitsu temple is in the Higashiyama district of the city of Kyoto. Hatano Yoshishige, Master Dogen's most powerful supporter, occupied a government office which was located nearby.

32. 1243.

[45]

菩提薩摩埵四摂法

BODAISATTA-SHISHOBO

Four Elements of a Bodhisattva's Social Relations

Bodaisatta *means "bodhisattva," a person who is pursuing the Buddhist truth;* ***shi*** *means "four"; and* ***shobo*** *means "elements of social relations" or "methods for social relations." The four are dāna, free giving; priya-ākhyāna, kind speech; artha-carya, helpful conduct; and samāna-arthatā, identity of purpose, or cooperation. Buddhism puts great value on our actual conduct. For this reason, our conduct in relating to each other is a very important part of Buddhist life. In this chapter Master Dogen preaches that these four ways of behaving are the essence of Buddhist life. He explains the real meaning of Buddhism in terms of social relations.*

[71] **First is free giving.** Second is kind speech. Third is helpful conduct. Fourth is cooperation.[1]

[72] *"Free giving"*[2] means not being greedy. Not being greedy means not coveting. Not coveting means, in everyday language, not courting favor.[3] Even if we rule the four continents, if we want to bestow the teaching of the right truth, we simply must not be greedy. That might mean, for example, donating treasures that are to be thrown away to people we do not know. When we offer flowers from distant mountains to the Tathāgata, and when we donate treasures accumulated in our past life to living beings, whether [the gift] is Dharma or material objects, in each case we are originally endowed with the virtue that accompanies free giving. There is a Buddhist

1. 四摂法 (SHI-SHOBO), the four methods for social relations, or the four elements of sociability (from the Sanskrit *catvāri saṃgraha-vastūni*—see Glossary), are listed and explained in chap. 66 of *Daichido-ron*. They are also mentioned in the *Devadatta* chapter of the Lotus Sutra (LS 2.208), and in the 11th chapter in the 12-chapter edition of Shobogenzo, *Ippyakuhachi-homyomon*. See Book 4, Appendices.

2. 布施 (FUSE), from the Sanskrit *dāna*.

3. Master Dogen first explains the Chinese characters, 布施 (FUSE), "free giving," with the Chinese characters, 不貪 (FUDON), "not being greedy," which he then explains using a Japanese word written in kana, むさぼる（貪） *(musaboru)*, "to covet." Finally he takes his explanation further using another colloquial Japanese word へつらう *(hetsurau)*, which means to curry favor through groveling, flattery, et cetera.

principle that even if things are not our own, this does not hinder our free giving. And a gift is not to be hated for its small value, but its effect should be real. When we leave the truth to the truth, we attain the truth. When we attain the truth, the truth inevitably continues to be left to the truth. When possessions are left to be possessions, possessions inevitably turn into gifts. We give ourselves to ourselves, and we give the external world to the external world. The direct and indirect influences of this giving pervade far into the heavens above and through the human world, even reaching the wise and the sacred who have experienced the effect. The reason is that in becoming giver and receiver, the subject and object of giving are connected; this is why the Buddha says, *"When a person who gives comes into an assembly, others admire that person from the beginning. Remember, the mind of such a person is tacitly understood."*[4] So we should freely give even a single word or a single verse of Dharma, and it will become a good seed in this life and in other lives. We should freely give even a single penny or a single grass-stalk of alms, and it will sprout a good root in this age and in other ages.[5] Dharma can be a treasure, and material gifts can be dharma—it may depend upon [people's] hopes and pleasures. Truly, the gift of a beard can regulate a person's mind,[6] and the service of sand can gain a throne.[7] Such givers covet no reward, but just share according to their ability. To provide a boat or to build a bridge are free giving as the dāna-pāramitā.[8] When we learn giving well, both receiving the body and giving up the body are free giving. Earning a living and doing productive work are originally nothing other than free giving. Leaving flowers to the wind, and leaving birds to time,[9] may also be the meritorious conduct of free giving. Both givers and receivers should thoroughly learn the truth which certifies that Great King Aśoka's being able to serve half a mango[10] as an offering for hundreds of monks is a wide and

4. Paraphrased by Master Dogen in Japanese from chap. 24 of *Zo-itsu-agon-gyo,* the fourth of the Āgama Sutras.

5. Traditionally *dāna* is categorized into *amisa-dāna,* 財施 (ZAISE), "giving of material gifts" (by lay Buddhists to monks) and *dharma-dāna,* 法施 (HOSE), "giving of dharma" (by monks to lay Buddhists). Master Dogen alludes to that distinction in these two sentences. A third category of *dāna* is sometimes added, namely *abhaya-dāna,* 無畏施 (MUI-SE), "giving of fearlessness." See, for example, LS 3.252.

6. Alludes to the story that when an officer in the court of the Tang emperor Taiso (reigned 627–649) fell sick and needed the ashes from a beard for medicine, Taiso burnt his own beard and gave the ashes to the officer.

7. The *Aiku-o-kyo (King Aśoka Sutra)* tells the story of a child who was playing in the sand when the Buddha came by on an alms round. The child put an offering of sand into the Buddha's food bowl, and by virtue of his giving he later became King Aśoka.

8. 檀度 (DANDO). 檀 (DAN) represents the sound of the Sanskrit *dāna.* 度 (DO), lit. "crossed over," represents the meaning of the Sanskrit *pāramitā,* which means lit. "gone to the far shore." See Book 1, Glossary.

9. Leaving owls to hoot at night, cocks to crow in the morning, et cetera.

10. 菴羅 (ANRA) represents the sound of the Sanskrit *āmra,* which means mango.

great service of offerings.[11] We should not only muster the energy of our body but should also take care not to overlook suitable opportunities. Truly, it is because we are originally equipped with the virtue of free giving that we have received ourselves as we are now. The Buddha says, *"It is possible to receive and to use [giving] even if the object is oneself, and it is all the easier to give to parents, wives, and children."* Clearly, to practice it by oneself is one kind of free giving, and to give to parents, wives, and children may also be free giving. When we can give up even one speck of dust for free giving, though it is our own act we will quietly rejoice in it, because we will have already received the authentic transmission of one of the virtues of the buddhas, and because for the first time we will be practicing one of the methods of a bodhisattva. What is hard to change is the mind of living beings.[12] By starting with a gift we begin to change the mental state of living beings, after which we resolve to change them until they attain the truth. At the outset we should always make use of free giving. This is why the first of the six pāramitās is the dāna-pāramitā.[13] The bigness or smallness of mind is beyond measurement, and the bigness or smallness of things is also beyond measurement, but there are times when mind changes things, and there is free giving in which things change mind.

[78] *"Kind speech"*[14] means, when meeting living beings, first of all to feel compassion for them and to offer caring and loving words. Broadly, it is there being no rude or bad words. In secular societies there are polite customs of asking others if they are well. In Buddhism there are the words *"Take good care of yourself!"*[15] and there is the disciple's greeting *"How are you?"*[16]

---

11. Alludes to a story in chap. 5 of the *Aiku-o-kyo.* King Aśoka is said to have become the ruler of a vast Indian empire 218 years after the Buddha's death, and to have reigned from 269 to 232 B.C., converting many peoples to Buddhism. He had edicts in local languages carved on rocks and specially-erected pillars throughout his empire. King Aśoka also sponsored the Third Council held in Patna in 235 B.C., during which the abidharma (commentaries) were added to the existing Theravada Canon of vinaya (precepts) and sutra (discourses).

12. Cf. *"That without constancy is the Buddha-nature. That which has constancy is the mind that divides all dharmas into good and bad."* (Master Daikan Eno, quoted in chap. 24, *Bussho.*)

13. The six *pāramitās* are *dāna-pāramitā* (giving freely), *śīla-pāramitā* (observance of precepts), *kṣānti-pāramitā* (forbearance), *vīrya-pāramitā* (diligence), *dhyāna-pāramitā* (the balanced state of Zazen), and *prajña-pāramitā* (wisdom).

14. 愛語 (AIGO), lit. "loving words," from the Sanskrit *priya-ākhyāna.*

15. 珍重 (CHINCHO), lit. "value [yourself] highly." This expression is used, for example, in chap. 30, *Gyoji,* para. [241], by Master Fuyo Dokai when finishing his talk and taking his leave.

16. 不審の孝行あり (FUSHIN *no* KOKO *ari*), lit. "there is the act of filial piety of '*it is not totally clear.*'" The expression 不審 (FUSHIN), "everything is not totally clear," or "I do not know everything in detail," appears at the beginning of a disciple's question to a master in many of the stories in Shobogenzo. See, for example, chap. 22, *Bussho,* para. [89]: "I wonder..." Master Dogen himself uses the expression rhetorically in chap. 21, *Kankin,* para. [188]. It is a kind of polite formula, and at the same time, a polite greeting from student to teacher.

Speaking with the feeling of *compassion for living beings as if they were babies*[17] is kind speech. We should praise those who have virtue and should pity those who lack virtue. Through love of kind speech, kind speech is gradually nurtured. Thus, kind speech which is ordinarily neither recognized nor experienced manifests itself before us. While the present body and life exist we should enjoy kind speech, and we will not regress or deviate through many ages and many lives. Whether in defeating adversaries or in promoting harmony among gentlefolk, kind speech is fundamental. To hear kind speech spoken to us directly makes the face happy and the mind joyful. To hear kind speech indirectly etches an impression in the heart[18] and in the soul. Remember, kind speech arises from a loving mind,[19] and the seed of a loving mind is compassion. We should learn that kind speech has the power to turn around the heavens; it is not merely the praise of ability.

[80] *"Helpful conduct"*[20] means utilizing skillful means[21] to benefit living beings, high or low; for example, by looking into the distant and near future and employing expedient methods[22] to benefit them. People have taken pity on stricken turtles and taken care of sick sparrows.[23] When they saw the stricken turtle and the sick sparrow, they did not seek any reward from the turtle and the sparrow; they were motivated solely by helpful conduct itself. Stupid people think that if we put the benefit of others first, our own benefit will be eliminated. This is not true. Helpful conduct is the whole Dharma. It universally benefits self and others. The man of the past who bound his hair three times in the course of one bath, and who spat out his food three times in the course of one meal,[24] solely had a mind to help others. There was never a question that he might not teach them just because they were the

17. Quotation from a Chinese text; source untraced.

18. 肝 (*kimo*) lit. means "the liver."

19. 心 (SHIN, *kokoro*) means not only "mind" but also "heart." In fact the Chinese character 心 is originally a pictograph of a heart. In this translation of Shobogenzo, 心 has almost always been translated as "mind," but the intended meaning is the subjective side of the whole human state, not only intellectual consciousness.

20. 利行 (RIGYO), "helpful conduct" or "beneficial conduct," from the Sanskrit *artha-caryā*, useful conduct. See Glossary.

21. 善巧 (ZENGYO), lit. "good skill"; short for 善巧方便 (ZENGYO-HOBEN), "skillful means," or "skillful expedients" from the Sanskrit *upāya-kauśalya*. See Book 1, Glossary.

22. 方便 (HOBEN), see note 21.

23. A Chinese chronicle called *Shinjo (History of the State of Shin)* says that a man called Koyu saved a turtle in distress and as a result of this good act he later became the governor of a district in the state. Another chronicle called *Taigu-nikki*, says that a nine-year-old boy called Yoho took care of an injured bird, and as a result of this good act his descendants ascended to three top positions in the Chinese government. See also chap. 30, *Gyoji*, para. [207].

24. The Chinese history *Shiki* says that when a king called Shuko appointed his son Hakukin as a district governor, Shuko told his son, "If three guests came while I was taking a bath, I would bind my hair three times to meet them, and if three guests came while I was eating, I would stop eating three times to meet them..."

people of a foreign land. So we should benefit friends and foes equally, and we should benefit ourselves and others alike. If we realize this state of mind, the truth that helpful conduct naturally neither regresses nor deviates will be helpfully enacted even in grass, trees, wind, and water. We should solely endeavor to save the foolish.

[82] *"Cooperation"*[25] means not being contrary.[26] It is not being contrary to oneself and not being contrary to others. For example, the human Tathāgata *identified*[27] himself with humanity. Judging from this identification with the human world we can suppose that he might identify himself with other worlds. When we know cooperation, self and others are oneness. The proverbial *harps, poems, and sake*[28] make friends with people, make friends with celestial gods, and make friends with earthly spirits. [At the same time,] there is a principle that people make friends with harps, poems, and sake, and that harps, poems, and sake make friends with harps, poems, and sake; that people make friends with people; that celestial gods make friends with celestial gods; and that earthly spirits make friends with earthly spirits. This is learning of cooperation. *"The task [of cooperation]"*[29] means, for example, concrete behavior, a dignified attitude, and a real situation. There may be a principle of, after letting others identify with us, then letting ourselves identify with others. [The relations between] self and others are, depending on the occasion, without limit. *Kanshi*[30] says: *"The sea does not refuse water; therefore it is able to realize its greatness. Mountains do not refuse earth; therefore they are able to realize their height. Enlightened rulers do not hate people; therefore they are able to realize a large following."* Remember, the sea not refusing water is cooperation. Remember also that water has the virtue of not refusing the sea. For this reason it is possible for water to come together to form the sea and for the earth to pile up to form mountains. We can think to ourselves that because the sea does not refuse the sea it realizes the sea and realizes greatness, and because mountains do not refuse mountains they realize mountains and realize height. Because enlightened rulers do not hate people they realize a

25. 同事 (DOJI), lit. "identity of task," from the Sanskrit *samāna-arthatā* which lit. means "identity of purpose," or "sharing the same aim" (see Glossary)—or to use a more colloquial expression, "being in the same boat." 同 (DO) means "same" and 事 (JI) means "thing," "matter," or "task."

26. 不違 (FUI). 違 (I), "different," or "contrary," is opposed to 同 (DO), "the same," in 同事 (DOJI).

27. 同ぜる (DO *zeru*). The character 同 (DO) is as in 同事 (DOJI).

28. The Taoist text *Gosha-inzui* says that harps, poems, and sake are [a hermit's] three friends. Master Dogen picks up this sentence and uses it to express the principles of mutual agreement between subject and object and identity of subject and object.

29. "The task [of cooperation]" is the character 事 (JI) of 同事 (DOJI). Real cooperation is not abstract but is always related to a concrete task.

30. 管子 (KANSHI) is the name of a Chinese Taoist text in 24 volumes attributed to Kanchu (Ch: Guan-tzu). Scholars suspect that there were actually several different authors.

large following. *"A large following"* means a nation. *"An enlightened ruler"* may mean an emperor. Emperors do not hate the people. They do not hate the people, but that does not mean there is no reward and punishment. Even if there is reward and punishment, there is no hatred for the people. In ancient times, when people were unaffected, nations were without reward and punishment—at least in as much as the reward and punishment of those days were different from those of today. Even today there may be people who seek the truth with no expectation of reward, but this is beyond the thinking of stupid men. Because enlightened rulers are enlightened, they do not hate people. Although people always have the will to form a nation and to find an enlightened ruler, few completely understand the truth of an enlightened ruler being an enlightened ruler. Therefore, they are glad simply not to be hated by the enlightened ruler, while never recognizing that they themselves do not hate the enlightened ruler. Thus the truth of cooperation exists both for enlightened rulers and for ignorant people, and this is why cooperation is the conduct and the vow of a bodhisattva. We should face all things only with gentle faces.

[85] Because these four elements of sociability are each equipped with four elements of sociability, they may be sixteen elements of sociability.

Shobogenzo
Bodaisatta-shishobo

Written on the 5th day of the 5th lunar month[31] in the 4th year of Ninji[32] by a monk who went into Sung China and received the transmission of the Dharma, śramaṇa Dogen.

---

31. 端午日 (TANGO *no* HI). The 5th day of the 5th lunar month was a day of celebration, referred to as 端午の日 (TANGO *no* HI). In Japan today, the term *tango no hi* is still sometimes used for the national holiday on May 5th (Children's Day).

32. 1243.

[46]

葛藤

KATTO

The Complicated

***Katsu** means "arrowroot" and **to** means "wisteria." Arrowroot and wisteria, being vines, are unable to stand by themselves but grow by entwining with other plants. Because of this, in China and Japan, arrowroot and wisteria are used as a symbol of something that is very complicated. Buddhist philosophy strives to describe what reality is. Because reality cannot be adequately expressed with words, it is sometimes described as "the ineffable." Here, Master Dogen uses the word **katto**, the complicated, to suggest reality, which is very direct, but complicated. He felt that the words "the complicated" express the nature of reality rather well.*

[87] **The experience and the transmission,** in the order on Vulture Peak, of Śākyamuni Buddha's right-Dharma-eye treasury and supreme truth of bodhi belongs only to the Great Master Mahākāśyapa. Authentically experienced in the transmission from rightful successor to rightful successor, it arrives at the twenty-eighth patriarch, the Venerable Bodhidharma. The Venerable One demonstrates in China the behavior of a patriarch, and transmits the right-Dharma-eye treasury and the supreme truth of bodhi to Great Master Taiso Shoshu Fukaku,[1] making him the second patriarch. We call the twenty-eighth patriarch, as the first in China to possess the behavior of a patriarch, "the First Patriarch"; and we call the twenty-ninth patriarch "the Second Patriarch." This is the custom in the eastern lands. The First Patriarch, under the Venerable Prajñātara in the past, has directly experienced, and has received the direct transmission of the Buddha's instruction and the bones of the truth. Using the original root he has experienced the original root, and made this into a base for branches and leaves. In general, although sacred beings all aim to learn the cutting of the roots of the complicated,[2]

---

1. Master Taiso Eka (487–593), the 2nd patriarch in China. Great Master Taiso Shoshu Fukaku is his posthumous title.

2. 葛藤 (KATTO). In colloquial modern Japanese, and also in zen teachings other than Master Dogen's, the word 葛藤 (KATTO) has negative connotations. *Kenkyusha* gives: "trouble(s), discord, dissension; complications." JEBD gives: "A derogatory word used to express complicated teachings." Further JEBD has the following dubious entry for 葛藤禅 (KATTO-ZEN): "Wordy zen. Zen which clings to words and letters and does not understand the great way of the Buddhas and patriarchs" (cf. words of Master Dofuku in para. [90]).

they do not learn that cutting means cutting the complicated with the complicated, and they do not know that the complicated is entwined with the complicated. How much less could they know that the succession of the complicated continues by means of the complicated? Few have known that the succession of the Dharma is the complicated itself. No-one has heard so. No-one has said so. Could many have realized so in experience?

[89] My late Master, the eternal Buddha, says, *"A bottle gourd vine entwines with a bottle gourd."*

This preaching has been neither seen nor heard in the orders in all directions of masters of all the ages. It has been preached by my late Master, for the first time, and by him alone. Bottle gourd vines intertwining with bottle gourd vines is Buddhist patriarchs investigating the state of Buddhist patriarchs and is Buddhist patriarchs experiencing the exact-same state of Buddhist patriarchs. It is the state, for example, of *the mind being transmitted by the mind.*[3]

[90] *The twenty-eighth patriarch says to his disciples, "The time is approaching.*[4] *Why don't you say what you have got."*

Then the disciple Dofuku[5] *says, "My view now is, without being attached to words or being detached from words, to perform the function of the truth."*

The Patriarch says, "You have got my skin."

The nun Soji[6] *says, "My understanding now is like that of Ānanda*[7] *seeing the land of Akṣobhya-Buddha.*[8] *Seen once, it is not seen again."*

The Patriarch says, "You have got my flesh."

---

3. 以心伝心 (ISHIN-DENSHIN). The phrase 以心伝心 (ISHIN-DENSHIN), or "intuitive communication from mind to mind," is common in everyday speech even among Japanese today. The Buddhist meaning of 以心伝心 (ISHIN-DENSHIN) can be represented with the metaphor of the sympathetic resonance of tuning forks.

4. Master Bodhidharma knew that the time of his death was drawing near.

5. Master Dofuku (464–524), successor of Master Bodhidharma. He traveled through many lands in search of a true teacher before finally meeting Master Bodhidharma and becoming his successor.

6. Nun Soji (dates unknown), successor of Master Bodhidharma. She was the daughter of Emperor Bu of the Liang dynasty (reigned 502 to 549). Nun Soji is her title, her monk's name being Myoren.

7. 慶喜 (KEIKI), "joy," represents the meaning, not the sound, of the Sanskrit *Ānanda.* The name is said to be derived from the fact that Master Ānanda's birthday was the day on which the Buddha first realized the truth.

8. In the mandala used by the Shingon Sect there are five Buddha-images, and the image on the eastern side is of Akṣobhya-buddha. This buddha is mentioned in Lotus Sutra, *Kejo-yu (The Parable of the Magic City): "Two of those śramaṇeras became buddhas in the eastern quarter. The first was named Akṣobhya and lived in the Land of Joy. The second was named Sumeru Peak."* (LS 2.66) In the story, the Buddhist land of Akṣobhya-buddha means an imaginary land or an ideal world.

The disciple Do-iku[9] says, "The four elements[10] are originally bare. The five aggregates[11] are not 'existence.' My viewpoint is that there is nothing to be got."

The Patriarch says, "You have got my bones."

Finally, Eka[12] does three prostrations and then stands at his place.

The Patriarch says, "You have got my marrow."

Consequently, he makes [Eka] the Second Patriarch, transmitting the Dharma and transmitting the robe.[13]

[92] Now, learn in practice, the First Patriarch's words *"You have got my skin, flesh, bones, and marrow"* are the Patriarch's words. The four disciples each possess what they have got and what they have heard. Both what they have heard and what they have got are skin, flesh, bones, and marrow that spring out of body and mind, and skin, flesh, bones, and marrow which drop away body and mind. We cannot see and hear the ancestral Master only by means of knowledge and understanding, which are but one move in a *go* game—not one-hundred-percent realization of subject-and-object, that-and-this. Nevertheless, people who have not received the authentic transmission think that there are degrees of intimacy in the understanding of each of the four disciples, and so the Patriarch also [expresses] differences of profundity between skin, flesh, bones, and marrow. Thinking skin and flesh to be further away than bones and marrow, [people] say that the Second Patriarch has received certification of getting the marrow because his understanding is superior. People who talk like this have never experienced learning in practice under the Buddhist patriarchs and have never received the authentic transmission of the Patriarch's truth. Remember, the Patriarch's skin, flesh, bones, and marrow are beyond shallowness and depth. Even if there is superiority and inferiority in understanding, the Patriarch's words are only about *getting me.* The point here is that the expression *"You have got my marrow"* and the expression *"You have got my bones"* are both beyond sufficiency and insufficiency, whether in teaching people or in receiving people, whether in picking up weeds or falling into grass.[14] [The Patriarch's expressions,] for example, are like picking up a flower and like transmitting the robe.[15] What [the Patri-

---

9. Master Do-iku (dates unknown), successor to Master Bodhidharma.

10. Earth, water, fire, and wind.

11. The five aggregates, or five skandhas, are matter, perception, thinking, action, and consciousness. The four elements and the five aggregates represent all physical things and mental phenomena in the Universe.

12. Master Taiso Eka. See note 1.

13. *Keitoku-dento-roku,* chap. 3. See also *Shinji-shobogenzo,* pt. 3, no. 1.

14. 拈艸落艸 (NENSO-RAKUSO), lit. "picking up weeds and falling into weeds," suggests miscellaneous cases of sincere active behavior and trivial passive behavior in everyday life.

15. Refers to the transmissions between the Buddha and Master Mahākāśyapa, and between Master Daiman Konin and Master Daikan Eno.

arch] expresses for the four disciples is, from the beginning, utterly the same. The Patriarch's expression is utterly consistent, but this does not necessarily mean that the four understandings are the same. Though the four understandings are individual and distinct, the Patriarch's expression is just the Patriarch's expression. Generally, speech and understanding cannot always be entrusted to each other. When the ancestral Master addresses each of the four disciples he is saying, for example, "You have got me as my skin." If there were hundreds of thousands of disciples after the Second Patriarch, there would have been hundreds of thousands of expressions; there would be no limit. There are only four disciples and so there are only the four expressions of skin, flesh, bones, and marrow, but there are many possible expressions left unexpressed. Remember, even in addressing the Second Patriarch, he could say *"You have got my skin."* Even if [the expression] were *"You have got my skin,"* [the First Patriarch] would be transmitting the right-Dharma-eye treasury to [Eka] as the Second Patriarch. Getting skin or getting marrow do not rely upon superiority or inferiority. Again, in addressing Dofuku, Do-iku, Soji, or others, he could say *"You have got my marrow."* Even if they are *my skin,* he must transmit the Dharma to them. Consider the body-mind of the ancestral Master: his skin, flesh, bones, and marrow are each the ancestral Master himself; it is never the case that marrow is close and skin is distant. Now, when one who is equipped with the eyes of learning in practice receives certification that *"You have got my skin,"* that is the ultimate realization of getting the ancestral Master. There is the ancestral Master whose thoroughly realized body[16] is skin; there is the ancestral Master whose thoroughly realized body is flesh; there is the ancestral Master whose thoroughly realized body is bones; there is the ancestral Master whose thoroughly realized body is marrow; there is the ancestral Master whose thoroughly realized body is mind; there is the ancestral Master whose thoroughly realized body is body; there is the ancestral Master whose thoroughly realized mind is mind; there is the ancestral Master who is the thoroughly realized ancestral Master; there is the ancestral Master whose thoroughly realized body gets me-and-you; and so on. If these ancestral masters manifest themselves together and address hundreds of thousands of disciples, they will say, as now, *"You have got my skin."* The hundreds of thousands of expressions will be the skin, flesh, bones, and marrow, but onlookers will excitedly consider them without reason to be expressions about skin, flesh, bones, and marrow. If there were six or seven disciples in the ancestral Master's order he might say *"You have got my mind,"* he might say *"You have got my body,"* he might say *"You have got my state of buddha,"* he might say *"You have got my eyes,"* and he might say *"You have got my real experience."* As regards *"you,"* there are times when it is the Patriarch and there are times when it is Eka. We

16. 通身 (TSUSHIN). See chap. 33, *Kannon.*

should also investigate in detail the truth of *"having got."* Remember, there are cases of *you have got me* and there are cases of *I have got you*. There are cases in which *getting me* is *you* and there are cases in which *getting you* is *me*. If, when we research the body-mind of the ancestral Master, we say that inside and outside cannot be oneness, or that the whole body cannot be the thoroughly realized body, we are not in the real land of Buddhist patriarchs. To have got the skin is to have got the bones, the flesh, and the marrow; to have got the bones, the flesh, and the marrow is to have got the skin, the flesh, and the countenance. How could this state only be the clear understanding that *"The whole Universe in ten directions is the real body"*?[17] It is utterly the skin, flesh, bones, and marrow themselves. For this reason, it is *getting my robe* and is *You have got the Dharma*. On this basis, even the speaking of words is individual instances of the springing out in which master and disciple experience the same state. And even the action of listening is individual instances of the springing out in which master and disciple experience the same state. Investigation of the same state by master and disciple is the entanglement[18] of Buddhist patriarchs. The entangled state of Buddhist patriarchs is the life-blood of their skin, flesh, bones, and marrow. The picking up of a flower and the winking of an eye are entanglement itself, and a face breaking into a smile is the skin, the flesh, the bones, and the marrow themselves. We should investigate further. In the seed of entanglement the potential exists here and now to lay bare the substance and it is by virtue of this that there are stems, leaves, flowers, and fruits entwining in the entangled; because these [real stems, leaves, flowers, and fruits] are beyond complicatedness and uncomplicatedness, Buddhist patriarchs are realized and the Universe is realized.

99] Great Master Shinsai of Joshu[19] preaches to the assembly, *"Mahākāśyapa gave the transmission to Ānanda. Say then, Bodhidharma gave the transmission to what person?"*

Then a monk asks, *"How about the Second Patriarch who got the marrow?"*

The Master says, *"Do not insult the Second Patriarch!"*[20]

On another occasion, the Master says, *"In Bodhidharma's words, someone who is outside gets the skin and someone who is inside gets the bones. Say then, someone who is still further inside gets what?"*

A monk asks, *"What does it mean to have got the marrow?"*

The Master says, *"Just be aware of the skin! The old monk here and now does not even broach the subject of marrow."*

---

17. Alludes to the words of Master Chosa Keishin. See chap. 50, *Shoho-jisso*.

18. 葛藤 (KATTO), or "the complicated," as in the chapter title.

19. Master Joshu Jushin (778-897), successor of Master Nansen Fugan. Great Master Shinsai is his posthumous title.

20. *Kosonshuku-goroku*, chap. 13.

The monk asks, *"But what is the marrow?"*

The Master says, *"If you are like that you cannot grope even for the skin."*

[100] So remember, when we cannot grope for the skin we cannot grope for the marrow, and when groping gets the skin it also gets the marrow. We should consider the truth of *being like that, unable to grope even for the skin.* When [the monk] asks, *"What does it mean to have got the marrow?"* the expression *"Just be aware of the skin! The old monk here and now does not even broach the subject of marrow"* is realized. In *'being aware of the skin,' 'not even broaching the subject of marrow'* is the real *meaning of having got the marrow.* On this basis, the question *"How about the Second Patriarch who got the marrow?"* has been realized. When we reflect exactly[21] the moment in which Mahākāśyapa gives the transmission to Ānanda, Ānanda is concealing his body in Mahākāśyapa and Mahākāśyapa is concealing his body in Ānanda. At the same time, in the moment of their meeting within the transmission, they are not beyond the sphere of concrete actions that change the countenance and change the skin, flesh, bones, and marrow. On this basis, [Joshu] preaches *"Say then, Bodhidharma gives the transmission to a What person."*[22] When Bodhidharma is giving the transmission he is Bodhidharma, and when the Second Patriarch is getting the marrow he is Bodhidharma. Relying on investigation of this truth, the Buddha-Dharma has remained the Buddha-Dharma to the present day. If it were otherwise, the Buddha-Dharma could not reach the present. Quietly endeavoring to master this principle, we should express it ourselves and should cause others to express it.

[102] *"Someone who is outside gets the skin and someone who is inside gets the bones. Say then, someone who is still further inside gets what?"* The meaning of the *outside* expressed now, and of the *inside* expressed now, should be extremely straight and direct. When we are discussing *outside,* skin, flesh, bones, and marrow each have an outside; when are discussing *inside,* skin, flesh, bones, and marrow each have an inside. This being so, the four Bodhidharmas have each mastered, instance by instance, the ascendant state of hundreds, thousands, and tens of thousands of skins, of fleshes, of bones, and of marrows. Do not think that there can be no state ascendant to the marrow; there are further concrete states of ascendance, numbering three or five. What the eternal Buddha Joshu has now preached to the assembly is the Buddha's truth. It is beyond others such as Rinzai, Tokuzan, Dai-i, and Unmon; they have never dreamt of it; how much less could they express it? The unreliable old veterans of recent times do not even know that it exists, and if we told them of it, they might be astonished and afraid.

---

21. 当観 (TOKAN). 当 (TO) means to be exact, especially with regard to timing, and 観 (KAN) means to reflect. The phrase is discussed in chap. 22, *Bussho,* note 19.

22. 什麼の人 (SHIMO *no* HITO) means 1) What person? and 2) a person whose state cannot be explained with words.

103] Zen Master Seccho Myokaku[23] says, *"The two 'Shu's,' Jo[shu] and Boku[shu],[24] are eternal Buddhas."*[25] So the eternal Buddha's words are evidence of the Buddha-Dharma and are a past expression of the self. Great Master Seppo Shinkaku[26] says, *"The eternal Buddha Joshu!"* A former Buddhist patriarch[27] has eulogized him with the eulogy *eternal Buddha* and a later Buddhist patriarch[28] has also eulogized him with the eulogy *eternal Buddha*. Clearly, in that which is ascendant to the past and present, [Joshu] is a transcendent eternal Buddha. In sum, the truth that skin, flesh, bones, and marrow are entangled is the standard for the state of *you have got me* which is preached by eternal Buddhas. We should endeavor to master this criterion.

105] Furthermore, some say that the First Patriarch has returned to the West, but we learn that this is wrong. What So-un[29] saw may not have been real. How could So-un see the leaving and coming of the ancestral Master? The true study is just to learn that after the ancestral Master passed away [his ashes] were deposited on Yuji-san mountain.[30]

Shobogenzo Katto

Preached to the assembly at Kannon-dori-kosho-horin-ji temple in the Uji district of Yoshu[31] on the 7th day of the 7th lunar month in the 1st year of Kangen.[32]

23. Master Seccho Juken (980–1052), successor of Master Chimon Koso. He was honored with the title Zen Master Myokaku during his lifetime. See, for example, chap. 19, *Shinfukatoku*.

24. Master Bokushu Domyo (780?–877?), successor of Master Obaku Ki-un. See, for example, chap. 30, *Gyoji*, para. [170].

25. From *Myokaku-zenji-goroku*, vol. 1.

26. Master Seppo Gison (822–907). The same quotation is discussed in chap. 44, *Kobusshin*.

27. Master Seppo.

28. Master Seccho.

29. The monk So-un was sent by imperial edict to India in 518 and he returned three years later with sutras and commentaries of the Mahāyāna. *Keitoku-dento-roku* says that three years after Master Bodhidharma's death, So-un and Bodhidharma met while So-un was returning to China along the silk road.

30. A mountain in China where Master Bodhidharma's stūpa was erected.

31. Corresponds to present-day Kyoto prefecture.

32. 1243.

[47]

三界唯心

SANGAI-YUISHIN

The Triple World is Only the Mind

***San** means "three" and **kai** means "world." So **sangai** means "the three worlds," or "the triple world." Traditionally, Buddhist theory looks at the world as the amalgamation of three worlds: the world of thinking, the world of feeling, and the world of action. In traditional Buddhist terminology these three worlds are called the worlds of volition, matter, and non-matter. The phrase "the three worlds," or "the triple world," is often used to mean this world here and now, the whole world, the real world, which includes the world of thinking, the world of feeling, and the world of action. **Yui** means "only," "solely," or "alone," and **shin** means "mind." So **sangai-yuishin** means "the triple world is only the mind" or "the triple world is the mind alone." The phrase "the triple world is only the mind" is often interpreted as an idealistic insistence that the whole world is produced by our mind. Historically, many Buddhist monks thought that this was the case. Master Dogen did not agree; he insisted that in Buddhism, the phrase "the triple world is only the mind" means something far more real. This phrase refers to the teaching that reality exists in the contact between subject and object. From this viewpoint, when we say that the world is only the mind, we also need to say that the mind is only the world, to express the fact that the relationship is a mutual one. In this chapter, Master Dogen explains the meaning of the phrase "the triple world is only the mind" from the Buddhist viewpoint, criticizing idealistic interpretations.*

07] **The Great Master Śākyamuni says,**

The triple world is only the one mind,
There is nothing else outside of the mind.
The mind, buddha, and living beings—
The three are without distinction.[1]

07] [This] one saying is the whole effort of [the Buddha's] lifetime. The whole effort of his lifetime is the complete wholeness of his total effort. While it is deliberate action, it may also be action in the natural stream of speech and action. Thus, the words now spoken by the Tathāgata, *"The triple*

---

1. The Garland Sutra says, *"[All] that exists in the triple world is solely the one mind,"* (part 37) and *"The mind, buddha, and living beings—the three are without distinction"* (part 10).

world is only the mind" are the whole realization of the whole Tathāgata, and his whole life is the whole of this one saying. The triple world[2] is the whole world; we do not say that the triple world is the same thing as mind. The reason is that however brilliant in all aspects the triple world is, it is still the triple world. Even if we misunderstand that it might be beyond the triple world, that is completely impossible. Inside, outside, and middle, beginning, middle, and end; all are the triple world. The triple world is as the triple world is seen, and a view of something other than the triple world is a mistaken view of the triple world. While in the triple world, we see views of the triple world as old nests and see views of the triple world as new twigs.[3] The old nests were visions of the triple world, and a new twig is also a vision of the triple world.

[110] For this reason...

The Great Master Śākyamuni says, *"It is best to see the triple world as the triple world."*[4]

This view is the triple world itself. This triple world is just as it is seen. The triple world is not original existence, the triple world is not present existence, the triple world is not fresh realization, the triple world does not arise from causes and conditions, and the triple world is beyond beginning, middle, and end. There is *getting free from the triple world,*[5] and there is *the triple world which is here and now.*[6] This state is the pivot meeting the pivot and entanglement promoting entanglement. The triple world here and now is the object seen as the triple world, and this object seen is [the agent's] *seeing it as the triple world. Seeing it as the triple world* is the realized triple world, is the triple world's realization, and is the realized Universe.[7] Being able to make the triple

---

2. 三界 (SANGAI), "the triple world," represents the Sanskrit *trayo-dhātavah*. The three worlds are *kāma-dhātu*, 欲界 (YOKKAI), "the world of desire or volition (thinking)"; *rūpa-dhātu*, 色界 (SHIKIKAI), "the world of matter or form (feeling)"; and *arūpa-dhātu*, 無色界 (MUSHIKI-KAI), "the world of non-matter or formlessness (action)." See Glossary.

3. While living in reality, we are constantly getting rid of views and opinions of reality, and at the same time, at every moment we are looking at reality directly.

4. Quoted from the *Nyorai-juryo (Tathāgata's Lifetime)* chapter of the Lotus Sutra (LS 3.18). See chap. 43, *Kuge*, note 49.

5. 出離三界 (SHUTSURI-SANGAI). The characters 出三界 (SHUTSU-SANGAI), "to get free from the triple world," appear several times in the 3rd chapter of the Lotus Sutra, *Hiyu (A Parable)*, in which a wealthy man causes his children to leave a burning house just as the Buddha causes living beings to get free from the suffering of the triple world (by seeing the triple world as it is). The characters 離三界 (RI-SANGAI), "to be free from the triple world," appear in the quotation in the following note.

6. 今此三界 (KONSHI-SANGAI), lit. "the triple world now and here," or "Now this triple world..." appears in the Lotus Sutra, *Hiyu: The Tathāgata, already free from / The burning house of the triple world / Lives serenely in seclusion / Abiding peacefully in forests and fields. / Now this triple world / All is my possession / And the living beings in it / All are my children."* (LS 1.198.)

7. The triple world is realized by the action of seeing.

world establish the mind, undergo training, [realize] bodhi, and [experience] nirvāṇa, is just the state in which *All is my possession.*

12] For this reason...
The Great Master Śākyamuni says,

Now this triple world
All is my possession
And living beings in it
All are my children.[8]

Because this triple world here and now is the Tathāgata's *own possession,* the whole Universe is the triple world. Because the triple world is the whole Universe, *here and now*[9] is the past, present, and future. The reality of past, present, and future does not obstruct *the here and now.* The reality of *the here and now* blocks off past, present, and future. *"My possession"* [expresses that] *The whole Universe in ten directions is a real human body,*[10] and *The whole Universe in ten directions is a śramaṇera's one eye.*[11] *"Living beings"* are the real bodies of the whole Universe in ten directions. Because there are many beings, each one with a life as a living being, they are *living beings. "All are my children"* is the truth that children themselves are the manifestation of all functions. At the same time, *my children* inevitably receive from a compassionate father their body, hair, and skin, which they neither injure nor lack, and this is seen as the child's realization.[12] That the state in the moment of the present is beyond the father being former and the child being latter, beyond the child being former and the father being latter, and beyond father and child being aligned together, is the truth of *"my children."* Without being given, this state is received, and without being taken by force it is acquired. It is beyond the forms of leaving and coming, beyond the scale of large and small, and beyond discussion of old and young. We should retain "old" and "young" as the Buddhist Patriarch retains "old" and "young." Sometimes a father is young and a child is old;[13] sometimes a father is old and a child is young; sometimes a father is old and a child is old; and sometimes a father is young and a child is young. One who imitates the maturity of a father is not being a

---

8. LS 1.198. See note 6.

9. 今此 (KONSHI), lit. "now this," (as in the Buddha's words) or "now and here."

10. Master Dogen frequently quotes this expression in Shobogenzo. It expresses oneness of the Buddhist state and the external world. In chap. 50, *Shoho-jisso,* Master Dogen attributes the expression to Master Chosa Keishin.

11. Master Chosa Keishin's words, quoted in chap. 60, *Juppo,* again expressing oneness of the Buddhist state and the external world.

12. This may allude to the Confucianist text called *Kokyo (The Book of Filial Piety),* which says that to be sincere to one's parents is not to injure or mutilate one's own body, hair, and skin.

13. This case is considered in the 15th chapter of the Lotus Sutra, *Ju-chi-yushutsu (Springing Out from the Earth): "The father young and the children old. / The whole world does not believe it."* (LS 2.318)

child, and one who does not pass through the immaturity of childhood will not be a father. We must consider and investigate in detail, without fail and without haste, the maturity and youth of a child and the maturity and youth of a father. There are [relations between] father and child that become apparent at the same time to father and to child, there are those that actually cease at the same time for father and for child, there are those that become apparent at different times to father and to child, and there are those that cease to be apparent at different times for father and for child. Though not restricting the compassionate father, we are realized as *"my children,"* and without restricting *"my children,"* the compassionate father is realized. There are mindful living beings and there are unmindful living beings; there are *"my children"* who are mindful of it and there are *"my children"* who are not mindful of it.[14] All such children—*"my children"* and *"childlike me's"*—are true heirs of the compassionate father Śākyamuni. Those living beings of the past, present, and future that exist throughout the Universe in ten directions are the past, present, and future buddhas of the Universe in ten directions. The buddhas' *"my children"* are living beings, and the compassionate fathers of living beings are the buddhas. This being so, the flowers and fruits of all things are the buddhas' *own possessions;* rocks and stones, large and small, are the buddhas' *own possessions; a peaceful abode* is *forests and fields*, and *forests and fields* are *already free.*[15] And though this may be so, the point of the Tathāgata's words is only to speak of *"my children."* We should investigate that he has never spoken of being the father.

[116] Śākyamuni Buddha says, *"Even the suitably transforming Dharma-bodies*[16] *of the buddhas do not leave the triple world. Outside the triple world there are no living beings, so what object could buddhas teach? For this reason, I say the doctrine that there is another world of living beings outside the triple world is a doctrine in the non-Buddhist Scripture of Great Existence,*[17] *and not the preaching of the Seven Buddhas."*[18]

[117] We should clearly realize in practice that *the suitably transforming Dharma-bodies of the buddhas* are all of *the triple world.* The triple world has *no outside,*[19] in the same way, for example, as the Tathāgata has *no outside*, and in

---

14. "Conscious" and "unconscious" are 有心 and 無心, lit. "with mind, without mind." This may allude to Lotus Sutra, *Hiyu: "All living beings / Are my children / [But] deeply attached to worldly pleasures / They do not have wisdom* (wisdom = lit. 'wise mind')." (LS 1.198).

15. See note 6.

16. 応化法身 (OKE-HOSSHIN). The phrase suggests the fact that buddhas manifest the Buddhist state in different forms as is appropriate to save different beings.

17. 外道大有経 (GEDO-DAI-U-KYO). It has not been established whether this refers to the proper name of a non-Buddhist scripture, or whether it is a general term.

18. *Ninno-gokoku-hannya-haramitsu-kyo*, pt. 1.

19. 無外 (MUGE). Master Dogen reversed the order of the characters in the sutra ("outside… there are no…") in order to suggest the state in which there is no object separate from the subject.

the same way as fences and walls have *no outside.* Just as the triple world has *no outside,* living beings have *no outside.* At the place where *there are no living beings, what is the object that buddhas teach?* The object of buddhas' teaching is always living beings. Remember, that which brings into existence another world of living beings outside the triple world is a non-Buddhist Scripture of Great Existence, and not a sutra of the Seven Buddhas. *The mind alone*[20] is beyond one or two; it is beyond the triple world and beyond leaving the triple world; it is free of error; it has thinking, sensing, mindfulness, and realization and it is free of thinking, sensing, mindfulness, and realization; it is fences, walls, tiles, and pebbles and it is mountains, rivers, and the Earth. The mind itself is skin, flesh, bones, and marrow; the mind itself is the picking up of a flower and a face breaking into a smile. There is conscious mind and there is unconscious mind; there is mind in which the body is present and there is mind in which no body is present; there is mind before the moment of the body and there is mind after the moment of the body. When the body is born, there are different kinds of birth—from womb, from egg, from moisture, and from transformation—and when the mind is born, there are different kinds of birth—from womb, from egg, from moisture, and from transformation. Blues, yellows, reds, and whites are the mind. The long, the short, the square, and the round are the mind. Living-and-dying and coming-and-going are the mind. Years, months, days, and hours are the mind. Dreams and fantasies, and flowers in space, are the mind. The spray of water, foam, and flame are the mind. Spring flowers and the autumn moon are the mind. Each moment is the mind. And yet it can never be broken. For this reason the real form of all dharmas is the mind, and buddhas alone, together with buddhas, are the mind.

[20] Great Master Shu-itsu[21] of Gensa-in temple asks Great Master Shin-o[22] of Jizo-in temple, *"How do you understand 'the triple world is the mind alone'?"*

Shin-o points to a chair and says, *"What does the Master call this thing?"*

The Great Master says, *"A chair."*

Shin-o says, *"The Master does not understand 'the triple world is the mind alone'."*

The Great Master says, *"I call this thing bamboo and wood. What do you call it?"*

Shin-o says, *"Keichin also calls it bamboo and wood."*

The Great Master says, *"If we search the whole Earth for a person who understands the Buddha-Dharma, it is impossible to find one."*[23]

---

20. 唯心 (YUISHIN), or "only the mind," as in the chapter title.

21. Master Gensa Shibi (835–907), successor of Master Seppo Gison. Great Master Shu-itsu is his posthumous title.

22. Master Rakan Keichin (867–928), successor of Master Gensa Shibi. Great Master Shin-o is his posthumous title.

23. *Keitoku-dento-roku,* chap. 11.

[121] As regards the question that the great Master now asks, *"How do you understand 'the triple world is the mind alone,'"* both *somehow understanding*[24] and *somehow not understanding* are *the triple-world-mind alone*,[25] and for this reason, they may not yet have become *"the triple world is the mind alone."* Shin-o, for this reason, points to a chair and says, *"What does the Master call this thing?"* Remember, [the meaning of] *"How do you understand?"* is *"What does the Master call this thing?"* As for the Great Master's words *"A chair,"* say, for the present, are they words that understand the triple world? Are they words that do not understand the triple world? Are they words of the triple world. Are they words beyond the triple world? Are they expressed by the chair? Are they expressed by the Great Master? We should investigate expression like this, *seeing if we can express something ourselves*.[26] We should have understanding, *seeing if we can understand something ourselves*. And we should have investigation in experience, *seeing if we can experience something ourselves*. Shin-o says, *"The Master does not understand 'the triple world is the mind alone.'"* This expression, for example, in expressing Joshu, is *"the east gate and the south gate,"* but there may also be *"a west gate and a north gate,"* and furthermore there is east Joshu itself and south Joshu itself.[27] Even if we have the state of *understanding "the triple world is the mind alone,"* we should also master *not understanding "the triple world is the mind alone."* Moreover, there is *the triple-world-mind alone* which is beyond both understanding and not understanding. The great Master says, *"I call this thing bamboo and wood."* We must completely master, both before it is voiced and after it becomes words, this unprecedented and unrepeatable[28] snippet of an expression. *"I call this thing bamboo and wood"*: prior to the naming that has now taken place, what was it called? In its former state of brilliance in all aspects, has it always been, in the beginning, middle, and end, bamboo and wood? Is to call it bamboo and wood now to express *"the triple world is the mind alone"*? Is it to leave unexpressed *"the triple world is the mind*

---

24. 作麼生会 (SOMOSAN-E) in Master Gensa's words means "How... understand?" Here the word 作麼生 (SOMOSAN), "how," suggests openness. It indicates that the understanding is real or intuitive rather than merely intellectually precise. See also end of chap. 35, *Hakujushi*.

25. 三界唯心 (SANGAI-YUISHIN). Here Master Dogen uses the phrase not as the statement "the triple world is the mind alone," but as a compound noun: "[the unity] of the triple world and the mind alone," i.e. one reality with the two faces of world and mind.

26. 試道看 *(kokoromo[ni] i[e] mi[n])*, "Try saying something!" or "See if you can express it yourself," is a phrase which appears in the preaching of Master Tendo Nyojo. See for example chap. 30, *Gyoji*, para. [264]: *"Try to express it yourself."* In the expressions which follow, Master Dogen substituted the words "understand" and "experience" for "express."

27. Master Joshu is asked by a monk, *"What is Joshu?"* The Master replies, *"The east gate, the south gate, the west gate, and the north gate."* See *Shinji-shobogenzo*, pt. 1, no. 46. Joshu is the name of the Master, a city, and a district where the Master lived. The monk's question suggests interest in Master Joshu's personality. Master Joshu's answer suggests that he was only conscious of living in reality.

28. 光前絶後 (KOZEN-ZETSUGO). This is a poetic variation on the expression 空前絶後 (KUZEN-ZETSUGO), which means "never before or since."

alone"? Remember, when *the triple-world-mind alone* is expressed in the morning it may be a chair, it may be the mind alone, and it may be the triple world, but when *the triple-world-mind alone* is expressed in the evening it comes out as *"I call this thing bamboo and wood."* Shin-o says, *"Keichin also calls it bamboo and wood."* Remember, though this is a conversation between master and disciple, it may also be a state of rightness from beginning to end which they are experiencing together. At the same time, we should investigate whether the Great Master's words *"I call this thing bamboo and wood,"* and Shin-o's words *"I also call it bamboo and wood,"* are the same or not the same, and whether they are adequate or not adequate. The Great Master says, *"If we search the whole Earth for a person who understands the Buddha-Dharma, it is impossible to find one."* We should also closely scrutinize and decide about this expression. Remember, the Great Master only calls it bamboo and wood, and Shin-o also only calls it bamboo and wood. They never understand *"the triple world is mind alone,"* they never negate understanding of *"the triple world is mind alone,"* they never express *"the triple world is mind alone,"* and they never negate expression of *"the triple world is mind alone."* Even so, I would like to ask Great Master Shu-itsu, "You say that *if we search the whole Earth for a person who understands the Buddha-Dharma, it is impossible to find one;* but see if you can answer this:[29] What is it that you call *'the whole Earth'*?" In conclusion, we should investigate it and make effort like this.

Shobogenzo Sangai-yuishin

Preached to an assembly on Yamashi peak in Etsu-u,[30] on the 1st day of the intercalary 7th lunar month in the 1st year of Kangen.[31]

---

29. 試道看 *(kokoromo[ni] i[e] mi[n]).* See note 26.
30. Corresponds to present-day Fukui prefecture.
31. 1243.

[48]

說心說性

SESSHIN-SESSHO

Expounding the Mind & Expounding the Nature

Setsu *means "teach," "explain," or "expound."* ***Shin*** *means "mind," and* ***sho*** *means "the essence," or "the nature." So* ***sesshin*** *means "expounding the mind" and* ***sessho*** *means "expounding the nature." Some Chinese Buddhist monks asserted that expounding the mind and expounding the nature belong within the sphere of intellectual effort, and so to make such effort to explain the mind and essence is not only unnecessary but also detrimental to attainment of the Buddhist truth. They believed that the Buddhist truth could never embrace intellectual understanding. Master Dogen had a different opinion. He thought that the concepts* ***sesshin*** *and* ***sessho*** *in Buddhist thought refer to something much more real. He understood* ***sesshin-sessho*** *as the manifestation of the mind and the manifestation of the nature in the real world. Master Dogen saw no reason to deny the concepts* ***sesshin*** *and* ***sessho****; instead he used them to explain the fundamental theory of Buddhism.*

27] **While Zen Master Shinzan Somitsu**[1] is walking with Great Master Tozan Gohon,[2] Great Master Gohon points to a nearby temple and says, *"Inside there is someone expounding the mind and expounding the nature."*

His elder brother[3] Somitsu says, *"Who is it?"*

Great Master Gohon says, *"Being asked one question by you, elder brother, I have directly attained the state of having died completely."*

Brother Somitsu says, *"That concrete state of expounding the mind and expounding the nature is who."*

Great Master Gohon says, *"In death I have come alive."*[4]

---

1. Master Shinzan Somitsu (dates unknown), successor of Master Ungan Donjo.
2. Master Tozan Ryokai (807–869), also a successor of Master Ungan Donjo, and the 38th patriarch in Master Dogen's lineage.
3. 師伯 (SHIHAKU), a term of respect for a senior member of one's master's order. 師 (SHI) means master or teacher. 伯 (HAKU), means elder brother or uncle.
4. *Shinji-shobogenzo*, pt. 1, no. 62.

[128] *Expounding the mind and expounding the nature*[5] are the universal basis of the Buddha's truth, by virtue of which every buddha and every patriarch is realized. Unless there is *expounding the mind and expounding the nature,* [buddhas and patriarchs] do not turn the splendid wheel of Dharma, do not establish the mind and undergo training, and do not realize the truth simultaneously with the whole Earth and all sentient beings; and all living beings do not realize the state of being without the Buddha-nature. Picking up a flower and winking an eye are *expounding the mind and expounding the nature*; a face breaking into a smile is *expounding the mind and expounding the nature*; doing prostrations and standing in place are *expounding the mind and expounding the nature;* the ancestral Master's entry into Liang[6] is *expounding the mind and expounding the nature;* and the transmission of the robe in the middle of the night is *expounding the mind and expounding the nature.* Holding up a staff is just *expounding the mind and expounding the nature.* Laying down a whisk is just *expounding the mind and expounding the nature.* In sum, the virtues which each buddha and each patriarch has are all just *expounding the mind and expounding the nature.* There is *expounding the mind and expounding the nature* by normality,[7] and there is *expounding the mind and expounding the nature* by fences, walls, tiles, and pebbles. [Moments] when the truth is realized that the arising of mind is the arising of miscellaneous real dharmas and the truth is realized that the passing of mind is the passing of miscellaneous real dharmas, are all moments when the mind is expounding and moments when the nature is expounding. Nevertheless, ordinary folk who do not penetrate the mind and do not master the nature, in their ignorance, not knowing *expounding the mind and expounding the nature* and not knowing discussion of the profound and discussion of the fine, say, and teach to others, that the truth of the Buddhist patriarchs should not include these things. Because they do not know *expounding the mind and expounding the nature* as *expounding the mind and expounding the nature,* they think of *expounding the mind and expounding the nature* as expounding about the mind and expounding about the nature.[8] And this is mainly because they do not think critically about whether or not they have penetrated the great truth.

---

5. 性 (SHO), lit. "nature," or "essence," means the natural state, or a natural function, in concrete reality. For example, in chap. 22, *Bussho,* Master Dogen explains 仏性 (BUSSHO), "the Buddha-nature," as the state of action.

6. Master Bodhidharma entered China during the time of the Liang dynasty (502–557). See chap. 30, *Gyoji.*

7. 平常 (HYOJO), frequently used in the phrase 平常心 (HYOJO-SHIN), "the normal mind," or "the everyday mind." See for example the opening paragraph of chap. 22, *Bussho.*

8. They think that real manifestation of the mind and the nature, which is done by action itself, means intellectual explanation.

[131] Latterly, a certain Soko, [titled] Zen Master Dai-e[9] of Kinzan mountain, has said, *"Because people today like to expound about the mind and expound about the nature, and they like to discuss the profound and discuss the fine, they are slow in attaining the truth. When we have simply thrown away the duality of mind and nature and forgotten both the profound and the fine, so that dualistic forms do not arise, then we really experience the state."* This [is the] insistence [of one who] has never known the thoughts[10] of the Buddhist patriarchs and has never heard of the royal lineage of the Buddhist patriarchs. As a result, because he understands that the mind is only thinking, sensing, mindfulness, and realization but does not understand that thinking, sensing, mindfulness, and realization are the mind, he speaks like this. Wrongly imagining *the nature* to be only clear, calm, peaceful, and quiet, he does not know the existence and non-existence of the Buddha-nature[11] and the Dharma-nature,[12] and he has never seen *the nature as it is*[13] even in a dream; therefore he has formed such a distorted view of the Buddha-Dharma. The mind that Buddhist patriarchs express is skin, flesh, bones, and marrow; the nature that Buddhist patriarchs retain is a bamboo cane and a staff; the profound that Buddhist patriarchs uniformly experience[14] is outdoor pillars and stone lanterns; and the fine that Buddhist patriarchs discuss is wisdom and understanding. Buddhist patriarchs who are really Buddhist patriarchs, from the beginning, hear in action, expound in action, practice in action, and experience in action this state of the mind and the nature. They retain and learn in action this state of the profound and the fine. People in the state like this are called children and grandchildren who are learning the Buddhist patriarchs. Those who are not like this are not learning the truth. For this reason, when it is time to attain the truth, they do not attain the truth, and when it is time to be beyond attainment of the truth they are not beyond attainment of the truth. They stumble through times of both attainment and non-attainment. The words *"to forget the duality of mind and nature,"* which that fellow [Soko] has spoken, are a partial attempt to ex-

---

9. Master Dai-e Soko (1089–1163), successor of Master Engo Kokugon. His history is recorded in chap. 75, *Jisho-zanmai*. His works included *Dai-e Shobogenzo (Dai-e's Right-Dharma-Eye Treasury)*. He was a major instigator of *koan-zen* (based on intentional consideration of questions and answers), as opposed to the *mokusho-zen* (silent, reflective Zazen) advocated by his contemporary Master Wanshi Shokaku.

10. 緗緗 (KENSHO). These characters, which are rare, lit. mean "blue thread," of the sort used in ancient times to bind Chinese texts. The words are therefore a concrete symbol of thoughts.

11. 仏性 (BUSSHO), see chap. 22, *Bussho*.

12. 法性 (HOSSHO), see chap. 54, *Hossho*.

13. 如是相 (NYOZESO) appears in Lotus Sutra, *Hoben* (LS 1.68). See also chap. 17, *Hokke-ten-hokke*, and chap. 50, *Shoho-jisso*.

14. 証契 (SHOKAI). 証 (SHO) means experience. 契 (KAI) means pledge, promise, accord, or binding agreement and, by extension, the state which is exactly the same as the state of Gautama Buddha. See also chap. 16, *Shisho*.

pound the mind—a hundredth, thousandth, ten-thousandth, or hundred millionth of a part. To speak of *"throwing away the profound and the fine,"* is a partial attempt to discuss the profound and the fine. When, not having learned this pivotal point, he stupidly speaks of forgetting, he thinks it means something leaving the hands; he understands that it means something having departed from the body.[15] He has not let go of the limited thinking of the small vehicle, so how could he penetrate the inner depths of the great vehicle, and how much less could he know the pivotal matter of the ascendant state?[16] It is hard to say that he has tasted the tea and meals of a Buddhist patriarch. To work earnestly under a teacher is to investigate physically, in the very moment of the body-mind, and is to investigate in experience, both before the body and after the body,[17] nothing other than *expounding the mind and expounding the nature*. There is no second or third different example at all.

[135] *Thereupon the First Patriarch says to the Second Patriarch,*[18] *"If you just let external involvements cease and have no panting and gasping in your mind, your mind will be like fences and walls, and you will be able to enter the truth." The Second Patriarch makes various efforts to expound the mind and expound the nature, but always fails to experience the state.*[19] *One day he suddenly attains reflection. At length he addresses the First Patriarch: "This time, for the first time, the disciple has let involvements cease." The First Patriarch, knowing that the other is already in the state of realization, does not examine him closely, but only says, "You have not realized cessation, have you?" The Second Patriarch says, "No."*[20] *The First Patriarch says, "What is the disciple's situation?" The Second Patriarch says, "I am always recognizing it very clearly, therefore I cannot express it with words." The First Patriarch says, "That is just the substance of the mind transmitted by the buddhas and patriarchs of the past. Now you have got it, you yourself must guard it well."*[21]

[136] There are those who doubt this story, and those who quote it. Among the stories of how the Second Patriarch served the First Patriarch, one story is like this. The Second Patriarch tried persistently to expound the mind and

---

15. To be conscious that something has gone is not to have forgotten it.

16. 向上の関棙子 (KOJO *no* KANREISU), the words of Master Obaku Ki-un, discussed at length by Master Dogen in the final paragraph of chap. 28, *Butsu-koji-no-ji*.

17. 身先身後 (SHINSEN-SHINGO), "before the body and after the body," suggests intuitive reflection immediately preceding and following an action. At the same time, it suggests endless continuation of Buddhist effort in eternity.

18. Master Bodhidharma says to Master Taiso Eka.

19. 相契 (SHOKAI). See note 14.

20. 無 (MU) expresses general negation: "No!" At the same time it lit. means "there is nothing," or "I have nothing."

21. *Keitoku-dento-roku*, chap. 3.

expound the nature, and at first his state did not match the state,[22] but he gradually accumulated merit and heaped up virtue until he finally attained the First Patriarch's state of truth. Common and stupid people have interpreted this as follows: "When at first the Second Patriarch expounded the mind and expounded the nature but did not experience the state, the fault was in the expounding of the mind and expounding of the nature. Later, when he abandoned expounding the mind and expounding the nature, he experienced the state." They speak like this because they have not mastered the teaching that *with minds like fences and walls we are able to enter the truth.* They are especially ignorant of stages in learning the truth. The reason [I say so] is this: From the time we establish the bodhi-mind and direct ourselves towards training in the way of Buddha, we sincerely practice difficult practices; and at that time, though we keep practicing, in a hundred efforts we never hit the target once. Nevertheless, *sometimes following good counselors and sometimes following the sutras,* we gradually become able to hit the target. One hit of the target now is by virtue of hundreds of misses in the past; it is one maturation of hundreds of misses. Listening to the teachings, training in the truth, and attaining the state of experience are all like this. Even though yesterday's attempts to expound the mind and to expound the nature were a hundred misses, the hundred missed attempts to expound the mind and to expound the nature yesterday are suddenly a hit today. When we are beginners in practicing the Buddha-way, even though, due to lack of training, we have not mastered the way, we can never attain the Buddha-way by abandoning the Buddha-way and pursuing other ways. It is hard for people who have not mastered the whole process of Buddhist training to clarify this situation as a fact. The Buddha-way, at the time of the first establishment of the will, is the Buddha-way; and at the time of realization of the right state of truth, it is the Buddha-way. The beginning, the middle, and the end are each the Buddha-way. It is like someone walking one thousands miles: the first step is one in a thousand miles and the thousandth step is one in a thousand miles. Though the first step and the thousandth step are different, the thousand miles are the same. Nevertheless, extremely stupid people think that when we are learning the Buddha-way we have not arrived at the Buddha-way; they think that it is the Buddha-way only in the time beyond realization of the effect. They are like this because they do not know that the whole way is expounding of the way, they do not know that the whole way is practice of the way, and they do not know that the whole way is experience of the way. Those who understand that only deluded people realize the great state of realization through Buddhist training and who neither know nor hear that people who are not deluded also realize the great state of realization through Buddhist training, express [the thoughts] described above. Even be-

---

22. 相契 (SOKAI), a variation of 相契 (SHOKAI); see note 14. 相 (SO) expresses mutual relation between two factors.

fore experience of the state, *expounding the mind and expounding the nature* is the Buddha-way; at the same time, it is by *expounding the mind and expounding the nature* that we experience the state. We should not learn that "experiencing the state" describes only a deluded person's first realization of the great state of realization. People in the state of delusion realize the great realization; people in the state of realization realize the great realization; people who are beyond realization realize the great realization; people who are beyond delusion realize the great realization; and people who are experiencing the state experience the state. Thus, to *expound the mind and expound the nature* is to be straight and true in the Buddha-way. Not having mastered this truth, Soko[23] says that we should not expound the mind and expound the nature, but his words are not a truth of the Buddha-Dharma. In the great kingdom of Sung today no-one has arrived even at Soko's level.

[140] The founding Patriarch, Great Master Gohon, as an Honored-One alone among the many patriarchs, has mastered the truth that *expounding the mind and expounding the nature* is *expounding the mind and expounding the nature*. The ancestral masters in all directions who have never mastered it have no expressions like his in the present story: While Brother Somitsu and the Great Master are walking along, [the Great Master] points to a nearby temple and says, *"Inside there is someone expounding the mind and expounding the nature."* Since the founding Patriarch manifested himself in the world, his Dharma-descendants have inevitably received the authentic transmission of this expression as the transcendent way of the patriarchs. Other lineages have not seen or heard it even in a dream. How much less could they know, even in a dream, the method of understanding it? [The method] has only been received in the authentic transmission to rightful successors. How could those who have not received the authentic transmission of this principle master the basis of the Buddha-way? The principle under discussion now is that [the unity of] *in* and *side*,[24] and [the unity of] *the existence of a human*[25] and *a human's existence*,[26] is *expounding the mind and expounding the nature*. [This unity] is

23. 杲公 (KOKO), lit. "Mister Ko." 杲 (KO) is from the name 宗杲 (SOKO). 公 (KO) is a title not generally used for monks.

24. 或裏或面 (WAKURI-WAKUMEN). In the story, "inside" is 裏面 (RIMEN). 裏 (RI) means "backside," or "inside." 面 (MEN) means "face," or "surface." In the story the compound 裏面 (RIMEN) is used colloquially, but here Master Dogen separates the characters 裏 (RI) and 面 (MEN) by the characters 或…或… (WAKU... WAKU...), which mean "either... or..." or "sometimes... and sometimes..." He thus suggests reality as the combination of meaningful content ("in") and objective form ("side").

25. 有人 (UNIN), translated in the story as "there is someone." 有 (U) means "there is," or "existence." 人 (NIN) means "person," or "human."

26. 人有 (NINU). By reversing the order of the characters in the story, Master Dogen again suggests two faces of reality—the idea of there being someone, and the concrete existence of a human being.

the-mind-as-surface-and-content expounding[27] and is *the-nature-as-surface-and-content expounding.*[28] We should investigate this and consider it. There has never been *expounding* that was separate from *the nature,* and *the mind* has never existed apart from *expounding.* "The Buddha-nature" describes all things expounding and "being without the Buddha-nature" describes all things expounding. Though we learn that the Buddha-nature is *the nature,* if we do not learn the Buddha-nature as existence, that is not learning the truth; and if we do not learn the Buddha-nature as being without, that is not learning the state in practice.[29] Those who learn in practice that *expounding* is *natural* are the legitimate descendants of Buddhist patriarchs. Those who believe that *the natural state* is *expounding* itself are Buddhist patriarchs who are legitimate descendants. To say that the mind is shaky but the nature is tranquil is the view of non-Buddhists. To say that the nature remains serene while form changes is the view of non-Buddhists. Buddhist learning of the mind and learning of the nature are not like that. Buddhist practice of the mind and practice of the nature are not the same as in non-Buddhism. Buddhist clarification of the mind and clarification of the nature are beyond non-Buddhists. In Buddhism there is expounding of the mind and expounding of the nature *there being someone,* and there is expounding of the mind and expounding of the nature *there being no-one;*[30] there is not expounding the mind and not expounding the nature *there being someone,* and there is not expounding the mind and not expounding the nature *there being no-one.* There is expounding the mind or failure to have expounded the mind and expounding the nature or failure to have expounded the nature. If we do not learn the expounding of the mind when there is no person, expounding of the mind has yet to reach fertile ground,[31] and if we do not learn the expounding of the mind when there is a person, expounding of the mind has yet to reach

27. 面裏心説 (MENRI-SHIN SETSU), lit. "the side-in mind expounding."

28. 面裏性説 (MENRI-SHO SETSU), lit. "the side-in nature expounding."

29. 有仏性 (UBUSSHO), "having the Buddha-nature" or "the Buddha-nature as concrete existence," and 無仏性 (MUBUSSHO), "being without the Buddha-nature" or "the Buddha-nature as the state of being without," are two contradictory expressions of the Buddha-nature (see chap. 22, *Bussho).* In this sentence, Master Dogen recommends us to realize the 性 (SHO) of 説心説性 (SESSHIN-SESSHO) as the 性 (SHO) of 仏性 (BUSSHO), realizing it not as a concept but as a real state which has two sides.

30. 無人 (MUNIN) is contrasted to 有人 (UNIN) in the story (see note 25). "Expounding of the mind and expounding of the nature there being no-one" suggests the manifestation of the Buddhist state by nature itself.

31. 未到田地 (MI-TO-DENCHI). 未 (MI) means "not yet." 到 (TO) means "reach." 田 (DEN), which means "paddy field," often represents a source of happiness—as for example in the poem in praise of the kaṣaya ("Formless, field of happiness, robe!"). 地 (CHI) means 1) earth, land, or ground; and 2) state [of body-mind].

fertile ground. We learn *the expounding of the-mind-in-which-there-is-no-person,*[32] we learn *the-state-in-which-there-is-no-person expounding the mind,*[33] we learn *expounding the mind as the concrete human state,*[34] and we learn *a concrete human being expounding the mind.*[35] The total effort that Rinzai expresses is only *"a true human being without rank,"*[36] but he has never mentioned *a true human being who has a rank.* We can say that he has not yet realized other study and other expressions, and that he has yet to reach the state of exploring the ultimate.[37] Because *expounding the mind and expounding the nature* is expounding the buddhas and expounding the patriarchs, we should meet it with the ears, and we should meet it with the eyes. Brother Somitsu, the story goes, says, *"Who is it?"* In realizing this expression, Brother Somitsu is able to exploit this expression in the former moment and he is able to exploit this expression in the latter moment. *"Who is it?"* is *expounding the mind and expounding the nature* which belongs to *that concrete situation.*[38] This being so, a moment in which *"Who is it?"* is expressed, or a moment in which *"Who is it?"* is concretely thought, is *expounding the mind and expounding the nature* itself. This *expounding the mind and expounding the nature* is something that people of other directions have never known. Because they forget the child and see it as the enemy, they deem enemies to be children.[39] The Great Master says, *"Being asked one question by you, elder brother, I have directly attained the state of having died completely."* Hearing these words, most ordinary practitioners think as follows: "Someone who expounds the mind and expounds the nature must directly attain the state of having died completely on being told *'it is who!'* The reason is that the words *'it is who!'* are [about] being face-to-face without consciousness of each other, [about] being totally without a view—so they may

---

32. 説心無人 (SETSU SHIN-MU-NIN), lit. "expounding the-mind-without-person." In chap. 3, *Genjo-koan,* for example, Master Dogen recommends us to realize the state in which we forget ourselves.

33. 無人説心 (MUN IN SESSHIN), lit. "no-person expounding the mind." In chap. 9, *Keisei-sanshiki,* for example, Master Dogen teaches that the voices of the river-valley and the form of the mountains manifest the Buddha-mind.

34. 説心是人 (SESSHIN-ZENIN), lit. "expounding the mind - concrete person."

35. 是人説心 (ZEN IN-SESSHIN), lit. "a concrete person expounds the mind." In chap. 72, *Zanmai-o-zanmai,* for example, Master Dogen says that sitting in the full lotus posture is the Buddha-mind-seal.

36. Quoted in *Rinzai-esho-zenji-goroku (A Record of the Words of Zen Master Rinzai Esho).*

37. 未到参徹地 (MI-TO-SAN TETSU-CHI). Alludes to the parallel phrase discussed in note 31. Here Master Dogen substitutes 参徹 (SANTETSU), "exploring the ultimate," for 田 (DEN), "paddy field."

38. 那裏 (NARI). 裏 (RI), lit. "the backside," or "the inside" (see note 24) means a concrete place or a concrete situation.

39. Because they do not understand that the straight and direct Buddhist state is like the state of a child who asks "Who is it?" they recognize as the Buddha's true disciples people who are causing complicated misunderstanding of the Buddha's teachings.

be a dead phrase."[40] That is not necessarily so. The people who have utterly mastered this *expounding the mind and expounding the nature* may be few. *Completely having died* is not to have died ten or twenty percent, and for this reason the *state of having died* is *complete*. At the very moment of *being asked* who can say that this state is not enclosing the whole sky and covering the whole earth? It may be that even illumination of the past is cut off, that even illumination of the present is cut off, that even illumination of the future is cut off, and that even illumination of this very moment is cut off.[41] Brother Somitsu says, *"That state of expounding the mind and expounding the nature is who."* Comparing the previous *"Who is it?"* and the present *"it is who,"* while the name is still the third son of Chang's, the man is the fourth son of Lee.[42] The Great Master says, *"Death itself has come alive."*[43] [With] this *death itself* he does not arbitrarily express *who it is*—hoping to indicate his *direct attainment of the state of having died,* and so directly indicating [his own] *concrete state of expounding the mind and expounding the nature*—for *it is who* has got rid of the *someone* who expounds the mind and expounds the nature.[44] There may be something to learn in practice in the assertion that we cannot always expect the complete state of having died.[45] The Great Master's words *"Death itself has come alive"* are the manifestation before us of the voice and form of *someone expounding the mind and expounding the nature.* At the same time, they may also be one or two concrete parts of the complete state of having died. *Liveliness,* though it is liveliness of the whole, does not manifest itself as liveliness through a transformation from death; it is simply liberated in the head-to-tail rightness of *coming alive.* In general, in the truth of the buddhas and the truth of the patriarchs, *expounding the mind and expounding the nature* exists and is investigated like this. Progressing further, through dying a complete death

---

40. 死句 (SHIKU), "dead phrase," means a comment which has no vital, concrete, or practical meaning. Ordinary practitioners do not notice the real meaning of Master Somitsu's straightforward question.

41. 際断 (SAIDAN), "cut off," means momentary. Each point of time is cut off from all other points in the past and future, and so all processes are momentary.

42. 是誰 (*ko[re] ta [zo]*; or ZESUI) "Who is it?", "Concretely who?", or "It is *who*", can be interpreted in at least two ways: 1) As a straightforward invitation to Master Tozan to make his words more concrete ("Who is it?" or "Concretely who?"), and 2) As a denial of the possibility of expressing in words the state of a person who expounds the mind and expounds the natural state ("It is *who*"). This sentence says the words 是誰 (ZESUI) are the same in both cases, but the meaning is different.

43. 死中得活 (SHICHU-TOKU-KATSU). In the story, read as *shichu [ni] katsu [o] e[tari],* these characters suggest the meaning "In death I have come alive." However, Master Dogen's interpretation is that there is no personal subject in the words 死中 (SHICHU), which lit. mean "the inside of death" and hence "the real state of death," or "death itself." In the context of the story, "death" represents the momentary extinction of all worries and fears.

44. In other words, the balanced state of action—not a personal subject—expounds the mind and expounds the nature.

45. Suggests the problem of attachment to the goal of detachment.

we realize the vivid state of coming alive. Remember, from the Tang dynasty until today, there have been many pitiable people who have not clarified the fact that *expounding the mind and expounding the nature* is the Buddha's truth and who, in their ignorance of *expounding the mind and expounding the nature* as teaching, practice, and experience, have produced outlandish explanations and confused sayings. We should save them both before the body and after the body. If I put it in words, *expounding the mind and expounding the nature* is the pivotal essence of the Seven Buddhas and the ancestral masters.

Shobogenzo Sesshin-sessho

Preached to the assembly at Kippo-ji temple in the Yoshida district of Etsu-shu,[46] Japan, in the 1st year of Kangen.[47]

46. Corresponds to present-day Fukui prefecture.
47. 1243.

[49]

仏道

BUTSUDO

The Buddhist Truth

***Butsu** means "Buddha" and **do** originally means "way," but also "morals" and "the truth." So **butsudo** means "the Buddha's truth" or "the Buddhist truth." The concept of "the Buddhist truth" is central to Master Dogen's theory, and it is helpful to examine the meaning from each of the four phases of Buddhist philosophy. In the first (subjective) phase, the Buddhist truth is embodied in the Buddhist philosophical system. In the second (objective) phase, the Buddhist truth is the external world, or nature. In the third phase (based on action), the Buddhist truth is ethical or moral conduct in everyday life; that is, everyday life as we live it. In the ultimate phase, the Buddhist truth is ineffable, the complicated; the state in Zazen, or reality itself. In this chapter, however, Master Dogen does not try to explain these meanings of "the Buddhist truth"; he simply asserts that there is only one Buddhism—that which was established by Gautama Buddha. Based on his assertion, although there are several Buddhist sects, we do not need to use the titles that these sects have been given. Master Dogen insists that the title "the Buddha's truth" or "Buddhism" is sufficient, and that it is wrong to use such titles as the Unmon Sect, the Hogen Sect, the Igyo Sect, the Rinzai Sect, and the Soto Sect. We usually think of Master Dogen as belonging to the Soto Sect, but he himself did not approve of the use of even the title "Soto Sect."*

[152] **The eternal Buddha Sokei**[1] on one occasion preaches to the assembly, "From Eno to the Seven Buddhas there are forty patriarchs."[2] When we investigate these words, from the Seven Buddhas to Eno are forty buddhas. When we count the buddhas and the patriarchs, we count them like this. When we count them like this, the seven Buddhas are seven patriarchs, and the thirty-three patriarchs are thirty-three buddhas. Sokei's intention is like this. This is the right and traditional instruction of the Buddha. Only the rightful successors of the authentic transmission have received the authentic transmission of this counting method. From Śākyamuni Buddha to Sokei there are thirty-four patriarchs. Each of the transmissions between these

1. Master Daikan Eno (638–713), successor of Master Daiman Konin. He is the 33rd patriarch, and the 6th patriarch in China.

2. Paraphrased in Japanese from *Rokuso-dankyo (The Sixth Patriarch's Platform Sutra).*

Buddhist patriarchs is like Kāśyapa[3] meeting the Tathāgata and like the Tathāgata getting Kāśyapa. Just as Śākyamuni Buddha learns in practice under Kāśyapa Buddha, each teacher and disciple exists in the present. Therefore, the right-Dharma-eye treasury has been personally transmitted from rightful successor to rightful successor, and the true life of the Buddha-Dharma is nothing other than this authentic transmission. The Buddha-Dharma, because it is authentically transmitted like this, is perfectly legitimate in its transmission. This being so, the virtues and the pivotal essence of the Buddha's truth have been faultlessly provided. They have been transmitted from India in the west to the eastern lands, a hundred thousand and eight miles, and they have been transmitted from the time when the Buddha was in the world until today, more than two thousand years. People who do not learn this truth in practice speak randomly and mistakenly. They randomly call the right-Dharma-eye treasury and the fine mind of nirvāṇa that have been authentically transmitted by the Buddhist patriarchs "the Zen Sect"; they call the ancestral Master "the Zen Patriarch"; they call practitioners "Zen students" or "students of dhyāna";[4] and some of them call themselves "the Zen schools." These are all twigs and leaves rooted in a distorted view. Those who randomly call themselves by the name "Zen Sect," which has never existed in India in the west or in the eastern lands, from the past to the present, are demons out to destroy the Buddha's truth. They are the Buddhist patriarchs' uninvited enemies.

[154] Sekimon's *Rinkanroku*[5] says: *Bodhidharma first went from the land of the Liang dynasty to the land of the Wei dynasty. He passed along the foot of Suzan mountain and rested his staff at Shorin [temple]. He just sat in stillness facing the wall, and only that—he was not learning Zen meditation. He continued this for a long time but no-one could understand the reason, and so they saw Bodhidharma as training in Zen meditation. Now, dhyāna*[6] *is only one of many practices: how could it be all there was to the Saint? Yet on the basis of this [misunderstanding] the chroniclers of that time subsequently listed him among those who were learning Zen meditation: they grouped him alongside people like withered trees and dead ash. Nevertheless, the Saint did not stop at dhyāna; and at the same time, of course, he did not go against dhyāna—just as the art of divination emerges from yin and yang without going against yin and yang.*[7]

---

3. Kāśyapa Buddha is the sixth of the Seven Ancient Buddhas, the seventh being Śākyamuni. See chap. 15, *Busso*.

4. 禅和子 (ZENNA-SU). 禅和 (ZENNA) is a transliteration of the Sanskrit *dhyāna*, lit. "thought or reflection." 子 (SU), lit. means "child," or "disciple."

5. *Sekimon-rinkanroku (Sekimon's Forest Records)* is a two-volume work which was first published in 1107. It was compiled by Master Kakuhan Eko (1071–1128); Sekimon was the name of the district where his temple was located.

6. 禅那 (ZENNA) is another transliteration of the Sanskrit *dhyāna*.

7. The same passage is quoted in chap. 30, *Gyoji*, para. [193].

155] Calling him the twenty-eighth patriarch is on the basis that the Great [Mahā]kāśyapa is the first patriarch. Counting from Vipaśyin[8] Buddha, he is the thirty-fifth patriarch. The Seven Buddhas' and twenty-eight patriarchs' experience of the truth should not necessarily be limited to dhyāna. Therefore the master of the past says, *"Dhyāna is only one of many practices; how could it be all there was to the Saint?"* This master of the past has seen a little of people and has entered the inner sanctum of the ancestral patriarchs, and so he has these words. Throughout the great kingdom of Sung these days [such a person] might be difficult to find and might hardly exist at all. Even if [the important thing is] dhyāna we should never use the name "Zen Sect." Still more, dhyāna is never the whole importance of the Buddha-Dharma. Those who, nevertheless, willfully call the great truth that is authentically transmitted from buddha to buddha "the Zen Sect" have never seen the Buddha's truth even in a dream, have never heard it even in a dream, and have never received its transmission even in a dream. Do not concede that the Buddha-Dharma might even exist among people who claim to be "the Zen Sect." Who has invented the name "Zen Sect"? None of the buddhas and ancestral masters has ever used the name "Zen Sect." Remember, the name "Zen Sect" has been devised by demons and devils. People who have called themselves a name used by demons and devils may themselves be a band of demons; they are not the children and grandchildren of the Buddhist patriarchs.

157] *The World-Honored One, before an assembly of millions on Vulture Peak, picks up an uḍumbara flower and winks. The assembly is totally silent. Only the face of the Venerable Mahākāśyapa breaks into a smile. The World-Honored One says, "I have the right-Dharma-eye treasury and the fine mind of nirvāṇa; along with the saṃghāṭī robe,[9] I transmit them to Mahākāśyapa.*[10]

The World-Honored One's transmission to the Great Mahākāśyapa, is *"I have the right-Dharma-eye treasury and the fine mind of nirvāṇa."* In addition to this there is no, "I have the Zen Sect and I transmit it to Mahākāśyapa." He says *"along with the saṃghāṭī robe;"* he does not say "along with the Zen Sect." Thus, the name "Zen Sect" is never heard while the World-Honored One is in the world.

158] The First Patriarch,[11] at that time, addresses the Second Patriarch: *"The buddhas' supreme and fine truth is to persevere for vast kalpas in difficult conduct and painful conduct, and to be able to endure what it is hard to endure. How can one hope to seek the true vehicle with small virtue and small wisdom, and with a trivial and con-*

---

8. Vipaśyin Buddha is the first of the Seven Ancient Buddhas. See chap. 15, *Busso.*

9. The large robe. See chap. 12, *Kesa-kudoku.*

10. Quoted from the *Nenge (Picking Up of a Flower)* chapter of *Daibonten-o-monbutsu-ketsugi-kyo.* See also *Shinji-shobogenzo*, pt. 3, no. 54, and Shobogenzo, chap. 68, *Udonge.*

11. Master Bodhidharma, the first patriarch in China.

ceited mind?"[12] On another occasion he says, *"The Dharma-seal*[13] *of the buddhas is not got from other people."* And on another occasion he says, *"The Tathāgata transmitted the right-Dharma-eye treasury to the Great [Mahā]kāśyapa."*

[159] What has been indicated now is *the supreme and fine truth of the buddhas, the right-Dharma-eye treasury, and the Dharma-seal of the buddhas.* At this time, there has been no instance at all of using the name "Zen Sect," and no cause of or condition for using the name "Zen Sect" has ever been heard. This *right-Dharma-eye treasury* has been passed on in the face-to-face transmission by the raising of an eyebrow and the winking of an eye; it has been given with body, mind, bones, and marrow; it has been received with body, mind, bones, and marrow; it has been transmitted and received *before the body and after the body;*[14] and it has been transmitted and received *on the mind and outside of mind.*[15] The name "Zen Sect" is not heard in the order of the World-Honored One and Mahākāśyapa; the name "Zen Sect" is not heard in the order of the First Patriarch and the Second Patriarch; the name "Zen Sect" is not heard in the order of the Fifth Patriarch and the Sixth Patriarch; and the name "Zen Sect" is not heard in the orders of Seigen and Nangaku.[16] There is nothing to indicate who began using the name, and from what time. People out to destroy the Dharma and to steal the Dharma, who could not be numbered as practitioners even though they were among practitioners, may have secretly initiated the name. If practitioners of later ages randomly use the name that Buddhist patriarchs have never permitted, they will corrupt the lineage of the Buddhist patriarchs. Further, there will appear to be another method called "the Zen Sect" besides the method of the buddhas and the patriarchs. If there is any method which is other than the truth of the Buddhist patriarchs, it may be a method of non-Buddhists. As already the children and grandchildren of Buddhist patriarchs, we should learn in practice the bones, marrow, and facial features of the Buddhist patriarchs. We have devoted ourselves to the Buddhist patriarchs' truth; we should not flee from this place and learn non-

---

12. This story is also quoted in chap. 30, *Gyoji,* para. [216]. The wording is slightly different in the two versions.

13. 法印 (HO-IN) represents the meaning of the Sanskrit *Dharmoddāna* or *Dharma-uddāna* (see Glossary). Sometimes three seals are enumerated, namely investigation of reality as *anitya* (inconstant, impermanent), as *an-ātman* (not self, non-spiritual), and as *nirvāṇa* (extinct, devoid of illusion). A teaching which does not bear these three 'seals,' or distinguishing features, is not regarded as the Buddha-Dharma.

14. 身先身後 (SHIN SEN-SHIN GO), "before the body and after the body," suggests the momentary continuation of Buddhist effort endlessly into the past and future. See also chap. 48, *Sesshin-sessho,* note 17.

15. 心上心外 (SHIN JO-SHIN GE), or "on [the basis of] the mind and outside [the conceptual area] of mind."

16. Master Seigen Gyoshi (died 740) and Master Nangaku Ejo (677–744) were both disciples of the sixth patriarch in China, Master Daikan Eno. Master Dogen's lineage is through Master Seigen. The Rinzai lineage is through Master Nangaku.

Buddhism. We have retained the rarely retained body-mind of a human being. This is by virtue of pursuing the truth in the past. If, having received this benevolent influence, we mistakenly promote non-Buddhism, we will not be repaying the benevolence of the Buddhist patriarchs. In great Sung [China] in recent ages, common folk throughout the country have heard this wrong name "Zen Sect," and so the vulgar usually use the wrong names "Zen Sect," "Bodhidharma Sect," and "Buddha's Mind Sect," rumors of which vie to be heard and to disturb the Buddha's truth. These [names] are the confused expressions of people who have never known the great truth of the Buddhist patriarchs, and who neither perceive nor believe that the right-Dharma-eye treasury even exists. How could anyone who knows the right-Dharma-eye treasury call the Buddha's truth by a wrong name?

[62] For this reason...

Great Master Musai[17] of Sekito-an temple on Nangaku-zan mountain, in formal preaching in the Dharma Hall, addresses the assembly as follows: *"My Dharma-gate*[18] *has been transmitted and received from past buddhas; it is, without discussing the balanced state of Zen or diligence,*[19] *solely to master the wisdom of the Buddha."*[20]

Remember, Buddhist patriarchs who possess the authentic transmission from the Seven Buddhas and the many buddhas speak like this. The only words realized are that *"My Dharma-gate has been transmitted and received from past buddhas."* There is no realization of the words "My Zen Sect has been transmitted and received from past buddhas." Without distinguishing separate instances of *the balanced state of Zen and diligence*, he causes us *solely to master the wisdom of the Buddha*. That which he has solely mastered—without spurning the balanced state of Zen and diligence—is the wisdom of the Buddha. This is expressed as *"I possess the right-Dharma-eye treasury and I transmit it."*[21] [Sekito's] *My*[22] is [the Buddha's] *"I possess."*[23] *The Dharma-gate* is *the right*

---

17. Master Sekito Kisen (700–790), successor of Master Seigen Gyoshi. Great Master Musai is his posthumous title.

18. 法門 (HOMON) may be interpreted as "gate to the Dharma," i.e. "way of teaching Buddhism." The translation "Dharma-gate" has been preferred, however, to avoid any suggestion of separation of means (gate) and end (Dharma). In *Fukan-zazengi* Master Dogen describes Zazen as 安楽法門 (ANRAKU *[no]* HOMON), "the peaceful and joyful gate of Dharma."

19. 禅定精進 (ZENJO-SHOJIN), "zen-balance and diligence," represent the Sanskrit *dhyāna* and *vīrya*. These are two of the six *pāramitā*, viz. *dāna* (free giving), *śīla* (moral integrity), *kṣanti* (fortitude), *vīrya* (diligence), *dhyāna* (balanced reflection), and *prajñā* (real wisdom).

20. *Keitoku-dento-roku*, chap. 14.

21. 吾有正法眼蔵付属 (GO-U-SHOBOGENZO-FUZOKU). These characters are taken from the Buddha's preaching quoted in para [157]: "I have the right-Dharma-eye treasury... and I transmit..."

22. 吾之 (GO-SHI). 之 (SHI) functions as a particle which makes 吾 (GO), "I," into "my."

23. 吾有 (GO-U), "I have," "I possess," or "my possession."

Dharma. "My," "my possession," and *"my marrow"*[24] are *the transmission*[25] which *you have got.*[26] Great Master Musai is a disciple of the founding patriarch Seigen, the only one to have entered Seigen's inner sanctum. And he is the Dharma-child of the eternal Buddha Sokei who shaved his head.[27] So the eternal Buddha Sokei is his forefather and his father, and the founding patriarch Seigen is his elder brother and his teacher. As a hero in the truth of the Buddha and in the order of the patriarchs, Great Master Musai of Sekito-an temple stands alone. Only Musai has *solely mastered* the authentic transmission of the Buddha's truth: every fruition and every element of the realization of his words is the timelessness of an eternal Buddha and the everlasting presentness of an eternal Buddha. We should see him as the eye of the right-Dharma-eye treasury, and we should not compare him with others. That people who do not know compare him with Daijaku of Kozei[28] is wrong. So remember, the Buddha's truth transmitted and received from past buddhas is not even called *"the balanced state of Zen"*; how much less could it be called, or discussed as, "the Zen Sect"? Clearly remember, to call it "the Zen Sect" is the most enormous error. Inept people, thinking that [the Buddha's truth] might be like a materialist sect[29] or an immaterialist sect,[30] regret that unless a name is given to a sect it is as if there is nothing to learn. The Buddha's truth cannot be like that. We should be absolutely certain that [the Buddha's truth] has never been called "the Zen Sect." Nevertheless, the common folk of recent ages, in their stupidity, do not know the old customs, and people who have not received the transmission of past buddhas wrongly say, "Within the Buddha-Dharma there are the lineages and customs of the five sects." This is a degeneration that has been left to follow its natural course. There has been not one person nor half a person to redeem it. My late Master Tendo, the eternal Buddha, is the first to have shown pity for this situation. This is his mission as a human being, and it is his mastery of the Dharma.

---

24. 吾髄 (GOZUI), "my marrow," alludes to Master Bodhidharma's words to Master Taiso Eka: 汝得吾髄 (NYOTOKU-GOZUI), "you have got my marrow." See chap. 46, *Katto.*

25. 付属 (FUZOKU), taken from the Buddha's words ("I transmit…"), suggests the transmission from the Buddha to Master Mahākāśyapa. The transmission from the Buddha, from Master Bodhidharma, and from Master Sekito Kisen, is the same transmission.

26. 汝得 (NYOTOKU). Master Bodhidharma's words 汝得吾髄 (NYOTOKU-GOZUI), "you have got my marrow," symbolize the state of oneness of subject and object in the transmission of the Dharma.

27. Master Daikan Eno died in 713, when Master Sekito was 13 or 14 years old. After that, Master Sekito became the disciple of Master Daikan Eno's successor, Master Seigen.

28. Master Baso Do-itsu (709–788), successor of Master Nangaku Ejo and a contemporary of Master Sekito. The Rinzai lineage is through Master Baso.

29. 有宗 (USHU). 有 (U) means existence or possession. 宗 (SHU) means sect or religion.

30. 空宗 (KUSHU). 空 (KU) means that which is empty, void, or immaterial: for example, spiritual essence or abstract ideals. The opposition of 空宗 (KUSHU) and 有宗 (USHU) suggests the opposing standpoints of idealism and materialism.

166] My late Master, the eternal Buddha, in formal preaching in the Dharma Hall, addresses the assembly as follows: *"That individuals today talk solely of there being differences in the customs of the lineages of Unmon, Hogen, Igyo, Rinzai, Soto, and so on, is not the Buddha-Dharma and is not the truth of the ancestral Master."*

The realization of these words is hard to meet [once] in a thousand years, for only my late Master expresses it, and is hard to hear through the ten directions, for only his consummate order hears it. This being so, among one thousand monks there is no listening ear and no seeing eye; how much less is there any who listens with the whole mind; and how much less is there any who listens with the body? Even if they listened with their whole body-mind for hundreds of millions of myriad kalpas, they could never utilize the thoroughly realized body-mind of my late Master to listen, to experience, to believe, and to get free. It is pitiful that everyone throughout the ten directions of the great kingdom of Sung has considered my late Master to be on a par with the old veterans of other districts. Should we see the people who think like this as equipped with eyes? Or should we see them as not equipped with eyes? Again, some have considered my late Master to be on a par with Rinzai and Tokuzan. It must be said that these people have never seen my late Master and have never met with Rinzai. Before I performed prostrations to my late Master, the eternal Buddha, I had intended to investigate the profound teachings of the five sects, but after performing prostrations to my late Master, the eternal Buddha, I clearly knew the principle that the five sects are random names. That being so, when the Buddha-Dharma flourished in the great kingdom of Sung there were no names of five sects. There was never an ancient who proclaimed the names of five sects or who mentioned sectarian customs. Since the Buddha-Dharma has weakened the names of five sects have occurred at random. The situation is like this because people are negligent in learning in practice and not keen in pursuing the truth. To each individual monk who pursues real mastery in practice, I issue a stern warning: Do not retain the random names of the five sects, and do not retain any concept of lineages or customs belonging to five sects. How much less should there be *the three kinds of profundity,*[31] *the three pivots,*[32] *the four thoughts,*[33] *the four relations between reflection and action,*[34] *the nine standards,*[35] and so on.

---

31. 三玄 (SANGEN), in *Rinzai-zenji-goroku (Record of the Words of Zen Master Rinzai).*

32. 三要 (SANYO), also contained in *Rinzai-zenji-goroku.*

33. 四料簡 (SHIRYOKEN), four ways of considering subject and object in Buddhist training: 1) to take away the person but not to take away circumstances; 2) to take away circumstances but not to take away the person; 3) to take away both person and circumstances; and 4) not to take away either person or circumstances. Also contained in *Rinzai-zenji-goroku.*

34. 四照用 (SHISHOYO) is another teaching of Master Rinzai concerning a master's guidance of a disciple: 1) reflect first, act later; 2) act first, reflect later; 3) reflect and act simultaneously; 4) reflect and act beyond simultaneousness.

How much less should there be *the three phrases*,[36] *the five relative positions*,[37] and *the ten kinds of shared true wisdom*.[38] The truth of Old Master Śākyamuni is not small thinking like that, and it does not esteem thinking like that as great. The words have never been realized. They have not been heard at Shorin [temple] or on Sokei [mountain]. It is pitiful that they are repeated by shavelings who, in the present degenerate age, do not hear the Dharma, their body-mind and eyes being dark. The children and grandchildren of the Buddhist patriarchs, and their embryos, must not express such words. Masters who abide in and retain the state of Buddhist patriarchs have never let these words of madness be heard. Recent second-rate teachers, people who have never heard the whole truth of the Buddha-Dharma, who lack complete devotion to the truth of the patriarchs, and who are ignorant in regard to their own state, being excessively proud of one or two mere trifles, establish names of sects like those mentioned earlier. Once the names of sects are established, small children, because they have not learned the way to pursue the substance, vainly follow the shadow. They do not have the spirit which adores the ancients; they have behavior which is corrupted by secular customs. Even secular people warn of the vileness of following the secular customs of the world.

[172] *The king Bunno*[39] *asks the minister Taiko, "Why is it that though a lord endeavors to employ sages, he does not reap the benefit, but social disorder gets more and more extreme, putting [the nation] in peril?"*

Taiko says, "He employs sages but does not use them. So although he employs wise advisers in name, he does not get the real effect of their wisdom."

Bun-no says, "Where does the fault lie?"

Taiko says, "The fault is in [the lord's] fondness for using those who are praised by the world, instead of obtaining for himself true sages."

Bun-no says, "What does it mean to like to use those who are praised by the world?"

Taiko says, "To like to listen to those who are praised by the world is to think the unwise wise, to think the unintelligent intelligent, to think the disloyal loyal, and to think the untrustworthy trustworthy. If the lord sees those who are praised by the world as wise and intelligent, and sees those who are reviled by the world as unworthy, people

---

35. 九帯 (KYUTAI), lit. "nine belts," nine standards established by Master Fuzan Ho-on for testing or guiding a disciple.

36. 三句 (SANKU). In the Unmon sect, for example, three short phrases conceived by Master Unmon were used in the training of monks.

37. 五位 (GO-I), five relative positions of the absolute and the relative, expounded by Master Tozan and modified by Master Sozan. See also chap. 66, *Shunju*.

38. 十同真智 (JU-DOSHINCHI), expounded by Master Fun-yo Zensho.

39. The Chou dynasty was the predominant dynasty in China for 867 years from the reign of the king Bu-o, which began in 1122 B.C. Bunno was Bu-o's predecessor as head of the Chou dynasty.

who have many accomplices will advance, and people who have few accomplices will recede. Thus, when the false band together and block out the wise, loyal retainers die having committed no crime, and false retainers use empty reputations to seek court rank. For these reasons social disorder becomes more and more extreme, and so the nation cannot escape peril."[40]

173] Even secular people regret it when their nation and their principles are in peril. When the Buddha-Dharma and the Buddha's truth are in peril, the Buddha's disciples must inevitably regret it. The cause of peril is arbitrary following of the customs of the world. When we listen to the praises of the world, we do not find true sages. If we want to find true sages, we should adopt a strategy of wisdom that illuminates the past and looks into the future. Those who are praised by the world are not always wise and not always sacred. Those who are reviled by secular people are not always wise and not always sacred. Observing three times the case in which the wise invite vilification and the case in which the false are praised, we should not confuse those cases. Not to use the wise is the nation's loss, and to use the unworthy is a matter for the nation's regret. The present establishment of the names of five sects is an aberration of the secular world. Those who follow the customs of this secular world are many, but those who have understood the secular as the secular are few. We should see those who reform the secular as saints. To follow the secular may be the utmost foolishness. How could people who are willing to follow the secular know the Buddha's right Dharma? How could they become buddhas and become patriarchs? [The Buddha-Dharma] has been received by rightful successor from rightful successor since the Seven Buddhas: how could this be similar to the establishment of the five versions of the vinaya[41] by people in India whose understanding depended upon sentences? So remember, the ancestral masters who made the right life of the Buddha-Dharma into [their own] right lives have never said that there are five sects. Someone who learns that there are five sects in Buddhism is not an authentic successor of the Seven Buddhas.

75] My late Master addresses the assembly: *"In recent years the truth of the patriarchs has degenerated. Bands of demons, and animals, are many. They frequently discuss the lineages and customs of five sects. It is very distressing, very distressing."*

Thus, clearly, the twenty-eight generations of India in the west and the twenty-two patriarchs of China in the east have never proclaimed five sects. All ancestral masters who are fit to be called ancestral masters are like this.

---

40. From the Taoist text *Rikuto (Six Strategies).*

41. 律の五部 (RITSU *no* GOBU). It is said that, by the time of Master Upagupta (the 4th patriarch in India), five separate versions of the vinaya had been established in India, namely: 1) the vinaya of the Dharmaguptakas; 2) the vinaya of the Sarvāstivādins; 3) the vinaya of the Mahīśāsakas; 4) the Prātimokṣa-sūtra of the Kāśyapīyas; and 5) the vinaya of the Vāsīputrīyas. See JEBD: 五部律 (GOBURITSU).

Those who uphold the names of five sects, claiming that each sect has its own fundamental principle, are those who *deceive and delude people of the world* and are those of *scant knowledge and sparse understanding.* If everyone in Buddhism established their own individual truth, how could the Buddha's truth have arrived at the present day? Mahākāśyapa would have established one of his own, and Ānanda would have established one of his own. If the principle of independent establishment were the right way, the Buddha-Dharma would have died out in the early days in India. Who could venerate principles that individuals had established independently? Among principles that individuals had established independently, who could decide between the true and the false? If unable to decide between the true and the false, who could consider [a principle] to be the Buddha-Dharma or not to be the Buddha-Dharma? Without clarifying this truth it is hard to call anything Buddhism. The names of the five sects were not established during the lifetimes of the respective ancestral masters. Since the deaths of the ancestral masters who are called the ancestral masters of the five sects, flotsam in the stream of their lineages—people whose eyes were not clear and whose feet did not walk—without asking their fathers, and going against their forefathers, have established the names. The principle is evident and anyone can know it.

[177] Zen Master Dai-en[42] of Dai-i-san mountain[43] is a disciple of Hyakujo Daichi[44] and he lives as master of Isan mountain at the time of Hyakujo, but he never says that the Buddha-Dharma should be called the Igyo[45] Sect. And Hyakujo does not say to Isan, "From your time onwards, living as master of Isan mountain, you should use the name 'Igyo Sect.'" Neither the Master[46] nor the Patriarch[47] uses the name, and so we should remember that it is a wrong name. And even though people arbitrarily use his name in the title of a sect, we should not necessarily single out Kyozan.[48] If it were appropriate [for Isan and Kyozan] to call [a sect] by their own names, they would use their own names. Because it is not appropriate to use personal names, personal names were not used in the past, and personal names are not used today. We do not speak of the Sokei Sect, the Nangaku Sect, the Kozei Sect, or

42. Master Isan Reiyu (771–853), successor of Master Hyakujo Ekai. The Tang emperor Senso awarded him the posthumous title Zen Master Dai-en.

43. 大潙山 (DAI-I-SAN), or Great Isan mountain. In Master Dogen's commentary Master Isan is referred to either as 潙山 (ISAN) or as 大潙 (DAI-I).

44. Master Hyakujo Ekai (749–814), successor of Master Baso Do-itsu. Zen Master Daichi is his posthumous title.

45. 潙仰 (IGYO). This represents the combination of the names of Master Isan Reiyu and his disciple Master Kyozan Ejaku—taking 潙 (I) from 潙山 (ISAN)and 仰 (KYO) from 仰山 (KYOZAN).

46. Master Isan.

47. Master Hyakujo.

48. Master Kyozan Ejaku (807–883), successor of Master Isan Reiyu.

the Hyakujo Sect.[49] It was impossible for Isan, in his time, to differ from Sokei; he could neither surpass Sokei nor be equal to Sokei. And the relation between Kyozan and one word or half a phrase spoken by Dai-i is not always one staff being carried on the shoulders of two men.[50] If people were going to establish the name of a sect, they should call it the Isan Sect, or they should call it the Dai-i Sect. There has never been any reason to use the name Igyo Sect. If it were appropriate to use the name Igyo Sect, the name should have been used when the two venerable patriarchs were in the world. What obstacle was it that caused them not to use a name that they might have used when they were in the world? Those who go against the truth of their father[51] and their forefather[52] and use the name Igyo Sect, which was not used when the two were in the world, are disloyal children and grandchildren. This name is neither the original hope of Zen Master Dai-i nor the original intention of Old Man Kyozan. It has no authentic transmission from a true master. The fact is evident that it is a wrong name used by a group of wrong people. Never let it be heard through the whole Universe in ten directions.

[80] Great Master Esho,[53] abandoning a sutra-lecturing school, became a disciple of Obaku.[54] He tasted Obaku's staff on three occasions, [receiving] sixty strokes altogether, and realized the state of realization while practicing in Daigu's order.[55] In the story he is in residence as the master of Rinzai-in temple in Chinshu. Though not having perfectly realized Obaku's mind, he still never says one word, or says half a word, to the effect that the Buddha-Dharma he has received should be called the Rinzai Sect; he does not [say so] by holding up a fist and does not [say so] by picking up a whisk. Nevertheless, flotsam among the members of his order, failing to preserve the conduct of their father and failing to keep the Buddha-Dharma, soon wrongly establish the name "Rinzai Sect." If it had been contrived during the human life of Great Master Esho there would have been discussion to prevent the establishment of that name—because it clearly goes against the teaching of the an-

---

49. These four names follow the lineage from Master Daikan Eno who lived on *Sokei* mountain, to Master *Nangaku* Ejo, to Master Baso Do-itsu who lived in *Kozei* district, to Master *Hyakujo* Ekai. Master Isan Reiyu, as a successor of Master Hyakujo Ekai, is a fourth-generation descendant of Master Daikan Eno.

50. In a monastery two monks might carry a heavy bucket of water, for example, by bearing each end of a staff on their shoulders. Master Dogen used this as a symbol of oneness of two factors.

51. Master Kyozan.

52. The Patriarch Isan.

53. Master Rinzai Gigen (815?–867), successor of Master Obaku Ki-un. Great Master Esho is his posthumous title.

54. Master Obaku Ki-un (died between 855 and 859), like Master Isan Reiyu, is a successor of Master Hyakujo Ekai.

55. Master Koan Daigu (dates unknown), successor of Master Kiso Chijo. See *Shinji-shobogenzo*, pt. 1, no. 27.

cestral patriarch himself. Moreover, as Rinzai is about to die, he entrusts [the Dharma] to Zen Master Sansho Enen,[56] saying, *"After my death, do not destroy my right-Dharma-eye treasury." Enen says, "How could I dare to destroy the Master's right-Dharma-eye treasury?" Rinzai says, "If someone suddenly questions you, how will you answer?" Enen at once lets out a yell. Rinzai says, "Who is there that knows that my right-Dharma-eye treasury, which is passing towards this blind donkey, will be destroyed."*[57]

[182] The words spoken by master and disciple are like this. Rinzai never says "Do not destroy my Zen Sect," never says "Do not destroy my Rinzai Sect," and never says "Do not destroy my sect." He only says, "Do not destroy my right-Dharma-eye treasury." We should clearly remember that the great truth authentically transmitted from buddha to buddha must not be called "the Zen Sect" and must not be called "the Rinzai Sect." We must never even dream of calling it "the Zen Sect." Though *cessation*[58] is the essence and form of the right-Dharma-eye treasury, the transmission is passed on like this. *Being destroyed as it passes towards a concrete blind donkey* is truly the *"Who knows?"* state of the transmission. In Rinzai's lineage Sansho is alone. We should neither associate him with nor align him with his elder and younger brothers in the Dharma; truly *his place is under a bright window.*[59] The story of Rinzai and Sansho is [a story of] Buddhist patriarchs. The Rinzai transmission today is the Vulture Peak transmission of olden days. Thus, the principle that we should not use the name "Rinzai Sect" is evident.

[183] Great Master Kyoshin[60] of Unmon-zan mountain practiced in the past under the venerable patriarch Chin,[61] and so he may have been a descendant of Obaku. Thereafter, he succeeded Seppo. This Master [Unmon] also does not say that the right-Dharma-eye treasury should be called "the Unmon Sect." But members of his lineage also, not knowing that the wrong names "Igyo Sect" and "Rinzai Sect" are wrong names, have established the new name "Unmon Sect." If the fundamental intent of Great Master Kyoshin aspired to a name that would establish a sect, then it would be difficult to

---

56. Master Sansho Enen (dates unknown), successor of Master Rinzai.

57. *Goto-eyo*, chap. 9.

58. 滅却 (MEKKYAKU), translated in the story as "destroy." 滅 (METSU) appears in the compound 生滅 (SHOMETSU) "arising and passing, " which expresses the instantaneousness of the Universe, and it is also the third of the Four Noble Truths, 苦、集、滅、道 (KU, SHU, METSU, DO), "suffering, accumulation, cessation, and the Way."

59. Under a bright window is a convenient location for reading sutras. These words might have been said to an attendant monk by a master who has recognized the potential of an excellent student. The source, however, has not been traced.

60. Master Unmon Bun-en (864–949), successor of Master Seppo Gison. Great Master Kyoshin is his posthumous title.

61. Master Bokushu Domyo (dates unknown), successor of Master Obaku Ki-un.

affirm that he was the body-mind of the Buddha-Dharma. When people now use the name of the sect, it is as if they are calling an emperor a peasant.[62]

[84] Zen Master Dai-Hogen[63] of Seiryo-in temple is the rightful successor of [the Master of] Jizo-in temple,[64] and a Dharma-grandchild of [the Master of] Gensa-in temple:[65] he possesses the fundamental teaching and is without wrongness. Dai-Hogen is the master's title he uses when signing his name. There is not one word in a thousand words, and not one saying in ten thousand sayings, in which he has advocated the establishment of the name "Hogen Sect," using his own title as a title for the right-Dharma-eye treasury. However, members of this lineage also have established the name "Hogen Sect." If Hogen could influence the present, he would eradicate the speaking of the present wrong name "Hogen Sect." Since Zen Master Hogen has passed away already, there is no-one to cure this disease. Even thousands or tens of thousands of years hereafter, people who wish to be loyal disciples of Zen Master Hogen must refuse to treat this name "Hogen Sect" as a name. That is to remain fundamentally loyal to Zen Master Dai-Hogen. Broadly, the likes of Unmon and Hogen are the distant descendants of the founding patriarch Seigen; the bones of the truth have been transmitted and the marrow of the Dharma has been transmitted to them.[66]

[86] The founding patriarch Great Master Gohon[67] received the Dharma from Ungan.[68] Ungan was the rightful successor of Great Master Yakusan.[69] Yakusan was the rightful successor of Great Master Sekito.[70] Great Master Sekito was the founding patriarch Seigen's only son: there was no second or third to equal to him; the conduct of the truth was authentically transmitted to him alone. That the right life of the Buddha's truth has survived in the eastern lands is by virtue of Great Master Sekito having faultlessly received the authentic transmission. The founding patriarch Seigen, at the time of the eternal Buddha Sokei, taught on Seigen [mountain] the teachings of Sokei. To be asked to manifest himself in the world[71] while [Sokei] was in the

62. 匹夫 (HIPPU), lit. "single husband"; that is, a man who is the husband of only one woman. To ancient Chinese, that represented a man of low social status.

63. Master Hogen Bun-eki (885–958), successor of Master Rakan Keichin. He received the title Zen Master Dai-Hogen by imperial decree during his lifetime.

64. Master Rakan Keichin (867–928), successor of Master Gensa Shibi. His posthumous title is Great Master Shin-o of Jizo-in.

65. Master Gensa Shibi (835–907), successor of Master Seppo Gison.

66. Whereas the lineages of Masters Isan and Rinzai stem from Master Nangaku Ejo, the lineages of Masters Unmon and Hogen stem from Master Seigen Gyoshi. Master Dogen's own lineage, that through Master Tozan Ryokai, also stems from Master Seigen Gyoshi.

67. Master Tozan Ryokai (807–869).

68. Master Ungan Donjo (782–841).

69. Master Yakusan Igen (745–828).

70. Master Sekito Kisen (700–790), successor of Master Seigen Gyoshi.

71. 出生 (SHUSSE), "to manifest oneself in the world," means to become a temple master.

world, and to experience manifestation in the world in that generation, he must have been a rightful successor above rightful successors and a founding patriarch among founding patriarchs: it is not true that the better course is learning under one's master and the inferior course is manifesting oneself in the world. [But] practitioners should take note that the average in those days would be outstanding today. When the eternal Buddha Sokei was about to teach human beings and gods by manifesting his parinirvāṇa,[72] Sekito, the story goes, steps up from his seat at the back[73] and asks whom he should rely upon as a teacher. The eternal Buddha then says *"Visit [Gyo]shi."* He does not say *"Visit [E]jo."* This being so, the eternal Buddha's right-Dharma-eye treasury is the authentic transmission of the founding patriarch Seigen alone. Although we acknowledge the excellent members of the order who attained the truth together with him, the founding Patriarch walks alone as a truly excellent member.[74] The eternal Buddha Sokei has made his own child into Seigen's child, who, as the father of the father of the father of the child [Tozan],[75] evidently had attained the marrow and evidently was the rightful successor of the ancestral patriarchs. Great Master Tozan, as the legitimate fourth-generation heir of Seigen, has received the authentic transmission of the right-Dharma-eye treasury, and has opened his eyes to the fine mind of nirvāṇa. Besides this, there is no separate transmission and no separate sect. The Great Master has never shown to the assembly any fist or wink of an eye that advocated the use of the name "Soto Sect." Furthermore, there was no flotsam mixed in among his disciples, and so there was no disciple who used the name "Tozan Sect." How much less could they speak of a "Soto Sect"? The name "Soto Sect" may be the result of including the name Sozan.[76] In such a case, Ungo[77] and Do-an[78] would have to be included too. Ungo is a guiding master in the human world and in the heavens above, and he is more venerable than Sozan. We can conclude, in regard to this name "Soto," that some stinking skin-bag belonging to a side lineage, seeing him-

72. When Master Daikan Eno was about to die.

73. At the time of Master Daikan Eno's death, Master Sekito would have been in his early teens, so he would have been seated relatively far from the Master.

74. 正神足の独歩なり (SHO-JINSOKU *no* DOPPO *nari*), lit. "he is a true mystical foot's solitary step." This is a play on the expression 神足 (JINSOKU), "mystical foot" (from the Sanskrit *ṛddipāda*), which was used to describe an excellent member of a Buddhist order. See Book 1, Glossary.

75. Master Sekito was the master of Master Yakusan Igen who was the master of Master Ungan Donjo who was the master of Master Tozan Ryokai.

76. Master Sozan Honjaku (840–901). The first character of 曹洞 (SOTO) is the "So" of Sozan and the second character is the "To" of Tozan. Master Sozan was a successor of Master Tozan, but Master Dogen's lineage is through another of Master Tozan's successors, Master Ungo Doyo.

77. Master Ungo Doyo (835?–902).

78. Master Do-an Dofu (dates unknown), successor of Master Ungo Doyo.

self as equal [to Tozan], has devised the name "Soto Sect." Truly, though the white sun is bright, it is as if floating clouds are obscuring it from below.

[89] My late Master says, *"Now there are many who ascend the lion's seats of many districts and many who act as teachers of human beings and gods, but there is no-one at all who knows the truths of the Buddha-Dharma."* Therefore, those who vie to uphold a sect among the five sects, and who remain wrongly stuck in words among sayings and words, are really the enemies of the Buddhist patriarchs. In another case, a school has been named after Zen Master Nan of Oryu,[79] and has begun to be called "the Oryu Sect," but before long that school will know their wrongness. In general, while the World-Honored One was in the world, he never named a "Buddha Sect," nor named a "Vulture Peak Sect," nor spoke of a "Jetavana Park Sect," nor spoke of a "My Mind Sect," nor spoke of a "Buddha's Mind Sect." In which of the Buddha's words is a Buddhist sect named? For what reason do people today use the name "Buddha's Mind Sect"? Why should the World-Honored One necessarily call the mind a sect? And why should a sect inevitably be related to the mind? If there is a Buddha's Mind Sect, there should be a Buddha's Body Sect, there should be a Buddha's Eye Sect, there should be a Buddha's Ear Sect, there should be sects for the Buddha's nose, tongue, and so on. There should be a Buddha's Marrow Sect, a Buddha's Bones Sect, a Buddha's Legs Sect, a Buddha's Realm Sect, and so on. Now there are no such things. Remember, the name "Buddha's Mind Sect" is a false name. When Śākyamuni Buddha cites that all dharmas through the whole of the Buddha-lands in ten directions are real form, and when he preaches the whole of the Buddha-lands in ten directions, he does not preach that in the Buddha-lands in ten directions he has established some sect. If the naming of sects were the method of Buddhist patriarchs, it would have taken place in the Buddha's reign. If it had taken place in the Buddha's reign, the Buddha would have preached it. The Buddha did not preach it. Clearly, it was not a tool in the reign of the Buddha. The patriarchs do not speak of it. Clearly, it is not a utensil in the domain of the patriarchs. You might not only be laughed at by others, but also thwarted by the buddhas, and even laughed at by yourselves. So, please, do not give names to sects, and do not say that there are five sects in the Buddha-Dharma.

[93] Latterly there has been an infantile man named Chiso[80] who made a collection of one or two sayings of ancestral masters and described the five sects. He called [this collection] "Eyes of Human Beings and Gods."[81] People have not recognized it for what it is; beginners and late learners have thought

---

79. Master Oryu Enan (died 1069 aged 68), successor of Master Jimyo So-en.

80. Also known as Zen Master Kaigen Chisho.

81. 人天眼目 (NIN DEN *[no]* GANMOKU), 3 volumes published in 1188. The first 2 volumes outline the so-called 5 Chinese sects and evaluate the words of ancient masters categorized as belonging to those sects.

it to be true, and there are even some who carry it hidden in their clothes. It is not the eyes of human beings and gods; it darkens the eyes of human beings and gods. How could it have the virtue of blinding the right-Dharma-eye treasury? The aforementioned Eyes of Human Beings and Gods was edited by veteran monk Chiso at Man-nen-ji temple on Tendai-zan mountain[82] in around the 12th lunar month of [the 6th year] of the Junki era.[83] Even a work produced latterly, if its words are true, should be approved. [But] this work is deranged and stupid. It has no eyes of learning in practice and no eyes of a journey on foot. How much less could it have the eyes of meeting Buddhist patriarchs? We should not use it. We should not call [the author] *Chiso*, which means Wise and Clear; we should call him *Gumo*—Stupid and Dark. One who does not know a true person, and who does not meet a person, has gathered together sayings without picking up the sayings of people who are true people. It is clear that he does not know a person.[84] The cause of students of the teaching in China using the names of sects was the presence of [masters of] this and that [lineage] who could rival each other. Now the transmission of the Buddhist patriarchs' right-Dharma-eye treasury has passed from rightful successor to rightful successor, with whom there can be no rival. There are no [other masters of] this and that [lineage] who might be included in the same class. Even so, unreliable old veterans today constantly use the names of sects at random. Scheming in their own interests, they are not in awe of the Buddha's truth. The Buddha's truth is not your own Buddha's truth; it is the Buddha's truth of the Buddhist patriarchs, and it is the Buddha's truth of the Buddha's truth. The minister Taiko says to the king Bunno, *"The whole country is not the whole country of one person: it is the whole country of the whole country."*[85] Thus, even a layman has this wisdom and has these words. Children in the house of the Buddhist patriarchs must not arbitrarily allow the great truth of the Buddhist patriarchs to follow the stupid and the dark, by calling themselves a sect. That is a great violation, and [one who commits it] is not a person of the Buddha's truth. If we should call ourselves by the name of a sect the World-Honored One himself would have used the name. Given that the World-Honored One did not name his own sect, what reason could we have, as his descendants, to use names after his death? What person could be more skillful than the World-Honored One? Those without skillfulness are likely to produce no benefit. Again, given that the Buddhist patriarchs have not contravened the time-honored truth by

---

82. A mountain in Chekiang province where Master Tendai Chigi (538–597) established the original training place of the Tendai Sect.

83. 1188. Here Master Dogen uses the Chinese dating system only.

84. 人をしる (*hito o shiru*), "to know a person" means the intuitive ability to know whether or not a person is true. Master Dogen esteemed this ability very highly. See end of chap. 52, *Bukkyo*.

85. From *Rikuto (Six Strategies).*

establishing their own sects, who among the Buddha's descendants could see their own sect as a sect? Learn in practice by illuminating the past and reflecting the present; do not be arbitrary. Hoping not to differ one jot from the World-Honored One when he was in the world, his bereaved disciples solely have in their mind the regret of not being able to achieve or the joy of having achieved, and the desire not to go against, even a millionth [of his teaching]. Thus we should vow to find him and to serve him in many lives. Thus we should desire to meet Buddha and to hear the Dharma in many lives. Those who would deliberately go against the teaching of the World-Honored One when he was in the world and establish the name of a sect are neither the disciples of the Tathāgata nor the descendants of the ancestral masters. [Their sin] is heavier than the heavy and the deadly [sins].[86] By rashly disregarding the importance of the Tathāgata's supreme truth of bodhi and by acting only in the selfish interests of their own sect, they make light of their predecessors and go against the predecessors. We can say that they do not even know the predecessors, and they do not believe in the virtues that were present in the World-Honored One's day. The Buddha-Dharma cannot abide in their houses. In conclusion, if you want to receive the authentic transmission of the conduct of the truth as one who follows the Buddha, do not see or hear the names of sects. That which every buddha and every patriarch transmits and authentically receives is the right-Dharma-eye treasury and the supreme truth of bodhi. The Dharma that the Buddhist Patriarch possessed has been transmitted in its entirety by buddhas, and there are no innovations to be added to the Dharma at all. This principle is the bones of the Dharma and the marrow of the truth.

Shobogenzo Butsudo

Preached to the assembly at Kippo-ji temple in the Yoshida district of Fukui prefecture, on the 16th day of the 9th lunar month in the 1st year of Kangen.[87]

86. 重逆 (JUGYAKU) stands for 十重罪 (JU-JUZAI), "the ten heavy sins," (i.e., killing, stealing, adultery, lying, sweet words, abusive speech, two-faced speech, greed, anger, and wrong views) and 五逆罪 (GO-GYAKUZAI), "the five deadly sins," (i.e., to kill one's mother, to kill one's father, to kill a sacred person, to cause the Buddha's body to shed blood, and to disrupt and divide a Buddhist order).

87. 1243.

[50]

諸法実相

SHOHO-JISSO

All Dharmas are Real Form

Sho *expresses plurality; it means "all," "various," or "many."* ***Ho*** *means "dharmas," both physical things and mental phenomena.* ***Jitsu*** *means "real."* ***So*** *means form. The Lotus Sutra teaches the most important and fundamental theory in Buddhism: that "all things and phenomena are real form." Because Buddhism is a philosophy of realism, its viewpoint is different from idealism and materialism. The idealist sees only phenomena, which cannot be confirmed to be substantially real. Idealists thus doubt that phenomena are real form. The materialist looks at the detail, breaking things into parts, thus losing the meaning and value that is included in the whole. Buddhism says that reality is all things and phenomena existing here and now and reveres them as real substance: reality itself. This teaching is found in the Lotus Sutra, expressed with the words "all dharmas are real form." In this chapter, Master Dogen explains the meaning of the Lotus Sutra's teaching.*

[01] **The realization of the Buddhist patriarchs** is perfectly realized real form. Real form is all dharmas. All dharmas are forms as they are,[1] natures as they are, body as it is, the mind as it is, the world as it is, clouds and rain as they are, walking, standing, sitting, and lying down, as they are; sorrow and joy, movement and stillness, as they are; a staff and a whisk, as they are; a twirling flower and a smiling face, as they are; succession of the Dharma and affirmation, as they are; learning in practice and pursuing the truth, as they are; the constancy of pines and the integrity of bamboos, as they are.

[03] Śākyamuni Buddha says, *"Buddhas alone, together with buddhas, are directly able to perfectly realize that all dharmas are real form. What is called 'all dharmas' is forms as they are, natures as they are, body as it is, energy as it is, action as it is, causes as they are, conditions as they are, effects as they are, results as they are, and the ultimate state of equilibrium of substance and detail, as it is."*[2]

The Tathāgata's words *the ultimate state of equilibrium of substance and detail* are the self-expression of *the real form of all dharmas*, are the self-expression of an ācārya, and are the learning in practice of total equilibrium. Because

---

1. 如是相 (NYOZE-SO) means "form as it is" or "forms as they are."
2. Lotus Sutra, *Hoben.* See LS 1.68.

learning in practice is in the state of total equilibrium, *buddhas alone, together with buddhas,* are *the real form of all dharmas;* and *the real form of all dharmas* is *buddhas alone, together with buddhas. Buddhas alone* are *real form,* and *buddhas together* are *all dharmas.* Hearing the words *"all dharmas,"* we should understand them neither as a description of the one nor as a description of the many. Hearing the words *"real form,"* we should learn them neither as a negation of voidness[3] nor as a negation of nature.[4] *The real* is *buddhas alone,* and *form* is *buddhas together. Directly being able* is *buddhas alone,* and *perfect realization* is *buddhas together. All dharmas* are *buddhas alone,* and *real form* is *buddhas together.* We call the state in which *all dharmas* are just *all dharmas "buddhas alone"* and we call the state in which *all dharmas* are just *real form "buddhas together."* Thus, there are *forms as they are* and there are *natures as they are* in which *all dharmas* exist as *all dharmas* themselves. And there are *forms as they are* and there are *natures as they are* in which *real form* is just *real form. Appearance in the world*[5] as *buddhas alone, together with buddhas,* is the preaching, practice, and experience of *all dharmas are real form.* This preaching is the *perfect realization* of *momentarily being able.* Though it is *perfect realization,* at the same time, it may be a *momentary ability.*[6] Because it is beyond beginning, middle, and end, it is *forms as they are* and *natures as they are,* and for this reason it is called *good in the beginning, middle, and end.*[7] The meaning of *perfect realization* as *momentarily being able* is *real form* as *all dharmas. Real form as all dharmas* is *forms as they are. Forms being as they are* is *momentarily being able to perfectly realize natures as they are.*[8] *Natures being as they are* is *momentarily being able to perfectly realize body as it is. Body being as it is* is *momentarily being able to perfectly realize energy as it is. Energy being as it is* is *momentarily being able to perfectly realize action as it is. Action being as it is* is *momentarily being able to perfectly realize causes as they are. Causes being as they are* is *momentarily being able to perfectly realize conditions as they are. Conditions being as they are* is *momentarily being able to perfectly realize effects as they are. Effects being as they are* is *momentarily being able to perfectly realize results as they are. Results being as they are* is *momentarily being able to perfectly realize the ultimate state of equilibrium of substance and detail as it is.* Because the expression *"the ultimate*

---

3. 虚 (KYO), "void," is opposed to the 実 (JITSU), "real," of 実相 (JISSO), "real form."

4. 性 (SHO), "nature," is opposed to the 相 (SO), "form," of 実相 (JISSO), "real form."

5. 出現於世 (SHUTSUGEN-O-SE). See, for example, LS 1.88–90.

6. 乃能 (NAINO), "momentary ability," is translated in the quotation as "are directly able." In the Lotus Sutra the function of 乃 (NAI, *sunawa[chi]*) is emphatic; thus in LSW, for example, the character is ignored in translation: *"Only a buddha together with a buddha can fathom the Reality of All Existence."* At the same time, 乃 (NAI, *sunawa[chi]*) expresses direct juxtaposition in a logical sequence ("accordingly") or direct juxtaposition in time ("whereupon"). By extension, in Master Dogen's usage, it expresses instantaneousness. The point of this sentence is that, even though buddhas have attained perfection, their ability is instantaneous or momentary.

7. 初中後善 (SHO-CHU-KO ZEN). See LS 1.40.

8. Reality itself, and the subject's ability to realize reality, cannot be separated.

state of equilibrium of substance and detail" is truly the realization of *reality as it is,*[9] *effects,* that is, individual and real effects,[10] are beyond the effects of 'cause and effect.' For this reason, the effects of cause-and-effect are just *effects,* that is, individual and real effects. Because these *effects* and *forms, natures, body,* and *energy* directly obstruct each other, the *form, nature, body,* and *energy,* and so on of *all dharmas*—however countless and boundless they may be—are *real form.* And because these *effects* do not restrict *forms, natures, body,* and *energy,* the *form, nature, body,* and *energy* of *all dharmas* each are *real form.* When these *forms, natures, body, energy,* and so on, and *effects, results, causes, conditions,* and so on, are left to obstruct each other, there is expression of eighty or ninety-percent realization. And when these *forms, natures, body, energy,* and so on, and *effects, results, causes, conditions,* and so on, are left not to restrict each other, there is expression of total realization. What has been called *"forms as they are"*[11] is not a single form, and *form as it is*[11] is not a uniform reality as it is: it is countless, boundless, inexpressible, and unfathomable reality as it is. As a measure, we should not use a measure of hundreds and thousands. We should use as a measure the measure of *all dharmas,* and we should use as a measure the measure of *real form.* The reason is that *buddhas alone, together with buddhas, can*[12] *perfectly realize that all dharmas are real form;* buddhas alone, together with buddhas, can perfectly realize that all dharmas are the real nature; buddhas alone, together with buddhas, can perfectly realize that all dharmas are real body; buddhas alone, together with buddhas, can perfectly realize that all dharmas are real energy; buddhas alone, together with buddhas, can perfectly realize that all dharmas are real action; buddhas alone, together with buddhas, can perfectly realize that all dharmas are real causes; buddhas alone, together with buddhas, can perfectly realize that all dharmas are real conditions; buddhas alone, together with buddhas, can perfectly realize that all dharmas are real effects; buddhas alone, together with buddhas, can perfectly realize that all dharmas are real results; and buddhas alone, together with buddhas, can perfectly realize that all dharmas are the real ultimate state of equality of substance and detail.

10] Because of the existence of truths like these, *the Buddha-lands of the ten directions*[13] are only *buddhas alone, together with buddhas,* and there is no-one, or even half a one, who is other than *buddhas alone, together with buddhas.* The relation between *alone* and *together* is, for example, *body* being provided with *body* and *forms* having experienced *forms.* Or it is like *natures,* through *body,*

---

9. 如是 (NYOZE), used here as a noun: "reality as it is." This usage also occurs, for example, in chap. 17, *Hokke-ten-hokke,* note 85.

10. 果果の果 (KAKA no KA), lit. "effects which are effect-effect." The point is to distinguish between effects as reality and effects as a concept.

11. 如是相 (NYOZE-SO). See note 1.

12. 乃能 (NAINO). See note 6.

13. 十方仏土 (JUPPO-BUTSUDO). See LS 1.106.

being maintained as *natures.*[14] On this basis [the Buddha] says, *"I, and buddhas in the ten directions, am directly able to know these things."*[15] Thus, the very moment of *directly being able to perfectly realize* and the very moment of *directly being able to know this* are both individual instances of existence-time. If *"I"* were different from *buddhas in the ten directions,* how could *"I"* realize the expression *"and buddhas in all directions"*? Because at this concrete place there are no 'ten directions,' *the ten directions* are this concrete place. Therefore, *real form* meeting *all dharmas* means spring getting into flowers, a person meeting spring, the moon illuminating the moon, and human beings meeting themselves. Again, a person looking into water is this same truth of mutual realization.[16] For this reason, we see the learning in practice of *real form* by *real form* as the Dharma-succession of Buddhist patriarchs by Buddhist patriarchs. It is the affirmation of *all dharmas* by *all dharmas. Buddhas alone* transmit the Dharma for the benefit of *buddhas alone. Buddhas together* receive the Dharma for the benefit of *buddhas together.* On this basis living-and-dying and coming-and-going exist. On this basis the establishment of the mind, training, bodhi, and nirvāṇa exist. Utilizing the establishment of the mind, training, bodhi, and nirvāṇa, we investigate in practice and clinch in action that *living-and-dying and coming-and-going are the real human body*; and as we do so, we hold firm and we let go. With this as their lifeblood, flowers open and fruits are borne. With this as their bones and marrow, Mahākāśyapa and Ānanda exist. *The forms as they are* of wind, rain, water, and fire are *perfect realization* itself. *The natures as they are* of the blue, the yellow, the red, and the white are *perfect realization* itself. Relying upon this concrete *body-energy,* we turn the common into the sacred. Relying upon these concrete *effects-and-results,* we transcend buddha and go beyond patriarchs. Relying upon these concrete *causes-and-conditions,* soil is grasped and made into gold. Relying upon these concrete *effects-and-results,* the Dharma is transmitted and the robe is given.

[213] The Tathāgata speaks of *"preaching for others the seal of real form."*[17] Let me interpret this: he practices for others the seal of real form; he hears for others the seal of real nature; and he experiences for others the seal of real body. We should investigate [his words] like this, and we should perfectly realize them like this. The state they indicate is, for example, like a pearl spinning

---

14. 性 (SHO) means "nature," or "essence." In Master Dogen's philosophy, however, 性 (SHO) means not an abstract essence but a natural state, or natural function, which includes both essential character and its physical manifestation in action. See, for example, chap. 22, *Bussho.*

15. 我及十方仏乃能知是事 (GA-GYU-JUPPO-BUTSU, NAI-NO-CHI-ZE-JI). See LS 1.70.

16. The person looks into the water and the water reflects the person.

17. Lotus Sutra, *Hoben: "I, body adorned with signs, / And brightness illuminating the world, / Am worshipped by countless multitudes / For whom I preach the seal of real form."* (LS 1.108.) "The seal of real form" is 実相印 (JISSO-IN), from the Sanskrit *dharma-svabhāva-mudrā* which lit. means "the seal of reality itself." See Glossary. A seal suggests the concrete as opposed to the abstract.

around a bowl and like the bowl spinning around the pearl.[18]

14] The Buddha Sun Moon Light[19] says:

The truth that all dharmas are real form
Has been preached for you all.[20]

Learning this expression in practice, we should realize that the Buddhist patriarchs have inevitably seen preaching the truth of real form as *the one great matter.*[21] Buddhist patriarchs proclaim the truth of real form in each of the eighteen spheres.[22] Before their body-mind, after their body-mind, and at the very moment of their body-mind, they preach real form, nature, body, energy, and so on. Those who do not perfectly realize real form, who do not preach real form, who do not understand real form, and who do not transcend understanding of real form, are not Buddhist patriarchs. They are bands of demons, and animals.

15] Śākyamuni Buddha says, *"The anuttara-samyak-saṃbodhi of all bodhisattvas totally belongs to this Sutra. This Sutra opens the gate of expedient methods and reveals true real form."*[23]

"All bodhisattvas" means all buddhas. Buddhas and bodhisattvas are not different species; they are without differences in maturity and without differences in excellence. This bodhisattva and that bodhisattva are not two people,[24] they are beyond self and others, and they are not personages of the past, present, and future; rather, becoming buddha is their Dharma-behavior of *practicing the bodhisattva-way.*[25] They realize buddha in their first establishment of the mind, and they realize buddha in the state of fine reflection.[26] There are bodhisattvas who have become buddha countless hundred thousand myriad koṭis of times. Those who say that after becoming buddha [bodhisattvas] cease practice and have nothing further to do are common men who have never known the truth of the Buddhist patriarchs. Those who

---

18. Alludes to the words of Master Engo Kokugon quoted in chap. 66, *Shunju.* A pearl spinning around a bowl and the bowl spinning around the pearl suggests a very vigorous situation in which subject and object are in mutual relation.

19. 日月燈明仏 (JITSU-GETSU-TOMYO-BUTSU), from the Sanskrit *Candra-sūrya-pradīpa Buddha.* See Glossary.

20. Lotus Sutra, *Jo: "When the Buddha [Sun Moon Light] had preached this Flower of Dharma / And caused the assembly to rejoice, / Then he, on that very day, / Proclaimed to the gathering of gods and people: / 'The truth that all dharmas are real form / Has been preached for you all…'"* (LS 1.58)

21. 一大事 (ICHIDAIJI). See LS 1.88–90.

22. The six sense organs, the six objects of the sense organs, and the six sense functions.

23. Lotus Sutra, *Hosshi.* See LS 2.156. "The gate of expedient methods" is 方便門 (HOBEN-MON), from the Sanskrit *dvāra-bhūtāni.* See Glossary.

24. They are in the same state.

25. 行菩薩道 (GYO-BOSATSUDO). See, for example, LS 3.20.

26. 妙覚地 (MYOKAKU-CHI), the ultimate state of a bodhisattva.

have been called *"all bodhisattvas"* are the original ancestors of all buddhas, and all buddhas are the original masters of all bodhisattvas. This supreme bodhi of the buddhas—whether they practice-and-experience it in the past or practice-and-experience it in the present or practice-and-experience it in the future, whether they practice-and-experience it in the moment before the body or practice-and-experience it in the moment after the mind—is in every case, in the beginning, middle, and end, *this Sutra*. The subject of *belonging* and the object of *belonging* are both *this Sutra*. At this very moment, *this Sutra* really experiences *all bodhisattvas*. The Sutra is not sentient, the Sutra is not insentient, the Sutra is not the product of doing and the Sutra is not the product of non-doing. Even so, when it experiences bodhi, experiences people, experiences real form, and experiences *this Sutra*, it *opens the gate of expedient methods. The gate of expedient methods* is the supreme virtue of the Buddha's ultimate state, it is *the Dharma abiding in the Dharma's place*, and it is *the form of the world abiding in constancy*.[27] The gate of expedient methods is not a temporary artifice; it is the learning in practice of the whole Universe in ten directions, and it is learning in practice that exploits the real form of all dharmas. Although this gate of expedient methods is manifesting itself such that it covers the whole Universe in ten directions with the Universe in ten directions, those other than *all bodhisattvas* are not in its orbit.

[219] Seppo[28] says, *"The whole earth is the gate of liberation, but people are not willing to enter even if they are dragged."*[29] So remember, even though the whole earth and the whole world is a gate, it is not left and entered easily, and the individuals who get out of it and get into it are not many. When people are dragged they do not get in and do not get out, and when they are not dragged they do not get in and do not get out. The progressive blunder and the passive falter. Going further, what can we say? If we take hold of the person and force it to leave or to enter the gate, the gate becomes more and more distant. If we take hold of the gate[30] and get it to enter the person, there are chances for departure and entry. *"Opening the gate of expedient methods"* means *revealing true real form. The revealing of true real form* covers the whole of time, and it is separated into moments of beginning, middle, and end. In *opening the gate of expedient methods,* the principle of momentary *opening* opens the gate of expedient methods through the whole Universe in ten directions. When, at this very moment, we glimpse the whole Universe in ten directions, the situation is one that we have never experienced before: by grasping the whole Universe in ten directions once and twice as a concept and a third and

---

27. Lotus Sutra, *Hoben (Expedient Means): "The Dharma abides in its place in the Dharma, /And the form of the world is constantly abiding. /Having recognized this in a place of the truth, /Guiding teachers teach it by expedient means."* (LS 1.120)

28. Master Seppo Gison (822–907), successor of Master Tokuzan Senkan.

29. *Rento-eyo*, chap. 21.

30 門を挙して (MON *o* KO *shi te*), "to take hold of the gate," means to focus on practice itself.

fourth time as a concrete thing, we cause it to open the gate of expedient methods. It may appear to follow from this that [the Universe in ten directions] is completely the same as *the opening of the gate of expedient methods,* but it seems to me that limitlessly abundant Universes in ten directions have borrowed a small fraction of *the opening of the gate of expedient methods* to use as their real features. Such elegance is entirely by virtue of *belonging to the Sutra. To reveal true real form* means to overhear the saying that *all dharmas are real form* spoken through the whole Universe, and to realize the truth through the whole Universe. It means making the truth that *real form is all dharmas* evident to the whole of humanity and making it manifest through the whole of the Dharma. In sum, the supreme truth of bodhi of the forty[31] buddhas and forty patriarchs totally belongs to *this Sutra.* It belongs to *this Sutra* and *this Sutra* belongs to it. The state in which a round cushion and a Zazen board[32] are the supreme truth of anuttara-samyak-saṃbodhi totally belongs to *this Sutra.* The picking up of a flower and a face breaking into a smile, and prostrations and attainment of the marrow, both *totally belong to this Sutra.* They are the belongings of *this Sutra.* They *open the gate of expedient methods and reveal true real form.*

[22] Nevertheless, recent unreliable people in the great kingdom of Sung, not knowing a place to settle down and not seeing the place of treasure, treat the words *real form* as if they were empty elaboration, and so they go on to study the sayings of Lao-tzu[33] and Chuang-tzu,[34] and they say that these are the same as the great truth of the Buddhist patriarchs. Furthermore, they say that the three teachings[35] may be of one conclusion. Or they say that the three teachings are like the three legs of a tripod, which would overturn if even one were missing. There is nothing to use as an example of the enormity of their foolishness. We should not concede that people in whom such words are present have ever listened to the Buddha-Dharma. Why? Because the origin of the Buddha-Dharma is India in the west. For eighty years in the world and for fifty years of preaching the Dharma, [the Buddha] did his ut-

---

31. Forty suggests the Seven Ancient Buddhas plus the historical patriarchs to the 33rd patriarch, Master Daikan Eno.

32. 禅版 (ZENPAN). This is a board used as a support in Zazen when a practitioner is sitting for a long time and gets tired. The board is held close to the body, with the chin resting on top of the board, and the bottom of the board resting in the hands. Traditionally its length is one *shaku* and seven or eight *sun* (about 55 cm), its width is two *sun* (6 cm), and its thickness is three or four *bu* (1.2 cm). It has a hole cut out at the top. In some temples the practitioner lays the board down on the Zazen platform, at right angles to the wall, and uses the hole to make a reference point on the floor for the eyes.

33. Lao-tzu (born c. 604 B.C., during the Chou dynasty), the founder of Taoism. His name 老子 (ROSHI) lit. means "aged child"; legend says that he spent 81 years in the womb and emerged with gray hair.

34. Chuang-tzu. Over a hundred thousand words of Taoist philosophy were attributed to him.

35. Buddhism, Taoism, and Confucianism.

most to educate human beings and gods; *he transformed all living beings and caused them all to enter the Buddha's truth.*[36] Thereafter the authentic transmission was received by the twenty-eight patriarchs. We esteem this as the utmost, as the subtle and fine, and as the supremely venerable. All kinds of non-Buddhists and celestial demons were completely defeated. Unknown numbers of human beings and gods realized buddha and became patriarchs. But they never said that, because they had not investigated Confucianism and Taoism in China, the Buddha's truth was insufficient for them. If the three teachings are inevitably of one conclusion, then when the Buddha-Dharma manifested itself Confucianism and Taoism should have manifested themselves in India at the same time. But the Buddha's Dharma is that *"In the heavens and under the heavens, I alone am the Honored-One."*[37] We should think back to the events of that time; we should not make mistakes through forgetfulness. Talk of the three teachings reaching one conclusion is worth less than the babbling of little children. It is [talk] of people who are out to destroy the Buddha-Dharma. People like this are very numerous. Some have manifested the purport of being the guiding teachers of human beings and gods, and some have become the masters of emperors and kings. It is the time of the degeneration of the Buddha-Dharma in great Sung [China]. My late Master, the eternal Buddha, strongly cautioned against this matter. Such people are the embryos of the two vehicles and non-Buddhists. Their kind has already passed two or three hundred years without even knowing that *real form* might exist. They speak only of learning the right Dharma of the Buddhist patriarchs in order to depart from the cycle of life and death. Many of them do not even know what it is to learn in practice the right Dharma of the Buddhist patriarchs; they believe that just to live in a temple is to emulate the ancients. It is pitiful that the truth of the ancestral patriarchs has died out. Venerable patriarchs in whom the truth is present greatly regret it. We should not listen to the sayings spouted by people like those mentioned earlier; we should feel sorry for them. Zen Master Engo[38] says, *"Living-and-dying, coming-and-going, is the real human body."* Picking up this expression, we should know ourselves and should consider the Buddha-Dharma. Chosa[39] says, *"The whole Universe in the ten directions is the real human body. The whole Universe in the ten directions is inside the brightness of the self."* Old veterans in all quarters of the great kingdom of Sung today generally do not even know that an expression like this is a truth to be learned; how much less could they

36. Alludes, for example, to Lotus Sutra, *Hoben*: *"[Buddhas] appear in the world because they desire to cause living beings to enter the truth that is the wisdom of Buddha."* (LS 1.88–90)

37. Legend says that when the Buddha was born he took seven steps in each of the four directions and, pointing to the sky with one hand and pointing to the ground with the other, he said these words.

38. Master Engo Kokugon (1063–1135), successor of Master Goso Ho-en.

39. Master Chosa Keishin (?–868), successor of Master Nansen Fugan. See chap. 60, *Juppo*.

[actually] learn it? If we quoted it to them, they would only go red in the face and be without words.

227] My late Master, the eternal Buddha, says, *"Old veterans in all directions today have no illumination of the past and no illumination of the present; they have never possessed the truths of the Buddha-Dharma.*[40] *The whole Universe in ten directions and suchlike are showing themselves like this! How can they be known? In other orders they seem never to have listened."* After hearing this I questioned old veterans in all directions and, in truth, few had listened. It is pitiful that they desecrate positions in which they have been installed without reason.

228] Zen Master O-an Donge[41] on one occasion addresses the venerable monk Tokki, *"If you want to understand easily, just keep facing the state of arising mind and moving images through the twelve hours.*[42] *When, just following this movement of images, you suddenly gain insight here and now, the ungraspable is like vast space. At the same time it is without spatial form and demarcation. Outside and inside are oneness. Intelligence and objects both disappear. Profundity and lucidity both vanish. The three times are in equilibrium. Those who arrive at this state*[43] *are called 'people at ease in the truth who are through with study and free of doing.'"*[44, 45]

These are words spoken by Old Man O-an in the state of using all his energy to express the truth. But it seems that he is only chasing shadows and never knows rest. When we are not in the state of *oneness of outside and inside,* can there be no Buddha-Dharma? What is this outside and inside? Furthermore, that "space has form and demarcation" is an expression of Buddhist patriarchs. What does he see as "space"? It may be supposed that O-an has never known space, has never seen space, has never grasped space, and has never struck space. He speaks of *"arising mind and moving images,"* but there is a truth that the mind never moves: how could there be *"arising mind"* through the twelve hours? 'Mind' cannot come into the reality of the twelve hours,[46] and 'twelve hours' do not enter the reality of the mind of the [concrete]

---

40. The truths of the Buddha-Dharma are, for example, the principle of practicing for the sake of practice itself, the law of cause-and-effect, the oneness of subject and object in action, and the principle that just sitting is beyond intellectual understanding.

41. Master O-an Donge (died 1163), successor of Master Kokyu Shoryu.

42. That is, the 24 hours, all day long.

43. 田地 (DENCHI). See chap. 48, *Sesshin-sessho,* note 31.

44. 絶学無為閑道人 (ZETSUGAKU MUI *[no]* KANDO-NIN). In the poem *Shodoka* Master Yoka Genkaku says: *"A person at ease in the truth, who is through with study and free of doing, does not try to get rid of delusion and does not want to get reality."*

45. *O-an-donge-zenji-goroku (Record of the Words of Zen Master O-an Donge),* chap. 7.

46. 十二時中 (JUNI-JI-CHU). In Master O-an's words 中 (CHU) means "during" or "through," but here Master Dogen uses the character to mean "the reality of." This usage of 中 (CHU) occurs frequently in Shobogenzo. See, for example, chap. 38, *Muchu-setsumu.*

twelve.[47] How much less could there be "arising mind"? And what are "moving images"? Do images move and not move, or are they beyond movement and non-movement? What is movement like? Again, what is non-movement like? What does he call "images"? Do images exist in the reality of the twelve hours? Do the twelve hours exist inside the image of reality?[48] Is it possible for there to be a time beyond the two factors? He says that *"if we just keep facing... through the twelve hours, it will be easy to understand,"* but what is the matter to be understood easily? Does "easy understanding" refer to the truth of the Buddhist patriarchs? If so, [he should know that] the Buddha's truth is beyond easy understanding and difficult understanding. That is why Nangaku and Kozei long pursued the truth following their masters. [O-an] speaks of *"suddenly gaining insight into the ungraspable,"* but he has never seen the truth of the Buddhist patriarchs even in a dream. How can one of such ability be up to *"wanting to understand easily"*? Clearly, he has not mastered the great truth of the Buddhist patriarchs. If the Buddha-Dharma were like that, how could it have reached today? Even O-an is like this. If we search among the old veterans of mountain-temples of the present for a person like O-an, even in consecutive kalpas we will not meet one. Even if we searched until our eyes were growing dim, we might not find another old veteran to equal O-an. Most people of recent times affirm O-an, but it is hard for me to affirm that the Buddha-Dharma reached him. I would say only that he is [worth] a junior's seat in the monastery and that he is of average standard. Why? Because O-an has the mental agility to be able to know a person. People today do not have the ability to know a person, because they do not know themselves. Even though O-an has not arrived, he has experience of learning the truth. The old veterans of today have no experience of learning the truth. O-an hears good words; it is just that they do not enter his ears and he does not see them with his ears: [further,] they do not enter his eyes and he does not hear them with his eyes.[49] Although O-an used to be like this, now, through his own efforts, he may be in the state of realization. Old veter-

---

47. 十二心中 (JUNI-SHIN-CHU). Here a definite number (twelve) represents the concrete and definite as opposed to the general.

48. 念裏 (NENRI). 裏 (RI) means "inside," "backside," or "in the concrete place of." See also chap. 48, *Sesshin-sessho,* notes 24 and 38. 念 (NEN) has two meanings: 1) abstract image, idea, thought, wish, et cetera. For example, in *Fukan-zazengi Shinpitsu-bon,* Master Dogen writes "Cease intellectual consideration of images, thoughts, reflections," and "If an image arises, just be conscious. If you are conscious of it, it will vanish at once." 2) The image, or the mental face of, reality itself. For example, in *Fukan-zazengi Shinpitsu-bon,* Master Dogen writes 正念現前 (SHONEN-GENZEN), "the right image manifesting itself before us." Further, in the corresponding section of the later *Fukan-zazengi Rufu-bon,* he writes of 正法自現前 (SHOBO-JI-GENZEN), "the right Dharma naturally manifesting itself before us." In this way, Master Dogen uses 念 (NEN), "image," and 法 (HO), "Dharma, reality," interchangeably, in order to describe the same experience in Zazen.

49. Seeing with the ears and hearing with the eyes suggests intuitive perception.

ans in the mountain-temples of great Sung [China] today do not glimpse the inside or the outside of O-an; their sounds and features are completely foreign to his state. Such people cannot even recognize whether the *real form* expressed by Buddhist patriarchs is the truth of the Buddhist patriarchs or is not the truth of the Buddhist patriarchs. For this reason, the old veterans and unreliable people of the last two or three hundred years have neither seen nor spoken of *real form* at all.

[234] My late Master Tendo, the eternal Buddha, says one night during informal preaching in the abbot's quarters:

> *There are calves*[50] *on Tendo mountain tonight,*
> *And golden-faced Gautama is manifesting real form.*
> *If we wanted to buy it, how could we afford the impossible price?*
> *The cry of a cuckoo above*[51] *a solitary cloud.*

Being like this, those who are accomplished in the Buddhism of venerable patriarchs speak of *real form*. Those who do not know the Buddha-Dharma, and in whom there is no learning in practice of the Buddha's truth, do not speak of *real form*. The above words [come about] as follows: It is approaching the fourth watch[52] of a night in the third lunar month in the spring of the second year of the great Sung era of Hogyo,[53] when three beats of the drum sound from above.[54] Taking the prostration cloth, and putting on the kaṣaya, I leave the Cloud Hall through the front entrance, and [find that] the sign for entry into the [Master's] room has been hung up. First I follow other monks to the vicinity of the Dharma Hall. Via the west wall of the Dharma Hall, I climb the west stairs of *Jakko-do*, the Hall of Serene Light.[55] I pass before the west wall of the Hall of Serene Light and climb the west stairs of *Dai-komyo-zo*, the Vault of Great Brightness.[56] The Vault of Great Brightness is the abbot's quarters. Via the southern end of a screen along the west side, I reach the incense stand, and burn incense and do prostrations. I am expecting that lines will have formed here for entry into the [Master's] room, but I do not see even one monk. *Myokodai*, the elevated stage,[57] has been

---

50. Calves symbolize Buddhist practitioners in a peaceful state.

51. 上 *(ue)*, "above," receives emphasis in the original Chinese by being the last character of the last line—the poem leaves the reader thinking upward and onward.

52. In China and Japan, the night was divided into five watches of two hours each.

53. 1226.

54. The abbot's quarters were located high up the mountain—see the traditional temple layout in Book 1, Appendices.

55. 寂光堂 (JAKKO-DO) is a proper name. The location of this hall would correspond to that of the Hall for Patriarchs' Images (3) or the Donors' Hall (9) in the ground plan shown in Book 1, Appendices.

56. 大光明蔵 (DAIKOMYO-ZO) is also a proper name.

57. 妙高台 (MYOKODAI) is lit. "Fine and High Stage." The abbot's quarters were likely divided, by bamboo blinds, into the elevated stage and an area for waiting and burning incense.

screened off by bamboo blinds. The Dharma-sound of the abbot, the Great Master, is faintly audible. Then Supervising Monk Sokon[58] from Saisen[59] arrives and he also burns incense and does prostrations. After that, peering stealthily towards the elevated stage, [we see that] monks are standing in a packed audience without regard to east or west. The informal preaching is now in progress, so we stealthily enter behind the other monks and, standing up, we listen. The story of the life in the mountains of Zen Master Hojo of Daibai[60] is quoted. At the part about his wearing clothes made from lotus leaves and eating pine nuts,[61] many of the monks shed tears. The story of Śākyamuni Buddha's retreat on Vulture Peak is quoted in detail. Many in the audience shed tears. *"The retreat on Tendo-zan mountain is approaching. Now it is spring, and it is neither cold nor hot. It is a lovely time to sit in Zazen. Brothers, how could we not sit in Zazen?"* After such informal preaching, there is the poem. On finishing the poem, [the Master] strikes the right arm of his Zazen chair once with his right hand and says, *"You may enter."*[62] For the interview, he says, *"A cuckoo cries and bamboos on the mountain split."* The words of the interview are [only] like this; there is no other talk. The monks present, though many, say nothing; they are just awed. This method of entering the [Master's] room was never practiced in other districts. Only my late Master Tendo, the eternal Buddha, practiced this method. During the informal preaching the [Master's] chair was surrounded by screens around which the monks stood in a crowd. All the monks remained standing while the interviews continued from whichever monk was ready to enter, and people who had completed their interview left through the doors of the abbot's quarters in the usual manner. The people who remained, still standing as before, could witness everything—the dignified behavior of stepping forward and stopping by the person entering for the interview, together with the behavior of the Venerable Abbot and his talk in the interview. This method has never been present in other districts, and it may be a method impossible for other old veterans to realize: During entry into the room of other masters, people wanted to enter the room before other people. In the case of this entry into the [Master's] room, people want to enter the room after other people. We

58. 維那 (INO). The Supervisor of monks in the Zazen Hall, or rector; represents the Sanskrit *karma-dāna*. The job of the *Ino* centers on maintaining discipline in the Zazen Hall.

59. A region of Szechwan (Sichuan) province in southwest China.

60. Master Daibai Hojo (752–839), successor of Master Baso Do-itsu. Master Dogen quotes the story in chap. 30, *Gyoji*, para. [141].

61. Master Daibai's poem says: *I shall never outwear the lotus leaves in the pond. / The flowers of a few pines are more than a meal. / Now my abode has been discovered by people in the world. / I shall move my shack deeper into seclusion.* Ibid.

62. 入室 (NYUSHITSU), "to enter the room," means to have an interview with the master of a temple. In this case, since the monks are already on the elevated stage with Master Tendo, it means to come forward one by one before the Master's chair. The Master's chair was likely surrounded by screens forming three sides of a square.

should not forget [that there are such] differences in people's minds and ways. From that time until this first year of the Japanese era of Kangen,[63] in an atmosphere of brightness, all of eighteen years have swiftly passed. I have no idea how many mountains and rivers there are between Tendo mountain and this mountain here, but the scene expressed as *real form* in those beautiful expressions and wonderful words has remained engraved on my body, mind, bones, and marrow. I imagine that the informal preaching and the entry into the [Master's] room that took place that night have been unforgettable for most of the monks present. On that night a crescent moon came peeping out from behind the high temple buildings, and even though the cuckoos were crying frequently, the night was silent.

[240] While Great Master Shu-itsu[64] of Gensa-in temple is preaching informally,[65] he hears the chirping of swallow chicks, and says, *"[This is] profound preaching of real form, and skillful expounding of the pivot of the Dharma."* He gets down from his seat.

Afterwards a monk requests instruction, saying *"I do not understand."*

The Master says, *"Go away! No one believes you."*[66]

As regards the meaning of *"profoundly preaching real form,"* we might interpret Gensa's words as saying that only the swallow chicks are profoundly preaching real form. But that is not so. During the informal preaching, the chirps of swallow chicks are heard. It is not that the swallow chicks profoundly preach real form, it is not that Gensa profoundly preaches real form, and it is not a cross between the two factors: rather, the ineffable state just in the moment is *profound preaching of real form.* We should take a short while to investigate this episode. Informal preaching is in progress. The chirping of swallow chicks is heard. The words *"profoundly preaching real form, and skillfully expounding the pivot of the Dharma"* are spoken. There is the act of getting down from the seat. Afterwards there is the monk's request for instruction: *"I do not understand."* And there is the Master's statement *"Go away! No one believes you." "I do not understand"* need not always be a request for instruction on real form, but it is the very lifeblood of the Buddhist patriarchs and the bones and marrow of the right-Dharma-eye treasury. Remember, even if this monk, in requesting instruction, says *"I have understood it"* or says *"I can expound it,"* in every case Gensa should still say to him *"Go away! No one believes you."* The reason he says *"Go away! No one believes you"* is not that [the monk] has understood but requests instruction by pretending not to understand. Truly, though it may be any third son of Chang or fourth son of

63. 1243.

64. Master Gensa Shibi (835–907), successor of Master Seppo Gison.

65. 参 (SAN) is short for 小参 (SHOSAN), which means unscheduled informal preaching, usually done in the master's room.

66. *Rento-eyo*, chap. 23, and *Shinji-shobogenzo*, pt. 3, no. 42.

Lee other than this monk, and though all [other] dharmas are [also] real form, at the time and place that someone cuts directly through to the lifeblood of the Buddhist patriarchs, learning in practice of real form is realized like this.[67] In Seigen's lineage this state has been realized.[68] Remember, real form is the right lifeblood that has been transmitted and received from rightful successor to rightful successor; all dharmas are the perfectly realized state of buddhas alone, together with buddhas; and the state of buddhas alone, together with buddhas, is the loveliness of form as it is.

Shobogenzo Shoho-jisso

Preached to the assembly at Kippo-ji temple in Esshu,[69] Japan, on a day in the 9th lunar month in the 1st year of Kangen.[70]

---

67. In the state of not understanding.

68. Master Gensa is a 7th-generation descendant of Master Seigen Gyoshi. Master Dogen also belongs to Master Seigen's lineage.

69. Corresponds to modern-day Fukui prefecture.

70. 1243.

[51]

密語

MITSUGO

Secret Talk

***Mitsu** means "secret," or "mystical," in the sense of not apparent to the senses or the intellect, but experienced directly or immediately—as if two things are touching. **Go** means "words" or "talk." So **mitsugo** means "secret talk," that is, something communicated directly without sound. In Buddhism it is said that there is secret talk that can be recognized and understood even though it has no sound. So "secret talk" suggests the existence of intuitive perception. It is a fact that we can sometimes discover meaning, or secrets, without receiving any external stimuli, but we need not see the fact as particularly mystical. An analogy that helps to understand such facts is the sympathetic resonance of tuning forks.*

3] **When the great truth,** *that which buddhas guard and desire,*[1] is realized as the real Universe, the state [expressed] *You are like this, I am like this,* and *each must guard it well,*[2] is experienced exactly in the present.

4] Great Master Kokaku[3] of Ungo-zan mountain, the story goes, is served offerings by a government official, who asks, *"The World-Honored One has secret talk;*[4] *for Mahākāśyapa nothing is concealed. What is the World-Honored One's secret talk?"*

The Great Master calls out, *"Minister!"*

The man responds.

---

1. Master Daikan Eno said to Master Nangaku Ejo, *"Just this untainted state is that which buddhas guard and desire. You are also like this. I am also like this. And the ancestral masters of India were also like this." Shinji-shobogenzo,* pt. 2, no. 1, and *Keitoku-dento-roku,* chap. 5. See also Shobogenzo, chap. 7, *Senjo.*

2. 善自護持 (ZEN-JI-GOJI). From Master Bodhidharma's words to Master Taiso Eka: *"That is just the substance of the mind transmitted by the buddhas and patriarchs of the past. Now you have got it, you yourself must guard it well."* See chap. 48, *Sesshin-sessho.*

3. Master Ungo Doyo (835?–902), successor of Master Tozan Ryokai.

4. 密語 (MITSUGO). 密 (MITSU) means "secret" or "close." Master Dogen explains later in this chapter that 密 (MITSU) describes the state of direct contact with reality, which is "secret" only in the sense that it is beyond explanation—it is not esoteric. 語 (GO) is lit. "words." Here it means not only verbal communication but "talk," as in the sense of "bird-talk," or as in the sense that a tree talks to us.

The Great Master says, *"Do you understand or not?"*

The official says, *"I do not understand."*

The Great Master says, *"If you do not understand, it is the World-Honored One's secret talk. If you understand, it is Mahākāśyapa's state of nothing being concealed."*

[5] The Great Master, manifesting himself as the legitimate descendant, after five generations, of Seigen,[5] is a master of gods and human beings and a great good counselor through the whole Universe in the ten directions. He transforms the sentient and transforms the insentient. As the forty-sixth buddha in the legitimate succession of buddhas, he preaches the Dharma for Buddhist patriarchs.[6] At his hermitage on Sanpo mountain, he was sent offerings from the kitchens of gods. But after receiving the transmission of the Dharma and attaining the truth, he transcended the state which is sent [heavenly] offerings.[7] The expression quoted now that *"The World-Honored One has secret talk; for Mahākāśyapa nothing is concealed,"* is the legacy of forty-six buddhas. At the same time, as the original features of the forty-six buddhas, *it is not got from others, it does not come from outside, it is not inherent,* and *it has never been something new.*[8] With regard to the realization of this matter of secret talk, not only the World-Honored Śākyamuni has secret talk: all the Buddhist patriarchs have secret talk. A world-honored one always has secret talk. And one who has secret talk inevitably has Mahākāśyapa's state of nothing being concealed. We should learn in practice and should not forget the truth that if there are a hundred thousand world-honored ones there are a hundred thousand Mahākāśyapas. "Learning in practice" means not intending to understand at once but striving painstakingly hundreds of times, or thousands of times, as if working to cut a hard object. We should not think that when a person has something to relate we will be able to understand at once. It may be that now, having already become the World-Honored One, [the Master of] Ungo-zan mountain is equipped with secret talk and possesses the state of Mahākāśyapa in which nothing is concealed. Do not learn that calling "Minister!" and the official's response, are secret talk itself.[9]

[7] The Great Master, in the story, says to the minister, *"If you do not understand, it is the World-Honored One's secret talk. If you understand, it is Mahākāśyapa's state of nothing being concealed."* We should resolve unfailingly to pursue the truth of this expression for many kalpas. He is saying "When you are

---

5. Master Seigen Gyoshi (died 740), successor of Master Daikan Eno.

6. Master Ungo is the 46th buddha in Master Dogen's lineage counting from Vipaśyin Buddha, the first of the Seven Buddhas. See chap. 15, *Busso.*

7. Alludes to the legend that when practitioners are pursuing enlightenment they are served meals by angels. See also chap. 30, *Gyoji,* para. [132].

8. These four aphorisms are in the style of quotations from Chinese, but their source has not been traced.

9. Secret talk is not just communication in words.

in the state beyond understanding, that is the World-Honored One's secret talk"; he does not call being momentarily dumbfounded "not understanding," and he does not call ignorance "not understanding." The principle of the words "If you do not understand..." is to sanction a course of quietly learning in practice. We should consider this through effort in pursuit of the truth.[10] Further, when he says "If you understand..." he is not discussing a state of now having understood already.[11] In learning the Buddha-Dharma in practice, there are many processes. Among them there are the pivotal matters of understanding the Buddha-Dharma and of not understanding the Buddha-Dharma. Those who, not having met a true teacher, do not even know that [these matters] exist, have misunderstood that secret talk exists at random, in conjunction with eyes and ears that are cut off from sight and hearing.[12] [Master Ungo] is not saying that you understanding is a condition for Mahākāśyapa's state of nothing being concealed: there are also cases of nothing being concealed in non-understanding. Do not learn that anyone can observe nothing being concealed: the state here and now is already nothing being concealed—[or] it may be that there is no place where nothing is concealed.[13] Just at the moment of the present we should investigate this by experiment. Thus, we have not been learning that states which are unknown to us are secret talk. The very moment of not understanding the Buddha-Dharma is one concrete instance of secret talk. It is, in every case, the World-Honored One's existence,[14] and the existent World-Honored One.[15]

[9] Nevertheless, people who do not hear the instruction of a true teacher, although they sit upon the lion-seat,[16] have never seen this truth even in a dream. They speak without reason as follows: *"The World-Honored One has secret talk" describes his picking up a flower and winking an eye before the assembly of millions on Vulture Peak. That is because verbal Buddhist preaching is shallow and seemingly concerned with name and form, but picking up a flower and winking an eye, being non-verbal preaching, are instances of establishing the teaching with secret talk. The assembly of millions cannot comprehend [the non-verbal preaching]. Therefore, for the assembly of millions, it is secret talk.*[17] *"Mahākāśyapa's state of nothing being concealed" describes Mahākāśyapa breaking into a smile as if he knew before-*

---

10. 工夫弁道 (KUFU-BENDO) means Zazen.

11. By "understanding" Master Ungo means practical realization in the moment, not intellectual understanding.

12. People misunderstand that secret talk is something esoteric. According to Master Dogen, however, secret talk is a mystery in that it is real, and therefore cannot be explained, but it is open to everyone—because reality is always talking secret talk.

13. Master Dogen described the same reality with two opposing expressions.

14. 世尊有 (SESON-U), translated in the story as "The World-Honored One has..."

15. 有世尊 (U-SESON).

16. 獅子座 (SHISHI-ZA) means a buddha's seat of preaching. See, for example, LS 2.186–88.

17. In this (wrong) view "secret" means esoteric, inaccessible to the uninitiated.

hand that the World-Honored One would pick up a flower and wink an eye. Therefore it is said that, to Mahākāśyapa, nothing is concealed. This is the true essence of the teaching, which has been transmitted and received one-to-one. People who believe this when they hear it are as [numerous as] rice plants, flax plants, bamboos, and reeds; they make up the monasteries of the nine states.[18] It is pitiful. That the truth of the Buddhist patriarchs has been ruined originally stems from this cause. A man of clear eyes should surely be able to defeat [these opinions] one by one. If the World-Honored One's speech is seen as shallow, picking up a flower and winking an eye must also be shallow. If people consider the speech of the World-Honored One to be [mere expression of] name and form, they are not students of the Buddha-Dharma. They know that speech is names and forms, but they have not yet realized that the World-Honored One is free of name and form: they have yet to shed the sentiments of the common man. All that is permeated by the body-mind of a Buddhist patriarch is liberation, is the preaching of Dharma, and is verbal preaching; and it turns the Dharma-wheel. Those who gain benefit from witnessing it are many. People of devotional practice[19] and of Dharma-practice[20] are covered by its influence at places where there are Buddhist patriarchs and they share in its influence at places where there are no Buddhist patriarchs. How could the assembly of millions fail to witness picking up a flower and winking an eye as picking up a flower and winking an eye? [The assembly of millions] may be on the same level as Mahākāśyapa and they may be living the same life as the World-Honored One. They may be experiencing the same state and establishing the mind at the same time as the assembly of millions. They are in the same state of truth and in the same national land. They are meeting Buddha and hearing the Dharma with knowing wisdom and they are meeting Buddha and hearing the Dharma with unknowing wisdom. Having initially met one buddha, they will go on to meet buddhas as numerous as sands of the Ganges. There may be multitudes [numbering] millions of koṭis in attendance at every single Buddhist gathering. Revelations by each of the buddhas of the picking up of a flower and the winking of an eye may all be witnessed taking place in the same moment. Eyes are not dim. Ears are sharp. We have mental eyes and physical eyes. We have mental ears and physical ears. How do those others understand Mahākāśyapa's breaking into a smile? Let them try to say something! If it is as they say, this [smile] should also be called "secret talk." But they call it "nothing being con-

---

18. 九州 (KYUSHU), nine states of China.

19. 信行 (SHINGYO), or "practice based on belief" suggests, for example, the practice of the Pure Land Sects.

20. 法行 (HOGYO), or "practice based on Dharma," suggests, for example, the practice of the so-called Zen sects.

cealed." This is doubly foolish.[21] Later the World-Honored One says, *"I have the right-Dharma-eye treasury, and the fine mind of nirvāṇa. I transmit them to Mahākāśyapa."* Is such an expression speech or is it non-verbal communication? If the World-Honored One hated speech but loved picking up flowers, he would have picked up a flower at the later time too. [And even in that case,] how could Mahākāśyapa fail to understand, and how could the assembly fail to hear? The tales told by the people described above are not to be relied upon.

4] In sum, the World-Honored One has secret talk, secret action, and secret experience. Stupid people, however, think that "secret" means other people do not know but the subject knows, and that there are initiated people and uninitiated people. Learning in practice of the Buddha's truth has never been present in those who have thought and said so in India in the west and in the eastern lands, from the ancient past till the present. In such a case, both in the secular world and beyond the secular world[22] there would be much secrecy among the uneducated and little secrecy among the learned. For people of wide learning can nothing be secret? Still more for those equipped with supernatural eyes, supernatural ears, Dharma-eyes, Dharma-ears, the Buddha's eyes, the Buddha's ears, and so on, we would have to say that there could be no secret talk and no secret will at all. Secret talk, secret will, secret action, and so on in the Buddha-Dharma are beyond such reasoning. When we meet a human being, that is just when we hear secret talk and talk secret talk. When we know ourselves, we know secret action. Moreover, a Buddhist patriarch is able thoroughly to penetrate and to discern the secret will and the secret talk described previously. Remember, in the momentary state of a Buddhist patriarch, secret words and secret acts vie to be realized. What has been described as "secret" is the truth of immediacy.[23] It is the absence of any gap. It is total containment[24] of a Buddhist patriarch, total containment of you, total containment of me, total containment of action, total containment of an age, total containment of virtue, and total containment of secrecy. Even the Buddha's eyes cannot glimpse the coming together of secret talk and a human being in the secret state. Action in the secret state is beyond the recognition of self and others; only I in the secret state can know it; and every other individual in the secret state *does not understand* it.[25] Because secrecy

---

21. The interpretation that "secret words" must mean non-verbal, esoteric conduct is foolish. But on the basis of that interpretation, the conduct of Master Mahākāśyapa should also be called "secret words," so to call it nothing being concealed is doubly foolish.

22. 世間・出世間 (SEKEN-SHUSSEKEN); that is, both among lay people and among monks.

23. 親密 (SHINMITSU). 親 (SHIN) means intimacy or familiarity. 密 (MITSU) means secrecy or closeness. 親密 (SHINMITSU) means intimacy, closeness, or immediacy.

24. 蓋 (GAI) as a noun means a lid or a cover, and as a verb means to cover as if with a lid; to cover totally.

25. 不会す (FU-E *su),* that is, "transcends understanding of it"—as in the story.

surrounds you, everything relies on secrecy, and a single or half a thing relies on secrecy. We should consider such truths in detail and learn them in practice. In conclusion, that places of teaching people and moments of intuition and affirmation are, in every case, the manifestation of secrecy, is the authentic tradition transmitted by buddhas and patriarchs. Because the present is an ineffable moment[26] it is secret to the self, it is secret to others, it is secret to Buddhist patriarchs, and it is secret to alien beings. For this reason, [the present,] on the basis of secrecy, is newly secret. Because teaching, practice, and experience like this are just the state of a Buddhist patriarch, they clear up and pass through the secrecy of a Buddhist patriarch, and thus they clear up and pass through secrecy itself.

[18] My Master's Master Seccho[27] addresses the assembly:

The World-Honored One has secret talk,
For Mahākāśyapa nothing is concealed.
Through the night a rain of falling flowers,
Water flowing through the city is fragrant.[28]

Here and now, Seccho's expression *"Through the night a rain of falling flowers; Water flowing through the city is fragrant"* is immediacy itself. Picking it up, we should examine the eyeballs and the nostrils of a Buddhist patriarch. It is beyond Rinzai and Tokuzan. We should explore the opening of nostrils in the eyes and should sharpen the tip of the nose in the ears.[29] Indeed, it is inside the ears, the nose, and the eyes that we realize the whole body-mind which is neither old nor new. We esteem this as the truth that *the raining of flowers is the occurrence of the world.*[30] In the Old Master's words *"Water flowing through the city is fragrant,"* the body is concealed yet its figure is ever more conspicuously revealed.[31] Thus, in everyday life inside the house of the Bud-

---

26. 甚麼の時節 (NAN *no* JISETSU), lit. "what time," that is, a time that cannot be expressed in hours and minutes, a real time.

27. Master Seccho Chikan (1105–1192), successor of Master Tendo Sogyoko. 師翁 (SHI-O), lit. "master old man," is a term of respect for the master of one's own master—Master Seccho was the master of Master Tendo Nyojo.

28. *Katai-futo-roku,* chap. 17.

29. We should make our sight (or intuition) and hearing (or discernment) vivid and accurate.

30. 華雨世界起 (KE-U-SEKAI-KI). The usual expression is 華開世界起 (KE-KAI-SEKAI-KI), *"the opening of flowers is the occurrence of the world."* These words of Master Prajñātara describe the oneness of phenomena and reality. Master Dogen substituted 雨 (U), "to rain," from Master Seccho's poem, for 開 (KAI), "to open."

31. 蔵身影弥露 *(mi o zo shi te kage iyo-iyo arawa ruru).* A related expression appears in chap. 28, *Butsu-kojo-no-ji,* para. [68]: "Doyo springs in through his brain and conceals himself in his body. And while concealed in his body, he conspicuously reveals his figure." Also, in chap. 46, *Katto,* para. [100], Master Dogen describes the transmission between Mahākāśyapa and Ānanda as Ānanda concealing his body in Mahākāśyapa and Mahākāśyapa concealing his body in Ānanda.

dhist patriarchs, we investigate and pass through *the World-Honored One's having secret talk* and *Mahākāśyapa's nothing being concealed.* The Seven World-Honored Buddhas each is learning it in practice as [we are] now. Mahākāśyapa and Śākyamuni alike have penetrated and discerned it as [we are doing] now.

Shobogenzo Mitsugo

Preached to the assembly at old Kippo temple in the Yoshida district of Esshu,[32] on the 20th day of the 9th lunar month in the 1st year of Kangen.[33]

32. Corresponds to modern-day Fukui prefecture.
33. 1243.

[52]

仏経

BUKKYO

The Buddhist Sutras

Butsu *means "Buddha" or "Buddhist," and* ***kyo*** *means "sutra" or "scripture." So* ***bukkyo*** *means Buddhist sutras. Shobogenzo chapter 24 is also called* ***Bukkyo****, but in that chapter,* ***kyo*** *is a different word, meaning "teaching." In Buddhism, there are fundamentally two ways that are useful in pursuing the truth. One is practicing Zazen, and the other is reading sutras. But some people emphasize the value of practicing Zazen so strongly that they are blind to the value of reading Buddhist sutras, and so they deny the value of reading them. They insist that Buddhism is not philosophical theories, and therefore that to attain the truth we need only practice Zazen, and that reading Buddhist sutras is useless or even detrimental to pursuing the truth. But Master Dogen did not think so. He esteemed the value of reading sutras, and he thought that it was necessary to read Buddhist sutras in order to attain the truth. Therefore he recorded the true meaning of reading Buddhist sutras in this chapter. Furthermore, in Master Dogen's thought, Buddhist sutras are not only Buddhist scriptures, but they are also the Universe itself, which shows us and teaches us the true meaning of our life.*

1] ***The method of teaching bodhisattvas,***[1] and the method of teaching buddhas, exist in the here and now.[2] They are both tools of the great truth. The tools accord with the master, and the master uses the tools. For this reason, at the very moment of *sometimes following a good counselor*[3] and *sometimes following the sutras*, which the Buddhist patriarchs of India and China have

---

1. 教菩薩法 (KYO-BOSATSU-HO), suggests the Lotus Sutra itself. See chap. 17, *Hokke-ten-hokke*, and for example, LS 1.52.

2. このなかに... *(kono naka ni)* means either "in this [time and place]" or "in these [Buddhist sutras]." Given that in this chapter reality and the Buddhist sutras are identified, both translations signify the same thing.

3. 知識 (CHISHIKI), lit. "acquaintance," is short for 善知識 (ZENCHISHIKI), lit. "good acquaintance," which represents the Sanskrit *kalyāna-mitra*. MW defines *kalyāna-mitra* as "a friend of virtue; a well-wishing friend; a good counselor." See Book 1, Glossary. *Kalyāna-mitra* is often translated as "spiritual friend," but in Master Dogen's philosophy 善 (ZEN), "goodness" or "virtue," is a practical rather than a spiritual matter. See, for example, chap. 10, *Shoaku-makusa*. "A good counselor" means a teacher who can give concrete practical guidance on how to apply the principles of Buddhism in daily life.

done without exception, establishment of the will, training, and experience of the effect, have no gap between each other at all. Establishing the will relies on the sutras and on a good counselor; training also relies on the sutras and on a good counselor; and experiencing the effect also is wholly intimate with the sutras and with a good counselor. The moment before, and a word after,[4] are both in the same state as the sutras and as a good counselor. The moment itself, and the inside of a word,[5] are both in the same state as the sutras and as a good counselor.

[23] Good counselors, in every case, are thoroughly versed in the sutras. "They are thoroughly versed" means that they see the sutras as their national land, and see the sutras as the body-mind. They have seen the sutras as the means of establishing the teaching for others, they have seen the sutras as their sitting, lying down, and walking, they have seen the sutras as father and mother, and they have seen the sutras as children and grandchildren. Because they have made the sutras into practice and understanding, good counselors have mastered the sutras. A good counselor washing the face and drinking tea[6] is the eternal Sutra itself. The saying that "the sutras produce good counselors" describes sixty strokes of Obaku's staff being able to produce children and grandchildren,[7] and three strikes [on a stone mortar] on Mt. Obai making possible the transmission of the robe and transmission of the Dharma.[8] It describes not only that: realizing the truth on seeing the peach blossoms, realizing the truth on hearing the sound of a bamboo,[9] and realizing the truth on seeing a bright star, are all examples of the sutras producing good counselors. There are skin-bags and fists who get eyes then get the sutras, and there are wooden dippers and lacquered tubs who get the sutras then get eyes. What has been called "the sutras" is the whole Universe in the ten directions itself; there is no time or place that is not the sutras. They use the characters of consummate philosophy and they use the characters of secular philosophy; they use the characters of the heavens above and they use the characters of the human world; they use the characters of the world of animals and they use the characters of the world of asuras;[10] they use the characters of the hundred weeds and they use the characters of ten thousand

---

4. 機先句後 (KISEN-KUGO), suggests action—intuition before, consideration after.

5. 機中句裏 (KICHU-KURI).

6. 洗面喫茶 (SENMEN-KISSA), alludes to a story about Master Isan Reiyu and his two disciples. See chap. 25, *Jinzu*, and *Shinji-shobogenzo*, pt. 1, no. 61.

7. Refers to the transmission between Master Obaku Ki-un and his disciples Rinzai Gigen, Bokushu Domyo et cetera. See also note 27.

8. Refers to the transmission between Master Daiman Konin and Master Daikan Eno, described for example in chap. 29, *Inmo*, para. [99].

9. The stories of Master Reiun Shigon and Master Kyogen Chikan realizing the truth in nature are recorded in chap. 9, *Keisei-sanshiki*.

10. Animals and asuras are two of the six states, 六道 (ROKUDO): gods, human beings, asuras (angry demons), animals, hungry ghosts, and beings in hell.

trees. Therefore, the long, the short, the square, the round, the blue, the yellow, the red, and the white, which are arranged in dense profusion throughout the Universe in ten directions, are all the characters of the sutras, and they are the concrete surface of the sutras. We see them as the tools of the great truth, as the Buddhist sutras. This Sutra is able to spread out over the whole of Time and to spread throughout entire nations. It opens the gate of teaching people and does not forsake any human household over the whole earth. It opens the gate of teaching things and saves material beings throughout the earth. In teaching buddhas and teaching bodhisattvas, it becomes the whole earth and the whole Universe. It *opens the gate of expedient methods,*[11] it opens the gate of *abiding in place,*[12] and, not forsaking one person or a half of one, it *reveals true real form.* To get this Sutra, at this very moment, with the thinking, sensing, mindfulness, and realization, and in the state without thinking, sensing, mindfulness, and realization, of buddhas or of bodhisattvas—though it is beyond the intentional doing of the individual—is the great aim of each person. The time of *decisively getting this Sutra*[13] is beyond past and present; because past and present are moments of getting the Sutra, what is manifested before our eyes as the whole Universe in ten directions is just *the getting of this Sutra.* When we read, recite, and become versed in this Sutra, the Buddha-wisdom, natural wisdom, and untutored wisdom[14] are realized prior to the mind and are realized prior to the body. At this time we do not have the doubt that [wisdom] may be a new and special state. When this Sutra is being received, retained, read, and recited by us, the Sutra is enfolding us. The situation before a line and around a word, and in scanning down and dwelling on a sentence, is, instantly, the scattering of blossoms and the making of garlands. We call this Sutra the Dharma itself, and in it there are eighty-four thousand accumulations of Dharma-preaching. In this Sutra there are characters which are buddhas who have realized the balanced and right state of truth, there are characters which are buddhas who are presently living in the world, and there are characters which are buddhas who have entered pari-nirvāṇa. The arriving of reality and the leaving of reality[15] are each a character in the Sutra and are a line of Dharma written on the Dharma. Picking up a flower and winking an eye, and a face breaking into a

---

11. Lotus Sutra, *Hosshi: "This Sutra opens the gate of expedient methods and reveals true real form."* See LS 2.156, and chap. 50, *Shoho-jisso.*

12. Alludes to Lotus Sutra, *Hoben: "The Dharma abides in its place in the Dharma, / And the form of the world is constantly abiding. / Having recognized this in a place of the truth, / Guiding teachers teach it by expedient means."* (LS 1.120).

13. 必得是経 (HITTOKU-ZEKYO). Source not traced.

14. 無師智 (MUSHI-CHI), lit. "no-master-wisdom," means wisdom that develops intuitively without being taught.

15. 如来如去 (NYORAI-NYOKO). 如来 (NYORAI), lit. "[One to whom] reality has arrived," representing the Sanskrit *Tathāgata,* is an epithet of the Buddha which is commonly used in the Buddhist sutras.

smile, are just the eternal Sutra authentically transmitted from the Seven Buddhas. Standing waist-deep in snow and cutting off an arm, doing prostrations and getting the marrow, are just the eternal Sutra transmitted from master to disciple. The subsequent transmission of the Dharma and giving of the robe are just the arrival of the moment in which all volumes of the universal scripture are entrusted. Three strikes of the mortar and three sifts of the rice in the winnowing basket[16] make the Sutra hold out a hand to the Sutra, and the Sutra thus rightly succeeds the Sutra. Furthermore, *"This is something coming like this"*[17] is a thousand sutras for teaching buddhas and is ten thousand sutras for teaching bodhisattvas. *"To explain a thing does not hit the target"*[18] nicely preaches the eighty thousand compilations and the twelve parts [of the sutras].[19] Furthermore, a fist and a heel, a staff and a whisk, are eternal sutras and new sutras, sutras of existence and sutras of emptiness. Being part of the assembly and pursuing the truth, making the effort of sitting in Zazen, are originally the Buddhist sutras that are right at the beginning and the Buddhist sutras that are right at the end. They are sutras written on leaves of the Bodhi tree, and sutras written on the faces of space. In sum, a Buddhist patriarch's one instance of movement and two instances of stillness, and his or her holding on and letting go, are naturally the closing and opening of the Buddhist sutras. Because we learn in practice that there being no ultimate extreme is the ultimate standard, we receive sutras and expel sutras through the nostrils and we receive sutras and expel sutras through the tips of the toes—[as] sutras were received and sutras were expelled before the birth of our parents and [as] sutras were received and sutras were expelled before the time of the King of Majestic Voice.[20] We receive sutras and preach sutras through mountains, rivers, and the Earth, and we receive sutras and preach sutras through the sun, moon, and stars. Sometimes we retain sutras and transmit sutras with the self that precedes the kalpa of emptiness, and sometimes we retain sutras and transmit sutras with the body-mind that precedes face and eyes. We cause sutras like these to appear by breaking atoms, and we cause them to appear by breaking the Dharma-world.

[30] The twenty-seventh patriarch, the Venerable Prajñātara, says:

---

16. Another reference to the transmission between Master Daiman Konin and Master Daikan Eno—see note 8, and chap. 29, *Inmo*.

17. Master Daikan Eno's words to Master Nangaku Ejo. See, for example, chap. 63, *Hensan*.

18. Master Nangaku Ejo's words to Master Daikan Eno. Ibid.

19. 十二部 (JUNI-BU), the twelve parts or divisions of the sutras, are explained in chap. 24, *Bukkyo*.

20. 威音王 (I-ON-NO), the name of an extremely old buddha, from the Sanskrit *Bhismagarjita-svara*. Lotus Sutra, *Jofugyo-bosatsu: "In the eternal past, countless infinite, inconceivable asaṃkhya kalpas ago, there was a buddha named King of Majestic Voice."* (LS 3.128).

My out-breath does not follow circumstances,
The in-breath does not belong in the world of aggregates.
I am constantly reciting sutras like this.
A hundred thousand myriad koṭis of scrolls.
Never only one scroll or two scrolls.[21]

Hearing these words of the ancestral Master, we should learn in practice that sutras are recited in exhalation and inhalation. If we know [this] reciting of sutras, we will know the place where sutras exist. Because it is the reciter and the recited, reciting sutras and sutras reciting, it may be total knowing and total seeing.

2] My late Master constantly said, *"In my order,*[22] *we do not rely on burning incense, doing prostrations, reciting names of buddhas, practicing confession, or reading sutras. Just sit, direct your energy into pursuing the truth, and get free of body and mind."*

Few people clearly understand an expression like this. Why? Because to call *reading sutras* "reading sutras" is to debase it, and not to call it "reading sutras" is to be perverse. *You are not allowed to talk and not allowed to be mute: say something at once! Say something at once!* We should learn this truth in practice. Because this principle [of reading sutras] exists, a man of old[23] has said, *"To read sutras we must be equipped with the eyes of reading sutras."* Remember, if there had been no sutras from ancient times till today, there could be no expression like this. We should learn in practice that there is reading sutras which is *getting free*, and there is reading sutras which is *non-reliance.*[24] This being so, each practitioner or half a practitioner who receives and retains the Buddhist sutras will inevitably become the Buddha's disciple. Do not learn at random the wrong views of non-Buddhists. Because the right-Dharma-eye treasury which is being realized in the present is itself the Buddhist sutras, all things that exist as Buddhist sutras are the right-Dharma-eye treasury. It is beyond unity and difference, and beyond self and others. Remember, the right-Dharma-eye treasury is limitlessly abundant, but you will not clarify it entirely. Even so, you are exhibiting the right-Dharma-eye treasury and you do not disbelieve it. The same should be true for the Buddhist sutras: they are limitlessly abundant, but you should hope to believe in and to practice a

---

21. Quoted from *Wanshi-juko (Wanshi's Eulogies of the Ancients)*, by Master Wanshi Shokaku. The poem is also quoted in chap. 21, *Kankin.*

22. 我箇裏 (GA-KORI), lit. "in my concrete place."

23. Master Unmon Bun-en (864–949), successor of Master Seppo Gison. Quoted in vol. 3 of *Unmon-kyoshin-zenji-koroku (General Record of Zen Master Unmon Kyoshin).*

24. 不用 (FUYO) generally means non-essential, needless, or useless. Here, however, 不用 (FUYO) suggests a state of transcendence. Master Tendo's words are not a denial of the value of reading sutras; they are a recommendation to get the real state of reading sutras. Similarly, in chap. 24, *Bukkyo,* 不要 (FUYO) means 1) unnecessary and 2) non-necessity.

single verse or a single saying; you will not be able to understand eighty thousand. As one who is not a complete authority on the Buddhist sutras, never rashly say that the Buddhist sutras are not the Buddha-Dharma. Although those others[25] can be heard boasting that they are the bones and marrow of the Buddhist Patriarch, when we look at them with right eyes they are just late learners who still rely on sentences. Some may be equal to those who have received and retained a single saying or a single verse, and there may be others who are inferior to those who have received and retained a single saying or a single verse. Never insult the Buddha's right Dharma on the basis of such sparse understanding. Nothing could have more virtue than the Buddhist sutras which are sound and form itself. Sounds and forms delude and disturb those others, who in any case still crave them. The Buddhist sutras do not delude and disturb those others. They should never insult the Buddhist sutras in their disbelief.

[35] Nevertheless, for the last two hundred years or so in the great kingdom of Sung, certain unreliable stinking skin-bags have said, *"We must not keep in mind even the sayings of ancestral masters. Still less should we ever read or rely upon the teaching of the sutras. We should only make our bodies and minds like withered trees and dead ash, or like broken wooden dippers and bottomless tubs."* People like this have vainly become a species of non-Buddhist or celestial demon. They seek to rely on what cannot be relied on, and as a result they have idly turned the Dharma of the Buddhist patriarchs into a mad and perverse teaching. It is pitiful and regrettable. Even broken wooden dippers and bottomless tubs are the Buddhist patriarchs' eternal Sutra itself. Few Buddhist patriarchs have completely enumerated and classified the scrolls of this Sutra. Those who say that the Buddhist sutras are not the Buddha-Dharma do not research the occasions on which the Buddhist patriarchs have relied upon the sutras, they do not study in practice the occasions on which Buddhist patriarchs manifest themselves following the sutras, and they do not know how deep the intimacy is between Buddhist patriarchs and the Buddhist sutras. Unreliable people like this are as [common as] rice, flax, bamboo, and reeds; they ascend the lion's seat, and establish monasteries throughout the country as the teachers of human beings and gods. Because the unreliable have learned from the unreliable, they know no truths other than the unreliable. And because they do not know [the truth], they do not aspire to it, but *they pass from darkness into darkness*. It is pitiful. Because they have never had the body-mind of the Buddha-Dharma, they do not know what the behavior of the body and working of the mind should be like. Because they do not clearly understand the principles of existence and emp-

---

25. なんだち *(nandachi)*, which lit. means "you" in the plural, here refers to those who affirm Master Bodhidharma's Zazen but negate study of the sutras, without understanding the true relation between Zazen and the sutras.

tiness, when someone asks them a question they randomly raise a fist, but they do not know the meaning of raising it. Because they do not clearly understand right and wrong ways, when someone asks them a question they hold up a whisk, but they do not know the meaning of holding it up. Sometimes, hoping to offer a guiding hand to others, they quote Rinzai's *four thoughts* and *four relations between reflection and action,* Unmon's *three phrases,* Tozan's *three paths* and *five relative positions,*[26] and so on, and see them as the standard for learning the truth. My late Master Tendo was constantly laughing at this, saying, *"How could learning the state of buddha be like that? We cause the great truth authentically transmitted by the Buddhist patriarchs to cover the mind and to cover the body again and again. When learning this state in practice, and aiming to master it, there is no time to spare; what free time could we have to fit in the sayings of later generations? Truly, we should know that old veterans in all directions have no will to the truth; it is evident that they do not learn in practice the body-mind of the Buddha-Dharma."*

] My late Master's preaching was like this. Truly, Rinzai was a junior[27] in Obaku's order; he received sixty strokes of the staff before he eventually visited Daigu[28] and had the conversation about the mind of an old granny, under the influence of which he reflected on his past conduct and went back again to Obaku. Because rumor of this episode has resounded like thunder, [people] have thought that the Buddha-Dharma of Obaku was transmitted to Rinzai alone. Moreover, [people] have thought that he was even more excellent than Obaku. That is not true at all. Rinzai had stayed a short while in Obaku's order and followed the other monks, but when Venerable Patriarch Chin[29] had prompted him, they say that Rinzai did not know what to ask. [Even] before clarification of the great matter, how could one who is standing on the ground to listen to the Dharma,[30] as a profound devotee of learning in practice, be dumbfounded like that? We should know that he is not of the highest makings. Further, Rinzai has never had more zeal than his Master, and sayings [of Rinzai] that surpass those of his Master have never been

---

26. These various categories are discussed in chap. 49, *Butsudo.*

27. 後生 (GOSHO). These characters are taken from the story of Master Rinzai's practice under Masters Obaku and Daigu which is recorded in *Shinji-shobogenzo,* pt. 1, no. 27. Master Dogen also describes the episode in chap. 30, *Gyoji,* para. [170]: *[Rinzai] was in Obaku's order for three years. Pursuing the truth with pure simplicity, three times he asked Obaku, at the instruction of the venerable patriarch Chin from Bokushu district, "What is the Great Intent of the Buddha-Dharma?" whereupon he tasted [the Master's] stick again and again, sixty times in all. Yet his zeal was not diminished. Then he went to Daigu and realized the great state of realization...*

28. Master Ko-an Daigu (dates unknown), successor of Master Kisu Chijo and, like Master Obaku, a second-generation descendant of Master Baso Do-itsu.

29. Master Bokushu Domyo (780?–877?), successor of Master Obaku. His secular name was Chin, and Venerable Patriarch Chin was his nickname.

30. 立地聴法 (RITSUCHI-CHOBO), "standing on the ground to listen to the Dharma" suggests the attitude of those who were eager to listen to the Buddha's preaching on Vulture Peak.

heard. Obaku has expressions that outshine his Master, he has great wisdom[31] surpassing that of his Master, he has expressed truth never before expressed by buddhas, and he has understood Dharma never before understood by patriarchs. Obaku is an eternal buddha who transcends past and present, he is even higher than Hyakujo, and he is even more of a genius than Baso. Rinzai does not possess such excellence of spirit. Why? [Because] Rinzai does not express any saying that has never been expressed before, even in a dream. He seems only to understand the many, forgetting the one, or to realize the one, forgetting the many. How could we see *the four thoughts* and so on as criteria[32] for learning the Dharma, as if the taste of the truth were present in them? Unmon is a disciple of Seppo;[33] though he has been able to operate as a great master to human beings and gods, it must be said that he is still at the learning stage.[34] How could we esteem these as having attained the root? They may be nothing more than sorry offshoots. Before Rinzai had arrived, before Unmon had appeared, what did Buddhist patriarchs rely upon as standards for learning the truth? So remember, in the houses of [Rinzai and Unmon], Buddhist conduct of the truth is not transmitted. Because [people] lack that which can be relied upon, they randomly expound such outlandish and confused theories. Such fellows recklessly ridicule the Buddhist sutras. Others must not follow the habit. If the sutras were to be discarded, Rinzai and Unmon might also need to be discarded. If we cannot rely upon the Buddhist sutras, we are without water to drink, and without a dipper to scoop water. There again, the founding Patriarch's *three paths* and *five relative positions*, as kernels [of the truth], are beyond the area which the unreliable can know. He has received the authentic transmission of the fundamental principles, and has directly indicated Buddhist conduct; his can never be the same as other lineages.

[43] Furthermore, unreliable people say that the teaching of the Tao, the teaching of Confucius, and the teaching of Śākyamuni may each amount to the same in their conclusion; they just have temporary differences in their gates of entry. Sometimes they compare it to the three legs of a tripod. This is a notion widely discussed by monks in the great kingdom of Sung today. When such people speak like this, the Buddha-Dharma has for them already vanished from the face of the earth. Further, we should say that not so much as an atom of the Buddha-Dharma has ever come to them. People like this,

---

31. 大智 (DAICHI), "Great Wisdom," is the posthumous title of Master Obaku's master, Master Hyakujo Ekai (749–814).

32. 指南 (SHI-NAN), lit. "pointing-south." 指南車 (SHI-NAN-SHA) was an ancient Chinese military vehicle topped by a wooden statue (on a magnetic base) whose arm always pointed south.

33. Master Seppo Gison (822–907), successor of Master Tokuzan Senkan.

34. 学地 (GAKUCHI), or "the learning state," is opposed to 無学 (MUGAKU), "being without study," a synonym for arhathood.

rashly attempting to express insight into the Buddha-Dharma, mistakenly say that the Buddhist sutras are not useful, and that in the lineage of the ancestral Master there is a fundamental teaching which is transmitted separately.[35] They are small in nature, because they have not glimpsed the boundaries of the Buddha's truth. They say that we should not rely on the Buddha's sutras: then if they had sutras by the Patriarch[36] would they rely on them, or would they not rely on them? There are many dharmas in the Patriarch's truth that are as described in the Buddhist sutras. Should they be relied upon or discarded? If the Patriarch's truth were said to be separate from the Buddha's truth, who could believe in the Patriarch's truth? The ancestral Master is the ancestral Master because he has received the authentic transmission of the Buddha's truth. If there were an ancestral master who had not received the authentic transmission of the Buddha's truth, who could call him the ancestral Master? We revere the First Patriarch because he is the twenty-eighth patriarch. If we spoke of a Patriarch's truth separate from the Buddha's truth, it would be difficult for there to be ten patriarchs or twenty patriarchs. That we revere the ancestral Master because he has received the transmission from rightful successor to rightful successor is due to the importance of the Buddha's truth. With what features could an ancestral master who had not received the authentic transmission of the Buddha's truth meet face-to-face with human beings and gods? It would be more difficult still to turn around the profound will that adores the Buddha in order to follow anew an ancestral master who did not belong to the Buddha's truth. That the unreliable madmen of today idly scorn the Buddha's truth is because it is impossible for them to decide which dharmas belong to the Buddha's truth. To compare, even for a moment, those teachings of the Tao and of Confucius, and the teaching of the Buddha, is not only pitifully stupid but is also the cause and conditions of wrong action and is the downfall of nations, because it is the undermining of the Three Treasures. The truths of Confucius and Lao-tzu[37] can never match the state of an arhat;[38] how much less could they equal the state of balanced realization or the state of fine realization?[39] [In] Confucianism and Taoism, they are able, barely, to discern in astronomical phenomena the vision and hearing of saints, but it is hard for them to clarify, in one life or in many lives, the cause-and-effect of the Great Saint. They are able, barely, to discern in non-doing the movement and stillness of the body-mind, but they can never clarify, in the limitlessness of the mo-

35. 別伝 (BETSUDEN) refers to the idea 教外別伝 (KYOGE-BETSUDEN), "the separate transmission outside the teachings." Master Dogen attacks this idea in chap. 24, *Bukkyo*.

36. "The Patriarch" means Master Bodhidharma. The people under discussion did not revere Buddhist sutras but claimed only to revere Bodhidharma's Zen.

37. Chinese philosopher of the 6th century B.C., known as the founder of Taoism.

38. The ultimate state of a śrāvaka, or intellectual Buddhist.

39. The penultimate and ultimate states of a bodhisattva.

ment,[40] the reality of the whole Universe in the ten directions. In short, the inferiority of the teachings of Confucius and Lao-tzu to the teaching of the Buddha does not deserve to be discussed in terms of the separation of heaven and earth. Randomly to discuss them as one is to insult the Buddha-Dharma and to slander Confucius and Lao-tzu. Though there is some accuracy in the teachings of Confucius and Lao-tzu, how could the old veterans of recent times understand even a fraction of them, much less grasp them as a great handle upon ten thousand ages? In those [teachings] too there is instruction and training which the flotsam of today could not easily enact. There is no-one who could even attempt to practice them. Not even a single atom can be identified with another atom; how much less could the late learners of today determine what the profound and mystical Buddhist sutras are? Not clearly understanding either of two factors, they just randomly express outlandish theories and confused words about unity.

[49] In great Sung [China] today such people sign their names under masters' titles and occupy positions of temple master. Without shame before the past and present, they stupidly make nonsense of the Buddha's truth. It is difficult to permit that the Buddha-Dharma is present in them. Old veterans like these, down to the last person, say: *"Buddhist sutras are not the original intention of the Buddha's truth; the Patriarch's transmission is the original intention. In the Patriarch's transmission the mysterious, the profound, and the fine have been transmitted."* Words like these are stupid in the extreme; they are the talk of madmen. There is no mystery in the authentic transmission from the ancestral Master that differs from the Buddhist sutras, or even from a single word or half a word therein. Both the Buddhist sutras and the Patriarch's truth have been authentically transmitted and have spread from Śākyamuni Buddha. The Patriarch's transmission has been received only by rightful successors from rightful successors, but how could [rightful successors] not know, how could they not clarify, and how could they not read and recite the Buddhist sutras? A past Master says, *"You delude yourself with the sutras. The sutras do not delude you."*[41] There are many stories about past masters reading sutras. I would like to say to the unreliable as follows: If, as you say, the Buddhist sutras should be discarded, then the Buddha's mind should be discarded and the Buddha's body should be discarded. If the Buddha's body-mind should be discarded, the Buddha's disciples should be discarded. If the Buddha's disciples should be discarded, the Buddha's truth should be discarded. If the Buddha's truth should be discarded, how could the Patriarch's truth not be discarded? If you discard both the Buddha's

40. 無尽際断 (MUJIN-SAIDAN), lit. "limitless separation," means the moment of the present which is completely cut off from past and future.

41. This probably alludes to the story about Masters Daikan Eno and Hotatsu. See chap. 17, *Hokke-ten-hokke*.

truth and the Patriarch's truth, you might become one person with a shaved head among a hundred secular people. Who could deny that you deserved to taste the stick? Not only would you be at the beck and call of kings and their retainers; you might also be answerable to Yama-rāja.[42]

Recent old veterans, on barely obtaining a note from a king or a retainer, proclaim themselves to be masters of Buddhist temples and on this basis they speak the insane words described previously. There is no-one to tell right from wrong. Only my late Master laughed at these people [whose wrongness] was totally unrecognized by the old veterans of other temples. In general, we should not think that because monks are from a foreign land they must inevitably possess clear understanding of the truth, or that because they teach the emperor of a great nation they must inevitably have accomplished something. The living beings of foreign lands do not all have the makings of monks; the good ones are good, and the bad ones are bad. It may be that types of living beings are the same in the limitless triple worlds of the Universe. Furthermore, those who possess the truth are not always chosen to become the teachers of the emperors of great nations; emperors also have difficulty knowing who possesses the truth. They make appointments merely on the basis of the recommendations they hear from their retainers. In the past and present there have been emperors' teachers who possessed the truth and many emperors' teachers who did not possess the truth. In a corrupt age, those appointed are people who do not possess the truth. In a corrupt age, those not appointed do possess the truth. What is the reason? It is because there are times in which a [true] person is known[43] and there are times in which a [true] person goes unknown. We should not forget the past example on [Mount] Obai of Jinshu.[44] Jinshu was the teacher of emperors; he lectured on the Dharma before bamboo screens, and preached the Dharma before bamboo blinds.[45] Moreover, he was the highest-ranking of seven hundred noble monks. We should believe in the past example on Obai of temple servant Ro.[46] By changing his occupation from woodcutter to temple servant he

---

42. *Yama* is the name of the god supposed by ancient Indians to rule the spirits of the dead. See Glossary.

43. 知人 (CHIJIN), "knowing a person," means the intuitive ability to know whether a person is true.

44. Ācārya Jinshu (died 706), successor of Master Daiman Konin. He was the most excellent of 700 monks in the order of Master Daiman Konin on Obai mountain, but could not match Master Daikan Eno who was living in the temple as a laborer. Posthumously titled Zen Master Daitsu. See also chap. 20, *Kokyo*.

45. Ācārya Jinshu was revered by the Tang emperor Chuso and the Empress Wu (who usurped the throne from Chuso for 20 years from 684). The screens and blinds were to veil the emperors from view.

46. 盧行者 (RO-ANJA). 盧 (RO) was the family name of Master Daikan Eno. 行者 (ANJA), "novice," or "temple servant," described someone who worked in the temple as a servant, either with a view to becoming a monk or as a livelihood.

had escaped from hauling firewood; still, he made it his job to pound rice. That his position was low is regrettable, but his leaving of secular life and transcendence of the monkhood, his attainment of the Dharma and reception of the robe, are an example unheard of since ancient times and absent even in India in the west; they are a rare and noble precedent set only in the eastern lands. It seems that even the seven hundred noble monks could not measure up to him, and that the dragons and elephants of the whole country could not follow in his traces. He is the Buddha's rightful successor, having properly taken his place in the succession as the thirty-third patriarch.[47] If the Fifth Patriarch were not a good counselor with the ability to know a person, how could it be so? Consider a truth such as this quietly; do not be hasty about it. Hope to get the ability to know people. To fail to know a person is a calamity for self and others, and a calamity for the whole nation. Wide knowledge and skill in handling important matters are not necessary, but we should urgently seek the eyes to know a person and the ability to know a person. Without the ability to know a person, we will sink into depression for long ages. In conclusion, we should know that in the Buddha's truth there are inevitably Buddhist sutras; we should learn in practice, as the mountains and the oceans, their universal text and their profound meaning; and we should make them our standard for pursuing the truth.

Shobogenzo Bukkyo

Preached to the assembly while lodging at Kippo-ji temple in the Yoshida district of Esshu,[48] in the 9th lunar month in the autumn of the 1st year of Kangen.[49]

47. Master Daikan Eno is the sixth patriarch in China, and the 33rd patriarch counting from Master Mahākāśyapa.

48. Corresponds to modern-day Fukui prefecture.

49. 1243.

[53]

無情説法

MUJO-SEPPO

The Non-Emotional Preaches the Dharma

Mujo *means the non-emotional and* ***Seppo*** *means to preach the Dharma. Originally,* ***mujo*** *means inanimate or insentient things, so* ***mujo-seppo*** *means inanimate things preach the Dharma. But Master Dogen's usage of the word* ***mujo*** *was wider than the usual usage, as if the words cover the whole of nature—human beings as well as mountains, rivers, and so on. Master Dogen insisted that even inanimate things can preach the Dharma, and at the same time he insisted that human beings can preach the Dharma when they are not emotional. He insisted that any thing that is not emotional can preach the Dharma—a viewpoint that profoundly expresses the true nature of Buddhist preaching.*

Preaching the Dharma in preaching the Dharma is the realized Universe that Buddhist patriarchs transmit to Buddhist patriarchs. This preaching the Dharma is the Dharma preaching. It is neither sentient[1] nor insentient.[2] It is neither intentional doing nor non-doing. It is not causally connected with doing and non-doing, and it is not something that arises from circumstances. At the same time, it does not follow the way of the birds; it is given to a Buddhist assembly. When the great state of truth is completely realized, preaching the Dharma is completely realized. When the Dharma treasury is transmitted, preaching the Dharma is transmitted. At the time of picking up a flower, preaching the Dharma is picked up, and at the time of transmitting the robe, preaching the Dharma is transmitted. For this reason, the buddhas and the patriarchs have, in like fashion, paid homage to preaching the Dharma since prior to the King of Majestic Voice,[3] and have practiced preaching the Dharma as their original practice since prior to the

1. 有情 (UJO). 有 (U) means "having." 情 (JO) means "feelings" or "emotion." In general 有情 (UJO) means "sentient beings," or "the sentient."

2. 無情 (MUJO). 無 (MU) mean "not having," or "without." Conventionally, opposed to "sentient beings," 無情 (MUJO) means "insentient things," or "the insentient"; that is, trees, rocks, fences, walls, et cetera. At the same time, in this chapter it also means "the non-emotional"; that is, the state without emotion, or reality, which is beyond emotion.

3. The name of a Buddha of the infinite past, mentioned at the beginning of the 20th chapter of the Lotus Sutra (LS 3.128).

buddhas themselves. Do not learn only that preaching the Dharma has been orchestrated by Buddhist patriarchs; Buddhist patriarchs have been orchestrated by preaching the Dharma. This preaching the Dharma is not merely the expounding of the eighty-four thousand gates of Dharma; it includes countless and boundless gates of Dharma-preaching. Do not learn that later buddhas preach as Dharma the Dharma-preaching of former buddhas. Just as former buddhas do not come back as later buddhas, so it is also in preaching the Dharma: former preaching of the Dharma is not used as later preaching of the Dharma. For this reason, Śākyamuni Buddha says, *"In the same manner that the buddhas of the three times preach the Dharma, so now do I also preach the Dharma that is without distinction."*[4] Thus, in the same way that buddhas utilize preaching the Dharma, buddhas utilize preaching the Dharma. And in the same way that buddhas authentically transmit preaching the Dharma, buddhas authentically transmit preaching the Dharma. Therefore, having been authentically transmitted from buddhas of the eternal past to the Seven Buddhas, and having been authentically transmitted from the Seven Buddhas to today, there exists *the non-emotional preaching the Dharma*. In this non-emotional preaching the Dharma the buddhas are present, and the patriarchs are present. Do not learn that *"I now preach the Dharma"* expresses an innovation that differs from the authentic tradition. And do not experience the time-honored authentic tradition as if it were an old nest in a demon's cave.

[61] *National Master Daisho*[5] *of Kotaku-ji temple in the Western Capital*[6] *in great kingdom of Tang, the story goes, is asked by a monk, "Can the insentient really preach the Dharma, or not?"*

The National Master says, "They are always preaching ardently; they preach without interval."

The monk says, "Why do I not hear it?"

The National Master says, "Whether or not you hear it yourself, you should not disturb others who do hear it."

The monk says, "I wonder what kind of person is able to hear it."

The National Master says, "Saints are able to hear it."

The monk says, "Does the Master hear it or not?"

The National Master says, "I do not hear it."

---

4. Lotus Sutra, *Hoben*. See LS 1.128.

5. Master Nan-yo Echu (died 755), successor of Master Daikan Eno. National Master Daisho is his posthumous title.

6. 西京 (SEIKYO), lit. "Western Capital." There were five cities in Tang China with this name, but here it refers to the city which is present-day Luoyang, in the Hwang basin in northern Honan, east China..

The monk says, "If the Master himself does not hear it, how does he know that the insentient preach the Dharma?"

The National Master says, "It is convenient that I do not hear it. If I heard it I would be on the level of the saints, and then you would not be able to hear me preaching the Dharma."

The monk says, "So living beings are without the means [to hear]."

The National Master says, "I preach for living beings. I do not preach for saints."

The monk says, "What are living beings like after they hear?"

The National Master says, "At that time they are beyond living beings."[7]

Beginners and later students who wish to learn in practice the non-emotional preaching the Dharma should get straight into diligent research of this story of the National Master. *"They are always preaching ardently; they preach without interval." "Always"* is a concrete time of many instants. *"They preach without interval"*: given that *preaching* is already manifest in reality, it is inevitably *without interval.* We should not learn that the manner in which *the insentient preach the Dharma* must necessarily be as in the case of the sentient.[8] [To suppose that the manner in which *the insentient preach the Dharma*] might accord with the voices of the sentient, and with the manner in which the sentient preach the Dharma, and thus to wrest voices from the sentient world and to liken them to the voices of the insentient world, is not Buddhism. *The insentient preaching the Dharma* may not always be sound as matter—just as the sentient preaching the Dharma is not sound as matter.[9] Now, asking ourselves and asking others, we must endeavor to learn in practice what is the sentient state and what is the insentient state. That being so, we should painstakingly apply our mind to learning in practice how the non-emotional might preach the Dharma. Stupid people think that the rustling of trees in the forest, and the opening and falling of leaves and flowers, are the non-emotional preaching the Dharma, but they are not practitioners of the Buddha-Dharma.[10] If it were so, who could fail to know the non-emotional preaching the Dharma, and who could fail to hear the non-emotional preaching the Dharma? Let us reflect for a while: in the non-emotional world are there any 'grass,' 'trees,' and 'forests' or not? Is the non-emotional world infiltrated by 'the emotional world' or not? [No.] To recognize, on the contrary,

7. A slightly different version of the story appears in *Keitoku-dento-roku,* chap. 28.

8. Because the state of the sentient (有情) is sometimes emotional, but the state of the insentient (無情) is always non-emotional, that is, balanced—in this part, Master Dogen distinguishes between the two states.

9. Just as a Buddhist lecture is not only sound but also has meaning, so a mountain stream not only produces sound but also expounds Buddhist teaching. See, for example, chap. 14, *Sansuigyo.*

10. In Master Dogen's view, nature can only teach us the truth when we ourselves are balanced (non-emotional).

that grass, trees, tiles, and pebbles are the non-emotional is to be incomplete in learning. And to recognize the non-emotional as grass, trees, tiles, and pebbles, is not to have experienced satisfaction. Though we shall now consider the grass, trees, and so on that are seen by human beings, and discuss them as the non-emotional, those very grass, trees, and so on are beyond the common intellect. For there are great differences between the forests of the heavens above and those of the human world; the produce of a civilized nation is not the same as that of a remote land; and grass and trees in the ocean are totally unlike those in the mountains. Still more, there are trees that grow in space and there are trees that grow in clouds. Among the hundred weeds and myriad trees that sprout and grow amid wind, fire, and so on, there are generally those that can be understood as sentient, those that are not recognized as insentient, and those weeds and trees which seem to be humans and animals: sentient and insentient have never been clearly distinguished. Still more, when we see a hermit's trees, stones, flowers, fruits, hot springs, and cool waters, they are utterly beyond doubt—but how could they not be difficult to explain? Barely having seen the weeds and trees of China, or having become familiar with the weeds and trees of Japan, do not think that similar situations may be present through the whole Universe in myriad directions.

[66] The National Master says, *"The saints are able to hear it."* That is, in orders where the non-emotional preaches the Dharma, the saints stand on the ground to listen.[11] The saints, and the non-emotional, both realize hearing and realize preaching. The non-emotional does indeed preach the Dharma to saints, but is it sacred[12] or is it common? [It is neither.] In other words, after we have clarified the manner in which the non-emotional preaches the Dharma, we are able to realize in physical experience that what the saints hear is as it is. Having attained realization in physical experience, we are able to fathom the state of the saints. Thereafter we should learn in practice, further, action on the road through the night which transcends the common and transcends the sacred. The National Master says, *"I do not hear it."* Do not suppose that even these words are easy to understand. Does he not hear because he transcends the common and transcends the sacred, or does he not hear because he rips apart the nests of the common and the sacred? With effort like this, we should realize the [Master's] expression. The National Master says, *"It is convenient that I do not hear it. If I heard it I would be on the level of the*

---

11. 立地聴 (RITSU-CHI-CHO), "standing on the ground," suggests politeness and eagerness to hear. Master Seppo said, *"The buddhas of the three times are inside the flame of the fire, turning the great wheel of Dharma."* Master Gensa replied: *"The flame is preaching Dharma for the buddhas of the three times, and the buddhas of the three times are standing on the ground to listen."* See chap. 23, *Gyobutsu-yuigi*.

12. 聖 (SHO) as a noun means "saint," or "sacred being" (as in the National Master's words), and as an adjective means "sacred."

saints." This elucidation is never one truth or two truths.[13] The *convenient I* is beyond the common and the sacred; might the *convenient I* be a Buddhist patriarch? Because Buddhist patriarchs transcend the common and transcend the sacred, [what they hear] may not be exactly the same as what the saints hear. Researching the truth of the National Master's words *"Then you would not be able to hear me preaching the Dharma,"* we should consider the Bodhi of the buddhas and the saints. The point is this: when the non-emotional preach the Dharma the saints are able to hear, but when the National Master preaches the Dharma that concrete monk is able to hear. Day upon day and month after month we should endeavor to learn this truth. Now I would like to ask the National Master: I do not ask what living beings are like after they hear, but what are living beings like just in the moment of hearing you preach the Dharma?

The founding Patriarch Great Master Tozan Gohon,[14] while practicing under the ancestral Patriarch Great Master Ungan, asks, "What people are able to hear the non-emotional preaching the Dharma?"

The ancestral Patriarch Ungan says, "The non-emotional are able to hear the non-emotional preaching the Dharma."

The founding Patriarch says, "Does the Master hear it or not?"

The ancestral Patriarch says, "If I hear it, then you will not be able to hear my preaching of the Dharma."

The founding Patriarch says, "If that is so, I would [rather] not hear the Master's preaching of the Dharma."

The ancestral Patriarch says, "You do not even hear me preaching the Dharma; how much less [do you hear] the non-emotional preaching the Dharma."

Then the founding Patriarch sets forth the following verse and presents it to the ancestral Patriarch:

> *How very wonderful! How very wonderful!*
> *The non-emotional preaching the Dharma is a mystery.*
> *If we listen with the ears, it is ultimately too difficult to understand.*
> *If we hear the sound through the eyes, we are able to know it.*[15]

The truth expressed now in the founding Patriarch's words *"What people are able to hear the non-emotional preaching the Dharma"* should be painstakingly

---

13. It is an expression of the whole truth of the National Master, who lived not by hard and fast rules, but by freely changing his behavior to suit circumstances—he kept his teaching at a level which could be understood by the listener.

14. Master Tozan Ryokai (807–869), successor of Master Ungan Donjo.

15. In general, ears represent intellectual understanding whereas eyes represent intuitive understanding, or the viewpoint of real experience. The story is recorded in *Shinji-shobogenzo*, pt. 2, no. 48, and *Keitoku-dento-roku*, chap. 15.

researched through the effort of one life and many lives. This question is also equipped with the virtue of an assertion.[16] And this assertion has the skin, flesh, bones, and marrow; it is not only *the mind being transmitted by the mind.*[17] Transmission of the mind by the mind is the pursuit of beginners and late learners, but there is a pivotal matter which has been authentically transmitted by means of the robe and authentically transmitted by means of the Dharma. How can people today expect to realize it as the ultimate in only three or four months of effort? The founding Patriarch has already experienced the principle expressed in the past by the National Master that *"The saints are able to hear the non-emotional preaching the Dharma,"* and yet he now asks further: *"What people are able to hear the non-emotional preaching the Dharma?"* Should we see this as affirmation of the National Master's words, or as non-affirmation of the National Master's words? Should we see it as a question or as an assertion? If he does not completely affirm the National Master, how could he speak words like these?[18] And if he completely affirms the National Master, how could he understand words like those?[19]

[70] The ancestral Patriarch Ungan says, *"The non-emotional are able to hear the non-emotional preaching the Dharma."* Following the authentic transmission of this lifeblood, there can be learning in practice that is free of body and mind. Saying *"The non-emotional are able to hear the non-emotional preaching the Dharma"* may be, in essence and in form, [the same as saying] "the buddhas are able to hear the buddhas preaching the Dharma." An assembly that listens to the non-emotional preaching the Dharma, whether of sentient beings or insentient beings, whether of common men or sages and saints, may just be the non-emotional itself. Relying upon its essence-and-form, we can tell the true from the false among [masters of] the past and present. Even if they have come from India in the west, if they are not true ancestral masters of the authentic transmission, we should not rely on them. Even if they have been learning continually for a thousand myriad years, if they have not received the transmission as rightful successor to rightful successor, we cannot succeed them. Now that the authentic transmission has already spread throughout the eastern lands, it may be easy to tell the true from the false. We might be able to receive the bones and marrow of the buddhas and the patriarchs even by listening to the expression "living beings are able to hear living beings preaching the Dharma." When we hear the words of the ancestral Patri-

---

16. 什麼人 (SHIMO-NIN), lit. "a what person" means a person in the ineffable state.

17. 以心伝心 (ISHIN-DENSHIN), describes intuitive communication among human beings. The phrase also appears in chap. 46, *Katto.*

18. Because Master Tozan completely affirms the National Master, he wants to investigate further the National Master's words that the saints are able to hear the non-emotional preaching the Dharma.

19. Because Master Tozan completely affirms the National Master, he absorbs the National Master's words without trying to understand them intellectually.

arch Ungan and listen to the words of the National Master Daisho, if we truly evaluate them, *the saints* expressed in *"The saints are able listen"* may be the non-emotional, and *the non-emotional* expressed in *"The non-emotional are able to hear"* may be the saints. What the non-emotional preaches is the non-emotional—because the non-emotional preaching the Dharma is the non-emotional itself. Thus, the non-emotional is the preaching of Dharma and the preaching of Dharma is the non-emotional. The founding Patriarch says, *"If that is so, I would [rather] not hear the Master's preaching of the Dharma."* The words *"If that is so,"* which we now hear, take up the principle that *the non-emotional are able to hear the non-emotional preaching the Dharma.* It is in accordance with the truth of *the non-emotional being able to hear the non-emotional preaching the Dharma* that *I do not hear*[20] *the Master's preaching of the Dharma.* The founding Patriarch at this time is not simply taking a back seat for the non-emotional preaching the Dharma; his own zeal to preach the Dharma to the non-emotional has shown itself and is piercing the sky. Not only does he physically realize that the non-emotional preaches the Dharma; in non-emotional preaching of the Dharma he has physically mastered [transcendence of] hearing and not hearing. Going further, in emotional preaching of the Dharma he has physically realized [transcendence of] preaching and not preaching—in preaching just past, preaching just now, and preaching just coming. And beyond that, in the preaching of the Dharma [which transcends] being heard and not being heard, he has completely clarified the truth [of knowing] that this is emotional and this is non-emotional.[21]

In general, hearing the Dharma is not confined to the spheres of the ear as a sense-organ or of auditory consciousness: we hear the Dharma with our whole energy, with the whole mind, with the whole body, and with the whole truth, from before the time our parents were born and from before the time of Majestic Voice until the limit of the future and into the limitless future. The Dharma is heard prior to the body and after the mind. There is benefit to be got in each of these cases of hearing the Dharma. Never say that there is no benefit in hearing the Dharma without the involvement of mind-consciousness. Those whose mind has ceased and whose body is spent[22] are

---

20. 不聞 (FUMON) sounds in the story like a statement of Master Tozan's willingness to forego hearing Master Ungan's preaching ("[I would rather] not hear"), but Master Dogen's interpretation here is that 不聞 (FUMON), "not hearing" or "being beyond hearing," expresses Master Tozan's non-emotional state.

21. The final sentence of the paragraph may be interpreted as an expression of Master Tozan's practice of Zazen (which is itself preaching of the Dharma). In the instructions for Zazen in *Fukan-zazengi Shinpitsu-bon,* Master Dogen writes: "If a thought, feeling, or emotion arises, just be aware of it."

22. 心滅身没のもの (SHINMETSU-SHINMOTSU *no mono*), or "mind-ceased body-sunk beings," suggests, for example, practitioners who feel too sleepy to concentrate on a Buddhist lecture.

able to benefit from hearing the Dharma, and those who are without mind and without body[23] are able to benefit from hearing the Dharma. The buddhas and the patriarchs, without exception, pass through series of such instants in becoming buddhas and becoming patriarchs. How can the common intellect be fully aware of the influence of the Dharma connecting with the body-mind? It is impossible for us fully to clarify the limits of the body-mind. The merit of hearing the Dharma, once sown as a seed in the fertile ground of the body-mind, has no moment of decay; sooner or later it will grow, and, with the passing of time, it is sure to bear fruit. Stupid people think: *Without progressing on the path of understanding, and unless our memory is good, even if we listen to the Dharma tirelessly there will be no benefit. The most important thing, whether in the human world or in the heavens above, is to devote one's body and mind to the pursuit of wide knowledge. If we immediately forget, and leave the seat a blank, what benefit can there be? What educational merit can it have?* They say this because they have not met a true teacher and have not seen a person of the fact. One who does not possess the traditional face-to-face transmission is said not to be a true teacher. One who has received the authentic transmission from buddha to buddha is a true teacher. [The time] that stupid people describe as [preaching the Dharma] being temporarily remembered in the mind-consciousness is the time when the merit of hearing the Dharma is subtly covering the whole mind and covering the whole consciousness. In this very moment, virtue is present which covers the body, which covers the moment before the body, which covers the mind, which covers the moment before the mind, which covers the moment after the mind, which covers causes, conditions, results, actions, forms, natures, substance, and energy, which covers buddhas, which covers patriarchs, which covers self-and-others, and which covers skin, flesh, bones, marrow, and so on. Realized throughout speaking and preaching and throughout [daily actions] such as sitting and lying down, the virtue pervades the meridians and pervades the sky. Truly, it is not easy to recognize such virtue of hearing the Dharma; nevertheless, if we come upon the great order of the Buddhist Patriarch and investigate the skin, flesh, bones, and marrow, there will be no time when the good influence of preaching the Dharma does not lead us, and there will be no place where we do not spread the Dharma-influence of hearing the Dharma. In this way, allowing moments and kalpas to be fleeting or slow,[24] we will see results become real. We should not deliberately throw

23. 無心無身のもの (MUSHIN-MUSHIN *no mono*) suggests practitioners who are in the state of action, and who are thus working as an integrated whole which is indivisible into "mind" and "body."

24. 時節劫波を頓漸ならしめて (JISETSU-KOHA *o* TONZEN *nara shime te*), "allowing moments and kalpas to be fleeting or slow," suggests patience in the face of passing time, which is sometimes fast (e.g. when we are lost in play) and sometimes slow (e.g. when we are waiting for something painful or boring to end).

away wide knowledge; at the same time, we do not see it, in isolation, as the pivot. Practitioners should know this. The founding Patriarch has realized it in physical experience.

8] The ancestral Patriarch says, *"You do not even hear me preaching the Dharma; how much less [do you hear] the non-emotional preaching the Dharma."* Here, [confronted] with the founding Patriarch's sudden manifestation of the state of continuing to experience, on the basis of real experience, the [Buddha's] state of real experience, the ancestral Patriarch loosens his collar, and seals and certifies the state as the bones and marrow of the forefathers. [He is saying,] "Even while I am preaching, you are beyond hearing!" He does not speak thus because [Tozan] is ordinary flotsam; he is certifying that the non-emotional preaching the Dharma, though multifarious, does not require the activation of the intellect. The succession that takes place at this time is truly a secret. Those in the states of the common and the sacred cannot easily arrive at it or glimpse it.

9] Then the founding Patriarch composes, and presents to the ancestral Patriarch Ungan, a verse which says that *the mystery*[25] *of the non-emotional preaching the Dharma* is *How very wonderful! How very wonderful!* So the non-emotional, and the non-emotional preaching the Dharma, are each difficult *to consider intellectually*.[26] How are we to see *the non-emotional* described here? We should learn in practice that it is beyond the common and the sacred, and beyond the sentient and the insentient. Common and sacred, sentient and insentient, are always, whether preached or not preached, within the orbit of intellectual consideration. The present *[non-emotional]*, which may indeed be *a mystery*, and *very wonderful*, and again *very wonderful*, is beyond the wisdom and the consciousness of common men and sages and saints, and is beyond the reckoning of gods and human beings.

] *"If we listen with the ears, it is ultimately too difficult to understand"*: Even with supernatural ears, or even with universal ears that pervade the whole world and all of Time, when we aim to listen with the ears, *it is ultimately too difficult to understand*. Even with an ear on a wall, or an ear on a stick, we cannot understand the non-emotional preaching the Dharma, because it is beyond sound as matter. It is not that there is no *possibility of listening with the ears*, but even if we exhaust hundreds of thousands of kalpas of effort, *it is ultimately too difficult to understand*. [The non-emotional preaching the Dharma] has the dignity of the undivided truth which is originally beyond sound and form; it does not reside in nests and dens near the common and the sacred.

---

25. 不思議 (FUSHIGI). As a compound these three characters mean mystery, wonder, miracle, marvel, et cetera. Individually, 不 (FU) means "not," or "beyond," 思 (SHI) means "think," and 議 (GI) means "discuss," "deliberate," or "consider intellectually."

26. 思議す (SHIGI *su*). See preceding note.

[82] *"Hearing its sound through the eyes, we are able to know it."* Interpreting this expression, certain individuals think: *The activity of grass, trees, flowers, and birds being seen in the present by human eyes may be described as "hearing sound through the eyes."* This point of view is completely mistaken and is not the Buddha-Dharma at all. The Buddha-Dharma has no such theory. When we learn in practice the founding Patriarch's words *hearing sound through the eyes,* the place where the sound of the non-emotional preaching the Dharma is heard, is the eyes[27] themselves; and the place where the sound of the non-emotional preaching the Dharma is realized, is the eyes themselves. We must investigate the eyes still more widely. "Hearing sound" through the eyes must mean the same as "hearing sound" through the ears; and for this reason, *hearing sound through the eyes* can never be the same as "hearing sound" through the ears. We should not learn that "there are ears in the eyes," we should not learn that "eyes and ears are one," and we should not learn that "sound is realized inside eyes." An ancient[28] says, *"The whole Universe in the ten directions is a śramaṇa's one eye."* We should not consider, by intellectual comparison, that to hear sound through this eye may be as in the founding Patriarch's words *hearing sound through the eyes.* Although we study the words of the ancient that *"the whole Universe in the ten directions is one eye,"* the whole of the ten directions is just one eye, and furthermore, there are thousands of eyes on the tips of the fingers, there are thousands of eyes of right Dharma, there are thousands of eyes in the ears, there are thousands of eyes on the tip of the tongue, there are thousands of eyes on the tip of the mind, there are thousands of eyes of the thoroughly realized mind, there are thousands of eyes of the thoroughly realized body, there are thousands of eyes on top of a stick, there are thousands of eyes in the moment before the body, there are thousands of eyes in the moment before the mind, there are thousands of eyes of death in death, there are thousands of eyes of liveliness in liveliness, there are thousands of eyes of the self, there are thousands of eyes of the external world, there are thousands of eyes in the concrete place of eyes, there are thousands of eyes of learning in practice, there are thousands of eyes aligned vertically, and there are thousands of eyes aligned horizontally. Thus, we study that the totality of eyes is the whole Universe, but still this is not physical mastery of *the eyes.* We should make it an urgent task to investigate, through the eyes, [the action of] just hearing the non-emotional preaching the Dharma. The point expressed now by the founding Patriarch is that it is difficult for the ears to understand the non-emotional preaching the Dharma. It is the eyes which hear the sound. Going further, there are in-

---

27. 眼処 (GENSHO), as in Master Tozan's words, lit. means "eyes-place." 処 (SHO), which means "place," or "seat," is suffixed to 眼 (GEN), "eyes," to indicate the eyes as the seat of sight; that is, the eyes as a concrete organ.

28. Master Chosa Keishin. See chap. 60, *Juppo.*

stances of the thoroughly realized body[29] hearing the sound and instances of the whole body[30] hearing the sound. Even if we fail physically to master hearing sound through the eyes, we must physically realize, and must get free from, [the truth that] *the non-emotional are able to hear the non-emotional preaching the Dharma,* for this is the truth that has been transmitted.

5] My late Master Tendo, the eternal Buddha, says, *"A bottle gourd vine entwines with a bottle gourd."*[31]

This is Dharma-preaching of the non-emotional state,[32] in which the ancestral Patriarch's right eyes have been transmitted and in which the bones and marrow have been transmitted. Relying upon the truth that all Dharma-preaching is in the non-emotional state, the non-emotional preach the Dharma, which is the ancient standard, and the non-emotional preaches Dharma to the non-emotional. What do we call *the non-emotional?* Remember, those who listen to the non-emotional preaching the Dharma are just it. What do we call *preaching the Dharma?* Remember, not knowing oneself to be the non-emotional is just it.

] Great Master Jisai[33] of Tosu-zan mountain in Joshu[34] (successor of Zen Master Suibi Mugaku, called Daido Myokaku in his lifetime, also called the eternal Buddha Tosu),[35] the story goes, is asked by a monk, *"What is the non-emotional preaching the Dharma?"* The Master says, *"No abusive language."*[36]

What Tosu expresses here is the very Dharma-plan of eternal buddhas and the ordinance of the patriarchs. Such [preaching] as the non-emotional preaching the Dharma, and Dharma-preaching of the non-emotional is, in short, *not to speak abusive language.* Remember, the non-emotional preaching the Dharma is the whole charter of the Buddhist patriarchs. Followers of Rinzai and Tokuzan cannot know it; only Buddhist patriarchs devote themselves to its investigation.

---

29. 通身処 (TSUSHIN-JO), or "the thoroughly realized body as a sense organ." The term 通身 (TSUSHIN), "the thoroughly realized body," is explained in chap. 33, *Kannon.* 処 (JO) is explained in note 27.

30. 徧身処 (HENSHIN-JO). Ibid.

31. Also quoted in chap. 46, *Katto.*

32. 説法無情 (SEPPO-MUJO). The reversal of 無情 (MUJO) and 説法 (SEPPO) makes the non-emotional the object preached as the Dharma instead of the subject that preaches the Dharma.

33. Master Tosu Daido (819–914), successor of Master Suibi Mugaku. Great Master Jisai is his posthumous title.

34. In present-day Anhui province in east China.

35. The explanation in parentheses, which appears in the source text in small characters, may have been added by an editor other than Master Dogen himself.

36. 莫悪口 (AKKU *na[shi]*), lit. "Not to bad-mouth." In the version of this conversation recorded in *Keitoku-dento-roku,* chap. 15, the Master's answer is given as only 悪 (AKU), "Bad." This probably reflects an error of omission by the editor of *Keitoku-dento-roku.*

Shobogenzo Mujo-seppo

Preached to the assembly at Kippo-ji temple in the Yoshida district of Esshu[37] on the 2nd day of the 10th lunar month in the 1st year of Kangen.[38]

37. Corresponds to modern-day Fukui prefecture.

38. 1243.

[54]

法性

HOSSHO

The Dharma-nature

Ho means Dharma, that is the Buddha's teaching, or the Universe itself. ***Sho*** *means essence, or nature. So* ***hossho*** *means the Dharma-nature, or the essence of the Universe. Needless to say, we are living in the Universe. Therefore what the Universe means is one of the most important philosophical problems in our life. Some people insist that the Universe is something spiritual. Others insist that the Universe is something material. But from the Buddhist standpoint, the Universe is neither spiritual nor material, but something real. It is, however, very difficult to express the Universe as something real using words, because reality usually transcends explanation with words. Master Dogen undertook this difficult task, in order to express the nature of the Universe, in this chapter.*

9] **When we learn in practice**, sometimes following the sutras and sometimes following good counselors, we realize the truth independently, without a master.[1] Independent realization without a master is the working of the Dharma-nature. Even the innately intelligent[2] should, without exception, visit a master and inquire into the truth. And even those without innate intelligence should, without exception, strive in pursuit of the truth. [But] what person is not innately intelligent?[3] Each follows the sutras and follows good counselors until arriving at the Buddhist effect, the truth of bodhi. Remember, getting samādhi as the Dharma-nature[4] from meeting the sutras and

---

1. 無師独悟 (MUSHI-DOKUGO). See also opening paragraph of chap. 16, *Shisho.*

2. 生知 (SHOCHI). This term, which may be Confucian in origin, is also discussed in the opening paragraph of chap. 26, *Daigo* and in chap. 90, *Shizen-biku.*

3. Cf. chap. 90, *Shizen-biku,* para. [54]: *"In the writings of Confucius there is the person of innate intelligence. In the Buddha's teaching there are no people of innate intelligence."* In that chapter, Master Dogen's point is to emphasize that intelligence or understanding comes with experience of life, not as a birthright. The point here is that every person's mind naturally inclines towards seeking out the truth.

4. 法性三昧 (HOSSHO-ZANMAI). 三昧 (ZANMAI) represents the Sanskrit word *samādhi,* which means the balanced state in Zazen. The word *samādhi* appears in the titles of three chapters of Shobogenzo: chap. 75, *Jisho-zanmai (Samādhi, State of Experiencing the Self),* expressing samādhi from the subjective side; chap. 31, *Kai-in-zanmai (Samādhi, State Like the Sea),* expressing samādhi as the mutual relation between subject and object in the moment of the present; and chap. 72,

good counselors is called "the innate intelligence" getting samādhi as the Dharma-nature from meeting samādhi as the Dharma-nature. It is to get wisdom that has abided from the past; it is to get the three kinds of illumination;[5] it is to experience [the supreme truth of] anuttara-samyak-saṃbodhi; it is to learn innate intelligence from meeting innate intelligence; and it is to receive the authentic transmission of untutored wisdom, or natural wisdom, through meeting untutored wisdom, or natural wisdom. If we were without innate intelligence, even if we met the sutras and good counselors we could not hear the Dharma-nature and could not experience the Dharma-nature. The great truth is not a [limited] principle like a person drinking water and naturally sensing whether it is cold or warm. All buddhas, together with all bodhisattvas and all living beings, by virtue of innate intelligence, are all realizing the great truth of all the Dharma-nature. To be realizing the great truth of the Dharma-nature by following the sutras and good counselors is to be realizing the Dharma-nature by ourselves. The sutras are the Dharma-nature, and they are the self. A good counselor is the Dharma-nature and is the self. The Dharma-nature is a good counselor and the Dharma-nature is the self. Because it is the self as the Dharma-nature, it is beyond the falsely-conceived selves of non-Buddhists and demons. In the Dharma-nature there is no "non-Buddhist" or "demon," but only *Come for breakfast! Come for lunch!* and *Come for tea!* Nevertheless, when people who call themselves twenty or thirty-year veterans witness discussion of the Dharma-nature, they stumble on through life in blank oblivion. They climb upon the [master's] round wooden chair, claiming to have become satisfied with monastic life, but when they hear the sound "Dharma-nature" or catch a sight of "Dharma-nature," their body-and-mind, object-and-subject, usually just bob in a pit of confusion. Their state is such that they deludedly imagine that after the triple world and the ten directions which we are experiencing in the present have suddenly dropped away, then the Dharma-nature will appear, and this Dharma-nature will be other than the myriad things and phenomena of the present. The true meaning of the Dharma-nature can never be like that. This Universe of things and phenomena, and the Dharma-nature, have far transcended discussion of sameness and difference and have transcended talk of disjunction or union. Because they are beyond past, present, and future, beyond separation and constancy,[6] and beyond matter, perception, thought, action, and consciousness, they are the Dharma-nature.

Zanmai-o-zanmai (The Samādhi That Is King of Samādhis), expressing the practice of Zazen itself. Together with the present chapter *Hossho,* which adds the objective viewpoint, these can be seen as forming one group of four chapters.

5. 三明 (SANMYO), from the Sanskrit *tisro vidyāh*: 1) knowing past lives, 2) supernatural vision, and 3) ability to end the superfluous.

6. 断常 (DANJO) means materialism and idealism. 断見 (DANKEN), lit. "view of separation," represents the view which sees all things as isolated instances of time and space, that is,

4] Zen Master Baso Daijaku[7] of Kozei in Koshu says, *"All living beings, for countless kalpas, have never left samādhi as the Dharma-nature; they are always in the reality of samādhi as the Dharma-nature: putting on clothes and eating meals, speaking and conversing, the working of the six sense organs, and all actions, are totally the Dharma-nature."*[8]

The Dharma-nature expressed by Baso is the Dharma-nature expressed by the Dharma-nature. It experiences the same state as Baso, and he is in the same state as the Dharma-nature. Having heard, how could we fail to speak? The Dharma-nature is riding on Baso.[9] People eat meals, and meals eat people. Since the beginning of the Dharma-nature they have never left samādhi as the Dharma-nature. After the Dharma-nature they will not leave the Dharma-nature. Before the Dharma-nature they did not leave the Dharma-nature. *The Dharma-nature* and *countless kalpas* are samādhi as the Dharma-nature itself; we call the Dharma-nature "countless kalpas." That being so, this place here and now is the Dharma-nature, and the Dharma-nature is this place here and now. *Putting on clothes and eating meals* are samādhi as the Dharma-nature putting on clothes and eating meals. The Dharma-nature as clothes is realized, the Dharma-nature as meals is realized, the Dharma-nature as eating is realized, and the Dharma-nature as dressing is realized. Without putting on clothes and eating meals, without speaking and conversing, without the working of the six sense organs, and without the performing of all actions, we are not in samādhi as the Dharma-nature and we have not entered the Dharma-nature. The realization of these words of the immediate present, handed on by the buddhas, arrives at Śākyamuni Buddha; and, authentically transmitted by the patriarchs, it has arrived at Baso. Handed on in the authentic transmission from buddha to buddha and from patriarch to patriarch, it has been authentically transmitted to samādhi as the Dharma-nature. The buddhas and the patriarchs, without entering it, cause the Dharma-nature to be a state of vigorous activity. Though literary Dharma-teachers have the word "the Dharma-nature," it is not the Dharma-nature expressed by Baso. Effort by living beings who never leave the Dharma-nature to be utterly beyond "the Dharma-nature"—even if [the effort] is successful—is three or four fresh instances of the Dharma-nature. Speaking, conversing, working, and acting that we think might be other than the Dharma-nature, may in fact be the Dharma-nature itself. The sun and moon for countless kalpas have been the instantaneous passing of the Dharma-nature. So

---

materialism. 常見 (JOKEN), lit. "view of constancy" or "view of eternity," represents idealism. 断見外道 (DANKEN-GEDO) and 常見外道 (JOKEN-GEDO) are traditional expressions of the two fundamental non-Buddhist viewpoints, materialism and idealism.

7. Master Baso Do-itsu (704–788), successor of Master Nangaku Ejo. Zen Master Daijaku is his posthumous title.

8. *Kosonshuku-goroku,* chap. 1.

9. 馬祖 (BASO) lit. means "Horse Patriarch."

they are in the present and so they will be in the future. When, seeing the quantity of the body-mind as the quantity of the body-mind, we think of it as far from "the Dharma-nature," this thinking is the Dharma-nature itself. When, not seeing the quantity of the body-mind as "the quantity of the body-mind," we think of it as beyond "the Dharma-nature," this thinking is the Dharma-nature itself. The thinking and the not thinking are both the Dharma-nature. Those who understand that, having been called "the nature," water will not flow, and trees will stop flourishing and withering, are non-Buddhists.

[98] Śākyamuni Buddha says, *"Form as it is, the nature as it is."*[10] So opening flowers and falling leaves are just the nature as it is.[11] Stupid people, however, think that in the world of the Dharma-nature there can be no opening flowers and falling leaves. Now, without directing a question to anyone else, imagine[12] your own doubt to be a statement. Treat it as the assertion of another person and investigate it three times over, and you may find that you are rid of it already. The aforementioned thought is not an evil thought; it is just a thought at a time before clarification. And at the time of clarification, there is no effort to get rid of this thought. Opening flowers and falling leaves are naturally opening flowers and falling leaves. Thinking in which it is thought that in the Dharma-nature there can be no "opening flowers and falling leaves," is the Dharma-nature itself. It is thinking which has got free of conceptualization,[13] and for this reason it is thinking as the Dharma-nature. Total thinking in thinking about the Dharma-nature has such features. Baso's expression *"the whole is the Dharma-nature,"*[14] truly, is eighty or ninety percent of realization. At the same time, there is much that Baso has not expressed. Namely, he does not say that all dharma-natures do not depart from the Dharma-nature, he does not say that the totality of all dharma-natures is the Dharma-nature, he does not say that all living beings do not depart from [being] living beings, he does not say that all living beings are in a small part of a dharma-nature, he does not say that all living beings are in a small part of all living beings, he does not say that all dharma-natures actually exist as a small part of a living being, he does not say that a concrete half of a living

10. 如是相、如是性 (NYOZE-SO, NYOZE-SHO), from Lotus Sutra, *Hoben*. In the Lotus Sutra, the subject is the reality called "all dharmas": *What is called "all dharmas" is form as it is, the nature as it is...* (LS 1.68.)

11. 開華葉落 (KAIKE-YORAKU), "opening flowers, leaves falling," represents the world of changing phenomenal forms which human thinking tends to oppose to the Universal essence.

12. 依模 (EMO). 依 (E) means depend on, follow, or be based upon. 模 (MO) means copy, imitate, or model after. 依模 (EMO) therefore suggests the forming of a model, image, representation, or conception of something based upon the thing itself.

13. 依模 (EMO). See preceding note.

14. 尽是法性 (JIN-ZE-HOSSHO). In the quotation, read as *kotogotoku kore hossho nari,* these characters mean "...are totally the Dharma-nature."

being is a concrete half of the Dharma-nature, he does not say that the state without "living beings" is the Dharma-nature itself, he does not say that the Dharma-nature is beyond "identity with living beings," he does not say that the Dharma-nature has got rid of "the Dharma-nature," and he does not say that living beings are free of "living beings." We can hear only that living beings do not depart from samādhi as the Dharma-nature; he does not say that the Dharma-nature cannot depart from the samādhi of living beings. There is no assertion that samādhi as the Dharma-nature leaves and enters samādhi as the state of living beings. Still less have we been able to hear that the Dharma-nature becomes Buddha, or to hear that living beings experience the Dharma-nature, or to hear that the Dharma-nature experiences the Dharma-nature. There is no expression about the non-emotional not leaving the Dharma-nature. Now, I would like to ask Baso: What is it that you call "living beings"? If what you call "living beings" is the Dharma-nature, the state is *"This is something coming like this."*[15] If what you call *"living beings"* is living beings, the state is *"To describe a thing does not hit the target."*[16] Speak at once! Speak at once!

Shobogenzo Hossho

Preached to the assembly at Kippo temple in Esshu[17] at the beginning of winter[18] in the 1st year of the Japanese era of Kangen.[19]

---

15. Master Daikan Eno's words on first meeting his disciple Master Nangaku Ejo. See *Shinji-shobogenzo*, pt. 2, no. 1 and, for example, Shobogenzo, chap. 63, *Hensan*.
16. Master Nangaku Ejo's words to Master Daikan Eno eight years later. Ibid.
17. Corresponds to present-day Fukui prefecture.
18. The 10th month of the lunar calendar.
19. 1243.

[55]

陀羅尼

DARANI

Dhāraṇī

The Chinese characters pronounced ***da-ra-ni*** *represent the Sanskrit dhāraṇī, which originally means a spell or incantation that is believed to have mystical omnipotence. But Master Dogen's interpretation was more concrete, and especially he esteemed the value of prostrations as dhāraṇī. In this chapter he explains the meaning of prostrations as dhāraṇī.*

03] **Those whose eyes of learning in practice are clear,** are clear in the eye of the right Dharma. Because they are clear in the eye of the right Dharma, they are able to be clear-eyed in learning in practice. The authentic transmission of this pivot is inevitably due to the influence of paying respect to a great good counselor, which is the great purpose itself and the great dhāraṇī itself. "A great good counselor" means a Buddhist patriarch, to whom, without fail, we should sincerely serve towel and flask.[1] Thus, in *bringing tea*,[2] and in *making tea*,[3] the *pivot of the mind*[2] is realized, and *mystical*

---

1. 巾瓶 (KINBYO), "towel and flask," are two of a monk's traditional possessions. See chap. 56, *Senmen*. Serving towel and flask means serving in daily life.

2. 擎茶来 (KEISA-RAI), lit. "holding up tea and coming," and 心要 (SHINYO), "the pivot of the mind," allude to a conversation between Master Ryutan Soshin and his Master, Tenno Dogo: *One day [Soshin] asked, "Since I came here I have not received any instruction about the pivot of the mind. [Do]go said, "Since you came I have done nothing but demonstrate the pivot of the mind to you." The Master [Soshin] said, "Where did you demonstrate it?" [Do]go said, "You came bringing tea, I received it for you. You came serving food, I received it for you. When you paid your respects [lit. "performed vandana"], then I lowered my head. Where did I not demonstrate the pivot of the mind?" The Master [Soshin] lowered his head for a while.* (*Keitoku-dento-roku*, chap. 14.)

3. 点茶来 (TENSA-RAI), "making tea," 神通 (JINZU), "mystical powers," 盥水来 (KANSUI-RAI), "bringing a tub of water," and 下面了知 (AMEN-RYOCHI), "witnessing everything from the wings," all allude to a story about Master Isan Reiyu and his disciples, Master Kyogen Chikan and Master Kyozan Ejaku: *After Master Isan had woken up from a nap Kyozan brought him a tub of water to wash his face. Kyogen said that he had been watching from the wings, and had witnessed everything clearly. Master Isan asked him to express his understanding of the situation. Kyogen went to make some tea. Isan praised them, saying, "The mystical powers and the wisdom of you two disciples are far superior to those of Śāriputra and Maudgalyāyana."* The story is recorded in Chinese characters in *Shinji-shobogenzo*, pt. 1, no. 61, and is paraphrased by Master Dogen in Japanese in Shobogenzo, chap. 25, *Jinzu*.

powers[3] are realized. *Bringing a tub of water,*[3] and *pouring water away,*[4] are the state of *not disturbing circumstances,*[4] and of *witnessing everything from the wings.*[3] [To perform such service] is not only to learn the pivot of the Buddhist patriarchs' mind; it is to meet, inside the pivot of the mind, with one Buddhist patriarch or with two Buddhist patriarchs. It is not only to receive and to use the Buddhist patriarchs' mystical powers; it is to have got, inside the state of mystical power, seven Buddhist patriarchs or Buddhist patriarchs. Thus, all the mystical power of the Buddhist patriarchs is perfectly realized in this one bundle. Every aspect of the pivot of the mind of the Buddhist patriarchs is perfectly realized in this one stroke. For this reason, although it is not wrong to use heavenly flowers and divine incense in paying respect to Buddhist patriarchs, to pay respect and to serve offerings with an act of dhāraṇī in the state of samādhi is just to be a child or grandchild of the Buddhist patriarchs.

[106] What I have called "the great dhāraṇī" is personal salutations.[5] Because personal salutations are the great dhāranī, we mutually encounter the reality of personal salutations. The word for personal salutations, *ninji,* which represents the sound of the Chinese word, has long been current in civilized society, but [the custom of personal salutations] was neither received from the Brahma Heavens nor received from the Western Heavens; its authentic transmission has been received from the Buddhist patriarchs. It is beyond the limited world of sound and form. Do not discuss it as before or after the Buddha King Majestic Sound. The personal salutations of which I speak are the burning of incense and prostration. We have as our original master the master who made us a monk, or the master who transmitted to us the Dharma. And sometimes the master who transmitted to us the Dharma is the master who made us a monk. Unfailingly to depend upon and pay respect to these original masters is a dhāraṇī that invokes their teaching. We should, as is often said, practice under them and serve them without wasting a single moment. At the beginning and end of the retreat, at the winter solstice, and at the beginning and middle of the month, we burn incense and do prostrations without fail. The method is as follows: Either before breakfast or just after breakfast, which are the established times, we visit the master's quarters dressed in the dignified manner. Dressed in the dignified manner means

4. 瀉水来 (SHA-SUI-RAI), "pouring water away," and 不動著鏡 (FU-DOJAKU-KYO), "not disturbing circumstances," allude to a story about Master Nansen Fugan and Master Godai Inpo (also known as To Inpo): *Nansen one day sees To Inpo approaching. He points to a water jar and says, "The jar is circumstances. Inside the jar there is water. Without disturbing the circumstances, bring some water to this old monk." In[po] then brings the jar of water before Nansen and pours. Nansen leaves it at that.* The story is recorded in *Shinji-shobogenzo,* pt. 1, no. 64, and in Shobogenzo, chap. 81, *O-saku-sendaba.*

5. 人事 (NINJI), refers to a monk's salutation to his or her master, by burning incense and doing prostrations.

wearing the kaṣāya, carrying the prostration cloth, and wearing sandals and socks;[6] dressed like this, and carrying a stick of aloes, sandalwood, or other incense, we proceed [to the master's quarters]. When we come in front of the master, we bow with joined hands.[7] Then the attendant monk prepares the incense burner and sets up a candle. If the master is already seated on the master's chair, we may burn incense at once. And if the master is behind the curtain,[8] we may burn incense at once. At times when the master is lying down, eating, or the like, we may burn incense straight away too. If the master is standing on the ground, as we bow with joined hands we should ask the master to be seated. Or we may ask the master to be comfortable: there are many formulas for asking the master to be seated. After we have got the master to sit on the master's chair, we bow with joined hands, bowing low according to the proper method. Having completed the greeting, we walk up to the front of the incense desk and place in the incense burner the stick of incense that we have been carrying. The incense to be used is sometimes tucked under the back of the collar, sometimes held in an inside breast pocket, and sometimes carried in the sleeves; it is a matter of individual preference. After the bow of greeting, we take out this piece of incense. If it is wrapped in paper, we turn our shoulders to our right hand side, and remove the wrapping paper. Then we lift the incense up with both hands and stand it in the burner. We should stand it up straight. Do not let it lean to one side. After setting up the piece of incense we fold the hands[9] and walk around to the right. When we arrive in front of the master we bow deeply with joined hands according to the proper method, spread the prostration cloth, and do prostrations. We do nine prostrations, or sometimes twelve prostrations. Having completed the prostrations, we fold the prostration cloth and bow with joined hands. In some cases, having spread the prostration cloth once and done three prostrations, we pay the compliments of the season. But for the nine prostrations [described] now, we should just do three rounds of three prostrations with the prostration cloth spread once,[10] and not say the season's greetings. The above formality has been transmitted

---

6. Socks of thick white material are still part of the formal attire of monks and priests in Japan today.

7. 問訊 (MONJIN), lit. to ask [how someone is] or to inquire after [someone's health], represents the Sanskrit *prati-sammodana*. Concretely, *monjin* means to bow either with the palms of the hands together (*gassho-monjin*) or with the left hand curled round the thumb and the right hand covering the back of the left hand (*shashu-monjin*).

8. The master's room would sometimes be divided by a cloth curtain thin enough to see through.

9. 叉手 (SHASHU). See note 7.

10. 一展三拝を三度あるべき (ITTEN-SANPAI *o* SANDO *arubeki*), "there should be three rounds of one spreading and three prostrations." Taken literally, this seems to suggest that the prostration cloth should be spread and folded three times, but it is natural to assume that the cloth was spread once for all nine prostrations.

from the Seven Buddhas in the distant past, and we have received its authentic transmission as the fundamental teaching. Therefore we practice this formality. Whenever the time comes to do prostrations like this, we do so without fail.

[110] In addition, we do prostrations whenever we have been covered by the benevolence of Dharma.[11] And we do prostrations in order to request the [master's] teaching on a story.[12] When, in the past, the second Patriarch presented his viewpoint to the first Patriarch, that was an example of doing three prostrations.[13] To exhibit the presence of the right-Dharma-eye treasury, we do three prostrations. Remember, prostration is the right-Dharma-eye treasury, and the right-Dharma-eye treasury is the great dhāraṇī. For prostrations when requesting the teaching, recently many people do one prostration in which the head bumps the ground,[14] but the traditional standard is three prostrations. The prostration of thanks for the benevolence of Dharma is not necessarily nine prostrations or twelve prostrations: it may be three prostrations, or one informal prostration,[15] or six prostrations. All of these are prostrations in which the head is bowed down to the ground[16]—in India these are called "the highest worship."[17] In doing six prostrations, for instance, we hit the ground with the head; that is, we strike the forehead upon the ground, even to the point of bleeding. For these prostrations also, the prostration cloth is laid out. Whether doing one prostration, three prostrations, or six prostrations, we hit the ground with the forehead. This is sometimes called "kowtowing."[18] Such prostration is present in secular society too; in secular society there are nine kinds of prostration. When [requesting] the benevolence of Dharma, we also have continuous prostra-

---

11. 法益 (HO-EKI), "Dharma-benevolence" means a master's preaching of Dharma.

12. 因縁 (INNEN), "causes and circumstances," originally meant the concrete causes and circumstances pertinent to a violation of the precepts (see explanation of *nidāna* in chap. 24, *Bukkyo*). By extension it came to mean any Buddhist story or episode such as the ones recorded by Master Dogen in *Shinji-shobogenzo*.

13. See chap. 46, *Katto*, para. [90].

14. 頓一拝 (TON-IPPAI). 頓 (TON) means a prostration in which one knocks one's head on the ground. 一拝 (IPPAI) means "one prostration."

15. 触礼一拝 (SOKURAI-IPPAI). 触 (SOKU) means to touch. 礼 (RAI) means bow. In this case, the prostration cloth, still folded into four, is placed on the ground, and only the forehead touches the prostration cloth. 触礼 (SOKURAI), lit. "touching bow," is opposed to 展拝 (TENPAI), lit. "unfolded prostration," which is a formal prostration done with the prostration cloth completely unfolded.

16. 稽首拝 (KEISHU-HAI). 稽 (KEI) means to strike, hit, or tap and 首 (SHU) means the head or the neck. 稽首 (KEISHU) represents the Sanskrit *vandana*. See Book 1, Glossary. In performing this prostration the forehead is lowered to the ground and the palms are turned upwards and raised as if to receive the feet of the person being bowed to.

17. 最上礼拝 (SAIJO-RAIHAI) represents the meaning of the Sanskrit *anuttara-pūja*. See Glossary.

18. 頓首拝 (TONSHU-HAI). 頓 (TON) is explained in note 14.

tions; that is to say, we do prostrations ceaselessly, continuing even for hundreds or thousands of prostrations. All of these are prostrations that have been practiced in the orders of Buddhist patriarchs. In general, we should practice these prostrations according to the proper method, observing the Master's directions. In general, while prostrations exist in the world the Buddha-Dharma exists in the world. If prostrations disappear, the Buddha-Dharma will perish.

[12] When we are prostrating ourselves to the master who transmitted to us the Dharma, we prostrate ourselves without selecting a time or worrying about the place: sometimes we do prostrations while [the master] is lying down or eating, or even while [the master] is going to the toilet; sometimes we prostrate from afar, with fences and walls between us, or with mountains and rivers between us; sometimes we prostrate with kalpas between us; sometimes we prostrate with living-and-dying and coming-and-going between us; and sometimes we prostrate with the state of bodhi, and nirvāṇa, between us. While the disciple performs these many kinds of prostration, the master does not return the prostration, but only joins hands.[19] Occasionally [the master] may do a single prostration, but as a general rule [the master] does not. At the time of such prostrations, we always prostrate ourselves facing north. The master, facing south, sits erect. The disciple stands on the ground before the master, facing north, and, aiming at the master, [the disciple] prostrates to the master. This is the original standard. It is an authentic tradition that when devoted right belief emerges in us, a prostration facing north is inevitably the first thing we do. Thus, in the day of the World-honored One, the human multitudes, celestial throngs, and dragon herds that devoted themselves to the Buddha all faced north to venerate and to do prostrations to the World-honored One. At the very beginning, the five companions[20]—Ājñāta-kauṇḍinya,[21] Aśvajit, Mahānāma, Bhadrika, and

---

19. 合掌 (GASSHO). In *gassho* the palms are brought together in front of the chest, with the tips of the fingers roughly in line with the nostrils. See also note 7.

20. The group of five ascetic practitioners whom the Prince Śākyamuni joined in ascetic training. It is said that when he left them to pursue the truth on his own, they felt he had given up. But when the Buddha returned after realizing the truth they were so struck by his dignity that they all prostrated themselves to him facing north. Then he preached the four noble truths to them, and they became the first members of the Saṃgha. Some sources give the fifth of the five not as Bāṣpa but as Daśabala-kāśyapa. In Pali, the five are Āññāta-koṇḍañña, Assaji, Makānāman, Bhadiya, and Vappa (or Dasabala-kassapa).

21. 阿若憍陳如 (A-NYA-KYO-JIN-NYO) represents in Chinese characters the sound of the original Sanskrit name Ājñāta-kauṇḍinya. Because he was the first to recognize the meaning of the Buddha's first teaching, Ājñāta, which means "known," was prefixed to his original name Kauṇḍinya. For each of the five names, the original text contains a note in small characters giving a Chinese abbreviation of the Sanskrit. In this case the abbreviated version is 拘隣 (KORIN).

Bāṣpa[22]—after the Tathāgata had realized the truth, rose unconsciously to face the Tathāgata and to offer their prostrations to him, facing north. When non-Buddhists and bands of demons devoted themselves to the Buddha, having discarded the false, they inevitably prostrated themselves facing north, even though they were caused to do so neither by themselves nor by others. Since that time, all those who have come to the orders of the twenty-eight generations of ancestral masters in the Western Heavens and the many generations of ancestral masters in the Eastern Lands, wishing to devote themselves to the right Dharma, have naturally prostrated themselves facing north. This is the state of compliance with the right Dharma; it is beyond the intention of master and disciple. This is the great dhāraṇī itself. *There is a great dhāraṇī, and it is called round realization.*[23] *There is a great dhāraṇī, and it is called personal salutations. There is a great dhāraṇī, and it is a realized prostration. There is a great dhāraṇī, and its name is the kaṣaya. There is a great dhāraṇī, and its name is the right-Dharma-eye treasury.* By this incantation, we have pacified and protected the whole Earth, we have pacified and established the whole Universe, we have pacified and manifested the whole sphere of Time, we have pacified and built the whole world of Buddha, and we have pacified and realized the inside of our huts and the outside of our huts. We should learn in practice, penetrate, and discern that great dhāraṇī is like this. All dhāraṇīs see this dhāraṇī as their mother-word. As dependents of this dhāraṇī, all dhāraṇīs are realized. All Buddhist patriarchs inevitably experience establishment of the mind, pursuit of the truth, realization of the truth, and turning of the Dharma wheel, through this gate of dhāraṇī. That being so, now that we are already the children and grandchildren of Buddhist patriarchs, we should painstakingly investigate this dhāraṇī.

[116] In sum, that which was covered by the robe of Śākyamuni Buddha is that which has been covered by the robes of all the Buddhist patriarchs of the ten directions. That which was covered by the robe of Śākyamuni Buddha is that which is covered by the kaṣaya. The kaṣaya is the banner of Buddhists. This conclusion is hard to arrive at and hard to meet. Though we are stupid, having received the rare human body in a remote land, the good influence of long-accumulated dhāraṇī has been realized, and we have been born to meet the Dharma of Śākyamuni Buddha. Though we do prostrations to the self-realized and externally-realized Buddhist patriarchs in a place of one hun-

---

22. 婆敷 (BAFU) is a transliteration of the Sanskrit *Bāṣpa*. The note in small characters, however, gives 力迦葉 (RIKI-KASHO). This stands for 十力迦葉 (JURIKI-KASHO), lit. "Ten-Powers Kāśyapa," that is, Daśabala-kāśyapa.

23. 有大陀羅尼、名為円覚 (U-DAI-DARANI, MYO-I-ENGAKU) alludes to the sutra *Dai-hoko-engaku-shuttara-ryo-gi-kyo* which says 無上法王有陀羅尼門 (MUJO-HO-O-U-DARANI-MON, MYO-I-ENGAKU), *"The supreme Dharma-King possesses the gate of dhāraṇī, which is called round realization."* In the sutra, 有 (U) means "possesses," but in Master Dogen's sentences, because there is no subject, 有 (U) means "there is."

dred weeds, it is Śākyamuni Buddha's realization of the truth, it is Śākyamuni Buddha's effort in pursuit of the truth, and it is the mystical transformation of dhāraṇī. Though we do prostrations to past buddhas and present buddhas in countless trillions of kalpas, they are a moment covered by Śākyamuni Buddha's robe. For the kaṣaya to cover the body once is already to have got Śākyamuni Buddha's body and flesh, hands and feet, head and eyes, marrow and brains, state of brightness, and turning of the Dharma-wheel. Such is the state in which we wear the kaṣaya. This is the realization of wearing the merit of the kaṣaya. We retain it and rely upon it, we love it and enjoy it, we preserve it and protect it as time passes, and we wear it to do prostrations and serve offerings to Śākyamuni Buddha. In so doing, we definitely realize and perfectly realize triple asaṃkhya kalpas of training. To do prostrations and serve offerings to Śākyamuni Buddha means, in some instances, to do prostrations and serve offerings to the master who transmitted to us the Dharma, or to do prostrations and serve offerings to the master who shaved our head. It is just to meet Śākyamuni Buddha, to serve Śākyamuni Buddha with an offering of Dharma, and to serve Śākyamuni Buddha with an offering of dhāraṇī. My late Master Tendo, the eternal Buddha, said in his preaching, *"Coming over the snow to do prostrations,*[24] *and remaining amid rice flour*[25] *to do prostrations, are excellent examples. They are the precedents of the ancestors. They are the great dhāraṇī."*

Shobogenzo Dhāraṇī

Preached to the assembly at Kippo-ji temple in Esshu,[26] in the 1st year of Kangen.[27]

---

24. It is said that when Master Taiso Eka first met Master Bodhidharma at Shorin Temple the mountain was covered in thick snow.

25. Master Daikan Eno, who was a woodcutter before entering the order of Master Daiman Konin, could not afford to live with the other monks, so he supported himself by pounding rice in a hut in the monastery.

26. Modern-day Fukui prefecture.

27. 1243.

[56]

洗面

SENMEN

Washing the Face

__Sen__ means to wash, and __men__ means the face. Idealistic religions generally revere only the spiritual side of the world; everyday activities such as eating meals, getting dressed, washing the face, and taking a bath are not considered to be religious practices. Buddhism, however, is a religion based on the real world; these everyday activities are important religious practices without which there can be no Buddhist life. This is why, when a Chinese Buddhist master was asked by his disciple, "What is the fundamental principle of Buddhism?" the master answered "Wearing clothes and eating meals." Master Dogen put the greatest value on the practice of washing the face. In this chapter he explains the Buddhist meaning in the daily activities of taking a bath and washing the face.

21] **The Sutra of the Flower of Dharma** says,

[The bodhisattva] applies oil to the body,
Having bathed away dust and dirt,
And puts on a fresh and clean robe:
Totally clean within and without.[1]

22] This is the Dharma that the Tathāgata, in the order of the Flower of Dharma, preaches to practitioners of the four peaceful and joyful practices.[2] It is not on the level of preaching in other orders, and it cannot be equaled by other sutras. So to bathe the body-mind, to apply fragrant oil, and to get rid

---

1. Lotus Sutra, *Anraku-gyo (Peaceful and Joyful Practice).* LS 2.258.

2. 四安楽行 (SHI-ANRAKU-GYO), *"the four peaceful and joyful practices,"* are described in detail in Lotus Sutra, *Anraku-gyo.* They are: 1) *peaceful and joyful practice through bodily action,* e.g., not associating closely with kings and ministers; preaching Dharma without expectation; always liking to sit in Zazen and to be in a quiet place; reflecting all dharmas as bare, as the form of reality as it is; etc. (LS 2.244–248), 2) *peaceful and joyful practice through speech,* e.g. not discussing other people's good and bad conduct or merits and demerits (LS 2.256), 3) *peaceful and joyful practice of mind,* e.g., to have great compassion for all living beings (LS 2.262), and 4) *peaceful and joyful practice through vowing,* namely vowing that, *"Though those people neither hear, nor believe in, nor understand this Sutra, when I attain the truth of anuttara-samyak-saṃbodhi, wherever I am, through mystical power and through the power of wisdom, I will lead them and cause them to be able to abide in this Dharma."* (LS 2.266)

of dust and dirt, are Buddha-Dharma of the highest priority. To put on a fresh and clean robe is a method of purification. When we bathe away dust and dirt and apply fragrant oil to the body, inside-and-outside will be totally clean. When inside-and-outside is totally clean, object-and-subject is pure and clean.

[123] Nevertheless, stupid people who neither hear the Buddha-Dharma nor enter into the Buddha's truth say: *Bathing merely washes the body's skin, but inside the body there are the five viscera*[3] *and six entrails.*[4] *Without bathing each of these, we cannot be pure and clean. So we need not necessarily bathe the body's surface.* People who speak like this have never known or heard the Buddha-Dharma, have never met a true teacher, and have never met a child or grandchild of the Buddhist patriarchs.

[124] Now, throwing away such words of people of wrong views, we should learn in practice the right Dharma of the Buddhist patriarchs. The limits of all dharmas have never been determined, and the inside and outside of the elements[5] are impossible to grasp. Therefore, the inside and outside of the body-mind also are impossible to grasp. Even so, when a bodhisattva in the ultimate body is just about to sit upon a bodhi-seat and realize the truth, [the bodhisattva] first washes the kaṣaya and then bathes the body-mind. This is the dignified behavior of the buddhas of the ten directions in the three times. Bodhisattvas in the ultimate body are different from other beings in all matters: their virtue, wisdom, and adornment of the body-mind, are all supremely venerable and supremely high. The same may be true of their methods of bathing and washing. Moreover, people's bodies and minds, and the limits thereof, differ according to time. It is said that during one sitting the three-thousand worlds are all sat away, and although, during that time, this is so, it is beyond the supposition of self or others: it is a virtue of the Buddha-Dharma. The dimension of the body-mind [that is bathed], again, is beyond 'five feet' or 'six feet,' because five feet or six feet are beyond what has been decided as 'five feet' or 'six feet.' The place where it exists also is beyond limited and unlimited areas such as 'this world,' 'the external world,' 'the whole world,' and 'the infinite Universe,' because *This concrete place is where something ineffable exists—explain it as fine or explain it as coarse.*[6] The

3. 五臓 (GOZO); the liver, heart, lungs, kidney, and spleen.

4. 六腑 (ROPPU); the throat, stomach, large intestine, small intestine, gall bladder, and bladder.

5. 諸大 (SHODAI). For example, 四大 (SHIDAI), "the four elements," from the Sanskrit *catvāri mahābhūtāni*, are earth, water, fire, and wind. 五大 (GODAI), "the five elements," from the Sanskrit *pañca mahābhūtāni*, are earth, water, fire, wind, and space. 六大 (ROKUDAI), "the six elements," from the Sanskrit *ṣaḍ dhātavaḥ*, are earth, water, fire, wind, space, and consciousness.

6. Alludes to an episode involving Master Rinzai Gigen and his disciple Koke Sonsho recorded in *Shinji-shobogenzo*, pt. 1, no. 96: *Fuke and Rinzai go to a patron's house for a midday meal. [Rinzai] asks, "A hair swallows the vast ocean and a mustard seed includes Mt. Sumeru.*

dimension of the mind, again, cannot be known by thinking and discriminating, and cannot be fathomed by not thinking and not discriminating. Because the dimension of the body-mind is like this, the dimension of bathing is also like this. To grasp this dimension and to practice-and-experience it is that which the buddhas and the patriarchs guard and desire. We should not see our conception of ourselves as foremost, and we should not see our conception of ourselves as real. Thus, when we bathe and wash like this we perfectly realize the dimension of body and the dimension of mind and we make them pure and clean. Whether [the body-mind] is the four elements,[7] the five aggregates,[8] or the immortal essence, in bathing it can be totally pure and clean. This is not to say that we should see ourselves as pure and clean only after we have brought water and washed. How could water be originally pure or be originally impure? Even if it is originally pure or originally impure, we do not claim that it causes the place we bring it to be pure or impure. The fact is simply that, when we maintain and rely upon the practice-and-experience of the Buddhist patriarchs, Buddha-methods such as using water to wash and bathing in water are transmitted. When we practice-and-experience on this basis, we transcend purity, pass through impurity, and get free of non-purity and non-impurity. Thus, the practice of washing and bathing even though we have not become dirty, and of washing and bathing even though we are already wholly pure and clean, is maintained and relied upon only in the Buddhist patriarchs' truth: it is beyond the knowledge of non-Buddhists. If it were as stupid people say, even if we ground the five viscera and six entrails to a dust as fine as air and used all the water of the great ocean to wash them, unless we also washed inside each particle of dust how could they be pure and clean? Without washing the inside of emptiness,[9] how can we realize *cleanness within and without?* Stupid fellows can never know the method of bathing emptiness. We utilize emptiness to bathe emptiness and utilize emptiness to bathe the body-mind. Those

---

Should we see this as 'the mystical powers and wondrous function' or should we see this as 'reality as it is.'" The Master [Fuke] duly overturns the dinner table. [Rin]zai says, "Very coarse person!" The Master [Fuke]says, "This concrete place is where it is—explain it as coarse or explain it as fine." Whereas here Master Dogen writes 什麽所在 (SHIMO *[no]* SHOZAI), in chap. 22, *Bussho*, para. [45], he writes 甚麽所在 (NAN *[no]* SHOZAI)," and the *Shinji-shobogenzo* version has simply 甚所在 (NAN *[no]* SHOZAI). Each of the three expressions means "the place where 'what?' exists," or "the place where something ineffable exists."

7. 四大 (SHIDAI): earth, water, fire, and wind. See note 5.

8. 五蘊 (GO-UN), from the Sanskrit *pañca skandha,* are form or matter (*rūpa*), perception or feeling (*vedana*), thinking (*saṃjñā*), action or formation of habits (*saṃskāra*), and consciousness (*vijñāna*). See chap. 2, *Maka-hannya-haramitsu.*

9. 空中 (KUCHU) means "the inside of emptiness" or "the real state of emptiness," that is, the balanced state in which things are allowed to be as they are. 空 (KU), "emptiness" or "the immaterial," expresses the mental face of reality: to be pure and clean is a matter of both mind and body.

who believe in bathing as the Dharma are maintaining and relying upon the practice-and-experience of the Buddhist patriarchs. That is to say, in the right Dharma authentically transmitted by rightful successors, buddha to buddha and patriarch to patriarch, when we practice bathing, the body-mind within and without, the five viscera and six entrails, the duality of object and subject, and the inside, the outside, and the middle of the Dharma-world and space, are instantly pure and clean. When we use incense or flowers for purification, the past, the present, and the future, causes-and-circumstances, and practice, are instantly pure and clean. The Buddha says,

> *Bathing three times, spreading fragrance three times,*
> *The body-mind is pure and clean.*[10]

Thus, the method of purifying the body and of purifying the mind is, inevitably, to bathe once and to spread fragrance once, and to do likewise again and again, *bathing three times, spreading fragrance three times,* then to bow to buddhas, to read sutras, to sit in Zazen, and to practice walking.[11] After walking, when we are ready once more to sit erect in Zazen, it is said that we must always wash the feet. Even though the feet are not dirty or defiled, the method of the Buddhist patriarchs is like this. In general, in the words *"Bathing three times and spreading fragrance three times,"* bathing once means taking one bath,[12] that is, bathing the whole body. After so doing, and getting dressed as usual, we burn some fine incense in a small censer and spread the fragrance inside the lapels, over the kaṣaya, around our sitting place, and so on. After that, we take another bath and spread fragrance again. To do this three times is a method that accords with the Dharma. At this time, although the six sense organs and their six objects do not newly arrive, the virtue of purity is present; it manifests itself before us and is beyond doubt. The fact that, although we had not intended to dispel the three poisons[13] and the four upset states,[14] the virtue of purity has manifested itself before us at once, is the Buddha-Dharma. Who could fathom it with the common intellect? What person could glimpse it with common eyes? For example, when we clean and purify aloes,[15] we must not break it into fragments to wash it and we

10. Source not traced.

11. 経行 (KINHIN), from the Sanskrit *caṅkrama.* The traditional rule for *kinhin* in Japan is 一息半歩 (ISSOKU-HANPO), "one breath per half-step."

12. Master Dogen explained the more general single character used in the verse, 沐 (MOKU), lit. "to wash," with a more specific compound 沐浴 (MOKUYOKU), "to bathe," or "to have a bath."

13. 三毒 (SANDOKU): 1) passion or greed (from the Sanskrit *rāga*), 2) hatred or anger (*dveṣa*), and 3) delusion or ignorance (*moha*).

14. 四倒 (SHITO): 1) seeing the impermanent as eternal, 2) indulging in suffering as if it were joyful, 3) seeing the impure as pure, and 4) seeing that which is without self as having self.

15. 沈香 (JINKO) was relatively expensive incense. 沈 (JIN) lit. means "sunk"; the incense was sometimes obtained from waterlogged wood.

must not grind it into particles to wash it; we can make it pure and clean by washing its body.

30] In the Buddha-Dharma, without fail, washing methods have been prescribed. We wash the body, wash the mind, wash the feet, wash the face, wash the eyes, wash the mouth, wash the anus and urethra, wash the hands, wash the pātra, wash the kaṣaya, and wash the head. All these are the right Dharma of the buddhas and the patriarchs of the three times. When we are going to serve offerings to Buddha, Dharma, and Saṃgha, bringing assorted incense, we first wash our hands, then rinse the mouth and wash the face, put on clean clothes, get some fresh water in a clean basin, and wash the incense; after that, we serve offerings to the domain of Buddha, Dharma, and Saṃgha. We hope to be able to serve to the Three Treasures offerings of sandalwood incense from the Malaya mountains,[16] washed in water of the eight virtues[17] from Lake Anavatapta.

32] Washing the face has been transmitted from India in the west, and it has spread through China in the east. Though [the method] is clarified in various collections[18] of the precepts, that which is transmitted and retained by the Buddhist patriarchs may be still more authentic and traditional. Not only has it been practiced by buddhas and by patriarchs for hundreds of years; it is spread throughout koṭis of thousand myriad kalpas of the past and future. Not only is it to get rid of grime and grease; it is the lifeblood of the Buddhist patriarchs. [Sutras] say that, without washing the face, it is wrong both to receive a prostration and to make a prostration to others.

I prostrate myself, and prostrate to him;
Subject of prostration and object of prostration:
[One] nature empty and serene,[19]
The nature is to get free.[20]

---

16. A mountain range in southern India famous for its sandalwood incense. See Glossary.

17. Water which has the eight virtues is sweet, cold, soft, light, clear, not brackish, not harmful to the throat, and not harmful to the stomach.

18. 部 (BU), lit. "part," here represents the Sanskrit *nikāya* which means a collection. See Glossary.

19. Master Dogen's record of his years in China, *Hogyo-ki (Hogyo Era Record)*, no. 10 says: *The Master [Tendo] once summoned me and preached, "Although you are a recent student, you possess in abundance the air of the ancients. You should just live in a secluded valley deep in the mountains and nurture the sacred womb of the Buddhist patriarchs. You will definitely arrive at the state experienced by the ancient masters." Then Dogen rose and made a prostration under the Master's foot. The Master called out, "Subject of prostration and object of prostration have a nature empty and serene. The empathy between us is difficult to think about." Then the Master widely preached the action of the Buddhist patriarchs of the Western Heavens and Eastern Lands. Dogen's tears of gratitude made his collar wet.* "Empathy" is 感応道交 (KANNO-DOKO), or "empathic communication of the truth"; the term is discussed in chap. 39, *Shinjin-gakudo.*

20. 性脱落 (SHO-DATSURAKU). 脱落 (DATSURAKU), "get free," or "drop off," usually appears

Therefore, we must unfailingly wash the face. As regards a time for washing the face, in some cases the fifth night watch,[21] and in some cases dawn, are the times. When my late Master was master of Tendo temple, he established the third period[22] of the third watch as the time. Carry skirt[23] and jacket[24] with you to the washstand. The hand-towel[25] is a sheet of cloth with a length of one *jo* and two *shaku*.[26] Its color must not be white; white is prohibited. The Sutra of Three Thousand Dignified Forms says, *"There are five points to observe in using the hand-towel: 1) Use the top and bottom ends for wiping. 2) Use one end for wiping the hands and the other end for wiping the face. 3) Do not wipe the nose with it. 4) Wash [the hand-towel] at once after it has been used to wipe grease or dirt. 5) Do not use it to wipe the body; when taking a bath, each person should have their own towel."* When carrying the hand-towel, hold it as follows: Fold the hand-towel in two and hang it over the left forearm near the elbow. Half the hand-towel is for wiping the face and half for wiping the hands. Not to wipe the nose means not to wipe the inside of the nose or nasal mucus. Do not use the hand-towel to wipe the armpits, the back, the belly, the navel, the thighs, or the lower legs. When it becomes soiled with dirt and grease, wash it. When it becomes wet or damp, dry it by a fire or in the sun. Do not use the hand-towel when taking a bath. The Cloud Hall washroom is the rear washstand,[27] and the rear washstand is located to the west of the Illuminated Hall[28]—this is the building layout which has been transmitted to us. For huts in the temple grounds and single quarters, [a washstand] is built at a convenient place.

---

in the description of Zazen as 身心脱落 (SHINJIN-DATSURAKU), "getting free of body and mind." "Getting free of body and mind" means experiencing the self as a whole and thereby getting free of the misconception of 'body' and 'mind' as separate entities.

21. The night was divided into five watches of two hours each, so the fifth watch was the last watch before dawn.

22. Each watch was further divided into five periods. So the third period of the third watch was the middle of the night.

23. 裙 (KUN), "skirt," or "hem"; more usually written as 裙子 (KUNZU), "hemmed thing," represents the Sanskrit *nivāsana* which lit. means "living, residing, passing time" (see Glossary). *Nivāsana* therefore seems to describe the *kunzu* as a garment worn in ordinary daily life.

24. 褊衫 (HENSAN), a long jacket usually of black cotton. The skirt and jacket may have been separate or they may have been sewn together as one long black gown with wide sleeves (*jikitotsu*) of the kind worn by monks and professional priests in Japan today. See also notes to chap. 7, *Senjo*.

25. 手巾 (SHUKIN). The *shukin* was used as a hand and face towel, and also as a sash to keep up the sleeves.

26. 一丈二尺 (ICHIJO-NISHAKU). One *jo* (9.94 ft.; 3.03 m.) is ten *shaku*, so the length of the towel is 11.93 ft., or 3.64 m.

27. 後架 (KOKA), so called because it is located to the rear of the Zazen Hall, is no. 48 on the temple ground plan in Book 1, Appendices.

28. 照堂 (SHODO). A senior monk would use this area for instructing other monks while the master of the temple was otherwise occupied. The Illuminated Hall (ibid. no. 57) directly separates the Zazen Hall and the washroom.

An abbot washes the face in the abbot's quarters. Washstands are suitably provided at the residences of aged monks and retired veteran monks. While lodging in the Cloud Hall, an abbot will wash at the rear washstand. When you arrive at the washstand, hang the center of the hand-towel around the back of your neck, and pull the two ends forward over the left and right shoulders. Then, with left and right hands, bring the left and right ends of the hand-towel under the left and right armpit and around to the back. Cross the two ends over behind your back, then bring the left end across to your right and the right end across to your left, and tie them together in front of your chest. Thus, the collar of the jacket is covered by the hand-towel, and the sleeves are tucked up above the elbows by the hand-towel. Below the elbows, the forearms and hands are exposed. For example, it is like having the sleeves tucked up by a *tasuki* sash.[29] After that, if in the rear washstand, take a washbowl to the cauldron and get a bowlful of hot water, then come back and place it on the washstand. If somewhere else, put hot water from a hot water tub into the washbowl.[30]

36] Next use the willow twig. In the mountain-temples of the great kingdom of Sung today the practice of chewing the willow twig, having long since died out, is not transmitted, and so they have no places for chewing the willow twig. But today at Eihei-ji temple on Kichijo-zan mountain[31] we have a place for chewing the willow twig—it is a new arrangement. On arriving there the first thing we should do is chew the willow twig. Taking a willow twig in the right hand, make a dhāraṇī-vow. The Pure Conduct chapter of the Garland Sutra says:

Taking the willow twig in the hand,
Pray that all living beings
Will get the right Dharma in their mind,
And be naturally pure and clean.

After reciting this sentence and before proceeding to chew the willow twig, recite as follows:

Chewing the willow twig at dawn,
Pray that all living beings

---

29. Whereas the (longer) hand-towel is knotted in front of the chest, a *tasuki* is knotted behind the back. The *tasuki* method would have been more familiar to Japanese of Master Dogen's time, and is still used in Japan today.

30. At a wash place that had no cauldron, there would be a tub which was filled with hot water from, for example, the kitchen.

31. According to the records at the end of the penultimate and final paragraphs of the chapter, this chapter was first preached in 1239, and preached for a second time in 1243, before Master Dogen moved to Eihei-ji. The third time it was preached, in 1250, Master Dogen was living at Eihei-ji. It seems probable that Master Dogen added this part during the third preaching of the chapter.

Get conquering teeth,
To chew up troubles.

After reciting this sentence, chew the willow twig. The length of the willow twig is the width of four fingers, of eight fingers, of twelve fingers, or of sixteen fingers. Precepts for the Great Saṃgha,[32] article 34, says, *"Use a twig for the teeth of suitable size, sixteen fingers at the longest, and four fingers at the shortest."* Remember, [the twig] should not be made shorter than four fingers, and longer than sixteen fingers is not a suitable size. The thickness is *the thickness of the little finger.* At the same time, there is nothing to prevent [the twig] being thinner. The shape is *the shape of the little finger:* one end is thick, the other end is thin. The thicker end is chewed into fine fibers. The Sutra of Three Thousand Dignified Forms says, *"The chewed end must not exceed three bu."*[33] Chew the twig thoroughly, and then rub and wash the front of the teeth and the back of the teeth, as if polishing them. Rub and polish, and wash and rinse, again and again. Thoroughly polish and wash the base of the teeth, above the gums. Carefully scrape clean the gaps between the teeth, and wash them clean. If the mouth is rinsed out repeatedly, [the teeth] will be rinsed clean. Next, scrape the tongue. The Sutra of Three Thousand Dignified Forms says, *"There are five points in scraping the tongue: 1) Do no more than three sets. 2) Stop if blood appears on the surface of the tongue. 3) Do not dirty the saṃghāṭī robe, or the feet, by waving the hand too far. 4) Do not throw away the willow twig on a path where people walk. 5) Always be in a secluded place."* "Three sets of scraping the tongue" means that we rinse the mouth with water then scrape and scrape the tongue, and repeat this three times. It does not mean to do [only] three scrapes. Heed the warning to stop if blood appears. Concerning the need to scrape the tongue thoroughly, the Sutra of Three Thousand Dignified Forms says, *"Cleansing the mouth means chewing the willow twig, rinsing out the mouth, and scraping the tongue."* Thus, the willow twig has been guarded and retained by Buddhist patriarchs and by the children and grandchildren of Buddhist patriarchs.

[139] *The Buddha was living at Veṇuvana park*[34] *in Rājagṛha,*[35] *together with one thousand two hundred and fifty bhikṣus. It was the 1st of December, on which day King Prasenajit*[36] *was preparing a meal. Bright and early in the morning, with his own*

---

32. 摩訶僧祇律 (MAKASOGI-RITSU), also quoted in chap. 7, *Senjo.*

33. 三分 (SANBU), three *bu,* is 0.36 inches (0.91 cm.).

34. 竹園 (CHIKU-ON), lit. "Bamboo Wood," represents the meaning of the Sanskrit *Veṇuvana.* This was a park which lay to the north gate of Rājagṛha and which the king Bimbisāra donated to the Buddha's order soon after the order's establishment.

35. 王舎城 (OSHAJO), "City of Royal Palaces," represents the Sanskrit *Rājagṛha,* the capital of the kingdom of Magadha. Its site is 70 km southwest of Patna, near the present-day small town of Rājgir. It was the most powerful royal city of northern India after Sāvatthi, the capital of the kingdom of Kosala.

36. King Prasenajit was the ruler of the kingdom of Kosala. See also chap. 59, *Baike.*

hand he offered the Buddha a willow twig. The Buddha accepted it and when he had finished chewing it he threw what remained onto the ground. It at once started to grow. With roots and shoots springing forth in profusion, and twigs and leaves spreading like a cloud, it rose to a height of five hundred yojanas. Its circumference was of the same order. By and by it produced flowers too, [each] as big as a carriage wheel. Finally it also bore fruits, [each] the size of a five-gallon jar.[37] *The roots, branches, twigs, and leaves were solely of the seven treasures, whose assorted colors shone with extraordinary beauty. Brightness emanating from the colors eclipsed the sun and moon. To the taste, the fruit was more delicious than nectar.*[38] *The fragrance filled the four quarters, and all who sensed it felt glad in their hearts. A fragrant breeze came blowing, whereupon, pushing and prodding each other, the twigs and leaves all gave out a melodious sound, which unfurled the pivot of Dharma, and which listeners never grew tired of hearing. The reverence and belief of all people who witnessed this transformation of the tree grew more and more pure and deep. The Buddha thereupon preached the Dharma, and their minds, receptive to his intention, were all enlightened. Those pursuing the state of Buddha attained the effect and were born in heaven—their numbers were very great.*[39]

2] The method of serving offerings to the Buddha and to the Saṃgha is, of necessity, to offer a willow twig at dawn. After that, various other offerings are prepared. There are many examples of willow twigs being offered to the Buddha, and many examples of the Buddha using the willow twig, but for now I shall just quote the story of King Prasenajit offering the willow twig with his own hand, and the story of the tall tree, because they deserve to be known. It was also on this day that the six non-Buddhist teachers[40] were each defeated by the Buddha; they ran away in astonishment and awe, and finally each of the six teachers *threw himself into a river to drown. Nine koṭis of followers of the six teachers all came seeking to be disciples of the Buddha. The Buddha said, "Welcome bhikṣus!" and their beards and hair fell away naturally, the Dharma-robe covered their bodies, and they all became śramaṇas.*[41] *The Buddha preached to them the Dharma and demonstrated the pivot of the Dharma. They ended the superfluous, dissolved [all] bonds, and attained arhathood.*[42] Thus, because the Tathāgata was already in the habit of using the willow twig, humans beings and gods of-

---

37. 斗 (TO), "gallon," is a measure of capacity which has varied from age to age.

38. 甘露 (KANRO), lit. "sweet dew," represents the Sanskrit *amṛta*, the nectar supposedly relished by ancient Indian gods.

39. Quoted from the chapter about how the Buddha defeated the six non-Buddhist teachers, in volume two of *Kengu-kyo (The Sutra of the Wise and the Stupid)*.

40. 六師外道 (ROKUSHI-GEDO): 1) Sañjaya-velaṭṭhiputa, a skeptic; 2) Ajita-kesakambarin, a materialist; 3) Makkali-gosāla, a fatalist; 4) Pūraṇa-kassapa, a negator of moral virtue, a moral relativist; 5) Pakuda-kaccāyana, a sensualist; and 6) Nigaṇṭha-nātaputta, the founder of Jainism.

41. The Sanskrit *śramaṇa* (lit. "striver") originally described a wandering mendicant who was not of the Brahmin caste—as distinct from a *parivrājaka*, a wandering religious mendicant of Brahmin origin. The Buddha applied the term *śramaṇa* to Buddhist monks.

42. Also quoted from *Kengu-kyo*.

fered the willow twig to him. Clearly, chewing the willow twig is a practice which buddhas, bodhisattvas, and the Buddha's disciples unfailingly retain. If we fail to practice it, the method will be lost. Would that not be regrettable?

[144] The Sutra of the Pure-Net Bodhisattva-Precepts says, *"Disciples of the Buddha! Always practice dhūta*[43] *in two periods of the year, sit in Zazen in winter and summer, and observe the summer retreat.*[44]*Always use the willow twig, [powdered] beans for washing, the three robes, a water bottle, the pātra, a prostration cloth, a staff,*[45] *an incense burner, a bag for filtering water, a hand-towel, a knife, a flint, tweezers, a rope stool,*[46] *sutras, precepts, a Buddha-image, and a bodhisattva-statue. When bodhisattvas go practicing dhūta, and when they travel, even if the journey is hundreds of miles or thousands of miles, these eighteen things should always go with them. The dhūta last from the 15th of the 1st lunar month to the 15th of the 3rd lunar month, and from the 15th of the 8th lunar month to the 15th of the 10th lunar month. During these two periods, the eighteen articles should always be with you. They should be as wings to a bird."*

[145] None of these eighteen articles should be missing. If any were missing, it would be like a bird having lost a wing. Even with one wing remaining, it could never fly. Its conditions would not be those of the way of the birds. Bodhisattvas are also like this. Unless equipped with these eighteen wings, they cannot practice the bodhisattva-way. And among the eighteen, the willow twig occupies first place: it should be supplied first. People who have clarified whether or not this willow twig is necessary may be bodhisattvas who have clarified the Buddha-Dharma. People who have never clarified [this matter] may never have seen the Buddha-Dharma even in a dream. This being so, to meet the willow twig is to meet the Buddhist patriarchs. For instance, if a person were to ask *"What is your intention?"* [I would reply,] *"You have been lucky to meet old man Eihei's chewing of the willow twig."* The buddhas and bodhisattvas of the past, present, and future, without exception, have received and retained, in the past, present, and future, these Pure-Net Bodhisattva-Precepts. That being so, they have also received and retained, in the past, present, and future, the willow twig.

---

43. 頭陀 (ZUDA), representing the Sanskrit *dhūta,* has two meanings: 1) the twelve ancient practices (recorded in chap. 30, *Gyoji*), and 2) the practice of begging for food every day and not accepting invitations, which is the first of the twelve *dhūta.* In this case, *dhūta* suggests the second meaning.

44. 夏安居 (GE-ANGO), "the summer retreat," from the Sanskrit *vārṣika* (which literally means "belonging to the rainy season") is described in detail in chap. 79, *Ango.*

45. 錫杖 (SHAKUJO), lit. "tin staff." Tin refers to metal rings which dangle from three holes in the embossed top of the stick. These jangle as the monk walks along, serving to scare away bears.

46. A folding stool with a rope seat.

7] *Pure Criteria for Zen Monasteries*[47] says, *"Read, recite, and thoroughly understand both the ten major precepts and the forty-eight minor precepts of the Pure-Net Sutra of the Great Vehicle, and thus know well what is observance and what is violation, what is permissible and what is forbidden. Rely only upon the sacred words of the golden mouth.*[48] *Do not follow ordinary people arbitrarily."*

Remember this. The principles authentically transmitted by the buddhas and the patriarchs are like this. Anything that goes against this is not the Buddha's truth, is not the Buddha-Dharma, and is not the truth of the patriarchs. Nevertheless, in the great kingdom of Sung today we do not see the willow twig at all. In the 4th lunar month of the 16th year of Kajo,[49] when I first visited the mountains and temples of great Sung [China], there was no monk who knew of the willow twig, and the whole nation, government and people, high and low, did not know of it. Because monks were completely ignorant of it, if I asked about the method of using the willow twig, they would grow pale and lose composure. It is pitiful that pure methods[50] have been lost. People who at least scantily rinse their mouths use [a device] in which hair from a horse's tail has been cut into lengths of an inch or so and then planted, like a horse's mane, into the top two inches of an ox-horn; this has been cut square in cross section to a thickness of approximately three *bu*,[51] and is six or seven *sun* in length.[52] They only clean the teeth with it. [But this] is hardly to be used as the utensil of a monk. It may be a vessel of impurity. It is not a vessel of the Buddha-Dharma. Even pious secular people might be disgusted by it. Such devices are used by both secular people and monks as a tool for sweeping dust off shoes; and also for brushing hair—there are slight variations in size, but it is the same thing. Even this device is used by only one person in ten thousand. So monks and lay people throughout the country have terribly bad breath. When people speak from two or three feet away, the stench from their mouth is difficult to bear. Even those famed as venerable patriarchs who possess the truth, and those titled as guiding teachers of human beings and gods, do not know even of the existence of the practices of rinsing the mouth, scraping the tongue, and chewing the willow twig. Judging from this situation, we cannot guess in how many ways the great truth of the Buddhist patriarchs may now visibly be degenerating. Even if, not begrudging our present dewdrop life to the thousands of miles of blue waves, we traverse the mountains and rivers of foreign lands,

---

47. 禪苑清規 (ZEN-EN-SHINGI), completed by Master Choro Sosaku in 1103. The work was based on Master Hyakujo's 古清規 (KO-SHINGI), "Old Pure Criteria."

48. 金口 (KINKU), "the golden mouth," means the mouth of the Buddha.

49. 1223.

50. 白法 (BYAKUBO), lit. "white methods."

51. 三分 (SANBU). See note 33.

52. 六七寸 (ROKU-SHICHI-SUN) is between and 7 and 9 inches. One *sun* (ten *bu*) is approximately 1.2 inches (3.03 cm.).

intending to search for the truth, the unfortunate situation [described above] will give us cause for sadness. How many pure methods have been lost already? It is regrettable. It is very regrettable. Through the whole of Japan, by contrast, both monks and lay people experience the willow twig. This may be to experience the Buddha's brightness. At the same time, our chewing of the willow twig does not accord with the proper method, and the method of scraping the tongue has not been transmitted to us, so it may be that we are slipshod. Even so, those who know the necessity of using the willow twig—in contrast to the Chinese who do not know of the willow twig—have naturally come to know a method of the excellent ones. In the methods of the mountain hermits,[53] too, they use the willow twig. Remember, it is, in all cases, an implement beyond dust,[54] and a tool of purification.

[151] The Sutra of Three Thousand Dignified Forms says, *"In using the willow twig, there are five points: 1) It should be cut to the proper scale. 2) It should be split according to the proper method. 3) The chewed end must not exceed three bu. 4) For odd teeth, it should be centered and chewed three times.*[55] *5) The sap should be used to bathe the eyes."*

Our present custom of cupping in the right hand, and bathing the eyes with, the water used in chewing the willow twig and rinsing the mouth, is originally just the teaching of the Sutra of Three Thousand Dignified Forms. Nowadays in Japan it has become a long-standing household tradition. The practice of scraping the tongue was imported by Master Eisai.[56] When you have finished using the willow twig, before throwing it away split the twig into two, tearing it with both hands from the chewed end. Place the sharp edge of the split twig crossways on the tongue's surface, and then scrape. That is to say, scoop water into the mouth with the right hand and rinse the mouth, then scrape the tongue. Repeatedly rinse the mouth and scrape the tongue, scraping and scraping with the edge of the split willow twig as if aiming to draw blood. While rinsing the mouth, secretly recite the following sentence: The Garland Sutra says:

---

53. 仙人 (SEN-NIN), or "mountain-dwelling wizard," expresses the ideal of the Taoist sage.

54. 出塵 (SHUTSU-JIN), lit. "getting out of dust," suggests, in general, transcendence of the secular world.

55. Where there is a gap between the teeth, the willow twig should be centered between upper and lower teeth, so as not to damage or loosen teeth by forcing the willow twig into a gap between them.

56. 僧正栄西 (SOJO-ESAI). 僧正 (SOJO) or "Chief Administrator of Monks" (see notes to chap. 8, *Raihai-tokuzui*) was the title of the highest ranking monk in the ancient Buddhist hierarchy (*sogo*) which was established in 624, based on the Chinese model. The system was formally abandoned following the Meiji Restoration of 1868. Master Eisai (1141–1215) went to China in the generation before Master Dogen, and introduced the teachings of the Rinzai Sect into Japan as the Master of Kennin-ji and other temples.

Washing out the mouth and cleaning the teeth,
Pray that all living beings
Proceed to the gate of pure Dharma
And realize ultimate liberation.

Repeatedly rinsing the mouth, use the flesh of the first, second, or third fingers of the right hand to cleanse inside and outside the lips, under the tongue, and to the roof of the mouth, leaving them as if thoroughly licked. Shortly after eating oily food, use honey locusts.[57] As soon as you have finished with the willow twig, throw it away in an unobtrusive place. Then, after disposing of the willow twig, snap the fingers three times. In the rear washstand there should be a box for discarded willow twigs. Elsewhere, discard [the twig] in some unobtrusive spot. Spit out the water used to rinse the mouth somewhere other than the washbowl.

53] Next, wash the face itself. Scooping hot water from the washbowl with both hands, wash all over, starting with the forehead, then the eyebrows, the eyes, the nostrils, the inside of the ears, the cheekbones, and the cheeks. First douse them thoroughly with hot water, and after that scrub and wash them. Do not let tears, spit, or nasal mucus fall into the hot water in the washbowl. While washing like this, do not use up the hot water immoderately, spilling or splashing it from the washbowl so that it runs out too soon. Wash until free of dirt and rid of grease. Wash inside the ears, for they are not [usually] able to contact water. Wash inside the eyes, for they cannot [be cleaned] through contact with sand. Sometimes we wash as far as the hairline or the scalp. This is dignified behavior itself. Having washed the face and thrown away the hot water left in the washbowl, again snap the fingers three times.

5] Next wipe the face dry with one end of the hand-towel. After that, take off the hand-towel again, then fold it into two and hang it over the left forearm. In the washroom behind the Cloud Hall there are face-towels for common use—a long bolt[58] of cloth is provided and there are charcoal braziers. Monks have no worries about lack [of a towel] for wiping the face. We may wipe the head and face with that [common towel], or we may use our own hand-towel; each is the proper method. While washing the face, do not make a noise by clanking the dipper loudly against the washbowl. And do not get the surrounding area wet by making a mess with the hot and cold water Secretly reflect that, although we were born after the five hundred years[59]

57. Honey locusts *(Gleditsia japonica)* are small, irregularly shaped green vegetables, roughly equal in size to green beans. Here they would be used to clean oil from inside the mouth. In chap. 7, *Senjo,* Master Dogen explains the use of honey locusts in washing the hands.

58. 一匹 (IPPIKI), one *hiki.* A *hiki* is a unit of cloth length. It is roughly the length of cloth needed to make one kimono; that is, just over 20 meters of cloth.

59. Alludes to the belief that in the age of right Dharma—the first five hundred years following the Buddha's death—the Dharma would flourish, after which it would decline.

and although we live on a remote island, the good we have accumulated in the past has not decayed; we should wholeheartedly rejoice that, receiving the authentic transmission of the dignified behavior of eternal buddhas, we can enjoy untainted practice-and-experience. On the way back to the Cloud Hall the footsteps should be light and quiet. The cottages of aged monks of long-accumulated virtue should always have a washstand. Not washing the face goes against the Dharma. There are methods for the use of facial medications at wash-time.

[156] In sum, chewing the willow twig and washing the face are the right Dharma of eternal buddhas and people who are devoted to practicing the truth with the will to the truth should practice and experience them. To use cold water when hot water is not available is an ancient custom, a time-honored method. If it is totally impossible to obtain hot water or cold water, then early in the morning we wipe the face thoroughly and apply fragrant herbs, powdered incense, or the like, after which we may bow to the Buddha, recite sutras, burn incense, and sit in Zazen. Before we have washed the face, to perform any of the various practices is impolite.

Shobogenzo Senmen

Preached to the assembly at Kannon-dori-kosho-horin-ji temple on the 23rd day of the 10th lunar month in the 1st year of En-o.[60]

[157] In India and China, kings, princes, ministers, and officials, lay people and monks, men and women of the government and the public, farmers and common folk, all wash the face. They possess washbowls, sometimes of silver and sometimes of tin, among their household goods. They perform the service of washing the face every morning at religious shrines and spirit-houses. They also offer the service of washing the face at the stūpas of Buddhist patriarchs. After they have washed their faces and straightened their clothing, lay people and monks bow to gods, bow to spirits, bow to their ancestors, and bow to their parents. They bow to their teachers, they bow to the Three Treasures, and they bow to the myriad souls of the triple world and the good guardians[61] of the ten directions. Nowadays, even farmers and workers in the fields, fishermen and woodcutters, never forget to wash the face. But they do not chew the willow twig. In Japan, kings and ministers, the old and the young, the government and the public, the high and the low among laymen and monks, all unfailingly chew the willow twig and rinse the mouth.

60. 1239.

61. 真宰 (SHINSAI) means gods and benevolent spirits who are imagined to guard and protect the Buddha-Dharma.

But they do not wash the face. Where they have one, they have lost the other. To maintain now both washing the face and chewing the willow twig is replenishment where there was insufficiency and is the illuminating presence of the Buddhist patriarchs.

Preached again to the assembly on the 20th day of the 10th lunar month in the 1st year of Kangen[62] at Kippo-ji temple in the Yoshida district of Esshu.[63]

Preached to the assembly on the 11th day of the 1st lunar month in the 2nd year of Kencho[64] at Eihei-ji temple on Kichijo-zan mountain in the Yoshida district of Esshu.

62. 1243.

63. Modern-day Fukui prefecture.

64. 1250.

[57]

面授

MENJU

The Face-to-Face Transmission

Men means face, and ju means transmission. Menju means the transmission of the Dharma from a master to a disciple face to face. In Buddhism, what is transmitted from a master to a disciple is not only abstract theory, but also something real, including actual conduct, physical health, and intuitional wisdom. Therefore the transmission of this real something cannot be actualized solely through explanations with words, or simply by passing on some manuscript. For this reason, the Dharma that Gautama Buddha taught has been transmitted in person from master to disciple since the days of Gautama Buddha. Without this personal contact, the Buddhist Dharma cannot be transmitted. In this chapter, Master Dogen praises the transmission of the Buddhist Dharma and explains its importance.

[61] ***Then Śākyamuni Buddha,*** *in the order on Vulture Peak in the western country, India, among an assembly of millions, picked up an uḍumbara flower and winked. At that time the face of the Venerable Mahākāśyapa broke into a smile. Śākyamuni Buddha said, "I possess the right-Dharma-eye treasury and the fine mind of nirvāṇa. I transmit them to Mahākāśyapa."*[1]

[62] This is the truth of the buddhas' and the patriarchs' face-to-face transmission of the right-Dharma-eye treasury. Authentically transmitted by the Seven Buddhas, it reaches the Venerable Mahākāśyapa. Through twenty-eight transmissions from the Venerable Mahākāśyapa, it reaches the Venerable Bodhidharma. The Venerable Bodhidharma personally descends into China and gives the face-to-face transmission to Great Master Shoshu Taiso Fukaku, the Venerable Eka.[2] Through five transmissions, it reaches Great Master Daikan Eno of Sokei-zan mountain. Through seventeen transmissions, it reaches my late Master, the eternal Buddha Tendo of Daibyakumyo-zan mountain in the district of Keigen-fu in the great kingdom of Sung. On the 1st day of the 5th lunar month, in the 1st year of the great Sung era of Hogyo,[3] Dogen first burns incense and does prostrations, on the elevated

1. *Daibonten-o-monbutsu-ketsugi-kyo (Sutra of Questions and Answers between Mahābrahman and the Buddha).* See also chap. 68, *Udonge.*

2. Master Taiso Eka. Great Master Shoshu Fukaku is his posthumous title.

3. 1225.

stage *Myokodai,* to the late Master Tendo, the eternal Buddha; and the late Master, the eternal Buddha, first looks at Dogen. Then, indicating the face-to-face transmission and bestowing it upon Dogen, he says, *"The gate of Dharma transmitted face to face by the buddhas and the patriarchs has been realized."* This is just the picking up of a flower on Vulture Peak, it is the attainment of the marrow on Suzan mountain,[4] it is the transmission of the robe on Obai mountain,[5] and the face-to-face transmission on Tozan mountain.[6] This is the face-to-face transmission of the eye-treasury of the Buddhist patriarchs. It is present only in our house; others have never experienced it even in a dream.

[164] This truth of the face-to-face transmission, because it was actually transmitted face to face to Śākyamuni Buddha in the order of Kāśyapa Buddha,[7] and because it has been maintained, is the face of the Buddhist Patriarch. Without the face-to-face transmission from the Buddha's face, we are not buddhas. Śākyamuni Buddha's direct meeting with the Venerable [Mahā]kāśyapa is the immediate transmission. Even Ānanda and Rāhula cannot match the intimacy[8] of the transmission to Mahākāśyapa. Even the great bodhisattvas[9] cannot match the intimacy of the transmission to Mahākāśyapa; they cannot sit in the seat of the Venerable Mahākāśyapa. The World-Honored One saw sharing his seat and sharing his robe with Mahākāśyapa as his lifetime of Buddha-behavior. The Venerable Mahākāśyapa, through face transmission, mind transmission, body transmission, and eye transmission, has intimately received the face-to-face transmission of the World-Honored One; he has served offerings to, venerated, made prostrations to, and served homage to the Buddha Śākyamuni. In thus pulverizing his bones and shattering his body, he has been through an unknown thousand myriad changes. His own countenance is beyond face and eyes; he has received the face-to-face transmission of the countenance of the Tathāgata. Śākyamuni Buddha really looks at the Venerable Mahākāśyapa. The Venerable Mahākāśyapa looks directly at the Venerable Ānanda. The Venerable Ānanda prostrates himself directly before the Buddha's face of the Venerable Mahākāśyapa. This is the face-to-face transmission. The Venerable Ānanda abides in and

---

4. Indicates the transmission between Master Bodhidharma and Master Taiso Eka.

5. Indicates the transmission between Master Daiman Konin and Master Daikan Eno.

6. Indicates the transmission between Master Tozan Ryokai and Master Ungo Doyo.

7. Kāśyapa Buddha is the sixth of the seven ancient buddhas, and Śākyamuni Buddha is the seventh. See chap. 15, *Busso.*

8. 親 (SHIN) means "immediate," "intimate," or "familiar" (see also notes to chap. 51, *Mitsugo*). Ānanda and Rāhula were blood relatives of the Buddha who became two of his ten great disciples. Ānanda was the Buddha's half-brother; he eventually became the second patriarch in India as the successor of Master Mahākāśyapa. Rāhula was the Buddha's son.

9. 大菩薩 (DAI-BOSATSU) indicates, for example, the Bodhisattva Mañjuśrī, who is usually depicted (mounted on a lion) as the left-hand attendant of Śākyamuni Buddha; and the Bodhisattva Samantabhadra, who is usually depicted (mounted on a white elephant) as the right-hand attendant of Śākyamuni Buddha.

maintains this face-to-face transmission and, through contact with Śāṇavāsa,[10] he transmits it face to face. The Venerable Śāṇavāsa directly serves the Venerable Ānanda, during which time *the face alone, together with the face*[11] transmits and receives the face-to-face transmission. In this way the true ancestral masters of successive generations have each passed on the face-to-face transmission through the disciple regarding the master and the master seeing the disciple. If even one ancestor, one master, or one disciple failed to give or to receive the face-to-face transmission they would not be the buddhas and the patriarchs. For example, in causing a stream of faith to develop by channeling water, or in keeping a light burning which makes brightness eternal—even in koṭis of thousand myriad cases—root and branch are one. At the same time, [the transmission] is fleeting moments of cheeping and pecking.[12] This being so, we have amassed an age of days and nights looking directly at Śākyamuni Buddha, and have amassed a generation of days and nights being illuminated by the presence of the Buddha's face. We do not know how countlessly many times this has continued, back and forth. We should quietly consider it, and be glad. It is the Buddha's eyes and the Buddha's countenance which have done prostrations to the Buddha-face of Śākyamuni Buddha, which have moved the Buddha-eyes of Śākyamuni Buddha into our own eyes, and which have moved our own eyes into the Buddha's eyes. That which has transmitted this state face to face until the present, without missing a single generation, is this face-to-face transmission. The present several tens of generations of rightful successors are individual instances of the Buddha's face, and they receive the face-to-face transmission from the original Buddha's face. To make a prostration to this traditional face-to-face transmission is just to make a prostration to the Seven Buddhas and to Śākyamuni Buddha. It is to make a prostration and to serve offerings to the twenty-eight Buddhist patriarchs from the Venerable Mahākāśyapa. The features and eyes of the Buddhist patriarchs are like this. To meet these Buddhist patriarchs is to meet Śākyamuni Buddha and the rest of the Seven Buddhas. It is the very moment in which Buddhist patriarchs intimately bestow the face-to-face transmission of themselves; and it is buddhas of the face-to-face transmission giving the face-to-face transmission to buddhas of the face-to-face transmission. Using the complicated, they give the face-to-face transmission to the complicated, without any interruption at all. Opening their eyes, they give the eye-to-eye transmission and receive the eye-to-eye transmission through the eyes. Showing their faces, they give the face-to-face transmission and receive the face-to-face transmission through the

---

10. The successor of Ānanda and therefore the third patriarch in India. See chap. 15, *Busso*.

11. 唯面与面 (YUIMEN-YOMEN) alludes to the familiar phrase from the Lotus Sutra; 唯仏与仏 (YUIBUTSU-YOBUTSU), *"buddhas alone, together with buddhas."*

12. 啐啄の迅機 (SOTSU-TAKU *no* JINKI) suggests the combined efforts of a baby chick and a mother hen to get the chick out of the egg—a metaphor for the efforts of disciple and master.

face—the face-to-face transmission is received and given at the place of the face. Utilizing the mind, they give the mind-to-mind transmission and receive the mind-to-mind transmission through the mind. Realizing the body, they give the body-to-body transmission of the body. Other nations in other directions also see this [transmission] as their original ancestor. [But] east of China the giving and receiving of the face-to-face transmission is present only in this house of the Buddha's right tradition. We have clearly received the transmission of the right eye with which to see the Tathāgata. When we do prostrations to the face of Śākyamuni Buddha, the fifty-one patriarchs[13] and the founding Seven Buddhas are neither aligned side by side nor aligned in succession; rather, their face-to-face transmissions are all present in the same moment. One who never in a lifetime meets a master is not a disciple, and one who never meets a disciple is not a master. When [master and disciple] have definitely seen each other, have been seen by each other, have given the face-to-face transmission, and have succeeded to the Dharma, that is the realization of the truth which resides in the patriarchs' face-to-face transmission. Thus, [master and disciple] have directly taken on the brightness of the Tathāgata's face. In sum, even after thousands of years, or myriad years, or hundreds of kalpas, or koṭis of kalpas, this face-to-face transmission is the appearance of the face of, and the realization of the transmission from, Śākyamuni Buddha.

[170] When this state of the Buddhist Patriarch has been realized, it is the realization of the images of the World-Honored One, Mahākāśyapa, the fifty-one patriarchs, and the Seven Founders; it is the realization of their brightness, the realization of their body, the realization of their mind, the appearance of the tips of their toes, and the appearance of the ends of their noses. Even before a word is comprehended and even before understanding of half a word is transcended, when the master has seen the back of the disciple's head, and the disciple has regarded the master through the crown of the head, that is the authentic face-to-face transmission. Revere a face-to-face transmission like this. Merely to appear to be manifesting a trace of the mind in the field of the mind is not always a great and valuable way of life. [But] the performance of the face-to-face transmission in the changing of the face,[14] and the presence of the face-to-face transmission in the turning of the head, may be face skin three inches thick[15] or face skin ten feet thin, and just this

13. From Master Mahākāśyapa to Master Dogen.

14. 換面 (KANMEN), or "changing the facial expression"—for example, genuinely smiling as Master Mahākāśyapa did on seeing the Buddha pick up an uḍumbara flower—is an example of an action which can only be done if there is both muscular movement and mental sincerity (oneness of body and mind).

15. 面皮厚三寸 (MENPI-KO-SANSUN), "face skin three *sun* thick," symbolizes something real and concrete.

skin of the face may be *the great round mirror of the buddhas.*[16] Because the great round mirror is seen as the skin of the face, *inside and outside have no flaws or blurs,* and great round mirrors have passed on the face-to-face transmission to great round mirrors. Those who have received the authentic transmission of the right Dharma that has met personally with Śākyamuni Buddha are even more familiar to us than Śākyamuni Buddha; and they cause to be visible, from the corner of the eye, Śākyamuni buddhas who are *three and three before and behind.*[17] Therefore those who revere Śākyamuni Buddha and long for Śākyamuni Buddha should revere and should honor this authentic tradition of the face-to-face transmission; we should do venerative prostrations to that which is hard to encounter and hard to meet. That is just to do prostrations to the Tathāgata, and to be given the face-to-face transmission by the Tathāgata. Those who directly meet the face-to-face transmission of the Tathāgata as a conspicuous state which is authentically transmitted and learned in practice, whether they are the self that we used to see as ourselves or whether they are others, should be cherished and protected. In the house [of Buddha] there is an authentic tradition that those who do prostrations before the eight stūpas[18] are liberated from hindrances of wrongdoing and are able to feel the effect of the truth. This [stūpa-prostration] concretely establishes the state of Śākyamuni Buddha's realization of the truth at the place of his birth,[19] at the place of his turning the Dharma-wheel,[20] at the place of his realization of the truth,[21] and at the place of his nirvāṇa;[22] it realized the great

---

16. Alludes to a poem by Master Geyāśata quoted in chap. 20, *Kokyo: "The great round mirror of the buddhas / Has no flaws or blurs, inside or outside. / [We] two people are able to see the same. / [Our] minds, and [our] eyes, are completely alike."*

17. 前後三三 (ZENGO-SANSAN) means concrete individuals as opposed to an abstract ideal. See *Shinji-shobogenzo,* pt. 2, no. 27, and Shobogenzo, chap. 42, *Tsuki,* note 2.

18. Shortly after the Buddha's cremation, various tribes laid claim to his ashes, which were therefore divided into eight parts. All recipients built a stūpa to bury their share of the relics.

19. Lumbinī, on the outskirts of the city of Kapilavastu (present-day Tilaurakoṭ in Nepal). This city was destroyed in a military campaign against the Śākyas at around the time of the Buddha's death. When refugee Śākyas returned from exile, they rebuilt Kapilavastu at another site (present-day Piprāvā in India) and it was in a stūpa here that the Śākyas deposited their share of the Buddha's relics.

20. The deer-park of Isipatana (present-day Sārnāth) near the ancient city of Vārāṇasī (Benares). The archaeological site at Sārnāth has the remains of two stūpas. The Dharmacakra Stūpa, dating from the time of King Aśoka (3rd century B.C.), is thought to mark the spot where the Buddha gave his first preaching. The Dharmarājika Stūpa, when demolished in 1794, was found to contain a stone urn which apparently contained a portion of the Buddha's ashes that Aśoka had brought to Sārnāth from another original burial place.

21. A bodhi tree on the bank of the Nairañjanā river near Uruvilvā (present-day Bodh-Gayā). Uruvilvā was a garrison town in the ancient kingdom of Magadha (the southern part of present Bihar). One of the portions of the Buddha's ashes was entrusted to King Ajātaśatru of Magadha.

22. A śāla grove at the southern edge of Kuśinagara, capital of the ancient kingdom of Malla. The Mallas of Kuśinagara carried out the cremation of the Buddha's body and buried all

Earth and realized the great space which have remained by the city of Kanyākubja[23] and remained in Āmrapālivana wood.[24] Through prostration to that which is realized as a stūpa by sounds, smells, tastes, sensations, substances, sights, and other objects, [the prostrater] really feels the effect of practice of the truth. Prostration to these eight stūpas is a discipline practiced throughout the western country, India; lay people and monks, celestial throngs and human multitudes, vie to prostrate themselves and to serve offerings [to the stūpas]. This is just the scroll of a sutra; Buddhist sutras are like this. There again, to practice the thirty-seven methods[25] and thereby to accomplish the Buddhist effect in each instant of living, is to propagate along the omnipresent routes of the ancients the traces of the eternal practice and discipline of Śākyamuni Buddha; because he has made [these traces] clear for eternity, we can realize the truth. Remember, those eight towers of many stories [have seen] innumerable renewals of frosts and flowers, and wind and rain have often tried to broach them, but they have left their trace in space and left their trace in matter; the freedom with which they bestow their virtue upon people of the present has not diminished. And when we apply ourselves in the present to practicing those roots, powers, truths, and paths[26]—although there are disturbances[27] and there is the obstacle of

---

the ashes at the cremation site. When other tribes laid claim to the Buddha's relics, however, the Mallas agreed to divide the ashes into eight portions, keeping one portion for their own stūpa at Kuśinagara. The names of the above four major sites of the Buddha's career are etched into the memory of monks in Japan who begin each formal meal by reciting: *Bussho-ka-pi-ra* (The Buddha was born in Kapilavastu), *Jo-do-ma-ka-da* (He realized the truth in Magadha), *Seppo-ha-ra-na* (He preached the Dharma in Vārānasī), *Nyu-metsu-ku-chi-ra* (And entered nirvāṇa in Kuśinagara)...

23. Kanyākubja, one of the great ancient cities of Middle India, was said to be the site of one of the eight stūpas. The city was situated on a Ganges tributary in the modern district of Farrukhabad.

24. A mango grove outside the city of Vesāli. One of the eight portions of the Buddha's ashes is said to have been allocated to the Licchavis of Vesāli, but no record that they built a stūpa at Āmrapālivana has been traced. However, HB states: "The covered bowl in which the Licchavis buried their share of the relics was unearthed in Vesāli in 1958." Āmrapālivana means "Āmrapāli's Wood." Āmrapāli was a Vesāli courtesan whose son by King Bimbisāra became a monk in the Buddha's order. It is said that when the Buddha and a following of monks reached Vesāli before the rains retreat in the last year of the Buddha's life, they camped at Āmrapālivana.

25. See chap. 73, *Sanjushichi-bon-bodai-bunbo.*

26. 根・力・覚・道 (KON, RIKI, KAKU, DO) refers to the following: the five roots, 五根 (GO RIKI): belief, diligence, mindfulness, balance, wisdom; the five powers, 五力 (GO RIKI) arising from those five roots: belief, diligence, mindfulness, balance, wisdom; the seven limbs of the balanced state of truth, 七等覚支 (SHICHI TO KAKU SHI): selection of Dharma, diligence, joy, entrustment, detachment, balance, and mindfulness; and the noble eightfold path, 八聖道 (HASSHO DO): right view, right thinking, right speech, right action, right livelihood, right effort, right mindfulness, right state of balance. These are the latter twenty-five of the thirty-seven methods. Ibid.

delusion[28]—when we practice-and-experience [the thirty-seven methods], their power is still fresh. Such is the virtue of Śākyamuni Buddha. Yet the present face-to-face transmission is beyond comparison with those [stūpas and methods]. The thirty-seven auxiliary bodhi-methods have this face of the Buddha—and the Buddha-mind, the Buddha-body, the Buddha's truth, the Buddha's brightness, the Buddha's tongue, and so on—as their original root. The accumulated virtues of the eight stūpas, likewise, have the Buddha's face and so on as their original foundation.

76] Now, as students of the Buddha-Dharma, if we are to walk the vigorous road of penetration and liberation, we should, in the peace and quiet of day and night, carefully consider and wholeheartedly rejoice that our country is superior to other countries and our truth alone is supreme. In other regions the people who do not equal us are many. The reason our country and our truth are supreme and honored alone is that although the multitudes assembled on Vulture Peak instructed others throughout the ten directions, the rightful successor at Shaolin temple was truly the educator of China, and the descendants of Sokei have passed on his face-to-face transmission to the present. This is an excellent time for the Buddha-Dharma to enter afresh into the mud and into the water. If we do not experience the effect at this time, when will we experience the effect? If we do not cut delusion at this time, when will we cut delusion? If we do not become buddha at this time, when will we become buddha? If we are not a sitting buddha at this time, when will we be an acting buddha? Consideration [of these questions] should be meticulous.

78] When Śākyamuni Buddha graciously gives the face-to-face transmission to the Venerable Mahākāśyapa, he says, *"I possess the right-Dharma-eye treasury and I transmit it to Mahākāśyapa."* At the order on Suzan mountain, the Venerable Bodhidharma actually addresses the Second Patriarch with the words *"You have got my marrow."* Clearly, that which gives the face-to-face transmission of the right-Dharma-eye treasury, and that which becomes the face-to-face transmission of *"You have got my marrow,"* is nothing other than this face-to-face transmission itself. At this very moment, when you see through and get free from your habitual bones and marrow, the face-to-face transmission of the Buddhist patriarchs is there. Even the face-to-face transmission of the great state of realization, and the face-to-face transmission of the mind-seal,

---

27. 煩悩 (BONNO) represents the Sanskrit *kleśa.* Traditional examples of *kleśa* are greed, anger, ignorance, arrogance, doubt, and false views. See Book 1, Glossary; see also notes to chap. 43, *Kuge.*

28. 惑障 (WAKU-SHO), or "layers of interference." 惑 (WAKU), "delusion," again represents the Sanskrit *kleśa.* 障 (SHO), "hindrance, obstacle," represents the Sanskrit *āvaraṇa* which means "obstruction," "covering," "outer layer," or "mental blindness." See Glossary, *kleśāvaraṇa.*

are a singular state at a definite place.[29] Although they are not the transmission of everything, we never enter into investigation of insufficiency of realization.[30] In conclusion, the great truth of the Buddhist patriarchs is nothing other than a face giving and a face receiving, and the reception of a face and the giving of a face, beyond which there is nothing surplus and nothing lacking. We should rejoice in, delight in, believe in, and serve whatever has had the opportunity to meet this face-to-face transmission, even if it is our own features. Dogen, on the 1st day of the 5th lunar month in the 1st year of the great Sung era of Hogyo,[31] prostrated myself to my late Master Tendo, the eternal Buddha, and received his face-to-face transmission for the first time; I was then allowed some access to his inner sanctum. Barely free of body and mind, yet being able to maintain and rely upon the face-to-face transmission, I came back[32] to Japan.

Shobogenzo Menju

Preached to the assembly at Kippo temple in the Yoshida district of Etsu-u,[33] on the 20th day of the 10th lunar month in the 1st year of Kangen.[34]

[180] Among those people who have never experienced and never learned in practice the truth that the face-to-face transmission of the Buddha's truth is like this, there was, during the Keiyu era[35] in the reign of the great Sung emperor Jin-so, a certain Zen Master Shoko[36] of Sempuku-ji temple.[37] In formal

---

29. 一隅の特地 (ICHIGU *no* TOKUCHI), lit. "a one-corner special state"—not a universal abstraction. The face-to-face transmission can take place in a stuffy office, in a temple set in fragrant tea fields, on a crowded train, et cetera, et cetera.

30. Because to have realized even ten percent is to have realized ten percent of the whole itself.

31. 1225.

32. The same characters 本来 (HONRAI), or "originally came," appear in the first line of an often-quoted poem by Master Bodhidharma: *"I originally came to this land / To transmit the Dharma and to save deluded emotional beings. / A flower is five petals opening; / The bearing of fruit is naturally realized."* See, for example, chap. 43, *Kuge.*

33. Modern-day Fukui prefecture.

34. 1243.

35. 1034 to 1037.

36. Sempuku Shoko (dates unknown). He lived by the stūpa of Master Unmon Bun-en, and was known by local people as "the Keeper of the Old Stūpa." He was already a Buddhist teacher when, on reading the record of Master Unmon's words, he felt he had finally attained clear understanding, and therefore called himself a successor of Master Unmon.

37. Located in Kiangsi province in southeast China.

preaching in the Dharma Hall he says: *"Great Master Unmon Kyoshin*[38] *is present just now. Do you all see him or not? If you are able to see him, then you are in the same state as this mountain monk. Do you see him? Do you see him? You should realize this matter directly, then you will have attainment for the first time, and it will be impossible for you to delude yourselves. Now, [consider] the example of Obaku in olden times. On hearing Master Hyakujo quote the story of the Great Master Ba[so]*[39] *letting out a yell, he chanced to have a great reflection. Hyakujo asked him: 'Disciple, would you not like to succeed the Great Master [Baso]?' Obaku said, 'Although I know of the Great Master, in short I have not met the Great Master. If I were to succeed the Great Master, I am afraid that I would forfeit my own children and grandchildren.' Members of this assembly! At that time, it was not even five years since the passing of the Great Master Ba[so], but Obaku himself confessed to not meeting. We should know that Obaku's viewpoint was not mature; in short, he only had one eye. This mountain monk is not like that. I am able to know Great Master Unmon, I am able to meet Great Master Unmon, and I am quite able to succeed Great Master Unmon. Yet given that it is already more than a hundred years since Unmon entered nirvāṇa, how can I today expound the principle of our intimate meeting? Do you understand it? People of penetration and men of attainment are able to certify it, but in the minds of the squinting and the inferior doubts and condemnation arise. Those who have been able to meet this state do not discuss it. Those who have not met it yet should look just now... You have been standing for a long time without questions. Thank you."*[40, 41]

3] Now [Shoko], even if we permit that you know Great Master Unmon, and that you see Great Master Unmon, does Great Master Unmon personally see you, or not? If Great Master Unmon does not see you, it might be impossible for you to succeed Great Master Unmon. Because Great Master Unmon has never sanctioned you, not even you claim that "Great Master Unmon sees me." It is evident that you and Great Master Unmon have never met each other. Among the Seven Buddhas and all the buddhas of the past, present, and future, is there any Buddhist patriarch who has succeeded to the Dharma without meeting with another as master and disciple? You must never call Obaku immature in his viewpoint. How could you fathom

---

38. Master Unmon Bun-en (864–949), successor of Master Seppo Gison. Great Master Unmon Kyoshin is his posthumous title.

39. 馬大師 (BA-DAISHI), lit. "the Great Horse Master." 馬 (BA) stands for 馬祖 (BASO), "the Horse Patriarch," which was the monk's name of Master Baso Do-itsu (709–788), successor of Master Nangaku Ejo. Master Baso was the master of Master Hyakujo Ekai (749–814), and the grandfather-master of Master Obaku Ki-un (died c. 855).

40. 珍重 (CHINCHO), lit. "value [yourselves]," or "take good care of yourselves," is a parting salutation. See, for example, chap. 30, *Gyoji*, para. [241] and chap. 45, *Bodaisatta-shishobo*, para. [78]. There were no questions from the audience, so Master Shoko finished his preaching and left the Dharma Hall.

41. Quoted from *Zokuto-roku (Supplementary Record of the Torch)*, one of the five Buddhist "records of the torch" compiled during the Sung era.

Obaku's actions? How could you fathom Obaku's words? Obaku is an eternal Buddha. He is at the limit of investigation[42] of the succession of the Dharma. You have never seen, heard, or learned in practice, even in a dream, the truth of the succession of the Dharma. Obaku has received the Dharma from his Master, and has maintained and relied upon the state of the Patriarch.[43] Obaku meets with his Master and sees his Master. You do not see a master, do not know a patriarch, do not know yourself, and do not see yourself, at all. And there is no master who sees you. You have never experienced the opening of a master's eyes; in truth it is you whose viewpoint is not mature and whose succession to the Dharma is never mature. Do you know, or do you not know, that Great Master Unmon is a Dharma-descendant of Obaku? How could you fathom the expressions of Hyakujo and Obaku? You cannot even fathom the expressions of Great Master Unmon. People who have the power of learning in practice take up the expressions of Hyakujo and Obaku, and people who have the directly accessible and settled state[44] can fathom those expressions. You, being without learning in practice and without the settled state, cannot know them and cannot fathom them. The words that "[Obaku] does not receive the Dharma from the Great Master Ba[so], even though *it is not even five years since the passing of the Great Master Ba[so],*" are truly not even worth laughing at. A person who deserves to succeed to the Dharma will be able to succeed to the Dharma even after countless kalpas. A person who does not deserve to succeed to the Dharma can never succeed to the Dharma, even if [the elapsed time] is [only] half a day or a minute. You are an utterly witless and stupid man who has never seen the face of the sun and the face of the moon in the Buddha's state of truth. You talk of succeeding to Unmon even though *it is already more than a hundred years since Great Master Unmon entered nirvāṇa*—is it by virtue of some momentous ability that you can succeed to Unmon? You are less reliable than a three-year-old child! People hoping to receive the Dharma from Unmon in another thousand years will probably have ten times your ability. Now I shall rescue you, so let us study for a while the story [of Hyakujo and Obaku].[45] Hyakujo's words *"Disciple, would you not like to succeed the Great*

42. 究参 (KYUSAN) is here used as an adjective. These characters usually appear the other way round, in the verb phrase 参究する (SANKYU suru), "to investigate," "to master," "to investigate in practice," "to master in experience," et cetera. 究 (KYU) means to investigate thoroughly. 参 (SAN) means to go, visit, enter into, participate, or devote oneself to. Master Dogen frequently uses 参 (SAN) in the compound 参学 (SANGAKU), "learning in practice," to indicate that Buddhist learning is a process to which the whole body-mind is devoted; it is not merely intellectual study of theoretical principles or scientific study of objective data.

43. Master Baso.

44. 直指の落処 (JIKISHI *no* RAKUSHO). 直指 (JIKISHI), lit. "directly indicated" or "directly indicatable," means not esoteric but open. The phrase appears in the final sentences of *Fukanzazengi*. 落処 (RAKUSHO), lit. "a place to settle down," suggests the balanced state of Zazen.

45. 話頭 (WATO). In the Rinzai sect, which traces its lineage directly back to Master Obaku

Master [Baso]?" never say "Go ahead and receive the Dharma from Great Master Ba[so]!"[46] Studying for a while the story of a lion mustering all its strength and speed,[47] and studying the story of a turtle trying to climb a tree upside down,[48] you should investigate the vigorous road of stepping forward and stepping back. In succession of the Dharma, the power of learning in practice like this exists. Obaku's words *"I am afraid that I would forfeit my own children and grandchildren"* are utterly beyond your comprehension. Do you know who is expressed in the words *"my own,"* and who the people described as *children and grandchildren* are? You should painstakingly study [Obaku's words] in practice. The words have been realized unconcealedly and conspicuously.

[86] Nevertheless, a certain Zen Master Bukkoku Ihaku,[49] being ignorant of the Buddhist patriarchs' succession of the Dharma, has listed Shoko among Unmon's Dharma-successors. This may be a mistake. Students of later ages must not unknowingly think that learning in practice might be present in Shoko. If it is possible for the likes of you, [Shoko,] to receive the Dharma by relying on written words, then do people who are enlightened by reading written sutras all receive the Dharma from Śākyamuni Buddha himself? That is never so. Enlightenment based upon written sutras always requires the seal of approval of a true teacher. Shoko, you have not even read the record of Unmon's words as thoroughly as you say. Only people who have penetrated Unmon's words have received the Dharma from Unmon. You have never seen Unmon with your own eyes, you have never seen yourself with your own eyes, you have never seen Unmon with Unmon's eyes, and you have never seen yourself with Unmon's eyes. There are many such things

---

as the master of Master Rinzai, so-called *koans* are called 話頭 (WATO)—see for example Master Sansho Enen's use of the word in chap. 20, *Kokyo*. In Shobogenzo Master Dogen usually refers to such stories as 因縁 (INNEN), "causes and circumstances."

46. Master Hyakujo simply recognized his disciple's great admiration of Master Baso. He did not recommend Master Obaku to transcend the face-to-face transmission.

47. 獅子奮迅 (SHISHI-FUNJIN) suggests the effort of one (like Master Obaku) who is more than up to the task in hand, but nonetheless devotes himself entirely to it. The words appear in Chap. 52 of the Chinese translation of the Mahā-prajña-parāmitā-sūtra, which uses the metaphor of a lion chasing small prey to explain the single-mindedness necessary to pursue the truth. The phrase 獅子奮迅 (SHISHI-FUNJIN) has remained a figure of speech used in modern Japanese; it means "like fury," or "with great power and speed."

48. 烏亀倒上樹 (UKI-TO-JOJU) suggests the effort of one (like Master Shoko) who is not up to the task in hand, but nonetheless devotes himself entirely to it. A related story appears in chap. 5 of a Chinese anthology called *Zen-rui (Zen Assortment)* and in *Zokuto-roku*, chap. 5: *[A monk] asks Zen Master Kyozan Unryo, "What is the meaning of Hyakujo rolling up his seat [to leave early] during Baso's formal preaching?" The Master says, "A mosquito climbing up the backside of an iron ox." [The monk] says, "What does that mean, in the end?" The Master says, "A black turtle climbing a tree upside down."*

49. Master Ho-un Ihaku, successor of Master Ho-un Hoshu. He completed the editing of the 30-chapter *Zokuto-roku* in 1101. Zen Master Bukkoku is his posthumous title.

that you have failed to investigate in experience. You should buy yourself new straw sandals, again and again, to search for a true teacher and receive the Dharma. You must not speak of succeeding Great Master Unmon. If you speak like that, you will just be a species of non-Buddhist. Even if Hyakujo himself were to speak as you have, it would be a great mistake.

[58]

坐禅儀

ZAZENGI

The Standard Method of Zazen

***Gi** means a form, or a standard of behavior. Therefore **Zazengi** means the standard method of Zazen. Master Dogen wrote several treatises about Zazen. First he wrote **Fukan-zazengi**, (The Universal Guide to the Standard Method of Zazen), in 1227, just after coming back from China. In Shobogenzo he wrote **Bendowa** (A Talk about Pursuing the Truth), **Zazenshin** (A Needle for Zazen), **Zanmai-o-zanmai** (The Samādhi That Is King of Samādhis), and this chapter, **Zazengi**. **Fukan-zazengi** was the first text Master Dogen wrote, and thus it was the first proclamation of his belief in Zazen. **Bendowa** was an introduction to Zazen written in an easy style and format to help us understand the fundamental theories of Zazen. **Zazenshin** contains a guiding poem on Zazen, and Master Dogen's interpretation of it. The reason Master Dogen used poetry to interpret the meaning of Zazen is that it is difficult to interpret the philosophical meaning of Zazen in prose, because the ultimate meaning of Zazen is something that cannot be explained with words. Master Dogen felt that it was appropriate to suggest the ultimate philosophical meaning of Zazen in poetry. But in this chapter, **Zazengi**, Master Dogen explained only the formal method of practicing Zazen. The existence of this chapter indicates how highly Master Dogen revered the formal standard of Zazen.*

] **To practice Zen is to sit in Zazen.**[1] For sitting in Zazen a quiet place is good. Prepare a thick sitting mat. Do not allow wind and smoke to enter. Do not allow rain and dew to leak in. Set aside an area that can contain the body. There are traces of those in the past who sat on a diamond [seat][2] or sat on a bed of rock;[3] they all were seated on a thick carpet of grass. The sitting place should be bright; it should not be dark, day or night. To be warm in winter

---

1. 参禅は坐禅なり (SAN ZEN *wa* ZAZEN *nari.*) 参 (SAN) lit. means visit, enter into, or participate in. 禅 (ZEN) represents the Sanskrit *dhyāna*, which means meditation, thought, reflection, or concentration—either the state or the practice thereof. 坐禅 (ZAZEN), "sitting dhyāna," means the concrete sitting practice itself.

2. The site of the Buddha's realization of the truth under the bodhi tree at present-day Bodh-Gayā.

3. Master Sekito Kisen, for example, built his hut on a large flat rock and sat in Zazen upon the rock.

and cool in summer is the way. Cast aside all involvements and cease the ten thousand things. Good is not considered. Bad is not considered. It is beyond mind, will, or consciousness, and beyond mindfulness, thought, or reflection. Do not try to become a buddha. Get free from sitting and lying down.[4] Take food and drink in moderation. Guard time closely. Love sitting in Zazen as if putting out a fire on your head. The Fifth Patriarch on Obai-zan mountain[5] had no other practices; he solely practiced Zazen.

[191] When sitting in Zazen, wear the kaṣaya and use a round cushion. The cushion does not support the whole of the crossed legs; it supports the backside. Thus the underside of the folded legs is on the mat, and the bases of the backbone[6] are on the cushion. This is the method of sitting used by the buddhas and the patriarchs when they sit in Zazen. Either sit in the half lotus posture or sit in the full lotus posture. To sit in the full lotus posture put the right foot on the left thigh and put the left foot on the right thigh. The toes of each foot should be symmetrically aligned with the thighs, not out of proportion. To sit in the half lotus posture just put the left foot on the right thigh. Let the robe and gown hang loosely and make them neat. Place the right hand on the left foot; then place the left hand on the right hand, with the tips of the thumbs resting against each other. Keeping the hands like this, draw them towards the body. Let the tips of the thumbs meet in line with the navel. Sit erect, letting the body be right. Do not lean to the left, incline to the right, slump forward, or arch backward. It is essential that the ears are aligned with the shoulders and the nose is aligned with the navel. Let the tongue spread against the roof of the mouth. Let the breath pass through the nose. Let the lips and the teeth each come together. And let the eyes be open; the eyes should be neither wide open nor half-closed. Having regulated the body-mind like this, let there be one complete exhalation. Sitting in balance in the mountain-still state, think the concrete state of not thinking. How can the state of not thinking be thought? It is non-thinking. This is the real secret of Zazen. Sitting in Zazen is not learning Zen meditation. It is the great peaceful and joyful gate of Dharma. It is untainted practice-and-experience.

---

4. 坐臥 (ZAGA), short for 行往坐臥 (GYO-O-ZAGA), "walking, standing, sitting, and lying down," the four kinds of daily activities.

5. Master Daiman Konin. See, for example, chap. 22, *Bussho*, and chap. 30, *Gyoji*.

6. 背骨のした (HAIKOTSU *no shita*). Anatomically speaking, this means the ischial tuberosities (the two knobbly protuberances at the bottom of the pelvis). These are the key weight-bearing points in sitting. If they are positioned optimally on the sitting cushion, then it is possible for the weight of the whole head, neck, and back to be effortlessly transmitted via the pelvis into the ground.

Shobogenzo Zazengi

Preached to the assembly at Kippo temple in the Yoshida district of Esshu,[7] in the 11th lunar month, in the winter of the 1st year of Kangen.[8]

7. Modern-day Fukui prefecture.
8. 1243.

[59]

梅華

BAIKE

Plum Blossoms[1]

Baike *means plum blossoms. Master Dogen loved plum blossoms very much and we can find many descriptions and poems about plum blossoms in his works. Master Tendo Nyojo, Master Dogen's master, also loved plum blossoms and so we can also find many poems about plum blossoms in his works. Plum blossoms may have been a great pleasure to Buddhist monks living in mountain temples when there were few consolations to relieve the hardship of winter—because plum blossoms bloom at the very beginning of spring, when there are no other flowers, and plum blossoms are both pretty and fragrant. In this chapter, Master Dogen described the real situation of nature, quoting Master Tendo Nyojo's poems and preachings on plum blossoms.*

5] **My late Master Tendo,** the eternal Buddha, is the thirtieth abbot and great master of Tendo Keitoku-ji temple on Daibyakumyo-zan mountain, in the great Sung district of Keigen-fu.[2] In formal preaching in the Dharma Hall he preaches to the assembly:

The first lines from Tendo this midwinter:[3]
Jagged and fanged[4] *is the old plum tree;*
Suddenly it flowers—one flower, two flowers,
Three, four, five flowers—countless flowers.
Its purity is not capable of pride.
Its fragrance is not capable of pride.

---

1. 梅華 (BAIKE). In Japan, the tree referred to as 梅 *(ume)* is accurately translated as a Japanese apricot *(Prunus mume)* in order to distinguish it from 李 *(sumomo)* which means plum, or Japanese plum. However, given that plum trees include numerous kinds of trees and shrubs of the genus *Prunus,* where no distinction is necessary 梅華 (BAIKE) has been translated as plum blossoms.

2. Present-day Ningpo in northern Chekiang province.

3. 天童仲冬第一句 (TENDO-CHUTO *[no]* DAI-IKKU). 天童 (TENDO) is the name both of Master Tendo Nyojo and of the temple. 仲冬 (CHUTO), "midwinter," means the middle of the three winter months, that is the 11th lunar month. 第一句 (DAI-IKKU), "first line(s) of verse" can be interpreted as a metaphor for the first branches of plum blossoms.

4. The branches and twigs of a plum (Japanese apricot) tree protrude at many irregular angles.

They spread out to create the look of spring and to
fan the grass and trees.

Patch-robed monks each with bald head.
Instantly changing are the raging wind and the hard rain,
While, wrapping the Earth in dragon-pattern robes,[5]
the snow is boundless.
The old plum tree is very unconstrained.
The freezing cold rubs the nostrils, and they sting.[6]

[197] *The old plum tree* that has been revealed now is very unconstrained; it suddenly flowers, and naturally bears fruit. Sometimes it makes the spring, and sometimes it makes the winter. Sometimes it makes a raging wind, and sometimes it makes a hard rain. Sometimes it is heads of patch-robed monks, and sometimes it is eyes of eternal buddhas. Sometimes it has become grass and trees, and sometimes it has become purity and fragrance.[7] Its instant mystical changes and mystical wonder are unfathomable: even the great Earth and the high heavens, the bright sun and the pure moon, have established their merits relying upon the tree-merits of the old plum tree, [whose state] is entanglement knotting and entwining with entanglement. When the old plum tree suddenly flowers, *"The opening of flowers is the occurrence of the world."*[8] A moment in which flowers opening is the occurrence of the world, is spring having arrived. At this moment *one flower* is present as *the opening of five petals.*[9] The Time of this one flower is able to include three flowers, four flowers, and five flowers; it includes hundreds of flowers, thousands of flowers, myriads of flowers, and koṭis of flowers; and it includes countless flowers. The opening of these flowers, in all cases, is the old plum tree's state of being unable to be proud of one twig, two twigs, or countless twigs. Uḍumbara flowers, Utpala[10] flowers, and so on, also are one twig or two twigs of flowers of the old plum tree. In sum, all cases of flowers opening are benevolent gifts of the old plum tree. The old plum tree is present in the

---

5. 袞 (KON) means the white ceremonial robes, gorgeously embroidered with dragon patterns, which were worn by ancient Chinese emperors.

6. *Nyojo-osho-goroku,* final volume.

7. In these sentences Master Dogen suggests that the plum tree is so conspicuously real in the scenery of nature that everything in nature depends upon it.

8. 華開世界起 (KE-KAI-SEKAI-KI), the words of Master Prajñātara, expressing the oneness of phenomena (flowers) and reality (the world).

9. Alludes to the words of Master Bodhidharma (quoted in full later in this chapter): *"I originally came to this land, / To transmit the Dharma and to save deluded emotional beings. / A flower is five petals opening, / The bearing of fruit is naturally realized."* See also chap. 43, *Kuge.*

10. *Uḍumbara* is the Sanskrit name for a fig tree of the mulberry family (see chap. 68, *Udonge*). *Utpala* is the Sanskrit name for the blue lotus flower. Uḍumbara and Utpala flowers are mentioned in the Lotus Sutra and other sutras, and as such they suggest flowers with special significance in Buddhism, not common or garden flowers.

human world and in the heavens above. It is in the reality of the old plum tree that the merits of human societies and of heavenly palaces are established. Flowers that number hundreds of thousands we call the flowers of human beings and gods. Flowers that number myriads of koṭis are the flowers of Buddhist patriarchs.[11] Such a moment we call *"the buddhas' appearance in the world,"*[12] and we call "the ancestral Master's *originally coming to this land."*

My late Master, the eternal Buddha, in formal preaching in the Dharma Hall preaches to the assembly:

> *It is the time when Gautama got rid of the Eye,*
> *In the snow, a single twig of plum blossoms*
> *Now every place has become a thorn*[13]
> *Yet [I] laugh at the swirling of the spring wind.*

Now that this eternal Buddha's Dharma-wheel has been turned in the farthest extremes of the Universe, it is the moment in which all human beings and gods attain the truth. Nothing is left uncovered by the benefit of [this] Dharma, which reaches even clouds, rain, wind, and water, and grass, trees, and insects. Turned by this Dharma-wheel, even the heavens, the earth, and national lands are the state of vigorous activity. "Hearing words never before heard" means listening to these words. "Attaining the unprecedented" means getting the present Dharma. It is a wheel of Dharma which, in general, cannot be seen or heard without dreamy good fortune. In and around the one hundred and eighty states of the great kingdom of Sung today there are mountain temples and village temples whose number is beyond calculation, and in which there are many monks. But most of them have never seen my late Master, the eternal Buddha; those who have seen him may be few. Those who have witnessed his words may be a still smaller minority. How then could the people who have met with him and saluted him be many? Those who have been allowed into his inner sanctum are not even a few. How much less could people be permitted to do prostrations to the late Master's skin, flesh, bones, marrow, eyes, and features? My late Master, the eternal Buddha, does not easily grant monks' requests to stay at the temple. He usually says, *"People who are accustomed to not having the will to the truth are not permitted in my place."* He sends them away at once. Having got rid of them he says, *"Without being a genuine person, what do they want to do? Dogs like that disturb others. They cannot stay."* I have actually witnessed this; I have heard it with my own ears. I secretly thought to myself: "What wrongness do they have not to be permitted to remain with us even though they are people of

11. To Buddhist patriarchs, reality displays limitless phenomena.

12. 諸仏出現於世 (SHOBUTSU-SHUTSUGEN-O-SE). This expression appears frequently in the Lotus Sutra. See, for example, LS 1.88–90.

13. 荊棘 (KEIKYOKU) means thorns, brambles, or "nettlesome circumstances." The harsh circumstances made Master Tendo worry about whether the plum flowers could survive.

this country? What luck do I have to be permitted not only to stay at the temple but also to come and go as I please in the [Master's] inner sanctum, to do prostrations to his venerable form, and to listen to his words of Dharma, though I am a native of a distant foreign country? This excellent connection which has formed between us, in spite of my dullness, cannot be pure imagination." While my late Master was spreading his influence through Sung China there were still people who were able to enter into [the truth] along with people who were unable to enter. Now that my late Master, the eternal Buddha, has departed Sung China, it may be darker than a moonless night. Why? I say so because at around the time of my late Master, the eternal Buddha, there were no other eternal Buddhas like my late Master, the eternal Buddha. That being so, in now aspiring to see and hear the foregoing [preaching], we students of a later age should be mindful. Do not imagine that human beings and gods in other directions might be able to see and to hear, or might be able to learn in practice, a wheel of Dharma like the present one.

[204] *Plum blossoms in the snow* are the one appearance of the uḍumbara flower.[14] How often does it recur in everyday life that, while looking at the right-Dharma-eye treasury of our Buddha-Tathāgata, we pass over the winking of an eye and do not break into a smile?[15] Yet just now we have received the authentic transmission of, and have been struck by, the realization that plum blossoms in the snow are the very Eye of the Tathāgata. Picking up this [realization], we make it into the eye on the forehead,[16] and we make it into the eyeballs in the eyes. Further, when we get inside plum blossoms themselves, and perfectly realize plum blossoms, doubtful causes or circumstances never appear at all. Just this is the eye of *"In the heavens above and under the heavens I alone am the Honored-One,"*[17] and it is honored throughout the reality of the Dharma-world. That being so, heavenly flowers in the heavens above, heavenly flowers in the human world, the mandārava flowers,[18]

14. 一現の曇華 (ICHIGEN *no* DONGE), "one appearance of the uḍumbara flower," or "the uḍumbara flower appearing in one moment," alludes, for example, to Lotus Sutra, *Hoben: "Wonderful Dharma like this the buddha-tathāgatas preach only occasionally, just as the uḍumbara flower appears only once in an age."* See LS 1.86–88.

15. Legend says that when the Buddha picked up an uḍumbara flower and winked an eye, Master Mahākāśyapa—seeing in these actions the essence of the Buddha's teaching (the right-Dharma-eye treasury)—broke into a smile. See, for example, chap. 68, *Udonge.*

16. The image of the Indian god Maheśvara, or Śiva, equipped with an intuitive third eye on the forehead, was sometimes used in Buddhism as a symbol of human intuition.

17. 天上天下唯我独尊 (TENJO-TENGE-YUI-GA-DOKU-SON). Legend says that when the Buddha was born, he took seven steps, and with one hand pointing to the heavens and the other pointing to the ground he said these words.

18. Flowers of the coral tree, mentioned for example in Lotus Sutra, *Nyorai-juryo: "This land of mine is tranquil / ...It is a place where living beings enjoy themselves. / The gods strike celestial*

mahā-mandārava flowers, mañjūṣaka flowers,[19] and mahā-mañjūṣaka flowers that rain from the heavens, together with the miscellaneous flowers of limitless lands in the ten directions, are all the dependents of plum blossoms in the snow; for they have bloomed by receiving a part of the benefit of plum blossoms. The hundreds of koṭis of flowers[20] are the dependents of plum blossoms; we should call them miniature plum blossoms. All other flowers, flowers in space, flowers on the ground, flowers in samādhi, and so on, are common flowers which are the large and small dependents of plum blossoms. Flowers that open in the lands which make up the hundreds of koṭis of lands inside a flower,[21] are all a portion of the benefit of these plum blossoms. Beyond the benefit apportioned by plum blossoms, there is no other raindrop or dewdrop of benefit at all; life-blood totally derives from plum blossoms. Do not learn that the place where *snow is boundless* is only the Shorin temple in the Suzan mountains:[22] *[snow is boundless]* is the Eye of the Tathāgata, it illuminates overhead and illuminates underfoot. Do not learn it as only the snow of a snow palace on a white mountain;[23] it is the Eye of the right-Dharma of the aged Gautama. The five eyes[24] are perfectly realized at this place. The thousand eyes[25] may be roundly realized in this Eye. Truly, there cannot be a single atom of *the real form of all dharmas* which the body-mind and the brightness of the aged Gautama do not perfectly realize. Though there are differences in the views of human beings and gods, and though the sentiments of the common and the sacred diverge, *the boundless expanse of snow* is *the Earth,* and *the Earth* is *the boundless expanse of snow.*[26]

---

drums, / And constantly make theater and music, / Showering mandārava flowers / On the Buddha and the great assembly." (LS 3.32.)

19. MW: *the name of a species of celestial flower.*

20. All phenomena in the world.

21. That countless worlds exist inside a flower is the characteristic teaching of the Avataṃsaka-sūtra, called in Chinese and Japanese 華厳経 (KEGON-KYO), lit. "Flower Adornment Sutra," and usually called in English "the Garland Sutra." The sutra emphasizes the interdependence of all things.

22. When Master Taiso Eka first visited Master Bodhidharma at the Shorin temple, *thenight snow fell as if without mercy, gradually piling up and burying him to his waist...* See chap. 30, *Gyoji,* para. [216].

23. 雪山雪宮 (SETSU-ZAN SETSU-GU), "snow-mountain, snow-palace," expresses an ideal place imagined by an immature viewpoint. Master Tendo's expression, in contrast, is an expression of what he actually realized.

24. 五眼 (GOGEN), the five eyes, or five intuitional states, are 1) the physical eye, 2) the supernatural eye, 3) the eye of wisdom, 4) the Dharma-eye, and 5) the Buddha-eye.

25. Suggests the thousand eyes of Bodhisattva Avalokiteśvara. See chap. 33, *Kannon.*

26. Master Tendo's poem says 乃至交袞大地雪漫漫 *(Naishi daichi ni ko-kon shi te yuki-man-man),* "...While, wrapping the Earth in dragon-pattern robes, the snow is boundless." Although Master Tendo thus describes 'the snow' as boundlessly covering 'the Earth,' the two elements 雪漫漫 (YUKI-MAN-MAN), "boundlessness of snow," and 大地 (DAICHI), "the Earth," are not separate.

Without *boundless expanses of snow*, there is no *Earth* in the Universe.[27] The getting together of the outside and the inside[28] of this *boundless expanse of snow* is just the Eye of Old Gautama. Remember, flowers and the ground are totally without appearance. Flowers are without appearance.[29] Because flowers are without appearance, the ground is without appearance. Because flowers and the ground are totally without appearance, the Eye is without appearance. The words "without appearance" express the supreme state of bodhi. What is seen just in the moment of this [supreme bodhi] is *a single twig of plum blossoms.* What is expressed just at this moment is *"In the snow, a single twig of plum blossoms!"* which is the vivid appearance[30] of ground and flowers. The reason this [scene] is described further as *"the boundless expanse of snow,"* is that its whole outside-and-inside is *the boundless expanse of snow.*[31] The whole Universe is the state of the mind, and the whole Universe is a scene of flowers.[32] Because the whole Universe is a scene of flowers, the whole Universe is plum blossoms. And because the whole Universe is plum blossoms, the whole Universe is Gautama's Eye. *The now, the place that has arrived*[33] is mountains, rivers, and the Earth. The present matter[34] and the present time[35] are the realization at the present place[36] of:

> *I originally came to this land,*
> *To transmit the Dharma and to save deluded emotional beings.*
> *A flower is five petals opening;*
> *The bearing of fruit is naturally realized.*[37]

---

27. Without manifestation of real phenomena, there could be no planet Earth.

28. 表裏 (HYO-RI), "outside and inside," means form and content.

29. 華無生 (KE-MUSHO), or "flowers are non-arising." 無生 (MUSHO) suggests 1) the instantaneousness of phenomena, and 2) the absence of illusory concepts such as "appearance" or "arising." In the latter meaning, 無生 (MUSHO) is sometimes used as a synonym for nirvāṇa (the state in which illusion has been extinguished). See also discussion of Master Taiso Eka's expression 華亦不曽生 (KE-MATA-FU-ZO-SHO), *"Flowers have never appeared"* in chap. 43, *Kuge,* para. [33].

30. 生生 (SHO-SHO), "appearance-appearance" or "life-life," is contrasted with 無生 (MUSHO).

31. Master Tendo's expression hit the target completely.

32. 華情 (KEJO). 情 (JO) means 1) feelings, emotion; 2) circumstances, conditions, scenery.

33. 而今の到処 (NIKON *no* TOJO). In Master Tendo's poem, 而今 (NIKON) is an adverb, "Now...," but here it is a noun, "the present" or "the now." 到処 (TO-JO, or *ita[ru] tokoro*), as a compound means "wherever one goes," that is, "everywhere," "every place." At the same time, 到 (TO, *ita[ru]*) means "to arrive " or "to have arrived" and 処 (JO, *tokoro*) means "place"; so 到処 (TO-JO) means 1) "every place," and 2) "the place which has arrived" or "the present place." The use of 到 (TO, *ita[ru]*) to indicate presence is also discussed in the notes to chap. 11, *Uji,* para. [44].

34. 到事 (TOJI), or "the matter which has arrived."

35. 到時 (TOJI), or "the time which has arrived."

36. 到処 (TOJO), or "the place which has arrived."

37. The words of Master Bodhidharma. See also chap. 43, *Kuge.*

Though there is coming from the west and there is movement to the east, they are the present place that is the now of plum blossoms. The state in which the realization of now is like this, is described as *realizing thorns.*[38] There is the now of old branches and new branches on big limbs, and there is the present place of old twigs and new twigs on small stems. We should learn *places* as *having arrived* and we should learn *having arrived* as *now.* The *inside*[39] of *three, four, five* and six flowers is the inside of *countless flowers.* A flower is equipped with inner virtues which are profound and universal, and it completely reveals outer virtues which are noble and great. This outside-and-inside[40] is the blooming of a flower. It is *a single twig,* and so there is no extraneous twig and no extraneous variety. He[41] who calls *the presence of one twig "the now"* is Old Man Gautama. Because [the transmission] is *a single twig,*[42] it is transmitted from rightful successor to rightful successor, and for this reason *"My existence*[43] *is the right-Dharma-eye treasury and its transmission to Mahākāśyapa,"* and *what you have got*[44] is *my marrow.*[45] Such realization of the present place is, wherever it occurs without exception, the great and valuable life, and therefore it is *five petals opening.* Five petals are a plum flower. On this basis,[46] the Seven Buddhist Patriarchs exist, and the twenty-eight patriarchs of India in the west, the six patriarchs[47] of the eastern lands, and nineteen[48] further patriarchs, exist. They are all five-petals opening on a single twig, and are a single twig of five-petals.[49] Having mastered *one twig,* and having mastered *five petals,* we meet the authentic transmission of *plum blossoms in the snow.* When we have transformed the body and transformed the mind inside the stream of the words *"a single twig,"* a cloud and the moon are

---

38. 成荊棘 (JO-KEIKYOKU). Read in the poem as *[to]na[ru],* 成 means "to become," but here, read as JO, 成 means "realization."

39. 裏 (RI, *ura*), lit. "backside," or "inside," here means the inner essence. Master Tendo's poem contains the phrase 雪裏 (SETSURI), "in the snow" or "inside the snow."

40. 表裏 (HYORI), oneness of outer form and inner essence.

41. Master Tendo.

42. The transmission is a single twig because transmitter, receiver, and that which is transmitted, are one. At the same time, the transmission is connected with individual concrete matters.

43. 吾有 (GO-U) means the Buddha himself. 吾 (GO) means "I" or "my," and 有 (U) means "possess" or "exist." The Buddha said, *"I possess the right-Dharma-eye treasury and the fine mind of nirvāṇa. I transmit them to Mahākāśyapa."* See, for example, para. [214], and the opening paragraph of chap. 57, *Menju.*

44. 汝得 (NYOTOKU) means what Master Taiso Eka got from Master Bodhidharma. See chap. 46, *Katto.*

45. 吾髄 (GOZUI) means Master Bodhidharma's marrow. Ibid.

46. On the basis of the oneness of the concrete individual many and the real inclusive whole.

47. From Master Bodhidharma to Master Daikan Eno.

48. From Master Daikan Eno to Master Dogen.

49. 五葉 (GOYO), "five-petals," means "flowers."

one, and the river-valley and the mountains are independent. Still, people who have never had eyes of learning in practice say: *The meaning of "five petals" is that the five patriarchs of the eastern lands, and the First Patriarch, make a flower. When we list those five generations they are beyond past and present, former and latter, and so we describe them as five petals.* These words are not even worth taking up to examine and defeat. Such people are not skin-bags who practice under buddhas and practice under patriarchs; they are pitiful. How could the truth that *five petals are a flower* be of only the five patriarchs? Are patriarchs after the Sixth Patriarch not to be mentioned? That is inferior to the talk of small children. We should not see or hear it, even in a dream.

[212] My late Master, the eternal Buddha, on the first morning of the year says in formal preaching in the Dharma Hall:

> *A New Year's morning is the start of happiness,*
> *The myriad things are totally fresh.*
> *With respect, monks of the assembly, [I say to you:]*
> *The plum tree reveals early spring.*[50]

Upon quiet reflection, even if the venerable old drills of the past, present, and future are liberated in body throughout the ten directions, if they do not have the expression *"The plum tree reveals early spring,"* who can call them individuals who have expressed the truth perfectly? My late Master, the eternal Buddha, stands alone as an eternal Buddha among eternal buddhas. His purport is that, embraced by the plum tree's blooming,[51] myriad springs have arrived early. Myriad springs are one or two of the virtues contained in a plum tree. Just one spring is able to make *the myriad things totally fresh,* and to make the myriad dharmas into *a New Year's morning. Starting of happiness* is rightness of the Eye. *"The myriad things"* expresses not only past, present, and future, but from before King Majestic Voice to the eternal future. He is saying that [this] immeasurable and infinite past, present, and future is totally fresh, and so this [real] freshness has got free of "freshness." On this basis, [Master Tendo speaks of] *treating the monks of the assembly with respect*—on the basis that his respectful treatment of the monks of the assembly is the state of the ineffable.

[214] My late Master Tendo, the eternal Buddha, says in formal preaching in the Dharma Hall:

---

50. In the lunar calendar, New Year's Day was the first day of spring; on that day the plum trees would already have been in bloom.

51. 開 (KAI, *hira[ku]*), means "to bloom," "to open," "to disclose" (see chap. 17, *Hokke-ten-hokke*), or "to reveal" (as in Master Tendo's poem).

If even a single word accords,[52]
The ten thousand ages do not move.[53]
Willow eyes are popping out on new twigs.
Plum blossoms are filling up old branches.[54]

That is to say, a hundred major kalpas of pursuing the truth[55] are—from beginning to end—*a single word according with [the Buddha's state].* And the effort[56] of one instant of consciousness is—both before and after—*the ten thousand ages not moving.* That which makes new twigs flourish and [willow] eyes pop out is the new twigs themselves, and at the same time it is the [willow] eyes themselves. The principle holds that [willow] eyes are nothing other [than willow eyes]; at the same time, we investigate them as the new twigs. We should learn *the new* in practice, as *the total freshness of the myriad things.* The meaning of *"Plum blossoms are filling up old branches"* is that plum blossoms are the whole of [each] old branch, that they thoroughly realize [each] old branch, and that [each] old branch is just plum blossoms—or, for example, that blossoms and branches have entered into practice together, that blossoms and branches have grown together, and that blossoms and branches have become full together.[57] Because blossoms and branches become full together, [the Buddha says:] *"I possess the right-Dharma-eye treasury and the fine mind of nirvāṇa, and I transmit them to Mahākāśyapa,"* [at which time] each face fills the picking up of a flower, and every flower fills the smiling face.

My late Master, the eternal Buddha, in formal preaching in the Dharma Hall says to all the monks of the assembly:

The willows[58] *are wearing belts;*[59]
The plum blossom is clad in bracers.[60]

---

52. 相契 (SOKAI, or *ai-kana[u]*), "mutually accord," means the accordance of a practitioner's state with the Buddha's state.

53. In other words, when a person manifests the Buddha's state in concrete form, even if the manifestation is only one word of speech, then eternity stands still.

54. The third and fourth line of the poem describe real facts in nature: willow buds grow on fresh green branches, whereas plum flowers grow on old brown or black branches.

55. 弁道 (BENDO).

56. 工夫 (KUFU). The words 弁道 (BENDO) and 工夫 (KUFU), which frequently appear together, both suggest the practice of Zazen.

57. "Together" is 同条 (DO-JO), lit. "the same twig." The point is that nothing is separate from anything else: the whole of the plum tree is contained in every part of the plum tree.

58. 楊柳 (YO-RYU). 楊 (YO) means purple willows and 柳 (RYU) means weeping willows.

59. The brown trunks of the willow trees showing between the green of the spring leaves and the green undergrowth looked like big leather belts.

60. Where the brown or black branches of the plum trees showed through the white or pink blossoms, they looked like bracers—i.e., the leather wrist or arm protectors worn by archers.

Those bracers are beyond Shoku brocade[61] and Benka's gem;[62] they are what the plum blossom reveals. What the plum blossom reveals is *I who am the marrow having got you.*[63]

[217] *King Prasenajit[64] invites the Venerable Piṇḍola[65] to a midday meal, upon which occasion the King asks, "I have heard that the Venerable One has intimately met Buddha. Is it true or not?" The Venerable One, lifting up an eyebrow with his hand, indicates affirmation.*

My late Master, the eternal Buddha, praises him as follows:

By lifting an eyebrow he answers the question in part.
He has met Buddha intimately, without any mutual deceit.
To this day he deserves offerings from the four quarters.
Spring is on the plum twigs, embraced by the coldness of the snow.[66]

[219] This is the story of King Prasenajit asking the Venerable One if he has met Buddha or not met Buddha. *"Meeting Buddha"* means becoming Buddha. To become Buddha means to lift an eyebrow. If the Venerable One had only experienced "the effect of arhathood,"[67] without being *a true arhat,*[68] he could not meet Buddha. Without meeting Buddha, he could not become Buddha. Without becoming Buddha, he might be unable to attain the state of Buddha which is the lifting of an eyebrow. So remember, as a disciple of Śākyamuni Buddha's face-to-face transmission, as one who, having already experienced the fourth effect, is awaiting his manifestation in the world as a later buddha, how could the Venerable One not be meeting Śākyamuni Buddha? This meeting Śākyamuni Buddha is not meeting with a buddha: we have learned

61. 蜀錦 (SHOKU-KIN). 蜀 (SHOKU) means Sichuan province which was famous for its gorgeous brocade. 蜀錦 (SHOKU-KIN), Shoku brocade, therefore, symbolizes something very desirable. 望蜀 (BO-SHOKU), lit. "desire for Shoku," means insatiable desire.

62. A huge gem found in ancient China during the Chou dynasty (1122 to 255 B.C.) by a man called Benka. Also mentioned in chap. 12, *Kesa-kudoku,* para. [127].

63. 髄吾得汝 (ZUI-GO-TOKU-NYO). These are Master Bodhidharma's words to Master Taiso Eka 汝得吾髄 (NYO-TOKU-GO-ZUI), *"You have got my marrow,"* in reverse order. They represent the unity of subject-object and object-subject in the transmission. See chap. 46, *Katto.*

64. King Prasenajit (Pali: Pasenadi), the ruler of the kingdom of Kośala, was a lay follower of the Buddha. He is described many times in the Pali Canon as a jovial character fond of rich living but at the same time a staunch supporter of the Saṃgha.

65. The monk Piṇḍola is remembered as one of the 16 arhats in the Buddha's order. His father, Bhāradvāja, was a Brahmin in the court of King Udayana of Kauśāmbī. King Udayana himself was not so sympathetic towards Buddhism; after his wives had gone to hear Piṇḍola preaching the Dharma while the King was asleep, Udayana reportedly threatened to have Piṇḍola thrown into a nest of red ants.

66. The story and Master Tendo's verse of praise are also quoted in chap. 61, *Kenbutsu.*

67. 阿羅漢果 (ARAKAN-KA) means the fourth stage of a śrāvaka, one who pursues the truth through intellectual study. See chap. 34, *Arakan.*

68. 真阿羅漢 (SHIN *[no]* ARAKAN) means a buddha. The phrase, which appears in Lotus Sutra, *Shinge* (LS 1.260), is also quoted in Shobogenzo, chap. 34, *Arakan.*

in practice that the state in which we meet Śākyamuni Buddha as Śākyamuni Buddha, is meeting Buddha.[69] King Prasenajit, having been able to open these eyes of learning in practice, encounters a skilled hand[70] lifting an eyebrow. [To grasp] the point of the words *"He has met Buddha intimately,"* we should quietly possess eyes that experience Buddha. This *Spring* is beyond the human world and it is not confined to the Buddha-land; it is *on the plum twigs*. How do we know that it is so? *The coldness of the snow* is the lifting of an eyebrow.[71]

1] My late Master, the eternal Buddha, says:

> *The original features are without life and death.*
> *Spring is in the plum blossoms, and has entered a picture.*

In picturing Spring we should not picture willows, apricot trees, peach trees, and plum trees; we should just picture Spring.[72] To picture willows, apricot trees, peach trees, and plum trees is to picture willows, apricot trees, peach trees, and plum trees; it is never to have pictured Spring. It is not true that Spring should not be pictured. Nevertheless, besides my late Master, the eternal Buddha, there is no-one, from India in the west to China in the east, who has pictured Spring. My late Master, the eternal Buddha, is the only sharp brush-tip to picture Spring. The Spring he is describing now is Spring as a picture, and, because it has entered a picture, he need not summon any extra effort. He has let plum blossoms enter a picture and let them enter trees only so that they may usher in Spring; it is a skillful means.[73] My late Master, the eternal Buddha, by virtue of his clarity in the right-Dharma-eye treasury, realizes the authentic transmission of this right-Dharma-eye treasury through Buddhist patriarchs assembled in the ten directions in the past, present, and future. Thus he has penetrated the Eye and has clarified plum blossoms.

---

69. 見仏 (KENBUTSU), "meeting Buddha," means realizing the state of Buddha as it is; it does not mean only seeing a buddha with the senses. See chap. 61, *Kenbutsu*.

70. 好手 (KOSHU), a good hand, a nice hand, or a fine hand, means a person who has practical ability.

71. The coldness of snow is reality—in the coldness of snow, we can experience the reality that the Master suggested by lifting an eyebrow.

72. We should realize Spring as an inclusive reality.

73. 善巧方便 (ZEN GYO-HOBEN), from the Sanskrit *upāya-kauśalya*. The use of words and imagery as a skillful means to lead us to the realization of reality which is beyond words and imagery, is explained by the Buddha in the Lotus Sutra. See, for example, LS 1.120; LS 3.16.

Shobogenzo Baike

On the 6th day of the 11th lunar month in the 4th year of the Japanese era of Ninji,[74] at Kitsu-rei-ji[75] temple in the Yoshida district of Esshu, deep snow, three-feet thick, covers the Earth in a boundless expanse.

[223] If by chance some demon of the self appears and the plum blossom seem not to be the Eye of Gautama, then think: what other dharma—perhaps having been cited as more apt than plum blossoms to be the Eye—could be seen as the Eye? And if at such a time we look for the Eye elsewhere, then every moment will be in the state of *being face-to-face without recognizing each other*—because mutual encounter[76] will not yet be realized. Today is not my today; it is the today of a great master. Simply let the Eye of the plum blossoms be clear. Stop searching for anything further.

[224] My late Master, the eternal Buddha, says:

It is patently clear.
Stop searching back and forth for something behind
the semblance of the plum blossom.
In the becoming of rain and the becoming of clouds
the past-and-present is naturally there.
The past-and-present being empty, what end-point could there be?

Thus, the becoming of clouds and the becoming of rain is the speaking and doing of the plum blossom. Floating clouds and falling rain are the plum blossom's thousands of twists and turns and myriad layers of color, its thousands of merits and myriad virtues. *The past-and-present being naturally there* is the plum blossom; the plum blossom is called *the past-and-present*.[77]

[225] In the past, Zen Master Ho-en[78] says:

The north wind mixes with snow and shakes the valley forest.
Though the myriad things have sunk under cover,
regret is not deep.

---

74. 1243.

75. 吉嶺寺 (KITSUREI-JI). 吉嶺 (KITSUREI) is almost certainly another name for 吉峰 (KIPPO), the temple in Esshu (modern-day Fukui prefecture) where Master Dogen preached the several chapters preceding this chapter. 嶺 (REI) and 峰 (HO, PO) both mean mountain peak.

76. 相逢 (SOHO), "mutual encounter," means getting rid of the illusion of separation of subject and object.

77. 古今 (KOKON), "past-present," means eternity.

78. Master Goso Ho-en (1024?–1104), successor of Master Haku-un Shutan.

The only presence is the mountain plum trees,
which are full of spirit.
Before December they are already spewing the mind for all the
coldness of the year.[79]

Now, without penetrating the concrete situation of plum blossoms it is hard to know the mind [that is ready] for all the coldness of the year. A bit of the virtue of the plum blossoms, mixed with the north wind, has become the snow. Clearly, that which draws the wind, makes the snow, brings order to the year, and causes the myriad things of the valley forest to exist, is totally the power of the plum blossoms.

[26] The veteran monk Taigen Fu[80] praised the realization of the truth as follows:

I remember at the beginning, before realization,
Each call of the painted long horn was a call of sorrow.
Now there are no idle dreams on my pillow.
I leave the plum blossoms to blow, in gusts large and small.

Veteran monk Fu was formerly a giver of lectures. Enlightened by the cook[81] of Kassan mountain,[82] he realized the great state of realization, which is the plum blossoms letting the spring wind blow, in gusts large and small.

---

79. Quoted from chap. 30 of *Zokuto-roku.*

80. Ācārya Taigen Fu (dates unknown), a successor of Master Seppo Gison (822–907). He traveled through many districts of China, not becoming the master of a temple.

81. 典座 (TENZO), the head cook, was one of the six main officers of a big temple. Master Dogen showed the importance he attached to this job by writing his own *Tenzo-kyokun (Instructions for the Cook).* The name of the cook referred to here has not been traced.

82. A temple was founded on Kassan mountain in 870 by Master Kassan Zen-e, a disciple of Master Sensu Tokujo.

[60]

十方

JUPPO

The Ten Directions

***Ju** means "ten" and **ho** means "direction," so **Juppo** means "the ten directions." The ten directions are east, west, south, north, northeast, southeast, southwest, northwest, and upward and downward. These represent all directions, the whole of space, or the whole world. In Buddhist philosophy the meaning of space is frequently discussed. In these discussions, the word **juppo**, "the ten directions," is often used as a concrete expression of space. In this chapter, Master Dogen picks up the word **juppo**, and uses it to discuss real space.*

A fist is just the concrete ten directions.[1] A moment of sincerity[2] is the brilliant ten directions. [With these words] the marrow has been struck out of the bones.

Śākyamuni Buddha tells a great assembly, *"In the Buddha-lands of the ten directions, there only exists the one-vehicle Dharma."*[3]

These *ten directions* have grasped *Buddha-lands* and made them into the concrete. Thus, unless we bring the Buddha-lands here, the ten directions never exist. Because they are the Buddha-lands, we see the Buddha as the ruler. This sahā-realm, it seems, is the Buddha-land of Śākyamuni. Taking up this sahā-world, and clearly noting that eight ounces is half a pound, we should learn in practice that the buddha-lands of the ten directions are of seven feet or of eight feet. These ten directions fit into a single direction and fit into a single buddha, and for this reason they have manifested the ten directions. Because they are the ten directions, one direction, this direction, [my] own direction, and the present direction, they are the direction of the eyes, the direction of a fist, the direction of an outdoor pillar, and the direction of a stone lantern. The buddhas of the ten directions in such buddha-lands of the ten directions never retain "great" and "small," or "pure" and "impure." For this reason, the *buddhas alone together with buddhas* of the ten

1. 十方 (JUPPO), from the Sanskrit *dāśa-diś*. Both the Sanskrit *diś* and the Chinese character 方 (HO) mean not only a direction but also a quarter, region, or district.

2. 赤心 (SEKISHIN), lit. "red mind," means naked mind or sincere mind.

3. Lotus Sutra, *Hoben*. See LS 1.106.

directions praise and admire each other. They never see maligning each other and discussing each others' relative merits or likes and dislikes as the turning of the Dharma wheel or as the preaching of Dharma. As buddhas and as the Buddha's disciples, they promote and salute [each other].[4] In receiving the Dharma of the Buddhist patriarchs, we learn under them like this, not criticizing each other as right and wrong and slandering and shaming each other, as if we were non-Buddhists or demons. When we open and peruse the Buddhist sutras that have now been transmitted to China, and glimpse the totality of the [Buddha's] lifetime of teaching, Śākyamuni Buddha never says that buddhas of other directions are inferior, never says that buddhas of other directions are superior, and never says that buddhas of other directions are not buddhas. In sum, what we can never find in [Śākyamuni Buddha's] lifelong preaching are words of the Buddha that criticize other buddhas. Words of buddhas of other directions that criticize Śākyamuni Buddha, similarly, have never been reported.

[7] Thus...

Śākyamuni Buddha tells a great assembly, *"I alone know concrete form, and the buddhas of the ten directions are also like that."*[5]

Remember, the *form* of *"I alone know concrete form"* is the enaction of round form.[6] Round form is *this bamboo being as long as this, and that bamboo being as short as that.*[7] The truth of the buddhas of the ten directions is the preaching that *"I alone know concrete form, and Śākyamuni Buddha is also like that."* It is *"I alone experience concrete form, and the buddhas of this direction*[8] *are also like that."* It is the form of *I*, the form of *knowing*, the form of *the concrete*, the form of *all*, the form of *the ten directions*, the form of the sahā-realm, and the form of Śākyamuni Buddha. This principle is the Buddhist sutras. Buddhas and their lands are beyond duality, they are beyond the sentient and beyond the insentient, they are beyond delusion and realization, they are beyond good, bad, and indifferent, they are beyond purity and beyond impurity, they are beyond creation, beyond existence, beyond destruction, and beyond empti-

---

4. 問訊 (MONJIN), lit. "to ask [how someone is]," in practice means to bow, either with the palms of the hands together (*gassho-monjin*), or with the left hand curled round the thumb and the right hand covering the back of the left hand (*shasshu-monjin*). See also chap. 55, *Darani.*

5. Lotus Sutra, *Hoben.* See LS 1.74.

6. 打円相 (TA-ENSO). In a verse quoted in chap. 22, *Bussho,* Master Nāgārjuna preaches that his body manifests 円月相 (EN-GETSU-SO), "the roundness of the moon." Here, as in that chapter, 円 (EN), "round," means not only circular but real.

7. Words of Master Suibi Mugaku. See *Shinji-shobogenzo,* pt. 1, no. 71.

8. 自方 (JIHO) means "the direction of [my]self"; that is, "this direction," or "this concrete place."

ness,[9] they are beyond constancy and beyond non-constancy, they are beyond existence and beyond non-existence, they are beyond self and beyond others; they have left behind the four lines[10] and transcended the hundred negations. They are nothing other than the ten directions and nothing other than the Buddha-lands. In sum, the ten directions are just folk who have heads and do not have tails.

Zen Master Chosa Keishin[11] addresses the assembly: *"The whole Universe in the ten directions is a śramaṇa's[12] eye."*[13]

What has been described now is one eye of the śramaṇa Gautama. The eye of the śramaṇa Gautama is *"I possess the right-Dharma-eye treasury."* It belongs to anyone,[14] and at the same time it is the eye of the śramaṇa Gautama. The whole Universe in the ten directions in its ragged and jagged state is Gautama's eye-organ. This *whole Universe in the ten directions* is one among a śramaṇa's eyes. And going up beyond this, there are *limitlessly abundant eyes.*[15]

"The whole Universe in the ten directions is a śramaṇa's everyday speech."

"Everyday"[16] means "ordinary" or, in colloquial Japanese, *"yonotsune."* So the ordinary speech of a śramaṇa's everyday life is the whole Universe in the ten directions; it is correctness in word and correctness in speech. We should clearly learn in practice the truth that because everyday speech is the whole

---

9. 成、住、壊、空 (JO, JU, E, KU), "creation, existence, destruction, emptiness," allude to the idea that there are four kalpas (of creation, existence, destruction, emptiness) between the establishment of one world and the establishment of the next world.

10. 四句 (SHIKU). Alludes to the philosophical system called 四句分別 (SHIKU-FUNBETSU), or "four-line discrimination." 1) 有 (U), "existence," "being," or "having," and 2) 無 (MU), "non-existence," "absence," or "being without," suggest two opposing approaches to describing reality—affirmative and negative. 3) 亦有亦無 (YAKU-U YAKU-MU), "both existence and non-existence," suggests concrete reality as inclusive of two sides. 4) 非有非無 (HI-U HI-MU), "neither existence nor non-existence," suggests reality as beyond affirmation and negation.

11. Master Chosa Keishin (died 868), successor of Master Nansen Fugan.

12. The Sanskrit *śramaṇa* (lit. "striver") originally described a wandering mendicant who was not of the Brahmin caste—as distinct from a *pārivrājaka* (lit. "wanderer"), a wandering mendicant of Brahmin origin. The Buddha applied the term *śramaṇa* to Buddhist monks. So *śramaṇa* means 1) a diligent practitioner, and 2) a monk.

13. This and the following quotations of Master Chosa's words appear together in *Keitoku-dento-roku*, chap. 10. See also chap. 36, *Komyo.*

14. 阿誰に付属す (ASUI *ni* FUSHOKU *su*). The Buddha said, *"I possess the right-Dharma-eye treasury and the fine mind of nirvāṇa. I transmit them to Mahākāśyapa"* (see chap. 68, *Udonge*). Here Master Dogen substituted 阿誰 (ASUI), "anyone," for *"Mahākāśyapa."* 阿誰 (ASUI) means 1) "who?" or "anyone," and 2) a person in the state that cannot be expressed with words. 付属 (FUSHOKU, or FUZOKU) here means "belong," but in the Buddha's words means "transmit."

15. 如許多眼 (NYOKYO-TA-GEN). See chap. 33, *Kannon.*

16. 家常 (KAJO) means, as an adjective, "everyday," and as a noun, "everyday life," or "the usual state." See chap. 64, *Kajo.*

Universe in the ten directions, the whole Universe in the ten directions is everyday speech. This *ten directions*, because it is without *limit*,[17] is [called] *the whole*[18] *ten directions*.[19] In everyday life we use this speech. It is as in the case of seeking a horse, seeking salt, seeking water, and seeking a pot, and as in the case of serving water, serving a pot, serving salt, and serving a horse.[20] Does anyone know that a great person who is free of thought transforms the body and transforms the brain within the stream of this speech, and transforms [even] speech in mid-speech. The correctness in word and straightness in speech of the ocean's mouth and the mountains' tongue is *everyday*. Thus, even if we cover our mouth and cover our ears, the ten directions are this real existence.

[13] *"The whole Universe in the ten directions is a śramaṇa's whole body."*

With one hand indicating the heavens as the heavens and with the other hand indicating the earth as the earth, [the Buddha says that,] although they are real as they are, "In the heavens and under the heavens, I alone am the Honored-One":[21] this state is the whole Universe in the ten directions as the śramana's whole body. Brain, eyes, and nostrils, skin, flesh, bones, and marrow: each is totally the śramaṇa's body as clarification and liberation of the whole ten directions. Without our moving the whole ten directions, it exists like this. Not depending upon intellectual thinking, but by mustering the śramaṇa's body which is the whole Universe in the ten directions, we realize the śramaṇa's body which is the whole Universe in the ten directions.

[14] *"The whole Universe in the ten directions is the brightness of the self."*[22]

"The self" means the nostrils that are prior to the birth of one's parents. And the condition in which the nostrils happen to be present in the hands of the self is called *"the whole Universe in the ten directions."* In that condition the self is realized and it realizes reality; it opens the Hall and meets Buddha. At

---

17. 尽 (JIN) here means "limit."

18. 尽 (JIN) here means "to the limit" or "whole."

19. The full sentence is: この十方、無尽なるがゆえに、尽十方なり (*Kono*JUPPO, MUJIN *naru ga yue ni*, JINJUPPO *nari*). 無尽 (MUJIN) means "without limit," and 尽十方 (JINJUPPO) means "the ten directions to the limit," i.e. "the whole of the ten directions." Ironically, therefore, this sentence says that because the ten directions are without 尽 (JIN=limit), they are 尽 (JIN=whole).

20. The word *saindhava*, or "product of the Indus river basin" is ambiguous, or inclusive, but a wise retainer knows from the real situation whether a king who requests saindhava wants a horse, salt, water, or a pot. See chap. 81, *O-saku-sendaba*.

21. Alludes to the legend that after his birth the Buddha took seven steps in each of the four directions and, pointing to the sky with one hand and pointing to the ground with the other, he said *"In the heavens and under the heavens, I alone am the Honored-One."* Source not traced. See also chap. 50, *Shoho-jisso*.

22. 自己の光明 (JIKO *no* KOMYO) means "the brightness of the self," or "my own brightness.

the same time, it is *someone having replaced the eyes with black beads.*[23] But there again, *when the face has split we may be able to meet with great masters.*[24] Moving on further, *to call someone to us is easy but to send them away is difficult.* Conversely, *when we get called we turn the head. What is the use of turning the head by oneself? In fact, I turn my head adhering to this concrete person.*[25] And *while a meal is waiting for someone to eat it and a robe is waiting for someone to wear it*—even if you seem to be groping in vain[26]—*I am afraid that I am already going to give you thirty strokes.*

6] *"The whole Universe in the ten directions exists inside the brightness of the self."*

An eyelid is called *"the brightness of self."* And its sudden opening is called *"existence inside."*[27] That which exists in eyes as a result of looking is called *"the whole Universe in the ten directions."* And though it is like this, *when we sleep on the same floor we know the holes in [each other's] covers.*[28]

7] *"In the whole Universe in the ten directions there is no-one who is not himself."*

So among individual excellent instructors and individual concrete fists, there is no instance of a *ten directions* who is not him or her self. Because of being itself, each individual self is totally the ten directions. The ten directions of each individual self directly restrict the ten directions. Because the lifeblood of each individual self is present in the hands of each individual, each returns to others the original cost of straw sandals.[29] How can it be that Bodhidharma's eyes and Gautama's nostrils are now newly conceived in the wombs of outdoor pillars? Because getting out and getting in are left utterly to the ten directions and ten aspects.

9] Great Master Shu-itsu[30] of Gensa-in temple says, *"The whole Universe in*

---

23. Having black beads for eyeballs means not being over-excited. The same expression is quoted in chap. 28, *Butsu-kojo-no-ji*, para. [65], but the original source has not been traced.

24. 劈面来大家相見 (HEKI-MEN-RAI-TAIKE-SOKEN), "the face having split, meeting with great masters," suggests the appearance of a new face, habitual imbalances having been transcended, and concrete entry into the real world of buddhas—which is not necessarily dependent on the opening of a Buddha Hall. The expression is in the style of a sentence written in Chinese (and has therefore been italicized), but a Chinese source has not been traced. The same applies to the expressions italicized in the remainder of the paragraph.

25. 著者漢廻頭 (*ko[no] kan [ni] tsui[te] ezu [suru]*), or "I turn my head adhering to this fellow," means "I turn my head by myself."

26. 模索不著 (MOSAKU-FUJAKU), lit. "groping without touching," suggests innocence, or immature effort.

27. 在裏 (ZAIRI), taken from Master Chosa's words, suggests concrete existence.

28. The four sentences of the paragraph exemplify the progress of Master Dogen's thoughts through the four philosophies of subject, object, synthesis in action, and ordinary reality.

29. To repay the cost of one's straw sandals means to have earned one's keep, to be worth one's salt. See also chap. 22, *Bussho*, para. [73].

30. Master Gensa Shibi (835–907). Great Master Shu-itsu is his posthumous title.

the ten directions is one bright pearl."[31]

Clearly, the one bright pearl is the whole Universe in the ten directions. Those with heads of gods or faces of demons have seen it as their cave, descendants of the Buddhist Patriarch have seen it as the Eye, men and women of human families have seen it as brains and fists, and beginners and late learners have seen it as wearing robes and eating meals. My late Master made it into a mud-ball with which to strike brothers senior and junior. Furthermore, although this was plain and simple placement of a piece,[32] it had scooped out the eyes of the ancestors. During the scooping, ancestors each lent a hand, and the insides of their eyes radiated light.

[20] *Master Kenpo,*[33] *the story goes, is asked by a monk, "'The bhagavats of the ten directions are on one road to nirvāṇa's gate.' I wonder where they are on the street." Kenpo draws a circle*[34] *with his staff and says, "They are right here."*[35]

"Being right here" is the ten directions. *"The bhagavats"* are a staff. *"A staff"* is being right here. *"One road"* is the ten directions. But[36] do not let a staff get lost inside "Gautama's nostrils," and do not let a staff get lost in "the nostrils of a staff": do not batter a staff into "the nostrils of a staff." And at the same time do not recognize that Old Man Kenpo has meditated on the bhagavats of the ten directions being on one road to nirvāṇa's gate": he only speaks of being right here. Being right here is not to be denied, and if Old Man Kenpo is, from the outset, not deluded by his staff, that is good. In sum we just learn in practice, as the ten directions, nostrils that are alive.

Shobogenzo Juppo

Preached to the assembly at Kippo temple in Esshu,[37] Japan, on the 13th day of the 11th lunar month in the 1st year of Kangen.[38]

---

31. *Keitoku-dento-roku,* chap. 18, and *Shinji-shobogenzo,* pt. 1, no. 15. See also Shobogenzo, chap. 4, *Ikka-no-myoju.*

32. 一著子 (ICHIJAKUSU) means one stone placed on a *go* board.

33. Master Esshu Kenpo (dates unknown), successor of Master Tozan Ryokai.

34. 画一画 (IKKAKU *[o] kaku [su]*), lit. "draw a drawing," in context suggests that the Master etched a circle in the ground with his staff, and said that the bhagavats of the ten directions existed inside the circle.

35. *Goto-egen,* chap. 13. See also *Shinji-shobogenzo,* pt. 1, no. 37.

36. The previous sentence has considered the meaning of concepts in the story. This sentence affirms the concrete existence of a staff.

37. Corresponds to present-day Fukui prefecture.

38. 1243.

[61]

見仏

KENBUTSU

Meeting Buddha

__Ken__ means "look at," "meet," or "realize the state of," and __butsu__ means "Buddha" or "buddhas." Therefore __kenbutsu__ means "meeting Buddha" or "meeting buddhas." In order to meet buddhas it is necessary first to become buddha, because buddhas can be seen only by buddhas. In this chapter, Master Dogen explained the real situation of meeting buddhas and the true meaning of meeting buddhas.

[3] **Śākyamuni Buddha addresses a great assembly:** *"If we see [both] the many forms and [their] non-form, we at once meet the Tathāgata.*[1]

To see the many forms and *to see [their] non-form*, as described now, is a liberated bodily experience, and so it is *to meet the Tathāgata.* Realization in which this Eye of meeting the Buddha is already open in experience is called *"meeting buddha."*[2] The vigorous way [called] *the Eye of meeting the Buddha* is eyes partaking in buddha. When we see in others our own buddha, and when we see our own buddha outside of buddhas,[3] although all things are a tangle, to have learned *meeting buddha* in practice, to be pursuing and realizing *meeting buddha*, to be getting free of *meeting buddha*, to be attaining the vivid state of *meeting buddha*, and to be utilizing *meeting buddha*, are the real manifestation of sun-faced-buddhas[4] and the real manifestation of moon-faced-buddhas. Meeting buddha like this, in each case, is meeting buddha

---

1. Quoted from *The Diamond Sutra (Kongo-hannya-haramitsu-kyo)*. 諸相 (SHOSO), "the many forms," means that which can be perceived by the senses. 非相 (HISO), "non-form," means that which cannot be perceived by the senses, i.e. meaning, essence, value.

2. 見仏 (KENBUTSU), lit. "seeing Buddha," means realization of the whole reality of the state of action which is called "buddha." It does not describe seeing the Buddha's form. 見 (KEN) has been translated as "see," "meet," "real manifestation," "view," and "realization," depending on the context.

3. An example might be leaving a Buddhist temple and receiving very helpful service from a lay person doing his or her daily job.

4. 日面仏見 (JITSU-MEN-BUTSU-KEN). When Master Baso Do-itsu was unwell a monk asked him how he was. The Master replied *"Sun-faced buddhas, moon-faced buddhas."* The story is quoted in *Eihei-koroku*, vol. 9, no. 80.

whose faces are limitless, whose body is limitless, whose mind is limitless, and whose hands and eyes are limitless. The effort in pursuit of the truth, and mastery of experience of the [Buddha's] state, which we are performing to the tips of the toes in the present and which we have continued since establishing the mind and taking the first step: all are vivid eyes and vivid bones and marrow running inside meeting buddha. This being so, the whole world of the self and all words in other directions, this individual and that individual, are all equally the effort of meeting buddha. When people without eyes of learning in practice take up the Tathāgata's words *"If we see the many forms [and] non-form..."* they think, "To see the many forms as non-form is just to see the Tathāgata." In other words, they think the words describe seeing the many forms not as forms but as the Tathāgata. Truly, a faction of small thinkers will [inevitably] study the words like that, but the reality of the words which the Buddha intended is not like that. Remember, to see the many forms, and to see [their] non-form, is to meet the Tathāgata at once. There is the Tathāgata and there is the non-Tathāgata.[5]

[26] Zen Master Dai Hogen[6] of Seiryo-in temple says, *"If we see the many forms [as] non-form, we are not then meeting the Tathāgata."*[7]

This expression of Dai Hogen now is an expression in the state of meeting buddha. In it, there is the expression of Hogen, and there is the expression of meeting buddha: conversing, they come head-to-head in competition and they extend hands in cooperation. We should listen to Hogen's expression with the ears, and we should listen to the expression of meeting buddha with the eyes. At the same time, [students] in the past who have learned this principle in practice have thought as follows: "The many forms are the form of the Tathāgata, and there is no instance of them having mingled with a form that is not the form of the Tathāgata. We should never see this concrete form as non-form. To see it as non-form is *leaving the father and running away.*[8]" They have asserted that, "Because this concrete form is just the form of the Tathāgata, we say that the many forms should be the many forms." This is truly a supreme discourse of the Great Vehicle, and the experience of the masters of many districts. Decisively determining it to be so, we should believe it and experience it. Do not be fluff following the wind to the east and to the west. *The many forms are the form of the Tathāgata, not non-form:* investi-

---

5. In other words, even the Buddha has both form and non-form.

6. Master Hogen Bun-eki (885–958), successor of Master Rakan Keichin. Dai Hogen Zenji (or "Zen Master Great Hogen") is his posthumous title.

7. *Wanshi-koroku*, chap. 3. In both the Buddha's words and Master Hogen's words, the characters of the first clause are exactly the same: 若見諸相非相, but in the first case they are read *"Mo[shi] shoso [to] hi-so [to o] mi[re ba]..."* and in the second case they are read *"Mo[shi] shoso [wa] hi-so [nari to] mi[re ba]"*

8. 捨父逃逝 (SHA-FU TOZEI). Alludes to Lotus Sutra, *Shinge*. See LS 1.224.

gating this and meeting buddha, deciding this and experiencing conviction, we should receive it and retain it, and we should recite it and become thoroughly versed in it. In so doing, we should make it seen and heard ceaselessly through our own ears and eyes, we should get free of it through our own body, mind, bones, and marrow, and we should make it clear through our own mountains, rivers, and Universe. Such is the action of learning the state of Buddhist patriarchs. Do not think that, because it is your own speech and conduct, it cannot make your own eyes clear. Being transformed by our own words of transformation,[9] we get free of the view of our own transformation into a Buddhist patriarch. This is the everyday state of Buddhist patriarchs. Therefore, there is only one way to comprehend the state in experience, namely: *the many forms are already beyond non-form, and non-form is just the many forms.* Because non-form is the many forms, non-form is truly non-form. We should learn in practice that the form called *"non-form"* and the form called *"the many forms,"* are both the form of the Tathāgata.[10] In the house of learning in practice, there are two kinds of texts: sutras that are seen, and sutras that are not seen. This is what eyes in the vivid state learn in practice. If we have never experienced the ultimate state of putting on the eyes and looking at these texts, [our eyes] are not eyes that experience the ultimate. If [the eyes] are not eyes that experience the ultimate, [the state] is not meeting buddha. In meeting buddha there are the many forms which are seen and non-form which is seen; the state is *"I do not understand the Buddha-Dharma."*[11] In not meeting buddha there are the many forms which are not seen and non-form which is not seen; which state *"People who understand the Buddha-Dharma have attained."* Hogen's expression, which is *eighty or ninety percent of realization,* is like this. At the same time, in regard to this *one great cause,*[12] we should say further, *"If we see the many forms as real form, we at once meet the*

---

9. 一転語 (ICHITENGO), or "a turning word." 一 (ICHI) means "one" or "the whole." 転 (TEN) means 1) "turn" as in 転機 (TENKI), "turning point," and 2) "move" or "change" as in 転身 (TENSHIN), "moving oneself (from A to B)" or "transforming one's body" (see also note 18 in chap. 62, *Hensan*). 語 (GO) means "word(s)." 一 (ICHI) can be understood as modifying 1) 転 (TEN), in which case 一転 means "complete transformation," or 2) 語 (GO), in which case 一語 means "one word" or "a word." See also chap. 20, Kokyo [155], and chap. 76, *Dai-Shugyo.*

10. The mental face of reality and the concrete face of reality are both faces of reality.

11. A monk asks Master Daikan Eno, *"What people attained Obai's teaching?"* The Master says [ironically], *"People who understood the Buddha-Dharma [intellectually] attained it."* The monk says, *"Did you yourself attain it, Master?"* The Master said, *"I did not attain it."* The monk says, *"Why did the Master not attain it?"* The Master says, *"I do not understand the Buddha-Dharma."* See *Shinji-shobogenzo,* pt. 1, no. 59.

12. 一大事因縁 (ICHIDAIJI-INNEN), "the one great cause," means the quotation from the Diamond Sutra. At the same time, it alludes to the passage in Lotus Sutra, *Hoben* which says that the buddhas appear in the world only on account of one great cause or one great purpose: to cause living beings to disclose, to be shown, to realize, and to enter, the Buddha's wisdom. See LS 1.88–90.

Tathāgata." An expression like this is totally by virtue of Śākyamuni Buddha's influence; it is the skin, flesh, bones, and marrow of no figure other than his.

[31] At that time Śākyamuni Buddha, on Vulture Peak,[13] addresses the great assembly through the Bodhisattva Medicine King:

If we are close to a teacher of the Dharma,
We instantly attain the bodhisattva-way.
And if we learn following this teacher,
We are able to meet buddhas
[numerous] as sands of the Ganges.[14]

"Being close to a teacher of the Dharma" describes the second Patriarch's eight years of serving his Master, after which he gets the marrow with his whole arm.[15] It describes Nangaku's fifteen years of pursuing the truth.[16] Getting the master's marrow is called *"being close." "The bodhisattva-way"* is *me being like this, and you also being like this.*[17] It is *instantly to attain* a limitlessly abundant tangle of action. *Instant attainment* is not the acquisition of that which has been manifested since ancient times, is not the first attainment of that which has never before occurred, and is not the rounding up of an amorphous state that exists in the present. Getting free of attainment of "being close" is called *instant attainment.* Therefore all attainment is *instant attainment.*[18] In regard to *"Learning following this teacher,"* being as if an attendant is the ancient example, and we should research it. Just at the moment of this action, direct experience of *being able to meet* is present. In that state *we meet buddhas [as numerous] as sands of the Ganges.* Buddhas [as numerous] as sands of the Ganges are just individual instances of the state of vigorous activity itself. Do not run cringing to meet buddhas [as numerous] as sands of the Ganges. First apply yourself to *learning following a teacher. To learn following a teacher* is *to attain the buddha-view.*[19]

---

13. 霊鷲山 (RYO-JUSEN), lit. "Sacred Vulture Peak." represents the Sanskrit *Gṛdhrakūṭa,* which lit. means "Vulture Peak." 霊 (RYO), "sacred," which was presumably added in the Chinese translation from the Sanskrit, has been omitted in the translation of this chapter.

14. The closing lines of Lotus Sutra, *Hosshi.* See LS 2.166.

15. Master Taiso Eka, the 2nd patriarch in China. Legend has it that he cut off his arm at the beginning of his practice under Master Bodhidharma; he was later affirmed with the words, *"You have got my marrow."* See chap. 30, *Gyoji* and chap. 46, *Katto.*

16. Master Nangaku Ejo pursued the truth for 15 years under Master Daikan Eno.

17. 吾亦如是、汝亦如是 (GO-YAKU-NYOZE, NYO-YAKU-NYOZE), or "I am also like this, and you are also like this." Alludes to the famous conversation between Master Daikan and Master Nangaku which is quoted in chap. 7, *Senjo,* chap. 62, *Hensan,* et cetera.

18. In other words, real attainment (experience which is not restricted by worrisome concepts such as "being close") can only take place in the present moment.

19. 得仏見 (TOKU-BUTSU-KEN), or "to attain buddha-realization." The last line of the quotation has 得見…仏 (TOKU KEN...BUTSU), "being able to meet buddhas...." Here Master Dogen

[4] Śākyamuni Buddha addresses the assembly, all of whom are experiencing the truth of bodhi:

> *Profoundly entering the balanced state of dhyāna,*
> *[We] meet the buddhas of the ten directions.*[20]

The whole Universe is *profound* because it is *in the buddha-lands of the ten directions.*[21] It is not wide, not great, not small, and not narrow. When we act, we *act following circumstances.*[22] This is called "total inclusion." This [action] is not of seven feet, eight feet, or ten feet; it is total inclusion with no outside, and is the one word *"enter."* And this *profound entry* is *the balanced state of dhyāna. To profoundly enter the balanced state of dhyāna* is *to meet the buddhas of the ten directions.* Because he is able to exist—*profoundly entering this place, with no-one contacting him*[23]—he *meets the buddhas of the ten directions.* Because *she will not receive it even if I take it,*[24] buddhas in the ten directions exist. *Profound entry* cannot manifest itself for a long, long time.[25] *Meeting the buddhas of the ten directions* is just *to see a reclining Tathāgata.*[26] *The balanced state of dhyāna* is impossible to get into or to get out of.[27] Neither disbelieving nor fearing the real dragon, in the present moment of meeting buddha we need endeavor no

---

reversed the order of the characters 見 (KEN) and 仏 (BUTSU).

20. Lotus Sutra, *Anraku-gyo*. See LS 2.282. The original subject in the Lotus Sutra is 読是経者 *(kono kyo o yoman mono)*, "a person who reads this Sutra."

21. 十方仏土中 (JUPPO-BUTSUDO-CHU) alludes to LS 1.106: *"In the Buddha-lands of the ten directions, / There only exists the one-vehicle Dharma."* In the Lotus Sutra 中 (CHU) is used here as a preposition, "in" or "within," but in Master Dogen's commentaries 中 (CHU) is frequently used as a noun, "the inside of," "the content of," or "the reality of." See, for example, the opening words of chap. 17, *Hokke-ten-hokke.*

22. 随佗挙 (ZUITAKO *su*) is a variation of the traditional phrase 随佗去 (ZUITAKO), which means "following others completely," or "just following circumstances." The latter phrase, which appears for example in chap. 24, *Bukkyo* [177], and chap. 37, *Shinjin-gakudo* [152], suggests a flexible attitude.

23. 深入裏許無人接渠 (SHIN-NYU-RIKO-MUNIN-SETSU-KYO) suggests the independence of a person who is absorbed in his or her own action. 渠 (KYO, *kare*), "him," is originally masculine in gender. The phrase is in Chinese characters only, but a source has not been traced.

24. 設使将来佗亦不受 (SETSU-SHI-SHORAI-TA-YAKU-FU-JU) suggests detachment. 佗 (TA), "he," "she," or "the other," is originally neutral in gender. The Chinese source has not been traced.

25. This expression 長長出 (CHO-CHO SHUTSU), lit. "long, long manifestation," also appears in chap. 3, *Genjo-koan*. In that chapter, Master Dogen says that we continue to manifest the state of realization for a long time (as a bell continues ringing after it has been struck). Here, however, he is interpreting 入 (NYU), "enter," not as an enduring state of having entered, but as the momentary action of entering.

26. Refers to a story about the first meeting between Master Joshu Jushin and Master Nansen Fugan. See chap. 35, *Hakujushi*.

27. In other words, dhyāna is just the state at the present moment. Entering, as action, can exist in the present moment. But entering into or getting out of a state, as processes over time, cannot exist in the present moment.

further to get rid of doubt. We meet buddha relying upon meeting buddha, and thus we profoundly enter the balanced state of dhyāna relying upon the balanced state of dhyāna. This truth of the balanced state of dhyāna, meeting buddha, profound entry, and so on, has not been produced in the past by folk who could ponder it at leisure, and then passed onto the folk of today. And it is not an innovation of the present. Rather, a truth such as this is inevitable. All transmissions of the truth and receptions of the behavior are like this. Initiation of causes and attainment of effects are like this.

[37] Śākyamuni Buddha addresses the Bodhisattva Universal Virtue:[28] *"If there is anyone who receives and retains, reads and recites, rightly remembers, practices, and copies this Sutra of the Flower of Dharma, we should know that that person is meeting Śākyamuni Buddha, and hearing this Sutra as if from the Buddha's mouth."*[29]

In general, all the buddhas say that *to meet Śākyamuni Buddha* and to realize the state of Śākyamuni Buddha is to realize the truth and to become buddha. Such behavior of buddhas is originally attained through each of these seven practices. A person who performs the seven practices is *that person* whom *we should know*,[30] and is *the very person here and now, as he or she is.*[31] Because this is just the state in which we meet Śākyamuni Buddha, it is directly *hearing this Sutra as if from the Buddha's mouth.* Śākyamuni Buddha, since having met Śākyamuni Buddha, is Śākyamuni Buddha. Thus, the form of his tongue universally enfolds the three-thousandfold [world]: what mountain or ocean could be other than the Buddha's sutras? For this reason, *the very person here and now* who copies is meeting alone with Śākyamuni Buddha. *The Buddha's mouth* is constantly open through the myriad ages: what moment could be other than the sutras? For this reason, the practitioner who receives and retains the sutras is meeting solely with Śākyamuni Buddha. The virtue of not only the eyes and ears but also the nose and so on, may also be like this.[32] The front and the back, the left and the right, taking and leaving, an instant of

---

28. 普賢 (FUGEN), from the Sanskrit *Samantabhadra.* He is often depicted, riding on a white elephant, as the right-hand attendant of the Buddha. See also chap. 17, *Hokke-ten-hokke.*

29. Lotus Sutra, *Fugen-bosatsu-kanpotsu.* See LS 3.330.

30. 当知是人 (TOCHI-ZENIN), "should know that person," is taken directly from the Lotus Sutra. 是人 (ZENIN), "that person," means a concrete person, a real person.

31. 如是当人 (NYOZE-TONIN). This is Master Dogen's characteristic variation using characters which appear in the Lotus Sutra. 如是 (NYOZE), used as an adjective, means "as it is," and used as a noun means "reality as it is." (See also chap. 17, *Hokke-ten-hokke* and chap. 50, *Shoho-jisso*). 当 (TO) originally means "to hit the target." Here it emphasizes the actual existence of the agent himself or herself. In the Lotus Sutra (read as *masa[ni]*) 当 means "should." 人 (NIN) means person or human being.

32. For example, the virtue of meeting Śākyamuni Buddha is to be had not only from reading the sutras and hearing their recitation but also from smelling incense, tasting tea, et cetera.

the present, also, are like this. We have been born to experience *this Sutra*[33] of the present: how could we not rejoice to be meeting Śākyamuni Buddha? Life is an encounter with Śākyamuni Buddha. People who, spurring the body-mind, *receive and retain, read and recite, rightly remember, practice, and copy this Sutra of the Flower of Dharma* may [already] *be meeting Śākyamuni Buddha.* They are *hearing this Sutra as if from the Buddha's mouth:* who could not vie to listen to it? Those who have no urgency and who do not apply themselves are wretched living beings without happiness or wisdom. One who *practices* is *that person whom we should know is meeting Śākyamuni Buddha.*

Śākyamuni Buddha addresses the great assembly: *"If good sons and good daughters, hearing my preaching of the eternity of [the Tathāgata's] lifetime, believe and understand it with a profound mind, then they will see the Buddha constantly existing on Mount Gṛdhrakūṭa, surrounded by an assembly of great bodhisattvas and many śrāvakas, and preaching the Dharma. And they will see this sahā-world with its land of lapis lazuli, even, level, and right."*[34]

This *"profound mind"* means *the sahā-world. "Belief and understanding"*[35] means the place of no escape. Who could not believe and understand the Buddha's words of real truth?[36] That we have met this Sutra is an opportune circumstance that we should believe in and understand. In order to believe in and understand with a profound mind this flower of Dharma, and in order to believe in and understand with a profound mind the eternity of [the Tathāgata's] lifetime,[37] we have longed to be born in this sahā-realm. The mystical power of the Tathāgata,[38] the power of his compassion, and the power of the eternity of his lifetime, are able, by means of mind, to make us believe and understand; are able, by means of body, to make us believe and understand; are able, by means of the whole Universe, to make us believe and understand; are able, by means of Buddhist patriarchs, to make us believe and understand; are able, by means of all dharmas, to make us believe and understand; are able, by means of real form, to make us believe and understand; are able, by means of skin, flesh, bones, and marrow, to make us believe and understand; and are able, by means of living-and-dying and go-

33. In Shobogenzo, the Lotus Sutra and the Universe itself are identified in the words 此経 (SHIKYO) or, as here, 此経典 (SHIKYOTEN), "this Sutra."

34. Lotus Sutra, *Funbetsu-kudoku.* See LS 3.56.

35. 信解 (SHINGE), "Belief and Understanding," is the title of the fourth chapter of the Lotus Sutra.

36. 誠諦 (JOTAI), "real truth," represents the meaning of the Sanskrit *bhūta,* which means "actually happened, true, real." See Glossary.

37. 如来寿量 (NYORAI-JURYO), "The Tathāgata's Lifetime," is the title of the 16th chapter of the Lotus Sutra.

38. 如来神力 (NYORAI-JINRIKI), "The Mystical Power of the Tathāgata," is the title of the 21st chapter of the Lotus Sutra.

ing-and-coming, to make us believe and understand. These instances of belief and understanding are the state of meeting buddha itself. Thus, clearly, when we possess the Eye of the mind we meet Buddha, and when we attain the Eye of belief and understanding we meet Buddha. That he speaks not only of "meeting buddha" but of seeing his *constant existence on Mount Gṛdhrakūṭa* may mean that the constant existence of Gṛdhrakūṭa Mountain is totally the same as the Tathāgata's lifetime. This being so, *seeing the Buddha constantly existing on Mount Gṛdhrakūṭa* describes the constant existence, in the past, both of the Tathāgata and of Gṛdhrakūṭa Mountain, and the constant existence, in the future, both of the Tathāgata and of Gṛdhrakūṭa Mountain.[39] The bodhisattvas and śrāvakas, similarly, may be constant existence, and preaching the Dharma also may be constant existence. We are looking at *the sahā-world with its land of lapis lazuli, even, level, and right.* Do not be disturbed in looking at the sahā-world: high places are level being high, and low places are level being low.[40] This ground is land of lapis lazuli.[41] Do not disdain eyes that see it as even, level, and right. Land in which the ground is of lapis lazuli is like this. If we saw this ground as other than lapis lazuli, Gṛdhrakūṭa Mountain would not be Gṛdhrakūṭa Mountain, and Śākyamuni Buddha would not be Śākyamuni Buddha. The belief and understanding that *the land is lapis lazuli* is just the form of profound belief and understanding, and is the state of meeting buddha itself.

[43] Śākyamuni Buddha addresses the great assembly:

And [when living beings], with undivided mind,
desire to meet buddha,
Without attaching to their own body and life,
Then I, with many monks,
Appear together on Vulture Peak.[42]

The *whole-heartedness*[43] described here is not the whole-heartedness discussed by the common man, the two vehicles, and the like. It is the whole-hearted state of meeting buddha. The whole-hearted state of meeting buddha is *Vulture Peak* and is *the accompanying many monks.* When each present

39. Not only the Tathāgata but also the concrete mountain is eternal; and not only the concrete mountain but also the Tathāgata is real.

40. Master Kyozan Ejaku, following his Master Isan Reiyu, is making a new paddy field. Master Kyozan says, *"This place is low like this. That place is high like that."* Master Isan says, *"Water is able to make things level. We will make it level just with water."* Master Kyozan says, *"There is no need to rely on water, Master. High places are level being high, and low places are level being low."* See *Shinji-shobogenzo*, pt. 1, no. 23.

41. 瑠璃 (RURI), from the Sanskrit *vaiḍūrya,* is a semiprecious stone that is usually rich azure blue. In ancient India it was a symbol of excellence (see Glossary).

42. Lotus Sutra, *Nyorai-juryo.* See LS 3.30.

43. 一心 (ISSHIN), lit. "one mind," translated in the quotation as "with undivided mind."

individual secretly arouses *the desire to meet buddha*, we are desiring to meet buddha through concentration of the Vulture Peak Mind. So *the undivided mind* is indeed *Vulture Peak* itself. And how could the undivided body not *appear together* with the mind? How could the state not be the undivided body-mind together? Just as body and mind are like this already, so too are lifetime and life like this. For this reason, we totally surrender our own *self-attachment* to the Vulture Peak state of solely attaching to the supreme truth. Thus, [the Buddha] expresses the state in which *I with many monks appear together on Vulture Peak* as the undivided mind of meeting buddha.

Śākyamuni Buddha addresses the great assembly:

If they preach this Sutra
Just this is to meet me,
The Tathāgata Abundant Treasures,
And many transformed buddhas.[44]

The preaching of this Sutra is *"I am always living at this place, [but] with mystical powers I make living beings who are upset still fail to see me though I am close."*[45] This Tathāgata-state of mystical powers apparent and hidden has the virtue of just this being to meet me and other [buddhas].

Śākyamuni Buddha addresses the great assembly:

One who is able to keep this Sutra,
Is already meeting me,
And also meeting the Buddha Abundant Treasures,
And those [buddhas] who are [my] offshoots.[46]

Because to keep this Sutra is difficult, the Tathāgata constantly encourages it. In the rare event that there is *one who keeps this Sutra*, the state is just meeting buddha. Clearly, if one is meeting buddha one is keeping the Sutra, and one who is keeping the Sutra is one who is meeting buddha. This being so, even to hear a single verse or a single line, and to receive and to retain them, is to be able to meet Śākyamuni Buddha, is also to meet the Buddha Abundant Treasures, is to meet the buddhas who are offshoots, is to receive the transmission of the treasury of the Buddha-Dharma, is to attain the Buddha's right Eye, is to be able to experience the Buddha's life, is to attain the

---

44. Lotus Sutra, *Ken-hoto*. See LS 2.194. The chapter describes countless buddhas emanating from the body of Śākyamuni Buddha and coming from all directions to hear the Dharma. These buddhas are called 化仏 (KEBUTSU), "transformed buddhas"; that is, transformations of Śākyamuni Buddha.

45. Lotus Sutra, *Nyorai-juryo*. See LS 3.30.

46. Lotus Sutra, *Nyorai-jinriki*. See LS 3.162. 分身 (BUNSHIN), "offshoots," means the same as 化仏 (KEBUTSU), "transformed buddhas," in the previous quotation.

Eye of the ascendant state of Buddha,[47] is to attain the Buddha's brain and eyes, and is to attain the Buddha's nostrils.

[47] The Buddha Constellation King of Flower-Wisdom with Voice of Thunder addresses the King Resplendent:[48] *"Remember, great king! A good counselor[49] is the great cause whereby we are educated and guided to be able to meet buddha and to establish the will to [the supreme truth of] anuttara-samyak-saṃbodhi."*[50]

The mats of this great order [described] now are not yet rolled up. Although we speak of *the buddhas of the past, the present, and the future,* [these past, present, and future] are not to be equated with the three times of the common man. [In the Buddha's order] what is called *"the past"* is matters in the mind, *"the present"* is a fist, and *"the future"* is the projections of the brain. This being so, the Buddha Constellation King of Flower-Wisdom with Voice of Thunder is an instance of meeting buddha realized in the mind. Commonly understood talk of meeting buddha is like this. *Education and guidance* is meeting buddha. Meeting buddha is *establishing the will to anuttara-samyak-saṃbodhi.* And establishment of the bodhi-mind is meeting buddha being right in the beginning and right at the end.

[48] Śākyamuni Buddha says:

Beings who practice all the virtues,
And who are gentle, simple, and straight,
All see my body,
Existing here and preaching the Dharma.[51]

What he calls *"all the virtues"* is dragging through the mud and staying in the water, or following ripples and chasing waves.[52] Those who practice this are called *beings who are gentle, simple, and straight—"As also I am, and as also you*

---

47. 仏向上眼 (BUTSU-KOJO-GEN) suggests the optimistic attitude which derives from the daily practice of Zazen. 仏向上 (BUTSU-KOJO), "the ascendant state of buddha," or "going beyond buddha," expresses the continuing daily practice of a Buddhist practitioner even after he or she has already realized the truth. In chap. 28, *Butsu-kojo-ji,* Master Dogen explains the term as follows: *What has been called 'the matter of the ascendant state of buddha' means, having arrived at the state of buddha, progressing on and meeting buddha again.* 眼 (GEN), "Eye," expresses the Buddhist view or attitude, in which is contained the whole body-mind of the practitioner.

48. 妙荘厳王 (MYO-SHOGON-O), from the Sanskrit *Śubha-vyūha-rāja.*

49. 善知識 (ZENCHISHIKI), from the Sanskrit *kalyāṇa-mitra,* in general means a teacher who gives practical guidance on how to apply the principles of Buddhism in daily life (see note 3 in chap. 52, *Bukkyo,* and Book 1, Glossary). In this specific episode in the Lotus Sutra, the King Resplendent has just praised his own sons as "good counselors," or "friends in virtue," for transforming his wrong mind, and causing him to be able to abide in the Buddha-Dharma and meet the World-Honored One.

50. Lotus Sutra, *Myo-shogon-o-honji.* See LS 3.306.

51. Lotus Sutra, *Nyorai-juryo.* See LS 3.32.

52. Common efforts in daily life.

are."[53] They have experienced this state of meeting buddha inside mud and have experienced this state of meeting buddha in the waves of mind; [thus] they witness [the Buddha] *existing here and preaching the Dharma.* On the other hand, in the great kingdom of Sung recently, cronies calling themselves "Zen Masters" are numerous. They do not know the length and breadth of the Buddha-Dharma, and their experience is very scant. Barely parroting two or three sayings of Rinzai or Unmon, they have considered these to be the whole truth of the Buddha-Dharma. If the Buddha-Dharma could be perfectly expressed by two or three sayings of Rinzai or Unmon, the Buddha-Dharma could not have reached the present day. It is hard to call Rinzai and Unmon venerable in the Buddha-Dharma. How much less [venerable] are the cronies of today who are inferior to Rinzai and Unmon; they are rabble who do not deserve to be mentioned. Because they are too stupid to understand the meaning of the Buddhist sutras for themselves, they randomly insult the Buddhist sutras, and neglect to practice and learn them. We should call them flotsam in the stream of non-Buddhism. They are not the children and grandchildren of Buddhist patriarchs. How much less could they arrive at the boundary of the state of meeting buddhas? They are rabble who cannot even attain the principles of Confucius and Lao-tzu. No child in the house of the Buddhist patriarchs should meet with those cronies who call themselves "Zen Masters." Just investigate in practice and realize in physical experience the eyes which are the Eye of meeting buddha.

My late Master Tendo, the eternal Buddha, quotes the following: *"King Prasenajit[54] asks the Venerable Piṇḍola[55] 'I have heard that the Venerable One has intimately met Buddha. Is it true or not?' The Venerable One, lifting up an eyebrow with his hand, indicates affirmation."*

My late Master praises [Piṇḍola] as follows:

By lifting an eyebrow he answers the question in part.
He has met Buddha intimately, without any mutual deceit.
To this day he deserves offerings from the four quarters.
Spring is on the plum twigs, embraced by the coldness of the snow.[56]

This *meeting buddha* is neither meeting our own state of buddha nor meeting the buddha in others; it is meeting Buddha. Because one branch of plum blossoms meets one branch of plum blossoms, the blooming of flowers is perfectly clear. The point of King Prasenajit's question is to ask whether the

---

53. 吾亦如是、如亦如是 (GO-YAKU-NYOZE, NYO-YAKU-NYÒZE). Master Daikan Eno's words to Master Nangaku Ejo. See note 17.

54. King Prasenajit was the ruler of the kingdom of Kosala, and a supporter of the Buddha's order. See also notes to chap. 59, *Baike.*

55. One of the 16 original arhats in the Buddha's order. Ibid.

56. *Nyojo-osho-goroku.* Also quoted in chap. 59, *Baike.*

Venerable One has already met buddha and whether he has become buddha. The Venerable One, unequivocally, has lifted an eyebrow. It is verification of meeting buddha, by which no one can be deceived, and to this day, it has not ceased: [Piṇḍola's] *deservedness of offerings*[57] is apparent without concealment. [And yet] we cannot trace his *meeting buddha,* which is *intimate experience.*[58] The meeting buddha of that master of three hundred million[59] is the meeting buddha of the present: it is beyond seeing the thirty-two signs. Who could be far from the state of seeing the thirty-two signs?[60] There may be many types of human beings, gods, śrāvakas, and pratyekabuddhas who do not know this principle of meeting buddha. It is similar, for example, when we say that those who stand up a fly-whisk are numerous, but those who stand up a fly-whisk are not many.[61] To be meeting buddha is to have been realized by the state of buddha. Even if the self wishes to conceal it, the state of meeting buddha has already leaked itself out—this is the principle of meeting buddha. We should investigate in detail the real features of this *lifting an eyebrow,* making effort with body-minds as numerous as the sands of the Ganges. Even if, for a hundred thousand myriad kalpas of days and nights, we have constantly lived together with Śākyamuni Buddha, if we lack the ability to lift an eyebrow, the state is not meeting buddha. Even if, more than two thousand years on, we are in a remote place more than a hundred thousand miles away, if we have intimately realized the ability to lift an eyebrow, it is realization of the state of Śākyamuni Buddha that precedes the King of Emptiness, it is realization of one branch of plum blossoms, and it is realization of *plum twigs* as *Spring.* This being so, *intimate experience of meeting buddha* is the performance of three prostrations, joining hands and bowing, a face breaking into a smile, a fist emitting a thunderclap, and crossed legs sitting on a round cushion.

---

57. 応供 (OGU). Read in the poem as KU *[ni] o[zu],* these characters mean "to deserve offerings." At the same time, 応供 (OGU) represents the Sanskrit term of reverence *arhat,* which means "one who deserves." Many temples in Japan have images of the 16 arhats, to which offerings continue to be served.

58. 親曾の見仏 (SHINZO *no* KENBUTSU), "meeting buddha as intimate experience," is the mutual relation between subject and object, and so we cannot witness it as a third party. 親 (SHIN) means familiar, intimate or immediate; it describes absence of separation into subject and object. 曾 (SO) means formerly, having taken place in the past; in the poem, read as *katsu[te]*, its function is to indicate the past tense, but in the compound 親曾 (SHINZO) it suggests experience. The phrase 親曾 (SHINZO), also appears in chap 25, *Daigo* [225] ("familiar experience"), chap. 36, *Komyo* [121], ("direct experience"), and chap. 57, *Menju* [170] ("familiar to us").

59. According to legend, Śrāvasti, the capital of the kingdom of Kośala, had a population of 900 million, one third of whom were Buddhists under the Venerable Piṇḍola.

60. Anyone could see the Buddha's physical form. Piṇḍola's meeting buddha was not only that, but also realization of the state of buddha.

61. Many set themselves up as Buddhist teachers but few really teach Buddhism.

The Venerable Piṇḍola goes to a great gathering at the palace of King Aśoka for a midday meal. After distributing incense, the King does prostrations and asks the Venerable One, "I have heard that the Venerable One has intimately met Buddha. Is it true or not?"

The Venerable One brushes up his eyebrow with his hand and says, "Do you understand?"

The King says, "I do not understand."

The Venerable One says, "When the Dragon King Anavatapta invited Buddha to a midday meal, I[62] *was also admitted among that number."*[63]

The point of King Aśoka's question is that the words *"Is it true that the Venerable One has intimately met Buddha?"* ask whether the Venerable One is already the Venerable One. Then the Venerable One at once brushes up his eyebrow. This causes the state of meeting buddha *to appear in the world;*[64] it causes act of becoming buddha to be *intimately experienced.* He says, *"When the Dragon King Anavatapta invited Buddha to a midday meal, I was also admitted among that number."* Remember, in a gathering of buddhas, *buddhas alone, together with buddhas,* may be as [abundant as] *rice, hemp, bamboo and reeds,*[65] [but śrāvakas of] the fourth effect and pratyekabuddhas cannot be admitted. Even if [śrāvakas of] the fourth effect and pratyekabuddhas have come, we cannot count them among the number of buddhas. The Venerable One himself has already declared, *"When Buddha was invited to a midday meal, I also was among that number"*—a natural self-expression which has emerged freely. The fact that he is meeting buddha is evident. *"Inviting Buddha"* means not only inviting Śākyamuni Buddha, but inviting all the countless and limitless buddhas of the three times and the ten directions. To be included in the number of invited buddhas is the state without hesitation, and the state beyond hesitation, of intimate experience of meeting buddha. Indication of meeting buddha, of meeting a teacher, of meeting myself, and of meeting you, in general, should be like this. The Dragon King Anavatapta is the Dragon King of Anavatapta Lake. Anavatapta Lake is called in this country "the Lake of No Suffering from Heat."

Zen Master Honei Nin-yu[66] praises [Piṇḍola] as follows:

---

62. 貧道 (HIN DO), lit. "poor way," a humble form used by a Buddhist monk. The same words are used by Master Prajñātara in chap. 22, *Kankin* [191].

63. *Aiku-o-kyo (Aśoka Sutra),* chap. 3.

64. 出現於世 (SHUTSUGEN-O-SE). These words appear frequently in the Lotus Sutra. See, for example, LS 1.88–90.

65. Both expressions in italics originate in the Lotus Sutra. See LS 1.68, LS 1.72.

66. Master Honei Nin-yu (dates unknown), successor of Master Yogi Ho-e. The poem is quoted from the one-volume record of his words, *Honei-nin-yu-zenji-goroku.*

Our Buddha intimately met with Piṇḍola
Whose eyebrows were long, hair short, and eyes rough.
Even King Aśoka doubted him.
Om maṇi śrī sūrya.[67]

This eulogy is not perfect in its expression, but I quote it because it is relevant research.[68]

[57] *Great Master Shinsai of Joshu,*[69] *the story goes, is asked by a monk, "I have heard that you intimately met Nansen. Is it true or not?"*

The Master says, "Chinshu district produces big radishes."[70]

The expression realized now is verification of *intimately meeting Nansen.* It is neither words that say something nor words that say nothing. It is neither words bestowed from above nor words of common parlance. It is neither the lifting of eyebrows nor the brushing up of eyebrows. It is intimate meeting with [Nansen's] eyebrows. Even though [Joshu] was an individual[71] of outstanding talent, without intimately meeting [Nansen], he could not be like this. This story of the big radishes produced in Chinshu is an account of the time when Great Master Shinsai was the abbot of Shinsai-in temple in Toka-en gardens in Chinshu. He was later given the title "Great Master Shinsai." Because he was like this, he received the authentic transmission of the Buddhist patriarchs' right-Dharma-eye treasury from his first opening in experience of the Eye of meeting buddha. When the authentic transmission of the right-Dharma-eye treasury is present, the dignified behavior is realized of a buddha manifesting an easy bearing, and the state of meeting buddha, at this place, is towering and magnificent.

---

67. The Sanskrit *om* is a word of affirmation often placed at the beginning of six-syllable Buddhist incantations called *vidyā shadakshari*; *maṇi* means jewel, gem, or pearl; *śrī* means to diffuse light; and *sūrya* means the sun. In the context of this poem, *Om maṇi śrī sūrya,* or "Truly, a pearl shines like the sun!" suggests the author's respectful affirmation of Master Piṇḍola.

68. 趣向の参学 (SHUKO *no* SANGAKU). 趣 (SHU, *omomuki*) means purport or gist, and 向 (KO, *mu[kau]*) means to direct towards; so 趣向の (SHUKO *no*) here means "being relevant to." In modern Japanese the compound 趣向 (SHUKO) means a plan, idea, design, scheme, or device. At the same time, as a traditional term representing the Sanskrit *prati-pādana* (see Glossary), 趣向 (SHUKO) sometimes means action itself, or conduct in the world. This meaning is retained for example in *Fukan-zazengi:* 趣向更是平常者也 (*shuko sarani kore hyojo naru mono nari*), "Actions are balanced and constant," or "Undertakings are balanced and constant."

69. Master Joshu Jushin (778–897), successor of Master Nansen Fugan. Shinsai-in was the name of his temple, and Great Master Shinsai is his posthumous title.

70. *Kosonshuku-goroku,* chap. 13.

71. 独歩 (DOPPO). 独 (DOKU) means alone, solitary, or independent, and 歩 (HO) means step or walk. In chap. 49, *Butsudo* [186], Master Dogen describes the singular excellence of Master Seigen Gyoshi by praising him as 正神足の独歩なり (SHO-JINSOKU *no* DOPPO), lit. "a solitary step of a true mystical foot."

Shobogenzo Kenbutsu

Preached to the assembly on Mt. Yamashibu on the 1st and the 19th days of the 11th lunar month in the winter of the 1st year of Kangen.[72]

72. 1243.

[62]

偏参

HENSAN

Thorough Exploration

Hen means "everywhere" or "widely," and ***san*** *means "to visit," or "to study through experience." Originally* ***hensan*** *described the custom Buddhist monks used to have of traveling around in order to meet excellent masters with whom they could be satisfied. But according to Master Dogen,* ***hensan****, or "thorough exploration," is accomplished not by traveling around, but by a Buddhist monk's thorough exploration of the Buddhist state under one true master. In this chapter, Master Dogen explains the true meaning of* ***hensan****.*

The great truth of Buddhist patriarchs is exploration of the ultimate state through and through, is *there being no strings under the feet,*[1] and is *the appearance of clouds under the feet.*[2] Still, although it is like this, *the opening of flowers is the occurrence of the world,*[3] and *"At this concrete place, I am always keen."*[4] For this reason, *"A sweet melon, right through to the stem, is sweet. A bitter gourd, right through to the root, is bitter."*[5] The sweetness of sweetness, right through to the stem, is sweet. We have been exploring in practice[6] the state like this.

---

1. *Keitoku-dento-roku,* chap. 15: Master Tozan is asked the meaning of action. He replies, *"Straightway there should be no strings under the feet."* In China captured birds had string tied around their feet to stop them flying away, so having no strings under the feet means being free of hindrances that pull one down. See also chap. 27, *Zazenshin* [44].

2. *Keitoku-dento-roku,* chap. 3, says, *"Haradai, having reverentially received the Master's instruction, said, 'Pray lend me your mystical power.' After he had spoken, clouds appeared under his feet."* Clouds appearing under the feet suggests the realization of concrete mystical power.

3. The words of the twenty-seventh Patriarch, Master Prajñātara, quoted in *Keitoku-dento-roku,* chap. 2, describe the oneness in reality of phenomena (flowers) and substance (the world).

4. Master Tozan's words quoted from *Keitoku-dento-roku,* chap. 15. See also *Shinji-shobogenzo,* pt. 1, no. 55, and Shobogenzo, chap. 40, *Gabyo* [211].

5. Words of Master Engo Kokugon, recorded in *Engo-zenji-goroku,* vol. 2.

6. "Exploring in practice" is 参学 (SANGAKU) usually translated as "learn in practice." 参 (SAN), translated in the chapter title as "exploration," lit. means "visit," but not in a sightseeing sense; it includes the meaning of participation in, experience of, or devotion to something. The character 参 (SAN) appears very frequently in Shobogenzo in the compounds 参学 (SANGAKU), "learn in practice" or "learn by experience," and 参究 (SANKYU), "investigate," "master in practice," et cetera. Master Dogen used it as a prefix to make a verb more suggestive of the real

[62] *Great Master Shu-itsu*[7] *of Gensa-zan mountain, the story goes, is summoned by Seppo, who says to the Master, "Bi of the dhūta!*[8] *Why do you not go widely exploring?" The Master says, "Bodhidharma did not come to the eastern lands; the Second Patriarch did not go to India in the west."*[9] *Seppo profoundly affirms this.*[10]

The principle of the state of thorough exploration described here is exploration of a somersault; it is the sacred truth, at the same time, not being practiced. *How could it have grades or ranks?* [11]

When Zen Master Nangaku Dai-e[12] first visits[13] the eternal Buddha of Sokei mountain,[14] the eternal Buddha says, *"This is something coming like this."*[15]

[Nangaku's] thorough exploration of this mud ball continues altogether for eight years. At last he expresses the conclusion[16] of his thorough exploration to the eternal Buddha, saying *"Ejo has understood [why], when I first came here, the Master received Ejo with [the teaching] 'This is something coming like this.'"*

The eternal Buddha Sokei says, *"How do you understand it?"*

Then Dai-e says, *"To describe a thing does not hit the target."* This is the realization of thorough exploration, and the realization of eight years.

The eternal Buddha Sokei asks, *"Do you rely upon practice and experience or not?"*

Dai-e says, *"It is not that there is no practice-and-experience, but to taint it is impossible."*

Thereupon Sokei says, *"I am like that, you are also like that, and the buddhas and patriarchs of India were also like that."*[17]

Buddhist process (i.e., not only learning knowledge but learning of a condition of body and mind). See also notes to chap. 57, *Menju* [183].

7. Master Gensa Shibi (835–907), successor of Master Seppo Gison. Great Master Shu-itsu is his posthumous title.

8. 備頭陀 (BIZUDA). 備 (BI) is from the name Shibi. 頭陀 (ZUDA) is a nickname derived from the Sanskrit word *dhūta*, which means a hard practice. The twelve *dhūta*, are listed in chap. 30, *Gyoji*. See also LS 2.310.

9. It was inevitable for Master Bodhidharma to come to China, and it was inevitable for the 2nd patriarch in China, Master Taiso Eka, to stay in China. They did not follow personal preferences.

10. *Keitoku-dento-roku*, chap. 18. See also Shobogenzo chap. 4, *Ikka-no-myoju*.

11. 何階級之有 *(nan no kaikyu ka kore aran)*, means in other words "How is it possible for any sub-divisions to exist?" The phrase suggests the holistic viewpoint. Chinese source not traced.

12. Master Nangaku Ejo (677–744), successor of Master Daikan Eno. Zen Master Dai-e is his posthumous title.

13. 参ずる *(sanzuru)* in this case includes the meaning of entering the Master's order as a disciple. See note 6.

14. Master Daikan Eno (638–713), successor of Master Daiman Konin.

15. Or "What is that comes like this?" See notes to chap. 29, *Inmo* [108].

16. 一著子 (ICHI-JAKUSU), "conclusion," lit. expresses placing a stone in a game of *go*.

17. *Shinji-shobogenzo*, pt. 2, no. 1. In the *Shinji-shobogenzo* version, Master Daikan Eno

After this, [Nangaku] thoroughly explores the state for another eight years. Counting from beginning to end, it is fifteen years of thorough exploration. [His] *"coming like this"* is thorough exploration. [His] opening the [Buddha] Hall and meeting the buddhas and patriarchs, in [the realization that] *describing a thing does not hit the target* is still exploration of *also being like that.* Since entering the picture and looking, he has thoroughly explored the state in sixty five-hundreds of thousand myriad koṭis of transformations of the body.[18] We do not esteem idly entering one monastery and leaving another monastery as thorough exploration. We esteem discovery with the whole of the eyes as thorough exploration. We esteem attainment of the ultimate through action as thorough exploration. To see, through to the end, how thick is the skin of the face: this is thorough exploration.

The point of Seppo's expression about thorough exploration is originally neither to encourage [Gensa] to leave the mountain nor to encourage him to travel north and south; it is to promote the thorough exploration which Gensa expresses as *"Bodhidharma did not come to the eastern lands; the Second Patriarch did not go to India in the west."* It is like saying, for example, *"How could [this] not be thorough exploration?"* Gensa's saying that Bodhidharma did not come to the eastern lands is not a random expression about coming and yet not coming; it is the truth that the Earth is without an inch of land. What we call *"Bodhidharma"* is an acute case of the lifeblood.[19] Even if the whole of the eastern lands suddenly sprang up in the extreme and waited upon him, that would not impinge upon his movement of his own body[20]—nor indeed upon his turning around in the stream of [others'] words.[21] Because he does not come to the eastern lands, he looks the eastern lands in the face. Although the eastern lands meet with a buddha's face and a patriarch's face, it is not that he has come to the eastern lands; it is that he has grasped the state of a Buddhist patriarch and lost [his own] nostrils. In sum, land is beyond east and west, and east and west are not connected with land. *"The Second Patriarch did not go to India in the west"*: in thoroughly exploring India, he does not go to India. If the Second Patriarch goes to India, [his state] is [only] having lost an arm.[22] Now, why does the Second Patriarch not go to India?

---

says, *"Just this untaintedness is that which buddhas guard and desire. You are like that, I am also like that, and the patriarchs of India were also like that."*

18. 転身 (TENSHIN) means 1) transforming one's physical state, e.g., by putting on the kaṣāya, going for a walk, or listening to words of transformation such as "Profoundly believe in cause and effect!"; 2) moving one's body (from A to B) or changing one's standpoint.

19. Master Bodhidharma is not only an abstract concept.

20. 転身 (TENSHIN), as in note 18. The point here is the independence of Master Bodhidharma's action.

21. 語脈の翻身 (GOMYAKU *no* HONSHIN), lit. "turning over his body in the stream of words," or "somersaulting in mid-speech," suggests a very flexible or accommodating attitude.

22. The fact that he cut off his arm would not have any meaning.

He does not go to India because he has sprung inside [Bodhidharma's] blue eyes. If he had not sprung inside those blue eyes, he would go to India without fail. We esteem gouging out Bodhidharma's eyes as thorough exploration. Going to India in the west and coming to the eastern lands are not thorough exploration. We do not esteem going to Tendai[23] or to Nangaku,[24] or traveling to Godai[25] or to the heavens above, as thorough exploration. If we fail to see through and get free from the four oceans and five lakes,[26] the state is not thorough exploration. Visiting the four oceans and five lakes does not cause the four oceans and five lakes to experience thorough exploration but only makes it slippery on the road and slippery underfoot, thus causing us to forget thorough exploration. In general, because we see it as thorough exploration to explore to the end that *"The whole Universe in the ten directions is the real human body,"*[27] we can investigate the real state in which *Bodhidharma did not come to the eastern lands and the Second Patriarch did not go to India in the west.* Thorough exploration is a big stone being big and a small stone being small. It is, without disturbing stones, to let the big experience themselves and the small experience themselves. To experience hundred thousand myriads of things at hundred thousand myriads of places is not yet thorough exploration. Performance of hundred thousand myriads of bodily transformations within the stream of half a word: this is thorough exploration. For example, to work the earth and only to work the earth is thorough exploration. To pass from once working the earth, to once working the sky, to once working the four quarters and eight aspects, is not thorough exploration. Gutei's[28] exploration of Tenryu,[29] and attainment of the one-finger state, is thorough exploration. *Gutei's only raising one finger*[30] is thorough exploration.

[70] Gensa preaches to the assembly, *"I and Old Master Śākyamuni have experienced the same state."*[31]

---

23. Tendai mountain in Chekiang province in east China, where Master Tendai Chigi established the training place which became the headquarters of the Tendai Sect.

24. Nangaku mountain is in Hunan province in southeast central China.

25. Godai mountain is in Shanxi province in northern China.

26. The four oceans means the oceans of the north, south, east, and west. The definition of the five lakes has changed from age to age.

27. In chap. 50, *Shoho-jisso,* Master Dogen attributes this expression to Master Chosa Keishin.

28. Master Gutei of Mt. Kinka (dates unknown), successor of Master Koshu Tenryu. He is said to have realized the truth when Master Tenryu showed him one finger. Thereafter, in answer to all question, Master Gutei just showed one finger.

29. Master Koshu Tenryu (dates unknown), successor of Master Daibai Hojo. He is famous for transmitting "one-finger Zen" to Master Gutei.

30. 倶胝唯豎一指 (GUTEI-YUI-JU-ISSHI). These characters appear in *Shinji-shobogenzo,* pt. 3, no. 46.

31. 同参 (DOSAN). 同 (DO) means "the same." 参 (SAN) is as in the chapter title. See note 6.

Then a monk steps forward and asks, *"I wonder what person you met."*

The Master says, *"The third son of the Sha family, on a fishing boat."*[32]

The head-to-tail rightness experienced by *Old Master Śākyamuni* is naturally the same as the experience of Old Master Śākyamuni himself. And because the head-to-tail rightness experienced by Old Man Gensa is naturally the same as the experience of Old Man Gensa himself, Old Master Śākyamuni and Old Man Gensa are experiencing the same state. Old Master Śākyamuni and Old Man Gensa are investigating to the limit the experience of satisfaction and the experience of dissatisfaction: this is the principle of thorough exploration. Because Old Master Śākyamuni experiences the same state as Old Man Gensa, he is the eternal Buddha. Because Old Man Gensa is in the same state as Old Master Śākyamuni, he is a descendant. We should thoroughly explore this truth, in detail. [Gensa meets] *"The third son of the Sha family, on a fishing boat":* we should clarify this point and learn it in experience. That is, in other words, to strive to thoroughly explore the moment in which Old Master Śākyamuni and Old Man Gensa simultaneously experience the same state. Old Man Gensa, who has met the third son of Sha on a fishing boat, is present, and is experiencing the common state. The third son of Sha, who has met a shaven-headed man on Gensa-zan mountain, is present, and is experiencing the common state. We should allow ourselves to consider, and should allow others to consider, experience of sameness and experience of difference. Old Man Gensa and Old Master Śākyamuni are experiencing the same state and thoroughly exploring it. We should thoroughly explore, and should commonly experience, the truth that "the third son of Sha" and "I" have met a *What person.*[33] Unless the truth of thorough exploration is actually manifest in the present, experience of the self is impossible and experience of the self is unsatisfactory; experience of others is impossible and experience of others is unsatisfactory; experience of *a person* is impossible, experience of "I" is impossible, experience of a fist is impossible, and experience of the Eye is impossible—lifting the self by fishing the self[34] is impossible, and rising up even before being fished is impossible.[35] When thorough exploration is perfectly realized already, it is free of "thorough exploration": *When the sea is dry its bottom is not seen; when human beings die no trace of their mind is retained.*[36] "The sea is dry" describes the whole sea having totally dried up. At the same

32. That is, Master Gensa himself. The story is recorded in *Rento-eyo*, chap. 23.

33. 甚麼人 (SHIMO-NIN), a person whose state cannot be expressed with words.

34. 自釣自上 (JI-CHO-JI-JO). 自 (JI) as a noun or pronoun means "self," "myself," "oneself," et cetera; and as an adverb means "by oneself," or "by itself"; that is 1) "independently," or 2) "naturally," "spontaneously." 釣 (CHO) means to fish, as in Master Gensa's words 釣魚船 (CHOGYO-SEN), "fishing boat." 上 (JO) means to go up.

35. 未釣先上 (MI-CHO-SEN-JO).

36. These are common expressions of a complete change. In the following sentences, Master Dogen considers the Buddhist meaning of each expression.

time, if the sea has dried up, a "sea-bed" is not seen. "Retaining no trace," and "total retention," are both in the human mind. When human beings die our mind does not remain: it is because we have grasped death that "mind" does not remain.[37] Thus, we can conclude that the whole human being is mind, and the whole of mind is a human being. We investigate in experience the front and back of each such partial thought.

[74] My late Master Tendo, the eternal Buddha, on an occasion when veterans of the truth from many districts have assembled to request his formal preaching in the Dharma Hall, gives the following formal preaching:

The great truth is gateless.
It springs out beyond your brains.
As space, it transcends any path.
[Yet] it has already got inside the nostrils of Seiryo.[38]
Meeting with it like this would be inimical to imitators of Gautama,
And a womb of trouble for those of Rinzai.
Aye...
A great master tumbles, dancing in the spring breeze.
Falling in amazement, apricot blossoms scatter a riot of crimson. [39]

For the present formal preaching in the Dharma Hall, the veterans of many districts have gathered at the time when my late Master, the eternal Buddha, is the abbot of Seiryo-ji temple in Kenko-fu city.[40] That they are *"veterans of the truth"* means that they have been either the Master's disciples or his companions on the Zazen platform. While [themselves] the masters of many districts, they are, in this way, his old friends. How could their number not be great? It is an occasion on which they have assembled to petition [the Master] for formal preaching in the Dharma Hall. Veterans who totally lack something concrete to say are not among his friends, and not in that number of petitioning friends who, despite being great and valuable themselves, wait upon him and request [his preaching]. In general, my late Master's state of thorough exploration is beyond the masters of other districts. In the last two or three hundred years in Great Sung China, there has been no eternal buddha to equal my late Master. *"The great truth is gateless"* describes four or five thousand willow quarters[41] and twenty or thirty thousand music halls. In *springing out* of such places with the whole body, we employ no methods other than *springing out beyond the brain,* and *getting inside the nostrils.* Both are learning in practice. Those who have never experienced springing

37. When we realize the state without illusion, the concept "mind" does not remain.

38. Seiryo means Master Tendo himself.

39. *Nyojo-osho-goroku,* vol.1.

40. To the south of present-day Nanking.

41. 華柳巷 (KARYUKO), lit. "blossom and willow quarter," means an area of pleasure houses, a red-light district.

free beyond the brain, and never experienced transformation of the body inside the nostrils, are not people of learning in practice, and are not men of thorough exploration. We should learn the meaning of *thorough exploration* only under Gensa. When the fourth Patriarch learned in practice for nine years under the third Patriarch,[42] that was just thorough exploration. Zen Master Nansen [Fu]gan's[43] living only in Chiyo district,[44] and not leaving the mountains for a small matter of thirty years, was thorough exploration. The efforts to learn in practice of Ungan, Dogo,[45] and the others, during forty years on Yakusan mountain, were thorough exploration itself. The second Patriarch learned in practice for eight years on Suzan mountain, and explored the skin, flesh, bones, and marrow to the limit. Thorough exploration is just sitting and getting free of body and mind. The state at the present moment in which going is going there and coming is coming here, there being no gap between them, is thorough exploration with the whole body, and it is the whole body of *the great truth*. Walking on, over Vairocana's head[46] is the state without emotion.[47] And decisive attainment of the state like this is the conduct of a Vairocana. When we have mastered thorough exploration of *springing out*, the state is that a gourd springs out of a gourd, and we have, for a long time, seen the top of a gourd as a practice-place for singling out the state of buddha. Life is like a thread,[48] and a gourd performs thorough exploration of a gourd. We have only seen that erecting a stalk of grass[49] is thorough exploration.

---

42. The 4th patriarch in China is Master Dai-i Doshin. His master, the 3rd patriarch, is Master Kanchi Sosan.

43. Master Nansen Fugan (748–834), successor of Master Baso Do-itsu.

44. In present-day Anhui province in east China.

45. Master Ungan Donjo (782–841) and Master Dogo Enchi (769–835) were two of the members of the order of Master Yakusan Igen.

46. 毘盧頂上行 (BIRU-CHOJO-GYO) alludes to *Shinji-shobogenzo*, pt. 1, no. 26: The Tang emperor Shukuso asks Master Nan-yo Echu, *"What is the state without conflict?"* The Master says, *"Walk on, treading on Vairocana's head!"* Vairocana is described in the Avataṃsaka-sūtra as ruling a realm of abundant time and space, where all things emit light and everything is contained in everything else.

47. The expression in the story, "the state without conflict" is 無諍三昧 (MUJO-ZANMAI), or "samādhi as the state without conflict." "The state without emotion" is 無情三昧 (MUJO-ZANMAI), or "samādhi as the state without emotion."

48. Master Daiman Konin said, *"The life of a person to whom the robe has been given is as if hanging by a thread."* In other words, the life of a Buddhist patriarch is very sincere. See *Keitoku-dento-roku*, chap. 3.

49. In chap. 69, *Hotsu-mujoshin*, Master Dogen describes picking up a stalk of grass and creating with it the sixteen foot golden body [image of Buddha]. Here "erecting a stalk of grass" represents one concrete action.

Shobogenzo Hensan

Preached to the assembly in a hut at the foot of Mt. Yamashibu on the 27th day of the 11th lunar month in the 1st year of Kangen.[50]

50. 1243.

[63]

眼睛

GANZEI

Eyes

__Ganzei__, which means "eyeballs" or "eyes," symbolizes the viewpoint of Gautama Buddha, that is, the Buddhist viewpoint. In this chapter, Master Dogen explains the meaning of the word __ganzei__, which appears frequently in Shobogenzo, quoting Master Tendo Nyojo, Master Ungan Donjo, Master Tozan Ryokai, and other Buddhist masters.

If koṭis of thousand myriad kalpas of learning in practice are gathered together into a happy circle, it will be eighty-four thousand Eyes.[1]

My late Master Tendo, the eternal Buddha, while the master of Zuigan-ji temple,[2] in formal preaching in the Dharma Hall addresses the assembly as follows:

Pure the autumn wind, bright the autumn moon.
Earth, mountains, and rivers are clear in the Eye;
Zuigan blinks and we meet afresh.
Sending staffs and shouts by turns, they test the patch-robed monk.[3]

"Testing the patch-robed monk" means verifying whether he is an eternal buddha. The hub of the matter is that [Earth, mountains, and rivers] send staffs and shouts charging forth by turns; and he calls this *"blinking."*[4] The vigorous state realized like this is the Eye. *Mountains, rivers, and the Earth* are a creative occurrence, such as clear manifestation of the Eye, not happening. This is the autumn wind being pure, which is perfect maturity. It is the autumn moon being bright, which is perfect immaturity. The autumn wind's state of purity is beyond comparison even with the four great oceans. The

---

1. In general 眼睛 (GANZEI) is capitalized in translation ("the Eye") when the sense of Buddhist viewpoint is stronger than that of concrete eyeballs.

2. In Chekiang province in east China.

3. This and the following quotations of Master Tendo's words are from *Nyojo-osho-goroku*, vol. 1.

4. 点瞎 (TENKATSU). 点 (TEN) means to let a drop fall, or to make a dot. 瞎 (KATSU) means blindness in an eye. 点瞎 (TENKATSU), "blinking," therefore suggests the momentary freshness of what is seen.

autumn moon's state of brightness is clearer than a thousand suns and moons. *Purity* and *brightness* are mountains, rivers, and the Earth which are the Eye. *The patch-robed monk* is a Buddhist patriarch. One who—without preferring great realization, without preferring non-realization, and without preferring before or after the sprouting of creation—is the Eye itself: this is a Buddhist patriarch. *Verification* is the clear manifestation of the Eye, is the realization of blindness,[5] and is the vivid Eye itself. *Meeting* is mutual encounter.[6] Meeting, or mutual encounter, is the Eye being sharp, and the Eye being a thunderbolt. In sum, do not think that the whole body is big but the whole Eye might be small. Even those considered in past ages to be venerable and great have understood that the whole body is big but the whole Eye is small. This is because they were never equipped with the Eye.

[83] *Great Master Tozan Gohon,[7] while in the order of Ungan,[8] comes upon Ungan making sandals, whereupon the Master says to Ungan, "I beg you Master for the Eye."*

Ungan says, "To whom did you give your own?"

The Master says, "I do not have it."

Ungan says, "You have. Where are you directing it?"

The Master is without words.

Ungan says, "The state of begging the Eye is itself the Eye, is it not?"

The Master says, "It is not the Eye."

Ungan criticizes this.[9]

Thus, learning in practice, when it is thoroughly conspicuous, *begs the Eye*. To pursue the truth in the Cloud Hall, to attend formal preaching in the Dharma Hall, and to enter the room [for questions] in the abbot's reception hall, are to beg the Eye. In general, to follow other monks in leaving a practice, and to follow other monks in coming to a practice, are naturally the Eye itself. The truth that the Eye is beyond subject and beyond object is evident. [The story] says that Tozan, already, has requested instruction[10] by *begging the Master for the Eye*. Clearly, one who is subjective will not be begged by others to instruct them, and one who is objective will not beg others for instruction.

---

5. 瞎 (KATSU), see note 4.

6. 相見は相逢なり (SOKEN *wa* SOHO *nari*). In other words, Master Tendo's expression 相見 (SOKEN), lit. "to see each other," describes not only sense perception but reciprocality of subject and object.

7. Master Tozan Ryokai (807–869), successor of Master Ungan Donjo and the 11th Chinese patriarch in Master Dogen's lineage. Great Master Gohon is his posthumous title.

8. Master Ungan Donjo (782–841), successor of Master Yakusan Igen.

9. *Keitoku-dento-roku*, chap. 14.

10. 請益 (SHIN-EKI), lit. means "to request the benefit [of a master's instruction]." See chap. 22, *Kankin* [219].

[Ungan] teaches, *"To whom did you give your own?"* There are times when the state is *your own*, and there are means of *giving it, to whomever*. [Tozan says] *"I do not have it."* These are words naturally expressed by the Eye itself. We should quietly investigate the principle of, and learn in practice, the realization of words like this. Ungan says, *"You have. Where are you directing it?"* The Eye of this expression is that the *not having*[11] in *"I do not have it,"* is to have it and to be directing it somewhere. And to be directing it somewhere is to have it. We should realize that the expression is like this. Tozan is without words. This is not bewilderment. It is a standard which his karmic consciousness has independently established. Ungan instructs, *"The state of begging the Eye is itself the Eye, is it not?"* This is a sentence which blinks the Eye. It is the vivid shattering of the Eye. The point expressed here by Ungan is that the Eye begs the Eye, water draws water, mountains line up with mountains; we go among alien beings,[12] and we live among our own kind.[13] Tozan says, *"It is not the Eye."* This is the Eye singing out by itself. Where body, mind, intellectual recognition, forms, and grades which are *not the Eye* are present, we should meet that state as the vivid Eye manifesting itself. The buddhas of the three times, standing on the ground, have listened to the Eye turning the great wheel of Dharma and preaching the great wheel of Dharma.[14] In conclusion, in the inner sanctum of investigation in practice, we establish the mind, undergo training, and experience the great truth of bodhi, by springing inside the Eye. This Eye is, from the beginning, neither subjective nor objective. Because there are no hindrances of any kind, a great matter like this also is without hindrances. For this reason, an ancestor[15] says, *"How wondrous are the buddhas in the ten directions! They are originally just the flowers in our eyes."*[16] What is expressed here is that the buddhas in the ten directions are the Eye, and flowers in the Eye are the buddhas in the ten directions. Our present backward steps and forward steps, sitting and sleeping, because they have received the power of the Eye itself, are all like this.[17] They are holding on and letting go inside the Eye.

---

11. 無 (MU), "not having" or "being without," suggests the balanced condition in which there is nothing superfluous and nothing lacking. See chap. 22, *Bussho*.

12. 異類中行 (IRUI-CHU-GYO), "going among alien beings," is an expression of independent action which appears often in Shobogenzo. See, for example, chap. 4, *Ikka-no-myoju* [101].

13. 同類中生 (DORUI-CHU-SHO), "living among one's own kind," expresses the Buddhist attitude from the other side—not only independence but also identification.

14. Seppo says: *"The buddhas of the three times are inside the flame of the fire, turning the great wheel of Dharma."* Gensa says: *"The flame is preaching Dharma for the buddhas of the three times, and the buddhas of the three times are standing on the ground to listen."* (*Shinji-shobogenzo*, pt. 3, no. 88). Master Dogen considers the story in detail in chap. 23, *Gyobutsu-yuigi*.

15. Master Roya Ekaku (dates unknown), successor of Master Fun-yo Zensho.

16. See chap. 43, *Kuge* [49].

17. They are all in the state without separation into subject and object.

[88] My late Master, the eternal Buddha, says, *"Gouging out Bodhidharma's Eye, I make it into a mud ball and work it into a person."* Loudly, he says, *"Yes! The sea has dried right to the bottom. Waves surge so high that they hit the heavens."*

He presents this teaching to a sea of monks[18] in the abbot's quarters of Seiryo-ji temple. So he speaks of *"working a person,"*[19] and this is as if to say "fashioning a person." Because of the work, each person possesses his or her own real features. He means, for example, that with Bodhidharma's Eye he has forged individual people. And he has forged people. The meaning of *"working a person"* is like this. Because each person is a person who has sat[20] with the Eye, a fist now striking people in the Cloud Hall, a staff striking people in the Dharma Hall, and a bamboo stick and a fly-whisk striking people in the abbot's quarters, are Bodhidharma's Eye itself. Having gouged out Bodhidharma's Eye, [Master Tendo] makes it into mud balls to work into people, but people today call this by such names as "having an interview and requesting the benefit [of instruction]," or "formal preaching in the morning and informal preaching in the morning," or "sitting and making effort." What sort of person does he fashion? *"Seas dry right to the bottom, and high waves hit the heavens."*[21]

[89] My late Master, the eternal Buddha, in formal preaching in the Dharma Hall, praises the Tathāgata's realization of the truth, saying:

Six years he stumbled in the undergrowth, the ghost of a wild fox.
The whole body that sprang free was just the state of entanglement.
He lost the Eye and had no object of pursuit.
Now he deceives people saying that he was enlightened by the bright star.

"He has been enlightened by the bright star" is the comment of an onlooker just at the moment when [the Tathāgata] loses the Eye. This is the entangled state[22] of *the whole body*, and so it is easily sprung. Pursuing the object we should pursue eliminates realization as an object of pursuit, and there is also nothing to pursue in non-realization.

[90] My late Master, the eternal Buddha, in formal preaching in the Dharma Hall, says:

---

18. 海衆 (KAISHU), lit. "sea-assembly," or "sea-saṃgha." The expression suggests the fact that there are no class distinctions among the members of a saṃgha.

19. 打人 (TA-NIN). 打 (TA) means to strike, hit, or hammer out. 人 (NIN) means a human being, a person, or people.

20. 打坐 (TAZA) means to sit in Zazen, as in the phrase 祇管打坐 (SHIKAN-TAZA), "just sitting." In this compound, 打 (TA) is a verb prefix that suggests concrete action.

21. Master Tendo fashioned people who were not worried by the impermanence of reality.

22. 葛藤 (KATTO), also translated as "the complicated." See chap. 46, *Katto*.

It is the time when Gautama lost the Eye,
In the snow, a single twig of plum blossoms!
Now every place has become a thorn.
Yet [I] laugh at the swirling of the spring wind.[23]

To comment in brief, Gautama's Eyes are not only one, two, or three. The *losing* [described] now refers to which Eye? It may be that there is an Eye which is called *"losing the Eye."* In the state like this, moreover, there is an Eye which is *a single twig of plum blossoms in the snow.* Stealing ahead of spring, it leaks the spirit of spring.

My late Master, the eternal Buddha, in formal preaching in the Dharma Hall, says:

Days and weeks of pouring rain!
Completely clear skies!
Croaking of bullfrogs.
Singing of earthworms.
Eternal buddhas have never passed away.
They are manifesting the diamond Eye.
Aah!
The complicated! The complicated![24]

"The diamond Eye" is days and weeks of pouring rain, is completely clear skies, is frogs croaking and worms singing. Because [eternal buddhas] have never passed away, they are eternal buddhas. And even when eternal buddhas pass away, [their passing] is never the same as the passing of people who are not eternal buddhas.

My late Master, the eternal Buddha, in formal preaching in the Dharma Hall, says:

The sun in the south grows distant.
Inside the Eye shines light.
Inside the nostrils passes breath.

The endless continuation of the present, the winter solstice and New Year's Day, the growing distant of the sun and moon: [all] are free of connectedness. Such is the shining of light inside the Eye, and the viewing of mountains in the sun. The dignified manner of being in such circumstances is like this.

My late Master, the eternal Buddha, while at Joji-ji temple in Rin-an city,[25] gives the following formal preaching in the Dharma Hall:

---

23. The same verse appears in chap. 59, *Baike* [200].
24. 葛藤 (KATTO). See note 22.
25. In Chekiang province in east China.

This morning is the first of the second moon.
The eyes of the fly whisk are bulging out;
As bright as a mirror, as black as Japanese lacquer.
Instantly they spring out,
And swallow the cosmos in one gulp.
Yet the students of this monk
Are still battering into fences and battering into walls.
In conclusion, what?
Having given all, I am laughing heartily,
And leave everything to the vagaries of the spring wind.

The *"battering into fences and battering into walls"* described now is the totality of fences themselves battering and the totality of walls themselves battering. There is this Eye. *This morning; the second moon; the first:* these are each concrete instances of the Eye, and they are called *"eyes of the fly whisk."* Because they spring out instantly, it is this morning. Because they swallow the cosmos hundreds of thousands of times, it is the second moon. A moment of giving all is the first. The realized vivid state of eyes is like this.

Shobogenzo Ganzei

Preached to the assembly under Yamashibu peak in Esshu[26] on the 17th day of the 12th moon in the 1st year of Kangen.[27]

26. Modern-day Fukui prefecture.
27. 1243.

[64]

家常

Kajo

Everyday Life

Ka *means "house" or "home," and* ***jo*** *means "usual" or "everyday." So* ***kajo*** *means "everyday" or "everyday life." People are often prone to think that religious matters should be different from daily life, being more sacred than and superior to daily life. But according to Buddhist theory, Buddhist life is nothing other than our daily life. Without daily life there can never be Buddhism. In China it was said that wearing clothes and eating meals are just Buddhism. In this chapter, Master Dogen explains the meaning of* ***kajo****, everyday life, on the basis of Buddhism.*

7] **In general, in the house of the Buddhist patriarchs,** [drinking] tea and [eating] meals are everyday life itself. This behavior of [drinking] tea and [eating] meals has long been transmitted and is realized in the present. Thus, the Buddhist patriarchs' vivid activity of [drinking] tea and [eating] meals has come to us.

8] *Master [Do]kai*[1] *of Taiyo-zan mountain asks Tosu,*[2] *"The ideas and words of a Buddhist patriarch are as everyday tea and meals. Beyond this, are there any other words with which to teach people or not?"*

Tosu says, "Say! The capital[3] *is under the Emperor's direct rule. Is there also any dependence upon [the ancient rulers] U, To, Gyo, and Shun,*[4] *or not?"*

Taiyo is about to open his mouth. Tosu covers the Master's mouth with his fly-whisk and says, "By the time you first established the will, you already deserved thirty strokes."

At this, Taiyo attains realization and does prostrations, then goes at once.

Tosu says, "Come back a while, Ācārya!"

Taiyo, in the end, does not turn his head.

---

1. Master Fuyo Dokai (1043–1118), successor of Master Tosu Gisei, and the 18th Chinese patriarch in Master Dogen's lineage.

2. Master Tosu Gisei (1032–1083), successor of Master Taiyo Kyogen.

3. 寰 (KAN) lit. means "the region around the capital which is ruled directly by the emperor." So Master Tosu's words are a truism.

4. Emperors Gyo and Shun ruled at the end of the legendary age of the Five Rulers (2852 to 2205 B.C.). Emperor U (ruled 2205 to 2197 B.C.) was the founder of the Hsia dynasty. Emperor To (ruled 1766 to 1753 B.C.) was the founder of the Shang dynasty.

Tosu says, "Has the disciple arrived at the state without doubt?"

Holding his hands over his ears, Taiyo leaves.[5]

[100] So we should clearly maintain and rely upon [the teaching that] a Buddhist patriarch's ideas and words are a Buddhist patriarch's everyday tea and meals. Coarse tea and plain food in everyday life are the ideas and words of a Buddhist patriarch. Buddhist patriarchs make tea and meals, and tea and meals maintain Buddhist patriarchs. That being so, we rely on no tea and meal energy outside of these [tea and meals], and we never waste the Buddhist patriarch energy in these [tea and meals]. *"Is there also dependence upon U, To, Gyo, and Shun, or not?"* We should strive to learn in practice this manifestation of the view. *"Beyond this, are there any other words with which to teach people or not?"* We should spring out in experience from the brains of this question. We should experiment and observe in experience whether we are able to spring out or unable to spring out.

[101] Great Master Musai[6] of Sekito-an hut on Nangaku-zan mountain says,

> *I thatched a hut and have no wealth.*
> *Having finished a meal, I calmly look forward to a nap.*[7]

[I] have finished a meal—[an experience] which he repeats, repeats again, and repeats over again—is the idea and words of a Buddhist patriarch who experiences meals. One who has not yet finished a meal is not yet satisfied with experience. At the same time, this truth of *calmness, having finished a meal,* is realized before a meal, is realized during a meal, and is realized after a meal. To misunderstand that, in the house of *having finished a meal,* there is [always] the eating of meals, is learning in practice of [only] four or five pints out of ten.

[102] My late Master, the eternal Buddha, preaches to the assembly: *"I remember the following: A monk asks Hyakujo, 'What is a miracle?' Hyakujo says, 'Sitting alone on Great and Mighty Peak.'*[8] *Monks, do not be disturbed. Let the fellow kill himself by sitting for a while. If someone today were suddenly to ask, 'Ācārya [Nyo]jo, what is a miracle?', I would only say to them, 'How could anything be a miracle?' Finally, what? The pātra of Joji*[9] *having passed to Tendo, I eat meals.'"*[10]

---

5. *Rento-eyo,* chap. 28.

6. Master Sekito Kisen (700–790), successor of Master Seigen Gyoshi and the 8th Chinese patriarch in Master Dogen's lineage.

7. *Keitoku-dento-roku,* chap. 30.

8. 大雄峰 (DAIYU-HO), or "Great and Mighty Peak" is another name for Hyakujo-zan mountain where Master Hyakujo had his order.

9. Master Tendo Nyojo left Joji temple in 1225 in order to become the master of Tendo temple, and he gave this preaching on the day he took up residence at Tendo temple. The pātra, the Buddhist food bowl, is the subject of chap. 78, *Hatsu-u.*

10. *Nyojo-osho-goroku,* vol. 2. Also quoted in chap. 78, *Hatsu-u.*

In the everyday life of a Buddhist patriarch there is always a miracle; it has been called, *"sitting alone on Great and Mighty Peak."* Even though we now hear *"Let the fellow kill himself by sitting,"* [his sitting] is still a miracle. And there is something even more miraculous than that; it has been called, *"the pātra of Joji passing to Tendo, and eating meals."* A miracle, in every instance and for every person, is always *eating meals.*[11] This being so, *sitting alone on Great and Mighty Peak* is just *eating meals.* The pātra is used for eating meals and what is used for eating meals is the pātra. For this reason [the Master speaks of] *Joji pātra* and *Tendo eating meals.*[12] After satisfaction, there is recognition of meals. After completely eating a meal, there is satisfaction. After recognition, there is satisfaction with meals. And after satisfaction there is still eating meals. Now then, what is the pātra? In my opinion, it is beyond [the description] *"It is only a piece of wood"* and it is not *as black as Japanese lacquer.*[13] How could it be unyielding stone? How could it be an iron man? It is bottomless,[14] and it is without nostrils. It swallows space in one gulp, and space receives it with joined hands.

[95] My late Master, the eternal Buddha, on one occasion while addressing an assembly in the abbot's quarters of Zuigan Jodo Zen-in temple in Daishu,[15] says, *"When hunger comes I eat a meal, when tiredness comes I sleep. Forges span the Universe."*

"Hunger coming" is the vivid state of a person who has eaten meals already. For a person who has not experienced eating meals, hunger is impossible. So remember, we for whom hunger may be an everyday state are, decidedly, people who *have finished a meal. "Tiredness coming"* may be further tiredness experienced in tiredness. It has totally sprung free from the top of the brains of tiredness. Therefore, it is a moment of the present when, in vivid activity through the whole body, the whole body is totally turned around. *"Sleeping"* is sleeping that borrows the eyes of Buddha, the eyes of

---

11. 喫飯 (KIPPAN), "eating meals," is here used as a representative example of a basic activity of everyday life.

12. 浄慈 (JOJI) and 天童 (TENDO) are the names of the two temples and at the same time the names of Master Tendo Nyojo himself. 浄慈鉢盂 (JOJI-HATSU-U), "Joji pātra," suggests the bowl not as an abstraction but as something actually used and realized in the life of the Master. 天童喫飯 (TENDO-KIPPAN), read in the quote as "... to Tendo, and [I] eat meals," here means "the eating of meals [realized by] Tendo," that is, real eating of meals.

13. 黒如漆 (KOKU-NYO-SHITSU), "as black as Japanese lacquer," are words used by Master Tendo himself to describe the *hossu,* or ceremonial fly-whisk (see chap. 63, *Ganzei* [94]). Master Dogen is suggesting here that the pātra is so profound that it defies any such description.

14. 無底 (MUTEI), means bottomless or without a base. The pātra is rounded at the bottom and therefore has no supporting rim or base; at the same time, the words 無底 (MUTEI) suggest that the state of a pātra is bottomless or unfathomable.

15. A coastal district of Chekiang province, bordering the East China Sea.

Dharma, the eyes of wisdom, the eyes of patriarchs, and the eyes of outdoor pillars and stone lanterns.

[106] My late Master, the eternal Buddha, upon proceeding from Zuigan-ji temple in Daishu to his assignment at Joji-ji temple in Rin-an-fu city,[16] says in formal preaching in the Dharma Hall:

Half a year I ate meals and sat on Banpo peak,
Shut off by thousand myriads of mists and clouds.
Suddenly, a thunderclap[17] *resounded.*
The color of Spring in the capital is apricot-blossom crimson.[18]

The teaching of the Buddhist patriarchs who administered the teaching during the age of the Buddha was, in every case, *sitting on Banpo peak and eating meals.* Mastery of the transmission of the Buddha's wisdom and life is just realization of the vivid state of *eating meals. Half a year of sitting on Banpo peak* is called *"eating meals." The enclosing mists and clouds* are incalculable. Though the *thunderclap* is *sudden,* the *Spring color* of *the apricot blossoms* is nothing other than crimson. *"The capital"* means each present instance of naked sincerity.[19] The ineffable state of these situations is *eating meals.* Banpo is the name of the peak [on which stands] Zuigan-ji temple.

[108] My late Master, the eternal Buddha, addressing the assembly on one occasion in the Buddha Hall of Zuigan-ji temple in Keigen-fu city[20] in Minshu, says:

The golden and fine form[21]
Is to get dressed and to eat meals.
That is why I bow to you.[22]
I sleep early and get up late.
Aye...
Talk of the profound and preaching of the fine are enormously free.
Sternly be on guard lest a twirling flower inflames you.

This instant, we should already have seen through the heavy burden. *"The golden and fine form"* describes getting dressed and eating meals. Getting

16. Also in Chekiang province.

17. The thunderclap symbolizes the invitation to become Master of Joji Temple.

18. *Nyojo-osho-goroku,* vol. 1.

19. 赤赤条条 (SEKISEKI-JOJO), lit. "red-red instance-instance," is a variation of the common expression 赤心片片 (SEKISHIN-HENPEN), lit. "red mind fragment-fragment," i.e. sincerity at every moment. See also chap. 20, *Kokyo* [162], and chap. 37, *Shinjin-gakudo* [156].

20. Present-day Ningpo in northern Chekiang.

21. Alludes to the golden hue of the Buddha, one of the 32 signs.

22. 因我礼伱 (*yo[tte] ware nanji o rai[su]*), "Therefore I bow to you," is thought to derive from a story involving Master Gensa Shibi, although a definitive source has not been traced. The point is that, in performing simple acts like getting dressed and eating meals, master and disciple are each furnished equally with Buddhist virtue.

dressed and eating meals are the golden and fine form. Never grope around asking what person gets dressed and eats meals. Do not say that someone else is the golden and fine form. Then your state will be this expression of the truth. [One to whom the Master says] *"That is why I bow to you"* is like that. When I have already started eating the meal, you bow with joined hands and eat the meal. Because we sternly guard against twirling flowers,[23] we are like that.

0] Zen Master Enchi Dai-an[24] of Chokei-in temple in Fukushu, says in formal preaching to the assembly in the Dharma Hall:

Dai-an lived on Isan mountain for thirty years,
Eating Isan meals,
Shitting Isan shit,
Not learning Isan Zen,
Just watching over a castrated water buffalo.
When it strayed into the grass, I dragged it out.
When it invaded another's seed patch, I whipped it.
Though disciplined for a long time already,
As a pitiful creature, it suffered people's remarks.
Now it has turned into a white ox on open ground.[25]
It is always before me.
All day long it is in a state of conspicuous brightness.
Even if driven away, it does not leave.[26]

We should clearly receive and retain this preaching. Thirty years of effort in an order of Buddhist patriarchs are eating meals, with no miscellaneous worries at all. When the vivid state of eating meals is realized, supervision of a castrated water buffalo is naturally the standard.

2] *Great Master Shinsai of Joshu*[27] *asks a newly arrived monk, "Have you ever been here before?"*

The monk says, "Yes, I have."

The Master says, "Have some tea."

---

23. 拈華 (NENGE), or "the picking up of a flower," alludes to the story of the transmission between the Buddha and Master Mahākāśyapa on Vulture Peak (see chap. 68, *Udonge*). Here it is an example of a stimulus which might tend to make a Buddhist practitioner feel spiritual.

24. Master Enchi Dai-an (793–883), successor of Master Hyakujo Ekai. He became a monk under Master Obaku, then joined Master Hyakujo's order along with Master Isan Reiyu. After Master Isan's death in 853, Master Enchi became the master of Isan mountain. Later he retired to Chokei-in temple. Zen Master Enchi is his posthumous title.

25. Alludes to the Lotus Sutra. See LS 1.166.

26. *Keitoku-dento-roku*, chap. 9.

27. Master Joshu Jushin (778–897), successor of Master Nansen Fugan. Joshu district is in modern-day Hupei province.

Later he asks another monk, "Have you ever been here before?"

The monk says, "No, never before."

The Master says, "Have some tea."

A chief of the temple office[28] *asks the Master, "Why [did you say] 'Have some tea,' to the monk who has been here before and also [say] 'Have some tea' to the monk who has never been here before?"*

The Master calls to the chief.

The chief answers.

The Master says, "Have some tea."[29]

"Here" is beyond the brain, is beyond the nostrils, and is beyond Joshu district. Because it springs free from "here," it *has already arrived here*[30] and it *has never been here before.*[31] *This place is the place where the ineffable exists,*[32] but they discuss it only as *having already arrived* and *never having been before.* For this reason my late Master says, *"What person in a painted tower*[33] *or a tavern could come to meet Joshu and enjoy Joshu's tea?"* In sum, the everyday life of Buddhist patriarchs is nothing other than drinking tea and eating meals.

Shobogenzo Kajo

Preached to the assembly under Yamashibu peak in Etsu-u on the 17th day of the 12th lunar month in the 1st year of Kangen.[34]

---

28. 院主 (INJU) also called 監寺 (KANSU), or "prior," is one of the main temple officers charged with general administration of the monastery.

29. *Shinji-shobogenzo*, pt. 3, no. 33, and *Rento-eyo*, chap. 6.

30. 曾到此間 (SO-TO-SHIKAN) in the story means "been here before," but the literal meaning of 到 (TO) is to arrive. Therefore 曾到此間 (SO-TO-SHIKAN), lit. "arrived here before," or "arrived here already," suggests the state at the moment of the present.

31. 不曾到此間 (FU-SO-TO-SHIKAN), "never been here before" or "never arrived here before," also describes the moment of the present.

32. In response to a question from Rinzai, Fuke overturns a dinner table. Master Rinzai says, *"Very coarse person!"* Fuke says, *"This place is the place where something ineffable exists. Explain it as coarse or explain it as fine." Shinji-shobogenzo,* pt. 1, no. 96. See also notes to chap. 56, *Senmen,* para. [124].

33. 画楼 (GARO) "painted tower" suggests a grand and luxurious building.

34. 1243.

[65]

龍吟

RYUGIN

The Moaning of Dragons

*Ryu means "dragons," and gin means "sing," "chant," or "moan." Dragons, of course, are not living animals, but are mythical animals. So it would be very strange for dragons to sing or moan; in short, it is impossible for dragons to sing or moan. But in ancient China people used the word **ryugin**, "the moaning of dragons" or "the whispers of dragons," as a symbol of something mystical in nature or in the Universe—for example, in the expression **koboku ryugin**. **Koboku** means "withered trees"; the words conjure an image of a lonely, desolate landscape of withered trees, where we feel we can hear something that is not a sound. This concept later entered into Buddhist explanations. The moaning of dragons is not a sound but something which cannot be heard with the ears alone; that is, quietness, nature, the Universe, or reality. Buddhism is not simple mysticism, and so we should not readily believe in the existence of something mystical. At the same time, we should not limit reality to the area of sensory perception. On this basis, Master Dogen explains the meaning of **ryugin** or "the moaning of dragons" in this chapter.*

6] **Great Master Jisai of Tosu-zan mountain in Joshu,**[1] the story goes, is asked by a monk, *"Among withered trees does the moaning of dragons exist or not?"*

The Master says, *"I say that inside of skulls exists the lion's roar."*[2]

Talk of withered trees and dead ash is the original teaching of non-Buddhists. But the withered trees of which non-Buddhists speak and the withered trees[3] of which Buddhist patriarchs speak may be very different.

---

1. Master Tosu Daido (819–914), successor of Master Suibi Mugaku. Great Master Jisai is his posthumous title. The simplicity of Master Tosu's life on Tosu-zan mountain in his home district of Joshu (in present-day Anhui province in east China) is mentioned in chap. 30, *Gyoji* [241]. See also chap. 42, *Tsuki*.

2. *Keitoku-dento-roku*, chap. 15.

3. 枯木 (KOBOKU), "withered trees" or "dead trees," in Buddhism symbolizes the vivid state of non-emotion, or people in the vivid state of non-emotion. The Zazen Hall of a Buddhist temple is sometimes called 枯木堂 (KOBOKU-DO), "The Withered Tree Hall." See, for example, chap. 30, *Gyoji* [241].

Even though non-Buddhists talk of withered trees, they do not know withered trees; how much less could they hear the moaning of dragons? Non-Buddhists have thought that withered trees might be trees in decay; they have understood that [withered trees] cannot meet spring. The withered trees of which the Buddhist patriarchs speak are in the learning in practice of *the sea having dried.*[4] The sea having dried is a tree having withered, and a tree having withered is [the vivid state of] *meeting spring.* A tree not being disturbed is the withered state. The mountain trees, ocean trees, sky trees, and other trees of the present, are just withered trees. Even a sprouting bud is the moaning of dragons among withered trees. Even [a tree] of a hundred thousand myriad fathoms is the descendant of withered trees. The form, nature, substance, and energy of the withered state are the withered stumps which Buddhist patriarchs have described, and are other than withered stumps—there are trees in mountains and valleys and there are trees in fields and villages. Trees in mountains and valleys are usually called "pines and oaks." Trees in fields and villages are usually called "human beings and gods." *Leaves spread out from roots:*[5] we call this state "a Buddhist patriarch." *Root and branch should return to the fundamental:*[6] this is just learning of the state. What exists in the state like this is the long Dharma-body of a withered tree, or the short Dharma-body of a withered tree. Those who are not withered trees never moan the moaning of dragons, and those other than withered trees do not get rid of "the moaning of dragons." *However many times [this withered tree] meets spring, it does not change its mind:"*[7] this is the moaning of dragons that has become totally dry. It does not belong on the scale *do, re, mi, fa,* and *so.* At the same time, *do, re, mi, fa,* and *so* are two or three former and latter instances of the moaning of dragons. That being so, this monk's expression *"Among withered trees does the moaning of dragons exist or not?"* which has been realized as a concrete question for the first time in countless kalpas, is the realization of a comment in itself.[8] Tosu's words *"I say that inside of skulls exists the lion's roar"*[9] mean, *Is there anything that is covered?* [They mean,] *The effort to curb ourselves*

4. 海枯 (KAIKO), "the sea has dried" represents a real situation that has changed completely (see also chap. 63, *Ganzei* [88]). The character for "withered" and for "dried" are the same: 枯 (KO).

5. 依根葉分布 *(ne ni yotte ha bunpu su).* Quoted from the poem *Sandokai (Experiencing the State)* by Master Sekito Kisen.

6. 本末須帰宗 *(honmatsu subekaraku shu ni kisu beshi).* Ibid. 本末 (HONMATSU) means root and branch, means and ends, substance and detail, or the important and the trivial.

7. 幾度逢春不変心 *(ikutabi ka haru ni au te kokoro o henze zu)* is the second line of the following verse by Master Daibai Hojo: *"A withered tree, broken and abandoned, in a cold forest, / However many times it meets spring, it does not change its mind. / Passing woodmen do not even look back. / Why should popular entertainers be keen to search it out?"* See chap. 30, *Gyoji* [141].

8. 話頭 (WATO) means a *koan;* that is, a comment or story in which the truth is expressed. See also notes to chap. 20, *Kokyo* [162], and chap. 36, *Komyo* [126].

9. 師小吼 (SHISHI-KU), "the lion's roar," symbolizes the Buddha's preaching.

and to promote others is ceaseless. [And they mean,] *Skulls are littering the whole countryside.*

9] Great Master Shuto[10] of Kyogen-ji temple, the story goes, is asked by a monk, *"What is the truth?"*

The Master says, *"The moaning of dragons among withered trees."*

The monk says, *"I do not understand."*[11]

The Master says, *"Eyes in skulls."*

Thereafter, a monk asks Sekiso,[12] *"What is the moaning of dragons among withered trees?"*

[Seki]so says, *"A trace of joy still being retained."*

The monk says, *"What are eyes in skulls?"*

[Seki]so says, *"A trace of consciousness still being retained."*

On another occasion, a monk asks Sozan,[13] *"What is the moaning of dragons among withered trees?"*

[So]zan says, *"The bloodline being unbroken."*

The monk says, *"What are eyes in skulls?"*

[So]zan says, *"Dryness being without limit."*

The monk says, *"I wonder if there are any who are able to hear."*

[So]zan says, *"Over the whole Earth there is no-one who does not hear."*

The monk says, *"I wonder what words the dragons moan."*

[So]zan says, *"Even without knowing the words, those who hear all share the loss."*[14]

] The listeners and moaners we are discussing now are beyond the level of moaners who moan about dragons. This melody is the moaning of dragons itself. *Among withered trees* and *in skulls* are beyond inside and outside and beyond self and others; they are the moment of the present and the moment of eternity. *A trace of joy still being retained* is horns growing further on a head. *A trace of consciousness still being retained* is skin having been shed completely. Sozan's words *"The bloodline being unbroken"* describe the truth being non-inimical, and the body being turned around in mid-speech.[15] *Dryness being*

10. Master Kyogen Chikan (died 818), successor of Master Isan Reiyu.

11. This line follows the version in *Keitoku-dento-roku*. In *Shinji-shobogenzo* the monk's second line is *"What is a person in the state of truth?"*

12. Master Sekiso Keisho (807–888), successor of Master Dogo Enchi.

13. Master Sozan Honjaku (840–901), successor of Master Tozan Ryokai.

14. This group of stories can be found in *Keitoku-dento-roku*, chap. 17. See also *Shinji-shobogenzo*, pt. 1, no. 28.

15. 語脈裏転身 (GOMYAKU-RI-TENSHIN), or "transforming the body inside the stream of words" expresses flexibility—maintenance of the purity of the Buddhist tradition does not call for a fighting attitude or a rigid outlook.

without limit is the sea having dried and the bottom not being reached.[16] Because not reaching the limit is dryness itself,[17] in the state of dryness we continue to dry.[18] Saying *"Are there any who hear?"* is as if to say "Are there any who cannot?" *Over the whole Earth there is no-one who does not hear.* I would like to ask further: Setting aside for a while *"there is no-one who does not hear,"* tell me, before "the whole Earth" exists, where then is the moaning of dragons? Speak at once! Speak at once! *I wonder what words the dragons moan.* We should ask this question. Moaning dragons are naturally a sound being voiced, or a matter being taken up, in the mud. They are the passing of air inside the nostrils. *We do not know what words these are*[19] describes the existence, in words, of dragons. *Those who hear all share the loss:*[20] how sorrowful it is! The moaning of dragons that has now been realized by Kyogen, Sekiso, Sozan, and the others, becomes clouds and becomes water.[21] Without speaking of the truth, without speaking of eyes or skulls, just this is the moaning of dragons in a thousand melodies and in ten thousand melodies. *A trace of joy still being retained* is the croaking of bullfrogs. *A trace of consciousness still being retained* is the singing of earthworms. Relying on this state, *the bloodline is unbroken,* and a gourd succeeds a gourd. Because *dryness is without limit,* outdoor pillars gestate and give birth and a stone lantern stands out against a stone lantern.[22]

---

16. 海枯不尽底 (KAI-KO-FU-JIN-TEI), or "the sea has dried and no sea-bed is reached," is a variation of the expression 海枯不見底 (KAI-KO-FU-KEN-TEI), "the sea has dried and no sea-bed is seen" (see note 3; see also chap. 62, *Hensan* [70]). Instead of 不見 (FUKEN), "not seeing," Master Dogen said 不尽 (FUJIN), "not reaching the limit."

17. 不尽是乾 (FUJIN-ZE-KAN). 不尽 (FUJIN), "not reaching the limit," suggests the Buddhist process as non-attachment to an end-result. 乾 (KAN), "dryness," also suggests non-attachment.

18. 乾上又乾 (KANJO-YU-KAN), lit. "on dryness, further drying."

19. 也不知是何章句 (MATA-FUCHI-ZE-KA-SHOKU), translated in the story as "Even without knowing the words..." is lit. "Even without knowing that these are what chapter and verse." 何章句 (KA-SHOKU), "what chapter and verse" or "what words," can be interpreted as *"What* words," that is "words of the ineffable."

20. 聞者皆喪 (MONSHA-KAI-SO), translated in the story as "those who hear all share the loss," is lit. "those who hear all mourn." 喪 (SO) means to mourn or to lose someone. At the same time, in the compound 喪失 (SOSHITSU) it means "to lose." The phrase 喪身失命 (SOSHIN-SHITSUMYO), "to lose body and life," is an ironic expression of attaining the state of realization. See, for example, chap. 67, *Soshi-sairai-no-i* [149].

21. くもをなし、みずをなす *(kumo o nashi, mizu o nasu),* "becoming clouds and becoming water," represents the unhindered working of Nature. In a poem in chap. 59, *Baike* [224], Master Tendo Nyojo uses the phrase "the becoming of rain and the becoming of clouds" to express Nature itself.

22. 燈籠対燈籠 (TORO-TAI-TORO), lit. "a stone lantern opposes a stone lantern," means a stone lantern exists conspicuously as it is. The name 燈籠 (TORO) is applied not only to the stone lanterns which are commonly seen in Japanese-style gardens but also to hanging lanterns, lanterns floated on water, et cetera. However, when Master Dogen uses the term 燈籠 (TORO) in Shobogenzo, it is assumed that he has in mind a stone lantern in the garden of a Buddhist temple.

Shobogenzo Ryugin

Preached to the assembly under Yamashibu peak in Etsu-u[23] on the 25th day of the 12th lunar month in the 1st year of Kangen.[24]

23. Modern-day Fukui prefecture.
24. 1243.

[66]

春秋

SHUNJU

Spring and Autumn

***Shun** means "spring" and **ju**, which is a corruption of **shu**, means "autumn." **Shunju**, spring and autumn, expresses the seasons. In this chapter Master Dogen describes the Buddhist attitude towards cold and heat. First Master Dogen quotes a famous conversation on this subject between Master Tozan Ryokai and a monk. Then he discusses the comments of some ancient masters in order to explain the true meaning of the story.*

Great Master Tozan Gohon,[1] the story goes, is asked by a monk, *"When cold or heat come, how are we to avoid them?"*

The Master says, *"Why do you not go to the place without cold and heat?"*

The monk says, *"What is the place without cold and heat?"*

The Master says *"When it is cold, kill the ācārya with cold.*[2] *When it is hot, kill the ācārya with heat."*[3]

Many have discussed this story in the past, and many should consider it in the present. Buddhist patriarchs inevitably have experienced it, and those who have experienced it are Buddhist patriarchs. Many Buddhist patriarchs of the past and present, in the Western Heavens and in the Eastern Lands, have seen this story as their real features. The realization of the features of this story is the reality of Buddhist patriarchs. That being so, we should clarify in detail the monk's question, *"When cold or heat come, how are we to avoid them?"* That means detailed examination in experience of the very moment in which cold has come and of the very moment in which heat has come. Both the totality of cold and the totality of heat, in this *cold and heat*, are cold and heat themselves. Because they are cold and heat themselves, when they have come, they have come from the very brains[4] of cold and heat themselves, and

---

1. Master Tozan Ryokai (807–869), successor of Master Ungan Donjo and the 11th Chinese patriarch in Master Dogen's lineage.

2. 闍梨 (JARI), represents the Sanskrit term of respect *ācārya*. In this case, it means "you."

3. *Shinji-shobogenzo*, pt. 3, no. 25.

4. 頂𩕳 (CHONEI), "brains," sometimes symbolizes the intellectual sphere, but in this case it means that which is fundamental or real as opposed to a concept.

they are manifest from the very eyes of cold and heat themselves. On these very brains is the place without cold and heat. In these very eyes is the place without cold and heat. The founding Patriarch's words, *"When it is cold, kill the ācārya with cold. When it is hot, kill the ācārya with heat"* are about the situation just at the moment of having arrived. *When it is cold,* the expression is *"killing with cold,"* but *when it is hot, "killing with heat"* need not always be the expression. Cold is utterly cold, and heat is utterly hot. Even if we have been able to discover myriad koṭis of methods of avoidance, they are all like replacing a tail with a head.[5] Cold is just the vivid eyes of the ancestral patriarchs. Heat is just the warm skin and flesh of my late Master.

[130] Zen Master Jo-in Koboku[6] (who succeeded Master Fuyo and who was known as Master Hojo) says, *"Some among the saṃgha interpret as follows: 'This monk's question has fallen into the relative already. Tozan's answer returns to the absolute. In [Tozan's] speech, the monk recognizes sound, and comes into the absolute. Tozan then exits via the relative.' Interpretations like this not only blaspheme the ancient saints but also daunt the perpetrators themselves. Have you not read the words that 'When we listen to the understanding of ordinary people, though the reds and blues [it excites] in the mind may be beautiful before the eyes, if it is stored for long it makes for disease.' In general, noble wayfarers, if you want to master this matter, first you must know the founding Patriarch's right-Dharma-eye treasury. The comments and teaching of other Buddhist patriarchs are something like the murmurs of hot [water] in a [lacquered] bowl. Even so, I dare to ask you, 'What, in conclusion, is the place without cold or heat? Do you understand or not?' A jeweled tower is a nest for a kingfisher, but a golden palace offers no shelter to a mandarin duck."*[7]

[132] This Master is a descendant of Tozan, a hero in the Patriarch's order. That being so, he clearly admonishes the many individuals who mistakenly prostrate themselves to Great Master Tozan, the founding Patriarch, inside the cave of the relative and the absolute. If the Buddha-Dharma were transmitted and received on the basis of limited consideration of the relative and the absolute, how could it have reached the present day? Wild kittens, barnyard bumpkins, who have never explored Tozan's inner sanctum, people who have not walked the threshold of the truth of the Buddha-Dharma, mistakenly assert that Tozan teaches people with his five positions of the relative and the absolute,[8] and so on. This is an outlandish insistence and a random

5. 以頭換尾 (I-TO-KAN-BI), "replacing a tail with a head," here suggests impracticality. Sometimes the same expression suggests changing from an intellectual attitude to a practical attitude.

6. Master Koboku Hojo (dates unknown), a successor of Master Fuyo Dokai (1043–1118) who was the 18th Chinese patriarch in Master Dogen's lineage. Zen Master Jo-in Koboku is his posthumous title.

7. *Katai-futo-roku,* chap. 26.

8. 偏正等の五位 (HENSHOTO *no* GO-I). See also chap. 49, *Butsudo* [166].

insistence. We should not see or hear it. We should just investigate the fact that the founding Patriarch possesses the right-Dharma-eye treasury.

Zen Master Wanshi[9] of Tendo-zan mountain in Keigen-fu city[10] (who succeeded Master Tanka and who was known as Master Shokaku) says, *"This episode, if we discuss it, is like a game of go between two players. If you do not respond to my move, I will fool you completely. If we experience it like this, we will begin to understand Tozan's intention. And Tendo cannot help adding a footnote:*

When we research it, this concrete place is without hot and cold.
Already the blue depths have dried to the last drop.
I tell you we can catch a giant turtle just by bending down.
You are a laugh, dallying in the sand with a fishing rod.[11]

Not denying the *game of go,* for the present, how are the *two players*? If we call it *"a game of go between two players,"* there might be a handicap of eight stones. With an eight-stone handicap, it is not a game of go, is it? If we are to discuss it, we should discuss it like this: the game of go is one player and an opponent meeting each other. Even so, we should mindfully consider, and should physically master, the state now expressed by Wanshi as *"you do not respond to my move." "You do not respond to my move"* says *"you can never be me."* Do not pass over *"I will fool you completely."*[12] In mud there is mud: those who tread in it wash their feet—and also wash their crown strings. In a pearl there is a pearl: when it shines it illuminates others and it illuminates itself.

Zen Master Engo[13] of Kassan mountain[14] (who succeeded Zen Master Goso Ho-en and who was known as Master Kokugon) says:

A bowl rolls around a pearl, and the pearl rolls around the bowl.
The absolute in the relative, the relative in the absolute.[15]

---

9. Master Wanshi Shokaku (1091–1157), successor of Master Tanka Shijun. He became a disciple of Master Tanka Shijun at the recommendation of Master Koboku Hojo. When he was 39 he became the Master of Keitoku-ji temple on Mt. Tendo, where he remained until his death.

10. Present-day Ningpo in northern Chekiang. Master Dogen was later to practice here on Mt. Tendo under Master Tendo Nyojo.

11. *Wanshi-koroku,* chap. 4.

12. Master Wanshi's words describe the serious state of action in daily life.

13. Master Engo Kokugon (1063–1135), successor of Master Goso Ho-en, and editor of *Hekigan-roku (Blue Cliff Record).* Both Master Engo and Master Goso are quoted in chap. 74, *Tenborin.*

14. In Hunan province in southeast central China.

15. 偏中正 (HEN-CHU-SHO) and 正中偏 (SHO-CHU-HEN) are the first two of Master Tozan's five positions. The other three are 正中来 (SHO-CHU-RAI), "the absolute coming to the middle," 偏中至 (HEN-CHU-SHI), "the relative arriving at the middle," and 兼中到 (KEN-CHU-TO), "both having arrived at the middle."

Of the antelope,[16] *carrying its horns, there is no trace.*
Hunting hounds circle the forest and emptily skulk.[17]

The present expression *"a bowl rolls around a pearl"* is unprecedented and inimitable, it has rarely been heard in eternity. Hitherto, [people] have spoken only as if the pearl rolling in the bowl were ceaseless. The antelope is now holding up its horns in the emptiness. And the forest is now circling the hunting hounds.

[137] Zen Master Myokaku[18] of Shisho-ji temple on Seccho-zan mountain in Keigen-fu city (who succeeded Master Hokuto [Ko]so,[19] and who was known as Master Juken) says:

A guiding hand[20] *is as a cliff of ten thousand feet.*
Why should the relative and the absolute always be neatly arranged?
A stately old mansion of lapis lazuli lights up a bright moon.
A black guard dog,[21] *hardy and keen, is vacantly padding up the steps.*[22]

Seccho is a third-generation Dharma-descendant of Unmon, and he may be called a bag of skin that has experienced satisfaction. Now, saying that *"A guiding hand is as a cliff of ten thousand feet,"* he indicates a singularly uncompromising standard, but [a guiding hand] may not always be like that. The present story of the monk's question and [To]zan's teaching is not necessarily about *bestowing a guiding hand or not bestowing a guiding hand,*[23] and not necessarily about *leaving the world or not leaving the world;* how much less does it rely on expression of the relative and the absolute. [People] seem unable to lay a hand upon this story without relying on the eyes of the relative and the absolute. That is because, lacking the nose-ring which is [got by] visiting [a master] and requesting [instruction], they do not arrive at the periphery of the founding Patriarch, and do not glimpse the great masters of the Buddha-Dharma. Picking up some new straw sandals, they should visit [a master] and request [instruction]. Stop recklessly saying that the

16. 羚羊 (REIYO, *kamoshika*), "a serow," is any of several goat-like antelopes (genus *Capricornis*) of eastern Asia which are usually rather dark and heavily built, and some of which have distinct manes [Webster's].

17. *Engo-zenji-koroku,* chap. 9, Eulogies of the Ancients.

18. Master Seccho Juken (980–1052).

19. Master Chimon Koso (dates unknown).

20. 垂手 (SUISHU), lit. "the hanging down of a hand," means practical guidance bestowed from a master to a disciple.

21. 韓獹 (KANRO). 韓 (KAN) was an area in China associated with this breed of dog. 獹 (RO) means black.

22. *Hekigan-roku (Blue Cliff Record),* no. 43.

23. 垂手不垂手 (SUISHU-FUSUISHU), lit. "hanging down a hand, not hanging down a hand," expresses a distinction between a master's instruction of others and his or her own practice. The phrase appears in the commentary of *Hekigan-roku,* 43: *"In the Soto lineage there is leaving the world and not leaving the world, and there is bestowing a guiding hand and not bestowing a guiding hand."*

Buddha-Dharma of the founding Patriarch is the five positions of the absolute and the relative.

Master Shutaku[24] of Tennei temple in Tokei district,[25] [titled] Zen Master Chorei, says:

Amid the relative exists the absolute; amid the absolute, the relative.
Thousands of centuries floating downstream in the human world.
How many times I have hoped to return, but to return has been impossible.
Before my gate, as ever, weeds are growing in abundance.[26]

He also cannot help mentioning the absolute and the relative, and yet he has picked up something. Not denying that he has picked up something, what is it that, *in the middle of the relative, exists?*[27]

Master Bussho[28] of Dai-i [mountain] in Tanshu[29] (who succeeded Engo and whose monk's name was Hotai) says:

Thanks to you,[30] *I have penetrated the place without cold or heat.*
A withered tree has bloomed again.
Laughable people who mark their boat in looking for a sword,[31]
Still today are in cold ashes.[32]

This expression has just enough power to tread upon the Board of Law[33] and to receive it upon the crown of the head.

Zen Master Tando Bunjun[34] of Roku-tan pond[35] says:

---

24. Master Chorei Shutaku (died 1123), successor of Master Oryu Isei.

25. 東京 (TOKEI) is lit. "the Eastern Capital." It corresponds to a district in present-day Honan province in east-central China.

26. *Chorei-shutaku-zenji-goroku (Record of the Words of Zen Master Chorei Shutaku).*

27. Master Chorei Shutaku's verse says 偏中有 (HEN-CHU-U), "In the relative, exists..." 偏 (HEN), "relative," originally means "one-sidedness." 中 (CHU), as a preposition means "in," "inside," or "in the middle of." The Middle Way is 中道 (CHUDO). Master Dogen picked up the three characters 偏中有 (HEN-CHU-U) to suggest real existence in the middle way between extremes.

28. Master Bussho Hotai (dates unknown), successor of Master Engo Kokugon (1063–1135).

29. In present-day Hunan province in southeast central China.

30. 君 *(kimi)*, a polite form for "you," here means Master Tozan.

31. The Chinese book 春秋 (SHUNJU), *"Spring and Autumn,"* by 呂子 (ROSHI) tells the story of a man who dropped his sword from a boat on a river, and tried to mark the place by putting a notch in his boat. He stubbornly searched under the notch, even though the boat had moved downstream.

32. *Zenshu-juko-renju-tsushu (Complete String-of-Pearls Collection of Eulogies to Past Masters of the Zen Sect)*, chap. 24.

33. 公安 (KOAN) represents 公案 (KOAN), which stands for 公府案牘 (KOFU ANTOKU), lit. "official government law-text." This name was given to a board on which a new law was displayed. It is thus a symbol of universal law, or Dharma; the Universe itself. See chap. 3, *Genjo-koan*.

In the moment of heat [I] kill [myself] with heat
and in the moment of cold with cold.
Where heat and cold come from I do not care at all.
Realizing the ends of space in action
and remembering worldly matters at will.
The old master is crowned with a boar-skin cap.[36]

Now let us ask: What is the truth of the state of *not caring*?[37] Speak at once! Speak at once!

[141] Zen Master Kazan Butto[38] of Koshu[39] (who succeeded Zen Master Bukkan Egon of Taihei mountain and who was known as Master Shujun) says:

Tozan spoke of the place without cold and heat.
Numerous Zen people have lost their way there.
When it is cold I get in front of a fire,
and when it is hot I employ means of keeping cool.
All my life I am able to avoid and escape cold and heat.[40]

[142] This Master [Shu]jun is a Dharma-grandson of Zen Master Goso Ho-en,[41] but his words are like those of a small child. Even so, in *"All my life I am able to avoid and escape cold and heat,"* there may be a hint of future mature realization. In that case, *"all my life"* means *"with my whole life,"* and *"escaping cold and heat"* means getting free of body and mind. In conclusion, although masters from many districts and in many ages have devoted themselves to flapping their lips like this, offering their eulogies to the ancients, they have never glimpsed the periphery of the founding Patriarch Tozan. The reason, if asked, is that they do not know what cold and heat are in the everyday life of a Buddhist patriarch, and so they randomly speak, for example, of *"employing means of keeping cool and getting in front of a fire."* It is especially pitiful that you [Shujun], though in the vicinity of venerable patriarchs, have not heard what *"cold and heat"* means. We should regret that the ancestral Master's truth has died out. Knowing the form and stages of this *cold and heat,*

---

34. Master Tando Bunjun (1060?–1115), successor of Master Shinjo Kokubun.

35. The name of a pond within the grounds of Tozan temple in Kiangsi province in southeast China.

36. *Zenshu-juko-renju-tsushu,* chap. 24.

37. 不干底 (FUKAN-TEI), or "the state beyond cares." Master Tando Bunjun said 不干 (FUKAN, *kan [se] zu*), "I do not care" or "I am not concerned." Master Dogen added the character 底 (TEI) "state," suggesting detachment as a concrete condition of the body-mind.

38. Master Kazan Shujun (1078?–1134). He was the successor of Master Taihei Egon, and at the same time he received the direct instruction of Master Engo Kokugon.

39. In present-day Chekiang province in east China.

40. *Zenshu-juko-renju-tsushu,* chap. 24.

41. Master Goso Ho-en (died 1104), successor of Master Haku-un Shutan. Master Goso was the master of Engo Kokugon.

having passed instantaneously through periods of cold and heat and having utilized cold and heat, we should praise over again, with eulogies of the ancients and discussions of the ancients, the truth that the founding Patriarch taught. Until we are at that level, the best thing for us is to know our own faults. Even the secular[42] are aware of the sun and the moon and they maintain and rely upon the myriad things, but there are differences among them between the sacred and the clever, between gentlefolk and stupid fellows. Do not misunderstand that cold and heat in the Buddha's truth are the same as the cold and heat of stupid fellows. Just be diligent in practice at once.

Shobogenzo Shunju

Preached to the assembly, a second time, deep in the mountains of Etsu-u in the 2nd year of Kangen.[43] At a Buddhist event,[44] I have preached a Buddhist Kirin Sutra.[45] An ancestral Master said, *"Though there are many horns in the herd, one kirin is enough."*[46]

42. 俗 (ZOKU), "the secular," often in Shobogenzo represents the teachings of Taoism and Confucianism. In this case, Master Dogen may have been thinking of the Taoist text 春秋 (SHUNJU), "Spring and Autumn."

43. 1244.

44. 仏事 (BUTSU-JI), a Buddhist event, suggests, for example, a memorial gathering on the anniversary of a person's death. Preaching by Master Tendo Nyojo at such an event is described in chap. 30, *Gyoji* [264].

45. The Taoist text 春秋 (SHUNJU), "Spring and Autumn," was also known as 麟経 (RINKYO), "the [Ki]rin Sutra." The kirin is a magical horned animal associated in Chinese legends with wise rule.

46. Master Seigen Gyoshi (died 740), successor of Master Daikan Eno. The quotation means *"To have just one outstanding student is enough."* It appears in *Keitoku-dento-roku* in the section about Master Seigen.

[67]

祖師西来意

SOSHI-SAIRAI-NO-I

The Ancestral Master's Intention in Coming from the West

So means "ancestor" or "patriarch" and ***shi*** *means "master"; thus* ***soshi*** *means "ancestral masters," or "the ancestral Master." The word sometimes, as in this case, indicates Master Bodhidharma.* ***Sai*** *means "west" and* ***rai*** *means "come."* ***I*** *(pronounced not as in white but as in green) means "intention" or "aim." So* ***Soshi-sairai-no-i*** *means Master Bodhidharma's intention in coming from the west. It is said that in the sixth century Master Bodhidharma went from India (the west) to China (the east) to spread Buddhism, and that this event marked the transmission of true Buddhism to China. Master Bodhidharma was then called the first Patriarch in China and so Chinese Buddhists thought it very important to discuss Master Bodhidharma's intention in coming from the west. In this chapter, Master Dogen picks up a famous discussion between Master Kyogen Chikan and his disciple to explain the real meaning of Master Bodhidharma's intention in coming from the west.*

Great Master Shuto[1] **of Kyogen-ji temple** (who succeeded Dai-i[2] and whose monk's name was Chikan) addresses the assembly: *"A person*[3] *has gone up a tree on a thousand foot precipice. In her mouth she is biting a branch of the tree. Her feet will not step onto the tree and her hands will not pull her onto the branch. Under the tree suddenly there appears [another] person who asks, 'What was the ancestral Master's intention in coming from the west?' Just at that moment, if she opens her mouth to answer the other she loses body and life, and if she does not answer she goes against what the other is asking. Now say, just at such a moment, what are you able to do?"*

---

1. Master Kyogen Chikan (died 898), successor of Master Isan Reiyu. Great Master Shuto is his posthumous title.

2. Master Isan Reiyu (771–853), successor of Master Hyakujo Ekai. He lived on Mt. Dai-i.

3. 人 (NIN, *hito*) means a person or a human being. In this case, it has been assumed that the person who has gone up the tree is a woman.

Then Ācārya Sho of Koto mountain steps out from the assembly and says, "I do not ask about when she has gone up the tree. Before she goes up a tree, please Master say, what is the situation then?"

The Master bursts into loud laughter.[4]

[148] The present story has appeared in many commentaries and discussions of the ancients, but the individuals who have expressed its truth are few; for the most part, it seems that [people] have been completely dumbfounded. Nevertheless, if we consider [the story] by utilizing *not thinking,* and by utilizing *non-thinking,*[5] effort on one round cushion with Old [Master] Kyogen will naturally be present. Once we are already sitting, in the mountain-still state, upon the same round cushion as Old Kyogen, we will be able to understand this story in detail even before Kyogen opens his mouth. Not only will we steal Old Kyogen's eyes and glimpse [the story]; drawing out Śākyamuni Buddha's right-Dharma-eye treasury, we will be able instantly to see through it.

[149] *"A person has gone up a tree on a thousand foot precipice."* We should quietly investigate these words. What is *"a person?"* We should not say that what is not an outdoor pillar is "a piece of timber."[6] We should not lose sight of the fact that even a buddha's face and a patriarch's face breaking into a smile are the meeting of a self and another. The present place where *a person goes up a tree,* is beyond "the whole Earth" and beyond "the top of a hundred foot pole"; it is just *a thousand foot precipice.* If there is dropping off,[7] it happens in the concrete reality of *a thousand foot precipice.*[8] We experience times of dropping and times of going up.[9] [The story] says that the person in the concrete reality of a thousand foot precipice *goes up a tree.* Remember that she has experienced a time of *going up.* That being so, it is *a thousand feet* up and it is *a*

---

4. *Wanshi-koroku,* chap. 3. See also *Shinji-shobogenzo,* pt. 3, no. 44.

5. *While Master Yakusan Igen is sitting, a monk asks him, "What are you thinking in the mountain-still mountain-still state?" The Master says, "Thinking about the concrete state of not thinking." The monk says, "How can the state of not thinking be thought about?" The Master says, "It is different from thinking."* The story is quoted in *Shinji-shobogenzo,* pt. 2, no. 24 and Shobogenzo, chap. 27, *Zazenshin.* See also *Fukan-zazengi Rufu-bon,* chap. 58, *Zazengi,* and chap. 72, *Zanmai-o-zanmai.*

6. 看橛 (MOKU-KETSU), or "wooden stake," here represents a general category. All wooden things are real entities, and so we should not always group them under a concept such as "wooden thing" or "piece of timber."

7. 脱落 (DATSURAKU), "dropping off," commonly appears in the phrase 身心脱落 (SHINJIN-DATSURAKU), "the dropping off of body and mind," or "getting free of body and mind." See, for example, chap. 72, *Zanmai-o-zanmai.*

8. 千尺懸崖裏 (SENJAKU-KENGAI-RI). Master Dogen suffixed the characters of the story 千尺懸崖 (SENJAKU-KENGAI), "a thousand foot precipice," with 裏 (RI), which lit. means "in the back of," or "inside of," and hence "in the concrete reality of."

9. 落時あり、上時あり (RAKU-JI *ari,* JO-JI *ari*), or "there is a time of dropping, and there is a time of going up."

thousand feet down. It is *a thousand feet* left and it is *a thousand feet* right. This place is *a thousand feet.* That place is *a thousand feet.* A real person[10] is *a thousand feet.* Going up a tree is *a thousand feet.* The foregoing *thousand feet* may be like this. Now let us ask: How long is *a thousand feet* ? We can say that it is as long as the eternal mirror,[11] as long as a brazier,[12] and as long as a tombstone.[13] *"The mouth is biting a branch of the tree."* What is *the mouth*? Even though we do not know the total extent of the mouth or the whole of the mouth itself, we may, for the present, know the location of the mouth by gradually moving along the branch of the tree, searching the branch and picking away leaves. It may be, for the present, that by gripping the branch of a tree, the mouth has been formed. Thus, the whole mouth is the branch, the whole branch is the mouth, the thoroughly realized body is the mouth, and the thoroughly realized mouth is the body. The tree steps upon the tree itself, and so [the story] says *"the feet will not step onto the tree."* It is like the feet stepping on the feet themselves. The branch pulls itself onto the branch, and so [the story] says *"the hands will not pull her onto the branch."* It is like the hands pulling themselves onto the hands. At the same time, the heels can still take forward steps and backward steps, and the hands can still make a fist and open a fist.[14] Now people—I and others—are prone to think, "She is hanging in space." But how could "hanging in space" be better than *biting the branch*?[15] *"Under the tree suddenly there appears a person who asks, 'What was the ancestral Master's intention in coming from the west?'"* This *under the tree suddenly there appears a person* seems to suggests that there are human beings inside the tree—as if it might be a man-tree. A human being suddenly appearing under a human being and asking is just such [a state of unity].[16] In that state the tree is asking the tree, the human being is asking the human being, the whole tree is asking a question, and the whole of [the ancestral Master's] intention in coming from

---

10. 如人 (NYO-NIN). In the story, read as *hito...[ga] goto[ki],* these characters mean "In the case that... a person." Here, however, 如 (NYO) means "real."

11. 古鏡 (KOKYO) symbolizes the mind. Masters Seppo and Gensa discuss the dimensions of the eternal mirror in *Shinji-shobogenzo,* pt. 2, no. 9. See also chap. 20, *Kokyo* [165].

12. 火炉 (KARO) is an object with a conspicuous physical presence. In *Shinji-shobogenzo,* pt. 1, no. 38, Master Seppo and Master Gensa discuss the fact that the buddhas of the three times are in a brazier, turning the great wheel of Dharma.

13. 無縫塔 (MUHOTO), lit. "seamless stūpa," is an oval tombstone carved in solid rock (hence "seamless") and placed on square steps, as a monument to a deceased monk. It is a concrete object with eternal meaning. Masters Seppo and Gensa discuss the dimensions of a tombstone in *Shinji-shobogenzo,* pt. 1, no. 60. See also chap. 32, *Juki* [38].

14. The self containment implied by "a tree stepping on itself," "feet stepping on themselves," and so on, does not imply any loss of freedom of movement.

15. As an expression of the state of action, Master Dogen preferred 銜樹枝 (KAN-JUSHI), "biting a tree-branch," over 掛虚空 (KA-KOKU), "hanging in space."

16. これ *(kore),* lit. "this," refers to 人樹 (NIN-JU), "man-tree," that is, the condition in which there is no separation between human beings and trees—because, for example, human ashes nourish trees and oxygen from trees nourishes human beings.

the west is asking [the ancestral Master's] intention in coming from the west. The questioner, in asking, is also biting the branch of the tree. Unless *the mouth is biting the branch,* there can be no asking, no voice that fills the mouth, and no mouth full of speech. When we ask about the [ancestral Master's] intention in coming from the west, we ask by biting onto [the ancestral Master's] intention in coming from the west. *"If she opens her mouth to answer the other, she loses body and life."* We should familiarize ourselves with the present words *"if she opens her mouth to answer the other..."* They suggest the possibility of answering the other without opening the mouth. In such an instance, she might not lose body and life. Even if there is [a choice between] opening the mouth and not opening the mouth, it cannot hinder the working of *a mouth biting the branch of a tree.* Opening and closing are not necessarily the whole of a mouth, but in a mouth there are both opening and closing. Thus, *biting the branch* is the everyday condition of a whole mouth, and it is impossible for opening and closing to hinder the working of a mouth. Does *"opening the mouth to answer the other"* mean disclosing the branch of the tree and answering the other, or does it mean disclosing [the ancestral Master's] intention in coming from the west and answering the other? Unless we disclose [the ancestral Master's] intention in coming from the west in answering others, we do not answer [the ancestral Master's] intention in coming from the west. Not to have answered others is to be holding onto life with the whole body; it cannot be called *losing body and life.*[17] [At the same time] if we have lost body and life already, to answer others is impossible.[18] Nevertheless, Kyogen's mind does not shrink from answering others: it may be that his state is just *having lost body and life.* Remember, when we have not yet answered others, we are preserving body and life. When suddenly we answer others, we turn around the body and invigorate life. In conclusion, the mouth of each person being full is the state of truth, [in which state] we should answer each other, should answer ourselves, should ask each other, and should ask ourselves. This is the mouth biting the truth. The mouth biting the truth is called *"the mouth biting the branch."* When [this state] answers others, over the mouth it further opens a mouth. When it does not answer others, even if it *goes against what others are asking,* it does not go against its own asking. So remember, the Buddhist patriarchs who have answered [the ancestral Master's] intention in coming from the west are all experiencing the moment of *being up a tree and biting in the mouth the branch of the tree,* and they are continuing to answer. The Buddhist patriarchs who have asked [the ancestral Master's] intention in coming from the west are all experiencing the moment of

17. 喪身失命 (SOSHIN-SHITSUMYO), "losing body and losing life," is used here as an ironic expression of attaining realization (i.e. getting into the activity of the moment and forgetting oneself).

18. In this sentence 喪身失命 (SOSHIN-SHITSUMYO), "losing body and losing life," may be understood literally or understood as suggesting loss of composure.

being up a tree and biting in the mouth the branch of the tree, and they are continuing to ask.

] Master Juken of Seccho,[19] the Zen Master Myokaku, says, *"To say something up a tree is easy. To say something under a tree is difficult.[20] This old monk will climb up the tree. Bring a question!"*[21]

[In response to] the present *"Bring a question!"* even if you bring one with all your effort, the question will come too late: I am afraid that you will be asking after the answer. I ask venerable old drills everywhere, past and present: Is Kyogen's loud laughter saying something up a tree or saying something under a tree? Is it answering [the ancestral Master's] intention in coming from the west, or is it not answering [the ancestral Master's] intention in coming from the west? See if you can say something![22]

Shobogenzo Soshi-sairai-no-i

Preached while deep in the mountains of Etsu-u on the 4th day of the 2nd lunar month in the 2nd year of Kangen.[23]

---

19. Master Seccho Juken (980–1052), successor of Master Chimon Koso. Zen Master Myokaku is his posthumous title. He is also quoted in chap. 66, *Shunju* [137].

20. It is easy to express peculiar ideas, but difficult to manifest the everyday state.

21. *Bukka-geki-setsu-roku (Record of Bukka's Attacks on Knotty Problems),* pt. 7.

22. 試道看 *(kokoromi[ni] i[e] mi[n])* was a phrase used by Chinese masters, including Master Tendo Nyojo, to elicit the expression of a student's understanding. 試 (SHI, *kokoro[miru]*), means to have a try, to make an attempt, 道 (DO, *i[u]*) means to speak, to say something, to express oneself, and 看 (KAN, *mi[ru]*) means to see, to watch, or to examine. Traditionally in Japan these words have been interpreted as "Try to say something, and I will examine you." but according to recent scholarly investigation the phrase as a whole means "Try to say something!" or "See if you can express yourself!" Cf. chap. 30, *Gyoji* [264]: *"Try to express it yourself"*; chap. 32, *Juki* [58]: *"Try to say something, and I will test you"*; chap. 47, *Sangai-yuishin* [121]: *"See if you can answer this"*; and chap. 51, *Mitsugo* [9]: *"Let them try to say something!"*

23. 1244.

[68]

優曇華

UDONGE

The Uḍumbara Flower

***Udonge** means the flower of a type of fig tree called uḍumbara in Sanskrit. The uḍumbara tree (Ficus glomerata) is a large tropical tree of the mulberry family (Moraceae). Its flowers grow around the fruit, so they look like peel rather than flowers. Because of this, people in ancient India considered the uḍumbara to be flowerless. Consequently, they used the uḍumbara flower as a symbol of something that rarely happens;[1] for example, the realization of the Buddhist truth. In a Buddhist sutra called Daibonten-o-monbutsu-ketsugi-kyo (The Sutra of Questions and Answers between Mahābrahman and the Buddha) there is a story that one day Gautama Buddha showed an uḍumbara flower to an audience. No-one could understand the meaning of Gautama Buddha's suggestion other than Master Mahākāśyapa, who smiled. In Chinese Buddhism this story symbolized the transmission of the truth. So Master Dogen used uḍumbara flowers to explain the meaning of the transmission. Because Daibonten-o-monbutsu-ketsugi-kyo was said to have been written in China, it was criticized by some Buddhists as not expressing Gautama Buddha's true intention. Master Dogen, however, insisted in Shobogenzo, chapter 74, Tenborin, that even if a Buddhist sutra was produced in China, after its words have been discussed by Buddhist masters it becomes a Buddhist sutra which expresses the true intention of Gautama Buddha; we need not worry whether or not it was written in India.*

Before an assembly of millions on Vulture Peak, the World-Honored One picks up[2] an uḍumbara flower and winks. Thereupon the face

1. See, for example, Lotus Sutra, Hoben: *"The Buddha addressed Śāriputra: 'Wonderful Dharma like this the buddha-tathāgatas preach only occasionally, just as the uḍumbara flower appears only once in an age.'"* (LS 1.88)

2. 拈 (NEN, *nen[jiru]*). This character is rarely seen in modern Japanese but it appears frequently in Shobogenzo. 拈 lit. means to pinch, to pick up something between one's finger and thumb (*tsumamu* in modern Japanese), or to twirl, twist, or twiddle (*hineru* in modern Japanese). In Shobogenzo it is also used with various wider meanings, including the following: 1) to take or to take up (e.g. chap. 14, *Sansuigyo* [195]: "the Buddhist patriarchs, when *taking up* water"; chap. 18, *Shin-fukatoku* [82]: "she should *take* three rice cakes and hand them over to Tokuzan"; chap. 30, *Gyoji* [241]: "to *take up* the clapper"), especially as a symbol of positive behavior (e.g. chap. 22, *Bussho* [35]: "we should quietly *take up* and let go of the sixth patriarch's words");

of Mahākāśyapa breaks into a smile. The World-Honored One says, *"I possess the right-Dharma-eye treasury and the fine mind of nirvāṇa; I transmit them to Mahākāśyapa."*[3]

The Seven Buddhas and the many buddhas are all in the same process of twirling flowers,[4] which they have practiced-and-experienced, and realized as twirling of flowers the ascendant state,[5] and which they have torn open and exposed as twirling of flowers down in the here and now.[6] Thus, inside the concrete reality of twirling flowers, every instance of ascending and descending, or towards the self and towards others, or outside and inwards, and so on, is the totality of flowers displaying itself.[7] It is the dimension of flowers, the dimension of buddha, the dimension of the mind, and the dimension of the body. All instances, however many, of the twirling of flowers, are individual instances of [the transmission from] rightful successor to rightful successor; they are the actual *existence* of the *transmission*.[8] Indeed, forget the World-Honored One's twirling of a flower! When, just now, a flower-twirling world-honored one appears, that is the succession of the World-Honored One. Because the time of twirling of flowers is the whole of Time itself, it is experience of the same state as the World-Honored One, and it is the same twirling of flowers. The meaning of *"twirling flowers"* is flowers

---

2) to hold something up to view, to display, to manifest (e.g. chap. 50, *Shoho-jisso* [234]: "golden-faced Gautama is *manifesting* real form"); 3) to take something up as an issue, to bring attention to, to discuss (e.g. chap. 20, *Kokyo* [166]: "In *taking up* this world, we see it as ten feet"; chap. 75, *Jisho-zanmai* [93]: "*discussions* of the ancients"); 4) to take into the mind, to gather, grasp, comprehend (especially in the compound 拈来 (NENRAI), e.g. chap. 69, *Hotsu-mujoshin* [171]: "To *grasp* snow mountains"); and 5) to summon up, muster, utilize (e.g. chap. 69, *Hotsu-mujoshin* [181]: "through the *mustering* of individual minds.") See also note 26.

3. *Shinji-shobogenzo,* pt. 3, no. 54. See also Shobogenzo, chap. 49, *Butsudo,* and chap. 57, *Menju.* The quotation paraphrases a section of the *Nenge (Twirling a Flower)* chapter of *Daibonten-o-monbutsu-ketsugi-kyo.*

4. 拈華 (NENGE), "twirling flowers," means 1) action that manifests real phenomena; and 2) real phenomena themselves in the world of action. See also note 9.

5. 向上の拈華 (KOJO *no* NENGE). 向上 (KOJO) means "ascending." In chap 28, *Butsu-kojo-no-ji* , Master Dogen describes this as a process which continues after realization of the truth. 向上の拈華 (KOJO *no* NENGE), "twirling of flowers in the ascendant state," suggests realization of phenomena in the continuing process of Buddhist practice-and-experience.

6. 直下の拈華 (JIKIGE *no* NENGE). 直下 (JIKIGE), means 1) "direct descent" (see, for example, chap. 25, *Jinzu* [186]: "Zen Master Dai-i is the thirty-seventh patriarch in the line of direct descent from Śākyamuni"), and 2) "the straight down"—a traditional expression of the here and now (see for example chap. 3, *Genjo-koan* [90] "the immediate present, and a single drop of water, are also like this"). 直下の拈華 (JIKIGE *no* NENGE) suggests actual realization of concrete phenomena here and now, in which illusory concepts such as "a continuing process of realizing phenomena" are seen through.

7. 渾華拈 (KON-GE-NEN), or "the totality of flowers, twirling," suggests all phenomena having entered into one vivid picture in the balanced state of action.

8. 付属有在 (FUZOKU-U-ZAI). In the quotation, 有 (U, *a[ru]*) means "I possess," but here it means "existence."

displaying flowers:[9] it is plum flowers, spring flowers, snow flowers, and lotus flowers. What has been called "the five petals of a plum flower"[10] is the more than three hundred and sixty orders,[11] is the five thousand and forty-eight scrolls,[12] is the three vehicles and the twelve divisions of the teaching, and is the three clever and ten sacred stages. Therefore it is beyond the three clever and the ten sacred stages. The Great Treasury[13] exists and miracles exist: they are described by *"The opening of flowers is the occurrence of the world."*[14] *"A flower is five petals opening and the bearing of fruit is naturally realized"*[15] describes the whole body already being hung upon the whole body.[16] Losing the eyes on seeing peach blossoms,[17] and having the ears disappear on hearing the green bamboo,[18] are present moments of twirling flowers. Being waist deep in snow and cutting off the arm, doing prostrations and attaining the marrow,[19] are flowers naturally opening. Pounding rice in a stone mortar and receiving the transmission of the robe in the middle of the night[20] are flowers having already twirled. These are instances of the life-source contained in the hand of the World-Honored One. In general, the twirling of flowers existed before the World-Honored One's realization of the truth, it was simultaneous with the World-Honored One's realization

---

9. 華拈華 (GE-NEN-GE), or "flowers twirling flowers," means phenomena manifesting themselves as they are.

10. 梅華の五葉 (BAIKE *no* GOYO), or "a plum flower as five petals," represents the oneness of the whole and its parts. In chap. 59, *Baike* [204], Master Dogen writes that all the Buddhist patriarchs of India and China exist on the basis of this oneness of five petals and a plum flower. See also notes 15 and 16.

11. *Kengo-kyo (Sutra of the Kalpa of Wisdom)* says, *"Among the many lineages of the all-embracing, there are more than three hundred and sixty orders, which are the causes and conditions of thousands of buddhas' establishment of the will."*

12. The Chinese chronicle 統記 (TOKI) says, *"The śramaṇa Chisho edited Kaigen-shakkyo-roku (Kaigen-era Records of Śākyamuni's Teaching), which is altogether 5,048 scrolls."*

13. 大蔵 (DAIZO), "the great treasury," stands for 大蔵経 (DAIZOKYO), "the great treasury of sutras" or "the whole of the sutras" (see, for example, chap. 21, *Kankin*). A monk asks Master Tosu Daido, *"In the teachings of the Great Treasury are there miracles or not?"* The Master says, *"To preach the teaching of the Great Treasury [is itself a miracle]."* See *Keitoku-dento-roku*, chap. 15.

14. 華開世界起 (KE-KAI-SEKAI-KI). These are the words of Master Prajñātara, Master Bodhidharma's master. See also chap. 43, *Kuge*, and chap. 59, *Baike*.

15. 一華開五葉、結果自然成 (IKKE-KAI-GOYO, KEKKA-JINEN-JO). These are the third and fourth lines of a four-line verse by Master Bodhidharma, quoted in chap. 59, *Baike* [204].

16. 渾身是已掛渾身 (KONSHIN-ZE-I-KAKONSHIN), "the whole body already being hung upon the whole body," suggests the state of wholeness that can be realized when sitting in the lotus posture.

17. Refers to the experience of Master Reiun Shigon. See chap. 9, *Keisei-sanshiki*.

18. Refers to the experience of Master Kyogen Chikan. Ibid.

19. Refers to the transmission from Master Bodhidharma to Master Taiso Eka. See chap. 30, *Gyoji*, and chap. 46, *Katto*.

20. Refers to the transmission from Master Daiman Konin to Master Daikan Eno. See chap. 29, *Inmo*.

of the truth, and it has existed since the World-Honored One's realization of the truth. Thus, flowers are realizing the truth. The twirling of flowers has transcended by far such separate periods of time. Every buddha's and every patriarch's establishment of the will to, first steps in, practice-and-experience of, and maintenance of [the truth], are twirling flowers dancing like butterflies in the spring wind. This being so, because World-Honored Gautama is now putting his body into flowers and has shrouded his body in space, we call being able to grasp nostrils, and call having grasped space,[21] "the twirling of flowers." Twirling flowers are twirled by eyes, twirled by mind-consciousness, twirled by nostrils, and twirled by flowers twirling. In general, the mountains, rivers, and the Earth; the sun and moon, the wind and rain; people, animals, grass, and trees—the miscellaneous things of the present displaying themselves here and there—are just the twirling of the uḍumbara flower. Living-and-dying and going-and-coming are also a miscellany of flowers and the brightness of flowers. Our learning in practice like this in the present is the continuing process of twirling flowers. The Buddha says, *"It is like the uḍumbara flower, which all love and enjoy."*[22] This *"all"* is Buddhist patriarchs of bodies apparent and hidden, and is the natural presence of brightness in grass, trees, and insects. *"All love and enjoy"* describes the skin, flesh, bones, and marrow of each individual just now being in the state of vigorous activity. Thus, all is totally the uḍumbara flower. And so we call just this "rare."

[165] *"A wink"* describes the moment in which, while [the Buddha] sat under the [bodhi] tree, the bright star took the place of his eyes. In this moment *the face of Mahākāśyapa breaks into a smile.* The face has broken already, and its place has been taken by the face of twirling flowers. In the moment of the Tathāgata's wink, we have already lost our eyes. This Tathāgata's wink is just the twirling of flowers. It is uḍumbara flowers opening at will. Even to the present it has not ceased to be that, just in the moment of the twirling of flowers, all Gautamas, all Mahākāśyapas, all living beings, and all of us, are each holding out a hand and twirling flowers as one. Moreover, because we have samādhi as containment of the body inside the hand,[23] we call it *the four elements and the five aggregates.*[24]

---

21. Master Shakkyo Ezo asks Master Seido Chizo, *"Do you understand how to grasp space?"* Seido says, *"I understand how to grasp it."* Shakkyo says, *"How do you grasp it?"* Seido clutches at space with his hand. Shakkyo says, *"You do not understand how to grasp space."* Seido says, *"How do you grasp it, brother?"* Shakkyo grabs Seido's nostrils and pulls them. See *Shinji-shobogenzo,* pt. 3, no. 49. The story is quoted in full in chap. 75, *Koku.*

22. The quotation appears to be from a sutra, but the source has not been traced.

23. 手裏蔵身三昧 (TERI-ZOSHIN-ZANMAI), "samādhi in which the body is contained inside the hand," or "samādhi as containment of the body inside the hand," suggests a state of total integration of the body-mind such that each part of the body contains the whole.

24. 四大 (SHIDAI), the four elements of earth, water, fire, and wind and 五陰 (GO-UN), the

7] *My possessing it* is the *transmission*, and the transmission is my possessing it. The transmission is inevitably restricted by my possessing it. "I possess" is cerebral. In order to understand it, we must understand it by getting a grip[25] on cerebral thinking. When we take[26] what I possess and change it into the transmission, that is maintenance of *the right-Dharma-eye treasury*. The ancestral Master's coming from the west was the coming of twirling flowers.[27] Twirling flowers is called "playing with the soul."[28] "Playing with the soul" means just sitting and dropping off body and mind. Becoming a buddha and becoming a patriarch is called "playing with the soul." Putting on clothes and eating meals is called "playing with the soul." In sum, the matter which is the ultimate criteria of a Buddhist patriarch is, in every case, playing with the soul. While we are being met by the Buddha Hall, or while we are meeting with the Monks' Hall, variety in their flowers becomes more and more abundant, and light in their colors deepens layer upon layer. On top of that, in the Monks' Hall now the plate is taken and it cracks into the clouds. In the Buddha Hall now a bamboo mouth organ is blown and it resounds to the water's bottom. At such times, [my late Master] would accidentally begin to play[29] a plum blossom tune. That is, my late Master, the eternal Buddha, would say:

> *It is the time when Gautama lost the Eye,*
> *In the snow, a single twig of plum blossoms!*

---

five aggregates of form (*rūpa*), feeling (*vedana*), thinking (*saṃjñā*), habit-formation (*saṃskāra*), and consciousness (*vijñāna*) represent total reality, which has not only phenomenal appearance but also real substance.

25. 巴鼻して (HABI *shite*), lit. "grasping by the nose," means keeping something in its place or restraining it within proper limits, as a water-buffalo is restrained when its nose-ring is grasped. See also chap. 44, *Kobusshin* [58].

26. 拈じて *(nenjite)* here means "taking" in the sense of using as a means. 拈じて *(nenjite)* thus sometimes functions as a prepositional phrase (e.g. *Fukan-zazengi*: "the changing of the moment, *through the means of* a finger, a pole, a needle, or a wooden clapper").

27. 拈華来 (NENGE-RAI), translated in the opening paragraph as "the process of twirling flowers."

28. 弄精魂 (ROZEIKON). 弄 (RO, *moteaso[bu]*) means to play or toy with: it suggests easy control and enjoyment. 精 (SEI) means spirit, energy, vitality. 魂 (KON, *tamashii*) means soul, spirit, or ghost, but the phrase 魂を入れる *(tamashii o ireru)*, lit. "to put soul into," means to give life to, to animate, to breathe life into. For the compound 精魂 (SEIKON), Spahn/Hadamitzky gives "energy, vitality." Nelson gives the phrase 精魂尽 (SEIKON *tsu[kiru]*), "to lose all one's energy." Thus, 精魂 (SEIKON) means the soul as *the animating principle, or actuating cause of an individual life; a person's total self* (Webster's)—that is, something vital, energetic, and whole rather than something ethereal. See also chap. 21, *Kankin* [199]; chap. 26, *Daigo* [127]; and chap. 28, *Butsu-kojo-no-ji* [59].

29. 吹 (SUI, *fu[ku]*), is lit. "to blow." Here it likens Master Tendo's poem to the playing of a wind instrument.

Now every place has become a thorn,
Yet [I] laugh at the swirling[30] *of the spring wind.*[31]

Now the Tathāgata's Eye has accidentally become plum blossoms, while the plum blossoms now have turned into all-pervading thorns. The Tathāgata is hiding his body in the Eye, and the Eye is hiding its body in the plum blossoms. The plum blossoms, having hidden their bodies in thorns, are now blowing back at the spring wind. And though it may be so, we can [simply] enjoy the music of the plum blossoms.

[169] My late Master Tendo, the eternal Buddha, says:

What Reiun has seen is peach blossoms blooming,
What Tendo has seen is peach blossoms falling.[32]

Remember, peach blossoms blooming are what Reiun has seen: *he has arrived directly at the present and has no further doubts.*[33] Peach blossoms falling are what Tendo has seen. Peach blossoms open at the prompting of the spring wind, and peach blossoms fall being hated by the spring wind. The spring wind deeply hates the peach blossoms, but as the peach blossoms fall we will drop off body and mind.

Shobogenzo Udonge

Preached to the assembly at Kippo temple in Etsu-u on the 12th day of the 2nd lunar month[34] in the 2nd year of Kangen.[35]

---

30. 繚乱吹 *(ryoran [to shi te] fu[ku koto]),* lit. "blowing in a whirl." 吹 *(fu[ku]),* "blowing," is as in the preceding note.

31. This verse also appears in chap. 59, *Baike* [200], and chap. 63, *Ganzei* [90].

32. *Nyojo-osho-goroku,* vol.2.

33. 直至如今更不疑 (JIKISHI-NYOKON-KO-FUGI). This is the last line of the following verse by Master Reiun Shigon: *For thirty years, a traveler in search of a sword. / How many times have leaves fallen and buds sprouted? / After one look at the peach blossoms, / I have arrived directly at the present and have no further doubts.* See chap. 9, *Keisei-sanshiki* [218].

34. The 2nd lunar month would have been around spring: plum blossoms would have already fallen, but peach blossoms might have been in bloom.

35. 1244.

[69]

発無上心

HOTSU-MUJOSHIN

Establishment of the Will to the Supreme

Hotsu *means "to establish,"* ***mujo*** *means "supreme," and* ***shin*** *means "mind" or "will."* ***Hotsu-mujoshin*** *means the establishment of the will to the supreme truth. In the original sentences of this chapter we do not find the words* ***hotsu-mujoshin****; but the words* ***hotsu-bodaishin****, which mean "the establishment of the bodhi-mind," appear many times. Therefore, the title* ***Hotsu-mujoshin*** *may have been selected to distinguish this chapter from the next chapter,* ***Hotsu-bodaishin.*** *Furthermore, the two chapters end with exactly the same words: "Preached to the assembly at Kippo temple in the Yoshida district of Esshu on the 14th day of the 2nd lunar month in the 2nd year of Kangen [1244]." We need to consider how the two chapters are related. Dr. Fumio Masutani has suggested that* ***Hotsu-mujoshin*** *was preached for lay people who were working on the construction of Daibutsu-ji temple (later called Eihei-ji temple), and that* ***Hotsu-bodaishin*** *was preached on the same day for monks. Unfortunately, there is no evidence to prove this theory conclusively, but the content of the two chapters does lend it some support. Both* ***hotsu-mujoshin*** *and* ***hotsu-bodaishin*** *mean the will to pursue the Buddhist truth, which can never be pursued for any purpose other than the truth itself. Master Dogen highly esteemed this attitude in studying Buddhism, and he explains the importance of establishing the will to the truth in these two chapters.*

[1] **The founding Patriarch** in the western kingdom[1] says, *"Snow mountains[2] are like great nirvāṇa."*[3]

Remember, he likens what should be likened. [Snow mountains and nirvāṇa] should be likened because they are experienced directly and are straightforward. To grasp what are called "snow mountains" is to liken them to snow mountains. To grasp great nirvāṇa is to liken it to great nirvāṇa.

[2] The first Patriarch in China says, *"The mind in every instance is like trees and stones."*[4]

---

1. 西国高祖 (SAIGOKU *[no]* KOSO) means Gautama Buddha.
2. 雪山 (SETSUZAN) means the Himalayas.
3. *Kosonshuku-goroku,* chap. 2.

What is described here as *"the mind"* is the mind as it is.[5] It is the mind as the whole Earth. Therefore it is the mind as self-and-others. *The mind in every instance*—the mind of a person of the whole Earth, of a Buddhist patriarch of the whole Universe in the ten directions, and of gods, dragons, and so on—is trees and stones, beyond which there is no mind at all. These trees and stones are naturally unrestricted by limitations such as "existence," "non-existence," "emptiness," and "matter." With this mind of trees and stones we establish the [bodhi-]mind and realize practice-and-experience—for the mind is trees and the mind is stones. By virtue of this trees as mind and stones as mind, thinking here and now about the concrete state of not thinking[6] is realized. After seeing and hearing the traditional teaching[7] of this trees as mind and stones as mind, we rise above the flotsam of non-Buddhism for the first time. Before that, we are not of the Buddha's truth.

[174] The National Master Daisho[8] says, *"Fences, walls, tiles, and pebbles are the mind of eternal buddhas."*[9]

We should examine exactly where the present fences, walls, tiles, and pebbles are, and we should ask *What is it that is being realized like this?*[10] The mind of eternal buddhas is not the other side of the King of Emptiness;[11] it is being satisfied with gruel and being satisfied with rice,[12] or being satisfied with grass and being satisfied with water.[13] To take in such truths and then to sit as buddha and become buddha is called establishment of the mind.

---

4. 心心如木石 (SHIN-SHIN-NYO-BOKUSEKI, or SHIN-SHIN *[wa]* BOKUSEKI*[no] goto[shi])*, lit. "mind-mind is like trees and stones." Ibid.

5. 心如 (SHIN-NYO). 如 (NYO, *goto[shi]*), which in the quotation means "is like," here means "as it is," or "itself."

6. 思量箇不思量底 (SHIRYO-KO-FUSHIRYO-TEI), "thinking the concrete state of not thinking," is Master Yakusan Igen's description of what he was thinking in Zazen. See, for example, chap. 27, *Zazenshin,* and chap. 58, *Zazengi.*

7. 風声 (FUSHO). 風 (FU) means atmosphere, style, customs, habits, and 声 (SHO) means voice. 風声 (FUSHO) therefore means the voice which emerges from the practice of Buddhist habits, that is, the traditional Buddhist teaching.

8. Master Nan-yo Echu (died 775), successor of Master Daikan Eno. National Master Daisho is his posthumous title.

9. *Keitoku-dento-roku,* chap. 28. See also Shobogenzo chap. 44, *Kobusshin.*

10. 是什麼物恁麼現成 *(ko[re] shimo-butsu inmo genjo)* is a variation of Master Daikan Eno's famous phrase 是什麼物恁麼来 (*(ko[re] shimo-butsu inmo rai)*, "What is it that comes like this?" or "This is something coming like this." See, for example, chap. 62, *Hensan.* Here Master Dogen substituted 現成 (GENJO), "to be realized," for 来 (RAI), "to come."

11. 空王 (KU-O) is identified with the King of Majestic Voice (from the Sanskrit *Bhīṣmagarjitasvara-rāja*), the first Buddha to appear in the Kalpa of Emptiness. See, for example, LS 3.128.

12. 粥足飯足 (SHUKU-SOKU HAN-SOKU), or "being satisfied with breakfast and being satisfied with the midday meal." This phrase appears elsewhere in Shobogenzo (e.g. chap. 22, *Bussho* [73], chap. 34, *Arakan* [91]).

13. 艸足水足 (SO-SOKU SUI-SOKU). This phrase does not appear elsewhere. It suggests, for

75] In general, in regard to causes of and conditions for establishing the bodhi-mind, we do not bring the bodhi-mind from elsewhere; we establish the mind by taking up the bodhi-mind itself. "To take up the bodhi-mind" means to take a stalk of grass and to make a Buddha, or to take a tree without roots[14] and to make a sutra. It is to serve sand to the Buddha,[15] or to serve rice-water to the Buddha.[16] It is to offer a ball of food to living beings,[17] or to offer five flowers to the Tathāgata.[18] To practice a bit of good at the prompting of another, or to be cajoled by a demon into doing prostrations to Buddha, are also the establishment of the bodhi-mind. It is not only that: it is *to know that a home is not one's home, to forsake one's home and to leave home, to go into the mountains and practice the truth, and to do devotional practice and Dharma practice;* it is to build Buddhas and to build stūpas; it is to read sutras and to be mindful of the Buddha;[19] it is to preach the Dharma to an assembly; it is to search for masters and research the truth; it is to sit in the full lotus posture; it is to make a prostration to the Three Treasures; and it is once to call *namas Buddha!*[20] The causes and conditions of eighty-thousand such Dharma-aggregates[21] are, in every case, the establishment of the mind. Some [people] have established the mind in a dream and attained the truth;[22] some have es-

---

example, the contented state of a castrated water buffalo—described by Master Enchi Dai-an in chap. 64, *Kajo* [110].

14. In a legendary conversation between a woman and the God Indra, a tree without roots is cited as something that cannot be. The story is recorded in *Rento-eyo,* chap. 1

15. Alludes to a story in the *Aiku-o-kyo (King Aśoka Sutra):* a child who is playing in the sand when the Buddha comes by on an alms round puts an offering of sand into the Buddha's food bowl, and by virtue of this giving he later becomes King Aśoka.

16. Chap. 8 of *Daichido-ron* records that an old woman served rice-water to the Buddha.

17. *Bibasha-ron* (from the Sanskrit *Abhidharma-mahāvibhāṣa-śāstra*) says, *"There was a person who, by offering a ball of food, was able to plant a good root of salvation."* In Thailand today, for example, monks eat rice from their pātra by forming it into a ball and picking it up in the hand.

18. *Zuio-hongi-kyo (Sutra of Auspicious Past Occurrences)* describes buying five flowers for five hundred silver coins and serving those flowers to Śākyamuni Buddha.

19. 念仏 (NENBUTSU), "mindfulness of Buddha," represents the meaning of the Sanskrit *Buddhānusmṛti.* Sometimes 念仏 (NENBUTSU) specifically means "to recite the Buddha's name" (see, for example, chap. 72, *Zanmai-o-zanmai* [233]); but here the literal translation has been preferred.

20. 南無仏 (NAMU-BUTSU), represents the sound of the Sanskrit devotional formula *namas Buddha.* The Monier-Williams Sanskrit dictionary defines *namas* as "bow, obeisance, reverential salutation, adoration (by gesture or by word)."

21. 法蘊 (HO-UN), "Dharma-aggregates," is here used as a general term for the elements of the Buddhist process which Master Dogen has just listed. 蘊 (UN) represents the Sanskrit *skandha,* which MW defines as "an aggregate, a part, a division, or (with Buddhists) a constituent element of being."

22. See, for example, Lotus Sutra, *Anraku-gyo: "And in the action of a dream the king of a nation / Forsakes his palace, his followers, / And the five desires for the superior and fine, / And he goes to a place of the truth. / At the foot of a Bodhi tree, / He sits on the lion-seat, / Pursues the truth for seven days, / And attains the wisdom of the buddhas."* (LS 2.282)

tablished the mind in drunkenness[23] and attained the truth; some establish the mind and attain the truth amidst flying flowers and falling leaves;[24] some establish the mind and attain the truth amidst peach blossoms and green bamboo;[25] some establish the mind and attain the truth in the heavens above;[26] and some establish the mind and attain the truth in the sea.[27] In all these cases, in the state of having established the bodhi-mind, the bodhi-mind is being established further. In the [oneness of] body-and-mind, the bodhi-mind is being established. In the body-mind of the buddhas, the bodhi-mind is being established.[28] In the very skin, flesh, bones, and marrow of the Buddhist Patriarch, the bodhi-mind is being established. Thus, our present building of stūpas, building of Buddhas, and so on, are just the establishment of the bodhi-mind itself. They are the establishment of the mind which leads directly to realization of buddha, and we must never abandon them midway. They are called merit achieved without doing,[29] and called merit achieved without becoming.[30] They are *the reflection of true reality,*[31] and

---

23. In 1837 Master Osen Mujaku published a 20-volume commentary on quotations contained in Shobogenzo. Out of humility he called it *Shoten-zoku-cho (lit. "A Commentary to Follow Martens").* This alludes to the Chinese saying "dogs' tails following martens' tails," which derided government officers who wore a marten's tail from their cap to denote high rank, but who were not capable officers. *Shoten-zoku-cho* traces the example of establishing the bodhi-mind in drunkenness to *Daichido-ron.*

24. 飛華落葉 (HIGE-RAKUYO). *Shoten-zoku-cho* traces these words to *Bibasha-ron.*

25. 桃華翠竹 (TOKA-SUICHIKU). 桃華 (TOKA), "peach blossoms," refers to the realization of Master Reiun Shigon, and 翠竹 (SUICHIKU), "green bamboo," refers to the realization of Master Kyogen Chikan. See chap. 9, *Keisei-sanshiki.*

26. *Shoten-zoku-cho* cites *Miroku-josho-kyo (The Sutra of Maitreya's Ascent and Birth [in Tuṣita Heaven]),* and *Shakubuku-rakan-kyo (The Sutra of the Defeat of the Arhat).*

27. *Shoten-zoku-cho* cites Lotus Sutra, *Devadatta*: *Mañjuśrī said, "I, in the sea, am constantly preaching only the Sutra of the Flower of the Wonderful Dharma."* (LS 2.218)

28. It may be helpful to remember, especially if reading the text aloud, that the "bo" of "bodhi" is pronounced not as in "body" but as in "abode."

29. 無為の功徳 (MUI *no* KUDOKU), or "merit achieved without artificiality." 為 (I), "doing," often carries the connotation of artificiality, intentionality, or interference. 無為 (MUI), "without doing," as an adjective means "without artificiality" or "natural," and as a noun means "non-doing," i.e., letting things be as they naturally are, not doing anything superfluous. In the poem *Shodoka* Master Yoka Genkaku speaks of 絶学無為閑道人 (ZETSUGAKU-MUI *[no]* KANDO-NIN), *"a person at ease in the truth, who is through with study and free of doing."* In the opening sentence of chap. 1, *Bendowa,* Master Dogen describes Zazen as 最上無為の妙術 (SAIJO-MUI NO MYOJUTSU), *"a subtle method which is supreme and without intention."* See also *asaṃskṛta* and *saṃskṛta* in Book 1, Glossary.

30. 無作の功徳 (MUSA *no* KUDOKU). 無作 (MUSA), "non-becoming," represents the negation of idealistic effort.

31. 真如観 (SHINNYO-KAN). *Yoraku-hongyo-kyo (The Sutra of Past Deeds as a String of Pearls)* says that 無相観 (MUSO-KAN), "reflection in which there are no [separate] forms," is called 真如観 (SHINNYO-KAN), "reflection of true reality."

the reflection of the Dharma-nature;[32] they are the buddhas' concentrated state of samādhi, they are the attainment of the buddhas' dhāraṇī, they are the anuttara-samyak-saṃbodhi-mind,[33] they are arhathood, and they are the realization of Buddha. Apart from this there is no method which is free of doing or free of becoming.

9] Nevertheless, stupid people of the small vehicle say: "The building of images and erecting of stūpas is achieved through intentional doing;[34] we should set it aside and not perform it. Ceasing thought and concentrating the mind is non-doing. Non-arising and non-becoming are true reality. Observing and practicing the real form of the Dharma-nature is non-doing." They have made such assertions into their custom in India in the west and in the eastern lands, from ancient times to the present. This is why, although they commit heavy sins and deadly sins, they do not build images or erect stūpas; and, although they dirty themselves in thickets of dusty toil, they are not mindful of the Buddha and they do not read sutras. These are people who not only ruin the potential of human beings and gods but also negate the Buddha-nature of the Tathāgata. It is truly regrettable that, having lived at the time of Buddha, Dharma, and Saṃgha, they have become enemies of Buddha, Dharma, and Saṃgha; that, having climbed the Three Treasure mountain, they return empty-handed; and that, having entered the Three Treasure ocean, they return empty-handed. Even if they meet the appearance in the world of a thousand buddhas and ten thousand patriarchs, they will have no chance of attaining salvation and they will lack the means of establishing the mind. They are like this because they do not follow the sutras and do not follow [good] counselors. Many are like this because they follow false teachers of non-Buddhism. We should quickly throw away views and opinions that efforts such as building stūpas are not the establishment of the bodhi-mind. Washing out the mind, washing out the body, washing out the ears, and washing out the eyes, we should not see or hear [those views and opinions]. We should just devote ourselves to the right Dharma, following the Buddhist sutras and following [good] counselors, and should practice the Buddha-Dharma.

1] In the great truth of the Buddha-Dharma, the sutras of the great thousandfold [world][35] are present in an atom, and countless buddhas are

32. 法相観 (HOSSHO-KAN). *Yoraku-hongyo-kyo* says that 一切種地観 (ISSAI-SHUCHI-KAN), "reflection of the causal grounds of all things," is called 法相観 (HOSSHO-KAN), "reflection of the Dharma-nature."

33. The will to the supreme right, balanced, and integrated state of truth. See Book 1, Glossary.

34. 有為 (U-I), lit. "with doing." 有為 (U-I) as an adjective means "artificial," and as a noun means "intentional doing," or "artificiality."

35. 大千 (DAISEN), "great thousand," stands for 三千大千世界 (SANZEN-DAISEN-SEKAI), "the three-thousand-great-thousandfold world," that is the domain of a buddha. Such a domain is

present in an atom. Each weed and each tree are a body-mind. Because the myriad dharmas are beyond appearance, even the undivided mind is beyond appearance.[36] And because all dharmas are real form, every atom is real form. Thus, one undivided mind is all dharmas, and all dharmas are one undivided mind, which is the whole body.[37] If building stūpas were artificial, buddhahood, bodhi, reality as it is, and the Buddha-nature, would also be artificial. Because reality as it is and the Buddha-nature are not artificial, building images and erecting stūpas are not artificial. They are the natural establishment of the bodhi-mind: they are merit achieved without artificiality, without anything superfluous.[38] We should definitely decide, believe, and understand that efforts such as building images and erecting stūpas are establishment of the bodhi-mind. Through these efforts hundred millions of kalpas of practice and vows will be promoted. [These efforts] are establishment of the mind which will not be overturned in hundred millions of koṭis of myriad kalpas. They are called *meeting Buddha and hearing the Dharma*. Remember, to build a Buddha or to build a stūpa by gathering wood and stone, by heaping up mud and earth, and by collecting gold, silver, and the seven treasures,[39] is to build a stūpa or to build an image by gathering undivided mind,[40] is to make a Buddha by accumulating emptiness upon emptiness,[41] is to build a Buddha through the mustering of individual minds,[42] is to build a stūpa by amassing stūpa upon stūpa,[43] and is to build a Buddha by causing momentary instances of buddha[44] to be realized. This is why a sutra says, *"At the time of this consideration, the buddhas of the*

---

thought to comprise one billion (one thousand to the power of three) worlds.

36. 不生 (FUSHO), "beyond appearance" or "not appearing," describes the state at the moment of the present. All things, even wholehearted devotion to Buddhist practice, are instantaneous. Master Dogen explains this meaning of 不生 (FUSHO), "not appearing," in chap. 3, *Genjo-koan* [87]. See also chap. 43, *Kuge* [40].

37. 全身 (ZENSHIN) suggests the Universe as the whole body of the Tathāgata. See chap. 71, *Nyorai-zenshin*.

38. 無漏 (MURO), lit. "without leakage," or "without excess," represents the Sanskrit *anāsrava* (see Book 1, Glossary). The Lotus Sutra begins by associating arhathood with the ending of 諸漏 (SHORO), "all excesses," or "all superfluities." See LS 1.8 and Shobogenzo, chap. 34, *Arakan*.

39. 七宝 (SHIPPO), "the seven treasures," or "the precious seven," from the Sanskrit *sapta ratnāni*, are for example gold, silver, coral, pearls, jewels, moonstones, and agates.

40. 一心 (ISSHIN).

41. 空空 (KU-KU).

42. 心心 (SHIN-SHIN).

43. 塔塔 (TO-TO).

44. 仏仏 (BUTSU-BUTSU). The elements 一心 (ISSHIN), lit. "one mind," 空空 (KU-KU), lit. "emptiness-emptiness" or "space-space," 心心 (SHIN-SHIN), lit. "mind-mind," 塔塔 (TO-TO), lit. "stūpa-stūpa," and 仏仏 (BUTSU-BUTSU), lit. "buddha-buddha," follow the characteristic progression of Master Dogen's thought from the general and inclusive, through the individual and increasingly concrete, to the suggestion of momentary realization of reality in action.

ten directions all appear."[45] Remember, when one individual's thinking is making a Buddha, thinking buddhas of the ten directions all appear. And when one dharma is being made into a Buddha, all dharmas are being made into a Buddha.

3] Śākyamuni Buddha says, *"When the bright star appeared, I, together with the Earth and all sentient beings, simultaneously realized the truth."*

So establishment of the mind, training, bodhi, and nirvāṇa may be [such] *simultaneous*[46] establishment of the mind, training, bodhi, and nirvāṇa. The body-mind of the Buddha's truth is grass, trees, tiles, and pebbles, and is wind, rain, water, and fire. Utilizing these so that the Buddha's truth is realized is just the establishment of the mind. Grasping space, we should build stūpas and build Buddhas. Scooping water from mountain streams, we should build Buddhas and build stūpas. This is establishment of the truth of anuttara-samyak-saṃbodhi, and it is hundred thousand myriads of establishments of the one establishment of the bodhi-mind. Practice-and-experience is also like this. When we hear, on the contrary, that the establishment of the mind is a one-off occurrence, after which the mind is not established again, and that training is endless [but] experience of the effect is a one-off experience, we are not hearing the Buddha-Dharma, we have not come upon the Buddha-Dharma, and we are not meeting the Buddha-Dharma. Thousands of koṭis of establishments of the mind are, inevitably, occurrences of the one establishment of the mind. Thousands of koṭis of people's establishment of the mind are occurrences of the one establishment of the mind. And one establishment of the mind is thousands of koṭis of establishments of the mind. Practice-and-experience, and preaching the Dharma, are also like this.[47] If it were not such things as grass and trees, how could the body-mind exist? If they were not the body-mind, how could grass and trees exist? Apart from grass and trees, there are no grass and trees; therefore [grass and trees] are like this. Sitting in Zazen and pursuing the truth is establishment of the bodhi-mind. Establishment of the mind is beyond oneness and difference, and sitting in Zazen is beyond oneness and difference; they are beyond repetition, and beyond division. All things should be investigated like this. If the whole process of gathering grass, trees, and the seven treasures, and building stūpas and building Buddhas, were inten-

45. 作是思惟時、十方仏皆現 (SA-ZE-SHI-I-JI, JUPPO-BUTSU-KAI-GEN), from Lotus Sutra, *Hoben* (LS 1.124). 是思惟 (ZE-SHI-I) means "this consideration" or "attention to the concrete."

46. 同時 (DOJI) here means "sameness in time"; that is, identity of subject and object in the present moment: the Buddha's realization of the truth had oneness of subject and object in the here and now, and our establishment of the will to the truth also has oneness of subject and object in the here and now.

47. かくのごとし *(kakunogotoshi)*, "like this," means in the state of total integration—all moments being contained in one moment and subject and object being indivisible.

tional doing and therefore useless for realizing the truth, then the thirty seven auxiliary bodhi methods[48] would also be intentional doing, and each instance of mustering the body-mind of a human being or god of the triple world in order to do training would be intentional doing, and realization of the ultimate state would be impossible. Grass, trees, tiles, and pebbles, and the four elements and five aggregates, are all equally *the mind alone*,[49] and are all equally *real form*.[50] The whole Universe in ten directions, and the true and real Buddha-nature, are both the Dharma abiding in the Dharma's place. In the true and real Buddha-nature, how could there be such things as "grass" and "trees"? How could grass, trees, and so on not be the true and real Buddha-nature? All dharmas are beyond "intentional doing" and beyond "non-doing"; they are real form. Real form is real form as it is, and the as-it-is is the body-mind here and now. With this body-mind we should establish the mind. Do not be averse to treading in water or treading on rocks. Just to take one stalk of grass and make it into the sixteen-foot golden body, or to take one particle of dust and construct an eternal buddha's stūpa or shrine, is the establishment of the bodhi-mind itself. It is to meet Buddha, to listen to Buddha, to meet Dharma, to listen to Dharma, to become Buddha, and to act as Buddha.

[187] Śākyamuni Buddha says, *"Upāsaka and upāsikā,*[51] *good sons and good daughters, serve to the Three Treasures offerings of the flesh of wives and children, and serve to the Three Treasures offerings of the flesh of their own bodies. When bhikṣus have received devout offerings, how could they be remiss in practice?"*

Clearly, to serve to the Three Treasures offerings of food and drink, clothes, bedding, medicine, monks' lodgings, fields and woods, and so on, is to serve offerings of the skin, flesh, bones, and marrow of one's own body and of wives and children. Those who have thus entered the ocean of virtue of the Three Treasures are of the one taste.[52] Because they are of the one taste already, they are the Three Treasures. [The condition] for the virtue of the Three Treasures actually to be realized in the skin, flesh, bones, and marrow of one's own body and of wives and children, is diligent effort in pursuing

---

48. 三十七品菩提分法 (SANJUSHICHI-BON-BODAI-BUNBO) is the title of Shobogenzo, chap. 73, *Sanjushichi-bon-bodai-bunbo.*

49. 唯心 (YUISHIN), see chap. 47, *Sangai-yuishin.*

50. 実相 (JISSO), see chap. 50, *Shoho-jisso.*

51. Lay men and lay women.

52. 一味 (ICHI-MI), lit, "[people of] one taste," is a term applied to people united by a common cause, e.g. a gang of conspirators or a group of partisans. At the same time, "the one taste" may be interpreted literally as the essence of the Dharma—in *Fukan-zazengi Shinpitsu-bon* Master Dogen writes of 法味資神 *(ho-mi shin [o] tasu[ke]),* "the taste of the Dharma lifting the spirit" or "the flavor of the Dharma soothing the soul."

the truth.[53] Now, upholding the nature and the form of the World-honored One, we must grasp the skin, flesh, bones, and marrow of the Buddha's truth. The devout offering of the present is the establishment of the mind. How could receiving bhikṣus be remiss in practice? We should be right from the head to the tail. Thus, at whatever moment a single particle of dust is established, the undivided mind will be established accordingly. If the undivided mind is established first, it will not be long before undivided space is established.

9] In summary, when the sentient and the insentient establish the mind, they are able to plant for the first time a seed of the Buddha-nature. If they [then] wholeheartedly practice by embracing the four elements and five aggregates, they will attain the truth. [Again,] if they wholeheartedly practice by embracing grass, trees, fences, and walls, they will be able to attain the truth—because the four elements and five aggregates,[54] and grass, trees, fences, and walls,[55] are experiencing the same state, because they share the same nature, because they are of the same mind and the same life, and because they are of the same body and the same makings. Thus, in the orders of Buddhist patriarchs, many have pursued the truth by taking up the mind of grass and trees. This is a characteristic of establishment of the bodhi-mind. The fifth Patriarch[56] at one time was a being who practiced the way by planting pines.[57] Rinzai experienced the effort of planting cedars and pines on Obaku-zan mountain.[58] There was the old man Ryu who planted pine trees

53. 精勤の辦道功夫 (SHOGON *no* BENDO-KUFU) suggests the daily practice of Zazen. 精勤 (SHOGON), "diligence," means steady application rather than short bursts of intense effort. 辦道 (BENDO) is written elsewhere in Shobogenzo as 弁道 (BENDO); see for example chap. 1, *Bendowa*. 弁 (BEN) is a simplified form of several old characters. The character used here 辦 (BEN), "to apply effort, to put one's energy into a certain task," in which the middle radical 力 represents strength. The compound 功夫 (KUFU), which is equivalent to 工夫 (KUFU) in modern Japanese, originally represented a craftsman's application of mental energy to the planning and performance of construction work. In Shobogenzo, 功夫 (KUFU) means 1) to strive, to make effort, and 2) to consider, to apply ones' mental faculties, to think out the means of doing something (see also notes to chap. 39, *Dotoku* [193]). Master Dogen often used 弁道功夫 (BENDO-KUFU), "effort in pursuing the truth," or "directing one's energy into practicing the truth," as an expression of Zazen itself.

54. 四大五蘊 (SHIDAI GO-UN), "the four elements and five aggregates," are the constituent elements of being in traditional Buddhist philosophy.

55. 艸木牆壁 (SO-MOKU-SHO-HEKI), "grass, trees, fences, and walls," are concrete objects familiar to everybody. Master Dogen saw these and the four elements and five aggregates as completely the same.

56. Master Daiman Konin, the 5th patriarch in China.

57. 栽松道者 (SAISHO-DOJA), or "pine-planting pilgrim." The words come from a story quoted in chap. 22, *Bussho* [22]. See also chap. 30, *Gyoji* [173].

58. See chap. 30, *Gyoji* [172].

on Tozan mountain.[59] By taking on the constancy of pines and oaks, they scooped out the Eye of the Buddhist patriarchs. This was real manifestation of the identity of power in playing with the lively Eye and clarification of the Eye. To build stūpas, to build Buddhas, and so on, are to play with the Eye,[60] are to taste the establishment of the mind, and are to use the establishment of the mind. Without getting the Eye of building stūpas and so on, there is no realization of the Buddhist patriarchs' truth. After getting the Eye of building Buddhas, we become buddhas and become patriarchs. The words that "building stūpas and so on eventually turns to dust and is not real merit, whereas training in which nothing arises is solid and enduring and is not tainted by dust and dirt,"[61] are not the Buddha's words. If stūpas turn to dust, the state without arising[62] also turns to dust. If the state without arising is beyond turning to dust, then stūpas also cannot turn to dust. *This is where something ineffable is taking place.* Explain it as intentional doing or explain it as non-doing![63]

[192] A sutra says, "*When bodhisattvas, in living and dying, first establish the mind, they solely pursue the truth of bodhi; they are steadfast and unshakable. The virtue of that single-mindedness is deep and vast without limit. If the Tathāgata were to analyze and explain it, even for whole kalpas, he would not be able to finish.*"[64]

Clearly know: to establish the mind by grasping life and death is *the sole pursuit of bodhi. That single-mindedness* must be the same as a single stalk of grass and a single tree—because it is a single moment of living and a single moment of dying. At the same time, the depth of its virtue is without limit, and the vastness of its virtue is without limit. Even if the Tathāgata analyzes this [virtue], making whole kalpas into words, there will be no finish. Because when the sea dries up the sea-bed remains and because even when a person dies the mind may remain, [all things] are *not able to be finished.* Just as

---

59. Old man Ryu is mentioned in *Keitoku-dento-roku,* chap. 17, in the section on Master Tozan Shiken. Tozan mountain was home to the order of Master Tozan Ryokai and Master Tozan Shiken.

60. 弄眼睛 (RO-GANZEI), "to play with the Eye," means to enjoy easy mastery of the viewpoint of action.

61. 塵埃 (JINNAI), "dust and dirt," alludes to the following verse by Ācārya Jinshu: "*The body is the bodhi tree, / The mind is like the stand of a clear mirror. / At every moment we work to wipe and polish it / To keep it free of dust and dirt.*" See chap. 20, *Kokyo* [134].

62. 無性 (MUSHO) means "non-arising," "non-appearance," or "non-birth." Sometimes 無性 (MUSHO) means "not being subject to re-birth on the wheel of saṃsāra," and as such is used as a synonym for nirvāṇa.

63. Alludes to *Shinji-shobogenzo,* pt. 1, no. 96: In response to a question from Rinzai, Fuke overturns a dinner table. Master Rinzai says, "*Very coarse person!*" Fuke says, "*This is where something ineffable exists. Explain it as coarse or explain it as fine.*"

64. *Shin-yaku Kegon-kyo,* lit. "the New Translation of the Flower-Adornment Sutra," is the name of the edition of the Garland Sutra translated during the years of the Chin dynasty (265 to 420 A.D.).

the depth and vastness of *that single-mindedness* are without limit, the depth and vastness of a weed, a tree, a rock, and a tile also are without limit. If a weed or a rock is seven feet or eight feet, *that single-mindedness* is seven feet or eight feet, and establishment of the mind is also seven feet or eight feet. In conclusion, to go deep into the mountains to consider the Buddha's truth may be easy, [but] to build stūpas and to build Buddhas is very difficult. Although each is accomplished through diligence and tirelessness, actively grasping the mind and being grasped by the mind may be much different. Through the piling up of such establishments of the bodhi-mind, Buddhist patriarchs are realized.

Shobogenzo Hotsu-mujoshin

Preached to the assembly at Kippo temple in the Yoshida district of Esshu[65] on the 14th day of the 2nd lunar month in the 2nd year of Kangen.[66]

65. Modern-day Fukui prefecture.
66. 1244.

[70]

発菩提心

HOTSU-BODAISHIN

Establishment of the Bodhi-mind

It is supposed that this chapter and the previous chapter originally had the same title, i.e., ***Hotsu-bodaishin****, "Establishment of the Bodhi-mind," but that the title of the previous chapter was changed to* ***Hotsu-mujoshin****, "Establishment of the Will to the Supreme," for the purpose of distinction. Dr. Fumio Masutani believes that the former chapter was a sermon for lay people and this chapter was a sermon given on the same day to monks and nuns. Whatever Master Dogen's intention was, one point is that this chapter includes a presentation of the "The Theory of the Momentary Appearance and Disappearance of the Universe." In Buddhist theory, action is esteemed highly; when we consider the meaning of life, we can consider that our life is just a series of moments of action. Why do we say that our life is momentary? Because once we have done an act we can never return to the past to undo it. At the same time, we can never perform an act until its time comes to the present. So an act is always done just at the moment of the present. Furthermore, the moment of the present is cut off from the moment immediately before it and the moment immediately after it, because we can never act in the past and we can never act in the future. According to Buddhist theory, then, our life is momentary, and the whole Universe appears and disappears at every moment. This theory, also known as "The Theory of Instantaneousness," is important in resolving the conflict between human freedom and the law of cause and effect; that is, free will versus determinism. In this chapter, Master Dogen clearly explains the theory.*

In general there are three kinds of mind. *The first, citta,*[1] *is here*[2] *called thinking mind.*[3] *The second, hṛidaya,*[4] *is here called the mind of grass and trees.*[5] *The third,*

---

1. MW defines *citta* as attending, observing; thinking, reflecting, imagining, thought; intention, aim, wish; memory; intelligence, reason. See also chap. 37, *Shinjin-gakudo* [144].

2. 此方 (SHIHO), lit. "this direction" or "this quarter," means the eastern lands, China and Japan. The sentences in italics are in the form of a quotation from a Chinese text.

3. 慮知心 (RYO-CHI-SHIN), lit. "considering and recognizing mind," in other words, reason.

4. MW defines *hṛidaya* as the heart (or region of the heart as the seat of feeling and sensations); soul, mind; the heart or interior of the body.

5. 艸木心 (SO-MOKU-SHIN), "the mind of grass and trees," describes the instinctive processes that exist in the "life force" itself and that are present prior to consciousness.

vṛiddha,[6] *is here called experienced and concentrated mind.*[7] Among these, the bodhi-mind is inevitably established relying upon thinking mind. *Bodhi* is the sound of an Indian word; here it is called "the truth."[8] *Citta* is the sound of an Indian word; here it is called "thinking mind." Without this thinking mind it is impossible to establish the bodhi-mind. That is not to say that this thinking mind is the bodhi-mind itself, but we establish the bodhi-mind with this thinking mind. To establish the bodhi-mind means to vow that, and to endeavor so that, *"Before I myself cross over,*[9] *I will take across all living beings."* Even if their form is humble, those who establish this mind are already the guiding teachers of all living beings. This mind is not innate and it does not now suddenly arise; it is neither one nor many; it is not natural and it is not formed; it does not abide in our body, and our body does not abide in the mind. This mind does not pervade the Dharma-world; it is neither of the past nor of the future; it is neither present nor absent; it is not of a subjective nature, it is not of an objective nature, it is not of a combined nature, and it is not of a causeless nature. Nevertheless, at a place where there is mystical communication of the truth,[10] establishment of the bodhi-mind occurs. It is not conferred upon us by the buddhas and bodhisattvas, and it is beyond our own ability. Establishment of the mind occurs during mystical communication of the truth, and so it is not inherent. This establishment of the bodhi-mind is most often able to occur in a human body, on the southern continent of Jambudvīpa. Rarely, it also occurs in the eight troubled worlds,[11] but not often. After establishing the bodhi-mind, we do training for three asaṃkhya kalpas, or for a hundred great kalpas. In some cases we practice for countless kalpas and become a buddha. In other cases we practice for countless kalpas to make living beings cross over before us, finally not becoming a buddha ourself but only taking across living beings and benefiting

---

6. MW defines *vṛiddha* as grown, become larger or longer or stronger, increased, augmented; great, large; grown up, full grown, aged, old, senior; experienced, wise, learned.

7. 積聚精要心 (SHAKUJU-SHOYO-SHIN) means the regulated mind of real wisdom, i.e. prajñā.

8. 道 (DO, or in Chinese *tao*) lit. means "way." In some cases 道 (DO) represents the Sanskrit *mārga,* as in the fourth noble truth 道諦 (DOTAI), from the Sanskrit *mārga-satya.* But in Shobogenzo, 道 (DO) usually represents the Sanskrit *bodhi,* which means the truth, or the state of truth. MW defines bodhi as "perfect knowledge or wisdom (by which a man becomes a Buddha); the illuminated or enlightened intellect." In Shobogenzo, however, wisdom is not intellectual, but is the harmonized state of the body-mind in Zazen; it is not a means to an end, but is complete in itself.

9. わたる *(wataru),* "to cross over," means to be delivered, to attain the truth.

10. 感応道交 (KANNO-DOKO) means 1) mystical communication of the truth to living beings, 2) empathy between a master and disciple. See also chap. 37, *Shinjin-gakudo* [144].

11. 八難処 (HACHI-NAN-SHO), lit. "the eight places of difficulty," or "the eight states of distress," represents the meaning of the Sanskrit *aṣṭākṣaṇāh.* The eight are: *naraka,* hell; *tiryañc,* animals; *preta,* hungry ghosts; *dīrghāyur-deva,* gods in heaven with interminably long lives; *pratyantajanapada,* remote or barbarian countries; *indriyavaikalya,* loss of power of the senses; *mithyādarśana,* pretentiousness; and *tathāgatānām-anutpāda,* absence of the Buddha. See Glossary.

living beings—this accords with the attitude of delight in bodhi. In general, the bodhi-mind ceaselessly operates through the three forms of behavior[12] so that all living beings may somehow be caused to establish the bodhi-mind and be led to the Buddha's truth. Vainly to confer worldly pleasures is not to benefit living beings. This establishment of the mind and this practice-and-experience have far transcended the facade of delusion and enlightenment, have risen above the triple world, and have surpassed all things. They are quite beyond śrāvakas and pratyekabuddhas.

"Bodhisattva Mahākāśyapa praises Śākyamuni Buddha in verse, saying:

Establishing the mind and the ultimate state: the two are
without separation.
Of these two states of mind the former mind is harder [to realize]:
It is to deliver others before attaining one's own deliverance.
For this reason, I bow to [your] first establishment of the mind.

With the first establishment, already the teacher of gods and men,
You rose above śrāvakas and pratyekabuddhas.
Such establishment of the mind surpasses the triple world,
Therefore we are able to call it the Supreme.[13]

"Establishing the mind" means establishing, for the first time, the will *to deliver others before attaining one's own deliverance;* this is described as *"the first establishment of the mind."* After establishing this mind, we then meet innumerable buddhas and serve offerings to them, during which time we meet Buddha and hear Dharma, and further establish the bodhi-mind—covering snow with frost. What has been called *"the ultimate state"* is Buddhahood, the state of bodhi. If we compare the state of anuttara-samyak-saṃbodhi and the first establishment of the bodhi-mind, they may be like the holocaust at the end of a kalpa and the fire of a firefly. At the same time, if we establish the will to deliver others before we ourselves attain deliverance, *the two are without separation.*

Constantly making this my thought:
How can I make living beings
Able to enter the supreme truth
And swiftly realize a buddha's body?[14]

This is the Tathāgata's lifetime itself. Buddhas' establishment of the mind, training, and experience of the effect, are all like this. Benefiting living beings means causing living beings to establish the will to deliver others before they attain their own deliverance. We should not expect to become buddha by virtue of having established the will to deliver others before we ourselves

---

12 三業 (SANGO): behavior of body, mouth, and mind.

13. *Daihatsu-nehan-kyo (Mahāparinirvāṇa-sūtra),* chap. 38.

14. Closing words of Lotus Sutra, *Nyorai-juryo.* See LS 3.36.

attain deliverance. Even if virtue which might make us buddha has matured and is about to be consummated, we turn it towards living beings' realization of buddha and attainment of the truth. This mind is not in the self, is not in others, and it does not appear, but after this establishment of the mind when we embrace the Earth it turns completely to gold and when we stir the ocean it at once becomes sweet dew. Henceforth, to take hold of soil, stones, sand, and pebbles is just to grasp the bodhi-mind; and to go exploring the spray of water, foam, and flame is to be carrying the bodhi-mind intimately. So to give away a nation, a city, a wife, a child, the seven treasures, a man, a woman, or one's head, eyes, marrow, brain, body, flesh, hands, and feet, is, in every case, the clamoring of the bodhi-mind and the vigorous activity of the bodhi-mind. Citta, the thinking mind of the present, is neither close nor distant and neither of the self nor of others; even so, if we turn this mind to the principle of delivering others before we attain deliverance ourselves, without regressing or straying, that is establishment of the bodhi-mind. When we thus give up for the bodhi-mind the grass, trees, tiles, pebbles, gold, silver, and precious treasures which all living beings of the present are clutching to themselves as their own possessions, how could that not be the establishment of the bodhi-mind itself? Because mind and real dharmas are both beyond subject, object, combination, and causelessness, if we establish this bodhi-mind for a single kṣaṇa,[15] the myriad dharmas will all become promoting conditions.[16] In general, establishment of the mind and attainment of the truth rely upon the instantaneous arising and vanishing[17] of all things. If [all things] did not arise and vanish instantaneously, bad done in the previous instant could not depart. If bad done in the previous instant had not yet departed, good in the next instant could not be realized in the present. Only the Tathāgata clearly knows the length of this instant. [The teaching that] *"Mind can produce one word of speech at a time, and speech can express one word of*

---

15. 刹那 (SETSUNA) represents the Sanskrit *kṣaṇa,* which as a noun means moment or instant and as an adverb means in a moment or instantaneously.

16. 増上縁 (ZOJO-EN). 増 (ZO) means to add on, to increase, or to promote; 上 (JO) means to go above, or to advance, to improve; and 縁 (EN) means a connection, an indirect or cooperating cause, a condition, a favorable circumstance. Therefore in context 増上縁 (ZOJO-EN) may be interpreted literally as "promoting conditions," i.e., circumstances which are favorable to attainment of the truth. At the same time, 増上縁 (ZOJO-EN) represents the Sanskrit *adhipati-pratyaya,* which is the fourth of the *catvāraḥ pratyayāh,* or four types of circumstance. The four are: *hetu-pratyaya,* circumstances directly responsible for the event; *samanantara-pratyaya,* circumstances immediately contiguous to the event; *ālambana-pratyaya,* circumstances indirectly connected with the event; and *adhipati-pratyaya,* overarching circumstances, all circumstances over and above the preceding. See Glossary.

17. 刹那生滅 (SETSUNA-SHOMETSU), or "appearance and disappearance in a kṣaṇa." This phrase introduces the "Theory of the Momentary Appearance and Disappearance of the Universe" mentioned in Nishijima Roshi's introduction to this chapter.

writing at a time."[18] is also of the Tathāgata alone—it is beyond the ability of other saints. In roughly the time it takes a man to click his fingers, there are sixty five kṣaṇas, [in each of which] the five aggregates arise and vanish, but no common man has ever sensed it or known it. Even common men have known the length of a tatkṣaṇa.[19] In the passing of one day and one night there are six billion, four hundred million, ninety-nine thousand, nine hundred and eighty kṣaṇas,[20] [in each of which] all five aggregates arise and vanish, but common men never sense or know it. Because they do not sense or know it, they do not establish the bodhi-mind. Those who do not know the Buddha-Dharma and do not believe the Buddha-Dharma do not believe the principle of instantaneous arising and vanishing. One who clarifies the Tathāgata's right-Dharma-eye treasury and the fine mind of nirvāṇa inevitably believes this principle of instantaneous arising and vanishing. Meeting now the Tathāgata's teaching, we feel as if we clearly understand, but we are merely aware of periods of a tatkṣaṇa or longer, and we only believe the principle to be true. Our failure to clarify and failure to know all the dharmas that the World-honored One taught is like our failure to know the length of a kṣaṇa: students must never carelessly become proud. We are not only ignorant of the extremely small; we are also ignorant of the extremely large. And yet, even ordinary beings, when we rely on the power of the Tathāgata's truth, see the three-thousandfold-world.[21] In sum, as we pass from living existence[22] into middle existence,[23] and from middle existence

---

18. *Daibibasha-ron (Abhidharma-mahāvibhāṣa-śāstra)*, chap. 15.

19. 恒刹那 (GO-SETSUNA). 恒 (GO), which means "constant," is thought to be a misprint of 怛 (TAN), which represents the sound of the Sanskrit *tat*. As a unit of measurement, the Sanskrit *tatkṣaṇa*, which lit. means "that moment," i.e., a definite period of time, is equivalent to one hundred and twenty kṣāṇas. See Glossary.

20. 六十四億九万九千九百八十の刹那 (ROKUJU-SHI-OKU, KYUMAN, KYUSEN, KYUHYAKU, HACHIJU *no* SETSUNA). "Six billion, four hundred million," i.e. 6,400 million, is expressed in Chinese and Japanese as 64 units of one-hundred million (億).

21. 三千界 (SANZENKAI), the whole world of one billion (one thousand to the power of three) constituent worlds.

22. 本有 (HON-U). Traditionally there are said to be four stages of life, known as 四有 (SHI-U), or "the four forms of existence." They are 生有 (SHO-U), "birth-existence," or existence at the moment of one's birth; 本有 (HON-U), "original existence," or the living of one's life; 死有 (SHI-U) "death-existence," existence at the moment of one's death; and 中有 (CHU-U), "middle-existence," an intermediate stage through which conscious beings are supposed to pass following the moment of death.

23. 中有 (CHU-U), "middle existence," represents the meaning of the Sanskrit *antarā-bhava*, which was originally a Brahmanistic concept describing the soul in an intermediate stage between death and regeneration. Buddhist masters utilized the concept to emphasize the importance of profound belief in cause and effect. See for example chap. 84, *Sanji-no-go* [44] and chap. 90, *Shizen-biku* [23].

into the next living existence,[24] all things move in a continuous process, kṣāṇa by kṣāṇa. Thus, regardless of our own intentions, and led by past behavior, the cycle of life and death continues without stopping for a single kṣāṇa. With the body-mind that is swept like this through life and death, we should establish at once the bodhi-mind which is the will to deliver others before we ourselves attain deliverance. Even if, on the way to establishing the bodhi-mind, we begrudge the body-mind, it is born, grows old, becomes sick, and dies; in the end, it is not our own possession.

[207] The ceaselessness and swiftness with which the course through life of living beings arises and vanishes:

While the World-honored One is in the world there is a bhikṣu who visits the Buddha, bows his head at the Buddha's two feet, then stands back to one side and addresses the World-honored One, saying, "How fast is the arising and vanishing of the course through life of living beings?"

The Buddha says, "Even if I could explain it, you could not know it."

The bhikṣu says, "Is there no allegory that can demonstrate it?"

The Buddha says, "There is, and I will tell it to you now. For example, four skilled archers each take a bow and arrow, stand together back to back, and prepare to shoot in the four directions. An agile man comes along and says to them, 'You may now shoot your arrows at once, and I will be able to catch each one before it falls to the ground.' What does it mean? Is he fast or not?"

The bhikṣu says to the Buddha, "Very fast, World-honored One."

The Buddha says, "That man is not as fast as earthbound yakṣas. Earthbound yakṣas are not as fast as skyborne yakṣas. Skyborne yakṣas are not as fast as the four heavenly kings.[25] Those gods are not as fast as the two wheels of the sun and the moon. The two wheels of the sun and moon are not as fast as the gods[26] who pull the chariot whose wheels are the sun and moon. Though the gods described here have become progressively swifter, the arising and vanishing of the course of a life is swifter still. [Life] flows at every instant, without the slightest pause."[27]

---

24. 当本有 (TO-HON-U). 当 (TO) means "the present," "this one"; at the same time, it sometimes stands for 当来 (TORAI), "the future."

25. 四天王 (SHI-TENNO), or "the four quarter kings," from the Sanskrit *catvāro mahā-rājikāḥ,* are four gods under the God Indra who inhabit the first and lowest of the six heavens in the world of desire and who each guard one quarter of the compass surrounding Mount Sumeru. Their names are *Dhṛtarāṣṭra,* the ruler of the eastern continent, *Virūḍhaka,* the ruler of the southern continent, *Virūpākṣa,* the ruler of the western continent, and *Vaiśravaṇa,* the ruler of the northern continent (who is mentioned by name in LS 3.252).

26. 堅行天子 (KENGYO-TENSHI), or "Firmly Going Sons of Heaven," probably represents the meaning of a Sanskrit proper name for these particular gods. However, such a name has not been traced.

27. *Daibibasha-ron,* chap. 136.

The swiftness of the arising, vanishing, and instantaneous flowing of the course of our life is like this. Moment by moment, practitioners should not forget this principle. While experiencing the swiftness of this instantaneous arising, vanishing, and flowing, if we arouse one thought of delivering others before we attain deliverance ourselves, the eternal lifetime will manifest itself before us at once. The buddhas of the three times and the ten directions, together with the Seven World-Honored Buddhas, plus the twenty-eight patriarchs of India in the east, the six patriarchs of China in the west, and all the other ancestral masters who have transmitted the Buddha's right-Dharma-eye treasury and fine mind of nirvāṇa, each has maintained and relied upon the bodhi-mind. Those who have never established the bodhi-mind are not ancestral masters.

Pure Criteria for Zen Monasteries,[28] question one hundred and twenty, says, *"Have you awakened the bodhi-mind, or not?"*

Clearly remember: in the Buddhist patriarchs' learning of the truth, to awaken the bodhi-mind is inevitably seen as foremost. This is the eternal rule[29] of the Buddhist patriarchs. *"To awaken"*[30] means to be clear in; it does not refer to the great realization of the truth[31] itself. Even those who have suddenly experienced the ten states[32] are still bodhisattvas. The twenty-eight patriarchs of India, the six patriarchs of China, and all the other great ancestral masters are bodhisattvas: they are not buddhas; and they are not śrāvakas, pratyekabuddhas, or the like. Among practitioners of this age there is not one person who clearly knows that [these patriarchs] are bodhisattvas, not śrāvakas. [Practitioners of this age] just randomly call themselves patch-robed monks and patch-robed disciples without knowing the reality of the matter, and so they have created confusion. It is pitiful that in a decadent age the truth of the patriarchs has degenerated. This being so, whether we are lay people or ones who have left home, whether in the heavens above or in the human world, whether in suffering or in happiness, we should quickly

---

28. 禅苑清規 (ZEN-EN-SHINGI). Its editing was completed by Master Choro Sosaku in 1103.

29. 常法 (JOHO). 常 (JO) means constant or eternal, and at the same time usual or everyday. 法 (HO) in this context means rule, method, or dharma.

30. 発悟 (HOTSU-GO). 発 (HOTSU) means to establish, to initiate, or to arouse, as in the chapter title. 悟 (GO, *sato[ru]*) means 1) to perceive, to realize, to wake up to, or to become conscious of something in a limited sense, with one's thinking mind; 2) to realize reality in the widest sense, through the whole body-mind. See chap. 26, *Daigo*.

31. 大覚 (DAIGAKU). 大 (DAI) means "great." 覚 (KAKU) means the state of truth, or realization of the state of truth.

32. 十地 (JUCHI), "the ten states," generally means 十聖 (JUSSHO), the ten sacred stages that constitute stages forty-one to fifty of the fifty-two stages through which bodhisattvas must pass before becoming buddhas. The first group of ten stages is 十信 (JISSHIN), ten stages of belief. The next three groups of ten stages are 三賢 (SANKEN), the three clever stages. The fifth group of ten stages is the ten sacred stages. The fifty-first stage is 等覚 (TOKAKU), "the balanced state of truth," and the fifty-second stage is 妙覚 (MYOKAKU), "the fine state of truth."

establish the will to deliver others before we attain deliverance ourselves. Although the world of living beings is beyond limit and beyond limitlessness, we establish the mind to deliver, ahead of ourselves, all living beings. This is just the bodhi-mind. When bodhisattvas one life away [from buddhahood][33] are about to descend to Jambudvīpa, they say in their ultimate teaching for the gods in Tuṣita Heaven:[34] *"The bodhi-mind is a gate of Dharma-illumination, for it prevents negation of the Three Treasures."*[35] Clearly, non-negation of the Three Treasures is by virtue of the bodhi-mind. After establishing the bodhi-mind we should steadfastly guard it, never regressing or going astray.

[212] The Buddha says, *"How do bodhisattvas guard the one matter, namely the bodhi-mind? Bodhisattva-mahāsattvas constantly endeavor to guard this bodhi-mind as worldly people protect an only child or as the one-eyed protect their remaining eye. Just as those who, journeying through a vast wilderness, protect their guide, bodhisattvas again guard the bodhi-mind like this. Because they guard the bodhi-mind like this, they attain the truth of anuttara-samyak-saṃbodhi. Because they attain the truth of anuttara-samyak-saṃbodhi, they are replete with constancy, happiness, autonomy, and purity,*[36] *which are Supreme and Great Parinirvāṇa. For this reason, bodhisattvas guard [this] one dharma."*[37]

[213] The Buddha's words on guarding the bodhi-mind are, evidently, like this. The reason we guard it and never permit backsliding is that, as popular custom has it, there are three things which, though born, do not reach maturity. They are fish eggs, āmra[38] fruit, and a bodhisattva who has established the mind. Because, in general, there are so many people who regress and lose

33. 一生補処の菩薩 (ISSHO-HOSHO *no* BOSATSU), lit. "a bodhisattva at the place of assignment in one life," means a bodhisattva who is living his or her last life in Tuṣita Heaven before descending to the world to become buddha. 一生補処 (ISSHO-HOSHO), "the place of assignment in one life" is identified with 妙覚 (MYOKAKU), "the fine state of truth," i.e., the last of the bodhisattva's fifty-two stages.

34. Tuṣita Heaven is usually listed as the fourth of 六欲天 (ROKU-YOKU-TEN), "the six heavens of [the world of] desire" (from the Sanskrit *kāmavacara*). The six heavens are inhabited by 1) *caturmahārāja-kāyikās* (deities attending the Four Quarter Kings; see note 25); 2) *trāyastriṃśās* (thirty-three gods living on top of Mt. Sumeru, eight in each quarter surrounding Indra in the center); 3) *yāmās* (deities under Yama, who rules the spirits of the dead); 4) *tuṣitās* (indeterminate celestial beings); 5) *nirmāṇa-ratayas* ("gods who enjoy pleasures provided by themselves"); 6) *paranirmita-vaśa-vartinas* ("gods who constantly enjoy pleasures provided by others"). MW has tuṣitās in the third heaven and yāmās in the fourth.

35. *Butsu-hongyo-jikkyo*. This part of the sutra is also quoted in *Ippyakuhachi-homyomon* in the 12-chapter edition of Shobogenzo. See Book 4, Appendices.

36. 常楽我浄 (JO-RAKU-GA-JO), "constancy, happiness, autonomy, and purity," are the four attributes of nirvāṇa.

37. *Daihatsu-nehan-kyo*, chap. 25.

38. The Sanskrit *āmra* means mango, a tree which produces many flowers, but relatively little fruit.

[the bodhi-mind], I have long feared that I also might regress and lose it. For this reason I guard the bodhi-mind. Bodhisattvas often regress or stray from the bodhi-mind when they are beginners because they do not meet a true teacher. Without meeting a true teacher, they do not hear the right Dharma. Without hearing the right Dharma, they are likely to negate cause and effect, to negate salvation, to negate the Three Treasures, and to negate all the dharmas of the three times. Idly craving the five desires[39] of the present, they lose the virtue for future [attainment of] bodhi. Sometimes, in order to hinder a practitioner, celestial demons, pāpīyas, and the like[40] will take on the shape of a buddha or will appear in the shape of a parent, a teacher, or relatives, gods, and so on; thus drawing near, they concoct fictions and prevail upon the bodhisattva, saying, *"The Buddha's truth is far distant. You would suffer long hardships and experience the deepest sorrow. The better course is to resolve our own life and death first and then to deliver living beings."* The practitioner, hearing these tales, regresses from the bodhi-mind and regresses in the conduct of a bodhisattva. Remember, talk such as the above is just the talk of demons. Bodhisattvas must recognize it and must not follow it. Just never regress or stray from your conduct and vow to deliver others before attaining deliverance yourself. Know [talk] that would turn you against the conduct and vow to deliver others before attaining deliverance yourself as the talk of demons, know it as the talk of non-Buddhists, and know it as the talk of bad companions. Never follow it at all.

There are four kinds of demon: The first is demons of hindrance, the second is demons of the five aggregates, the third is demons of death, and the fourth is celestial demons.[41]

"Demons of hindrance"[42]*—of what are called the one hundred and eight hindrances and so on*[43]*—discriminate eighty-four thousand miscellaneous hindrances.*

---

39. 五欲 (GOYOKU), "five desires," are desires for pleasure through sight, sound, smell, taste, and touch. They are also categorized as desires for property, sexual love, food and drink, fame, and sleep.

40. 天魔波旬等 (TENMA-HAJUN-TO). 天魔 (TENMA), "celestial demons," generally refers to the demons who rule Paranirmita-vaśa-vartin Heaven, which was thought to house the palace of Māra, or Māraḥ-pāpīyān, the king of demons. 波旬 (HAJUN) represents the sound of the Sanskrit *pāpīyas*, which means "most wicked ones." 天魔波旬 (TEN-MAHAJUN) may be understood as one concept, "celestial māraḥ-pāpīyas," and as referring to one individual, "the celestial Māraḥ-pāpīyān." Here, however, 等 (TO) indicates plurality. See Glossary.

41. This section (one paragraph in the source text) is from *Daichido-ron* (from the Sanskrit *Mahā-prajñā-pāramitopadeśa*), chap. 68. The original Mahā-prajñā-pāramitopadeśa is a commentary attributed to Master Nāgārjuna, the 14th patriarch. It was translated into Chinese by Kumārajīva in c. 405 A.D.

42. 煩悩魔 (BONNO-MA), from the Sanskrit *kleśa-māra*. Kleśa means affliction, trouble, the cause of suffering, that which disturbs our balance and hinders our action.

43. 百八煩悩等 (HYAKUHACHI-BONNO-TO) refers to lists in Buddhist commentaries enumerating six or ten *mūla-kleśa*, basic causes of suffering, and varying numbers of *upakleśa*, secondary

"Demons of the five aggregates"[44] are the primary and cooperating causes which combine to produce hindrances. We have got this body of the four elements;[45] together with matter made from the four elements and matter [sensed through] the eyes and other organs, this is called "the aggregate of matter."[46] The sum of feelings such as those of the one hundred and eight hindrances is called "the aggregate of feeling."[47] Differentiation and synthesis of the countless thoughts, great and small that we have is called "the aggregate of thought."[48] Through the occurrence of pleasure and displeasure, there can arise habits which accommodate or do not accommodate mental states such as greed, anger, and so on: this is called "the aggregate of conduct."[49]

---

hindrances. According to JEBD, in the Vijñānavāda tradition the six mūla-kleśa are enumerated as *rāga*, craving; *pratigha*, anger; *mūḍha*, ignorance; *māna*, arrogance; *vicikitsā*, doubt, and *ḍrṣṭi*, wrong view (of which there are five categories—the *pañca ḍrṣṭyah*), while the Abhidharma-kośa-śāstra lists the following nineteen upakleśa: *pramāda*, negligence; *kausīdya*, indolence; *āśraddha*, unbelief; *styāna*, sloth; *auddhatya*, disdain; *āhrīkya*, shamelessness; *anapatrāpya*, lack of reserve; *krodha*, wrath; *mraksa*, hypocrisy; *mātsarya*, meanness; *īrṣyā*, envy; *pradāsa*, affliction; *vihiṃsā*, tendency to do harm; *upanāha*, continual enmity; *māya*, duplicity; *śāṭhya*, roguery; *mada*, presumption; *middha*, drowsiness; and *kaukṛtya*, remorse. MW cites ten kleśas listed in the Sarvadarśana-saṃgraha and refers to "twenty-four minor evil passions" listed in the Dharma-saṃgraha. See Glossary.

44. 五衆魔 (GOSHU-MA) from the Sanskrit *pañca-skandha-māra*. The pañca skandha are the five constituent elements of being. MW lists them as 1) *rūpa*, 'bodily form'; 2) *vedana*, 'sensation'; 3) *saṃjñā*, 'perception'; 4) *saṃskāra*, 'aggregate of formations'; and 5) *vijñāna*, 'consciousness or thought-faculty.' Thich Nhat Hanh *(The Miracle of Mindfulness)* lists them as 1) form, or bodily and physical forms; 2) feeling(s); 3) perception(s); 4) mental functioning(s); and 5) consciousness. T. R. V. Murti *(The Central Philosophy of Buddhism)* lists them as 1) matter, or material forms; 2) feeling; 3) ideation; apprehension of determining marks; 4) the forces, mental and material, that condition existential entities; and 5) consciousness, or pure awareness without content. Ven. Dr. U. Rewata Dhamma, translating from the Pali *(The First Sermon of the Buddha)*, lists them as 1) matter; 2) sensations or feelings; 3) perceptions, or sense recognition following the arising of sensations; 4) mental formations, i.e., all our actions and reactions in daily life; 5) consciousness. Ven. Rewata Dhamma notes that sensations and perceptions are not volitional actions and so do not produce any karmic force, whereas *saṃskāra* produces actual karmic effects.

45. 四大 (SHIDAI), "the four elements," from the Sanskrit *catvāri mahābhūtāni*, are 1) earth (representing the qualities of heaviness and lightness—ibid.); 2) water (cohesion or fluidity); 3) fire (heat and cold); and 4) wind (motions and movements).

46. 色衆 (SHIKI-SHU). 色 (SHIKI) is lit. "color" or "form."

47. 受衆 (JU-SHU). 受 (JU) is lit. "receive," "accept," or "take in." Master Nāgārjuna's comment confirms that the term *vedana* embraces all feelings, not only physical or sensory (sensing of external stimuli) but also mental or emotional (greed, anger, pride, doubt, et cetera).

48. 想衆 (SO-SHU). 想 (SO), is lit. "idea," "conception," or "thought." For *saṃjñā* as one of the skandhas MW gives "perception," but his general definition of the term includes "clear conception" and "direction." See Glossary.

49. 行衆 (GYO-SHU). 行 (GYO) means going, conducting oneself, acting, carrying out, performing, becoming operative, being translated into action. For *saṃskāra* as one of the skandhas, MW gives "mental conformation or creation of the mind," but he defines *saṃskāra* in general as forming well, accomplishment, forming the mind, training, education. In Master Nāgārjuna's

Combination of the six senses[50] *and their six objects*[51] *gives rise to the six kinds of consciousness.*[52] *The countless and limitless states of mind which are the differentiation and synthesis of these six kinds of consciousness are called "the aggregate of consciousness."*[53]

"Demons of death,"[54] *through the impermanence of direct and cooperating causes, break the momentary succession of the lives of the five aggregates and utterly remove three things: consciousness, heat, and life. Therefore we call them "demons of death."*

"Celestial demons,[55] *as rulers of the world of desire,*[56] *deeply attach to worldly pleasures and rely upon expectation of gain;*[57] *therefore, they give rise to wrong views. They hate and envy all sages' and saints' ways and methods of nirvāṇa. We call these "celestial demons."*

---

explanation *saṃskāra* indicates concrete self-conduct as the criterion of formation of good or bad habits.

50. 六情 (ROKU-JO), usually called 六根 (ROKKON), represents the Sanskrit *ṣad indriyāṇi.* The six sense organs are *cakṣus,* the eyes; *śrotra,* the ears; *ghrāṇa,* the nose; *jihvā,* the tongue; *kāya,* the body; and *manas,* the mind as a sense organ. According to MW, manas originally means mind in a wide sense as applied to all mental faculties—intellect, understanding, perception, motor-sense, conscience, et cetera. In Buddhist philosophy the mind as a sense organ is sometimes sub-divided into two components (see also note 51).

51. 六塵 (ROKU-JIN), also called 六境 (ROKKYO), represents the Sanskrit *ṣad viṣayaḥ.* The six objects are *rūpa,* form; *śabda,* sound; *gandha* , odor; *rasa,* taste; *sparśa,* tangible objects; and *dharma,* objects of the mind such as thoughts, wishes, ideas, attributes, patterns, movements, et cetera.

52. 六識 (ROKU-SHIKI), "the six kinds of consciousness," are the momentary consciousness which arises in the eyes seeing a visible object, the ears hearing a sound, the nose smelling an odor, the body touching a tangible object, and the mind meeting a mental object. Sub-division of the mind into kinesthetic and intellectual faculties results in seven kinds of consciousness, as mentioned in chap. 28, *Butsu-kojo-no-ji* [63].

53. 識衆 (SHIKI-SHU). 識 (SHIKI), "consciousness," thus defined as the combination of subject and object, is the basis of the teaching of 唯識 (YUI-SHIKI), "consciousness-alone" (Sanskrit: *vijñāna-mātratā*). This teaching, elucidated in the so-called Yogācāra-Vijñānavāda school (stemming from the 21st patriarch Vasubandhu), affirms the all-embracing reality of consciousness, whereby grass, trees, stars, pebbles, and so on, are all seen as manifestations of seeds of store-consciousness *(ālaya-vijñāna).*

54. 死魔 (SHIMA) represents the Sanskrit *mṛityu-māra.* See Glossary.

55. 天子魔 (TENSHIMA), lit. "demons who are the sons of heaven," represents the Sanskrit *devaputra-māra.* Here the term refers to demons in Paranirmita-vaśa-vartin Heaven, the sixth and highest heaven in the world of desire. See note 40.

56. 欲界 (YOKKAI), "the world of desire or volition," represents the Sanskrit *kāma-dhātu.* See chap. 47, *Sangai-yuishin.*

57. 有所得 (USHOTOKU) means having an ulterior motive or idealistic aim in mind—a tendency which Master Dogen sometimes attributes to celestial demons; see, for example, chap. 8, *Raihai-tokuzui* [194]. The antonym 無所得 (MUSHOTOKU), "non-gaining" or "non-attainment," describes the action of one who is living fully in the present moment. See also chap. 87, *Kuyo-shobutsu* [131].

Māra[58] *is an Indian word; in China it is called a being which is able to steal life. Only demons of death can actually steal life, but the others also are able to produce the direct and cooperating causes of the taking of life; moreover, they take away the life of wisdom. For this reason we call them killers.*

Someone asks, "One category, the demons of the five aggregates, covers the other three kinds of demon. Why do you separate them and explain the four?" The answer is as follows: "In fact it is one demon. [But] for the purpose of analysis, there are the four."

[219] The foregoing is the teaching of the ancestral Master Nāgārjuna. Practitioners should know it and should diligently learn it. Never idly be worried by demons into regressing or straying from the bodhi-mind. This is to guard the bodhi-mind.

Shobogenzo Hotsu-bodaishin

Preached to the assembly at Kippo temple in the Yoshida district of Esshu on the 14th day of the 2nd lunar month in the 2nd year of Kangen.[59]

58. 魔 (MA), hitherto translated as "demon," represents both the sound and the meaning of the Sanskrit *māra*, which means 1) killing, and 2) demon. See Glossary.

59. 1244.

[71]

如来全身

NYORAI-ZENSHIN

The Whole Body of the Tathāgata

***Nyorai** represents the Chinese translation of the Sanskrit word **tathāgata**, which means a person who has arrived at the truth. Sometimes, as in this case, **nyorai** means Gautama Buddha himself. **Zenshin** means "the whole body." In this chapter, Master Dogen teaches that Buddhist sutras are Gautama Buddha's whole body, using the word "sutras" to express the real form of the Universe. Thus Master Dogen insists that the Universe is Gautama Buddha's whole body.*

[1] **At that time, Śākyamuni Buddha** was living on Mount Gṛdhrakūṭa[1] at Rājagṛha.[2] He addressed the Bodhisattva Medicine King, saying: *"Medicine King! In every place where [this sutra] is preached, or read, or recited, or copied, or where volumes of the sutra are kept, we should establish a stūpa[3] of the seven treasures, making it most high, wide, and ornate. [But] there is no need to place bones[4] in it. Why? [Because] in it there is already the whole body of the Tathāgata. This stūpa should be served, revered, honored, and extolled with all kinds of flowers, fragrances, strings of pearls,[5] silk canopies, banners, flags, music, and songs of praise. If any people, being able to see this stūpa, do prostrations and serve offerings to it, know that they are all close to anuttara-samyak-saṃbodhi."*[6]

---

1. The Sanskrit *Gṛdhrakūṭa,* here represented phonetically, means "Vulture Peak." This mountain, a natural platform overlooking the Rājagṛha valley, was the stage on which was set the Buddha's preaching of the Sutra of the Lotus Flower of the Wonderful Dharma; i.e., the Sutra of the Lotus Universe, the Lotus Sutra. See LS 1.8.

2. 王舎城 (OSHAJO), lit. "City of Royal Palaces," represents the meaning of the Sanskrit *Rājagṛha,* which was the name of the capital of the ancient kingdom of Magadha.

3. 塔 (TO), lit. "tower." On the one hand, LSW notes that the Sanskrit text of the Lotus Sutra here has caitya. Furthermore, LSW notes that, from this place on, the Lotus Sutra stresses the building of caityas (pagodas for sutras) as opposed to stūpas (pagodas for relics). On the other hand, the Monier-Williams Sanskrit-English dictionary suggests that the two terms, *caitya* and *stūpa*, are interchangeable. See Book 1, Glossary. Master Dogen discusses the problem further in chap. 87, *Kuyo-shobutsu,* [160]. In general, we have translated 塔 (TO) as "stūpa."

4. 舎利 (SHARI) represents the Sanskrit *śarīra,* which means body, dead body, or bones.

5. 瓔珞 (YORAKU), lit. "necklaces," represents the Sanskrit *muktāhāra,* which means a string of pearls or jewels worn by royalty and nobility in ancient India.

6. Lotus Sutra, *Hosshi.* See LS 2.154.

[222] What has been called *"volumes of the Sutra"* is concrete preaching itself,[7] is concrete reading itself, is concrete reciting itself, and is concrete copying itself. *Volumes of the Sutra* are real form itself.[8] *There will be established the Stūpa of the Seven Treasures:*[9] this expresses real form as a stūpa. The *height and width* of *utmost making* are inevitably the dimensions of real form. *In this*[10] *there is already the whole body of the Tathāgata:* for volumes of the Sutra are the whole body itself. Thus, concrete preaching, concrete reading, concrete reciting, concrete copying, and so on, are themselves the whole body of the Tathāgata. We should serve, revere, honor, and extol them with all kinds of flowers, fragrances, strings of pearls, silk canopies, banners, flags, music, and songs of praise. Those may be celestial flowers, celestial fragrances, celestial canopies, and so on, all of which are real form. Or they may be the choice flowers, choice fragrances, fine robes, and fine clothes of the human world—these are all real form. Serving offerings and showing reverence are real form. We should establish the Stūpa, *"but there is no need to place bones in it:"* clearly, volumes of the Sutra are themselves the bones of the Tathāgata and the whole body of the Tathāgata. These are the golden words of the Buddha's own mouth; there can be no virtue greater than seeing and hearing them. We should be quick to accumulate merit and to heap up virtue. If any people do prostrations and serve offerings to this Stūpa, remember, *they are totally close to anuttara-samyak-saṃbodhi.* When we are able to see this Stūpa, we should wholeheartedly do prostrations and serve offerings to this Stūpa; just those

---

7. 若説 (NYAKU-SETSU). In the Lotus Sutra quotation, 若 *(moshi[ku wa])* is used as the conjunction "or," but here Master Dogen uses the character as an intensifier to suggest real preaching as it is. The same applies to reading, reciting, and copying. Similar usage of 若 (NYAKU) occurs in chap. 20, *Kokyo* [153] and in chap. 22, *Bussho* [14].

8. 経巻は実相これなり (KYOGAN *wa* JISSO *kore nari*). Master Dogen saw 妙法蓮華経 (MYOHO-RENGE-KYO), "the Sutra of the Lotus Flower of the Wonderful Dharma," as an expression of the Universe itself. Therefore, 経巻 (KYOGAN), "volumes of the Sutra," means not only copies of the Sutra of the Lotus Universe, but also the concrete manifestations of this Lotus Universe as a Sutra. 実相 (JISSO), "real form," also means the Universe itself, or reality itself (see chap. 50, *Shoho-jisso*).

9. 応起七宝塔 (O-KI-SHIPPO-TO). The meaning suggested in the Lotus Sutra is "we should erect a stūpa of the seven treasures." But in Master Dogen's interpretation 七宝塔 (SHIPPO-TO), "the Stūpa of the Seven Treasures," is used as another figurative expression of the substantial form of the real Universe. Here, 応起 (O-KI) means not only "[we] should erect" but also "[there] will arise"; i.e., it suggests not only the propriety of building a stūpa out of bricks et cetera, but also the inevitability of the momentary establishment of the real Universe.

10. 此中 (SHICHU), "in this," means "in this concrete reality here and now." 此 (SHI), "this," may therefore be interpreted as referring to 1) volumes of the Lotus Sutra; 2) action; 3) real form or reality; 4) the Stūpa of the Seven Treasures. In the first sentence of this paragraph Master Dogen has identified 1) and 2); in the second sentence 1) and 3); in the third sentence 3) and 4); and in the fourth sentence 2) and 3). In this sentence he says that in each of these four elements, which he has thus directly or indirectly identified with each other, there is the whole body of the Tathāgata.

actions may be *total closeness* to *anuttara-samyak-saṃbodhi. Being close* is neither closeness following separation nor closeness following coming together. Anuttara-samyak-saṃbodhi is called *"total closeness."* Our own experience here and now of receiving, retaining, reading, reciting, interpreting, and copying is *being able to see this Stūpa.* We should rejoice: it is the total closeness of anuttara-samyak-saṃbodhi.

So the volumes of the Sutra are the whole body of the Tathāgata. To do prostrations to volumes of the Sutra is to do prostrations to the Tathāgata. To have met volumes of the Sutra is to be meeting the Tathāgata. The volumes of the Sutra are the bones of the Tathāgata. Because this is so, bones may be this Sutra.[11] Even if we know that volumes of the Sutra are the bones, if we do not know that bones are volumes of the Sutra, that is not yet the Buddha's truth. The real form of all dharmas here and now is volumes of the Sutra. The human world, the heavens above, the ocean, space, this land, and other realms all are real form, are volumes of the Sutra, and are bones. Receiving, retaining, reading, reciting, interpreting, and copying bones we should disclose realization: this is [called] *"sometimes following the sutras."* There are bones of eternal buddhas, bones of present buddhas, bones of pratyekabuddhas, and bones of wheel-rolling kings. There are lion bones, there are wooden buddha bones and painted buddha bones, and there are human bones. In the great kingdom of Sung today, several generations of Buddhist patriarchs are manifesting their bones while they are living; and many have yielded their bones after cremation.[12] These cases are all volumes of the Sutra.

Śākyamuni Buddha addressed the great assembly, saying, *"The lifetime which I have realized by my original practice of the bodhisattva-way is not even yet exhausted but will still be twice the previous number."*[13]

The eighty-four gallons of bones of the present are just the Buddha's lifetime itself. The lifetime of *original practice of the bodhisattva-way* is not confined to the three-thousand-great-thousandfold world; it may be incalculable. Such is the whole body of the Tathāgata. Such are the volumes of the Sutra.

The Bodhisattva Wisdom Accumulation said, "I have seen [how] Śākyamuni Tathāgata, during countless kalpas of hard practice and painful practice, accumulating merit and heaping up virtue, has pursued the bodhisattva-way and has never ceased. I have observed that in the three-thousand-great-thousandfold world, there is no place even the size of a mustard seed where he has not abandoned his body and life

---

11. 舎利は此経なるべし (SHARI *wa* SHIKYO *naru beshi*). 舎利 (SHARI), "bones," are here a symbol of the concrete, and 此経 (SHIKYO), "this Sutra," means "a Sutra of this concrete reality."

12. 闍維 (JA-I) represents the pronunciation of the Prakrit *jhāpita*, which means cremation.

13. Lotus Sutra, *Nyorai-juryo*. The *"previous number"* refers to the astronomically large number of kalpas which had passed since the beginning of the Buddha's buddhahood. See LS 3.12, LS 3.20.

as a bodhisattva for the sake of living beings. After acting thus, he was then able to realize the truth of bodhi."[14]

Clearly, this three-thousand-great-thousandfold world is a single instance of red mind, is a single concrete space, and is the whole body of the Tathāgata, which can never depend upon abandonment or non-abandonment. Bones are neither prior to the Buddha nor subsequent to the Buddha; nor are they arranged side by side with the Buddha.[15] Countless kalpas of hard practice and painful practice are the vivid activity of the Buddha's womb or the Buddha's abdomen; they are the Buddha's skin, flesh, bones, and marrow. It says *"he has never ceased":* having attained buddhahood he practices all the more vigorously, and having educated the great-thousandfold world he is still going forward. The vigorous activity of the whole body is like this.

Shobogenzo Nyorai-zenshin

Preached to the assembly at Kippo temple in the Yoshida district of Esshu on the 15th day of the 2nd lunar month in the 2nd year of Kangen.[16]

---

14. Lotus Sutra, *Devadatta*. See LS 2.218–220.
15. Concrete bones and the Buddha cannot be separated.
16. 1244.

[72]

三昧王三昧

ZANMAI-O-ZANMAI

The Samādhi That Is King of Samādhis

Zanmai** is the Japanese pronunciation of the phonetic rendering in Chinese of the Sanskrit word "samādhi," which means the state in Zazen; that is, the balanced state of body and mind.* ***O *means "king." We can consider that there are many kinds of samādhi in our daily lives. However, according to Buddhist theory the most important and best samādhi is just the samādhi that we can experience in Zazen. Therefore, we call the state in Zazen "the king of samādhis." In this chapter, Master Dogen explains what Zazen is, and so he chose the title* ***Zanmai-o-zanmai****, The Samādhi That Is King of Samādhis.*

To transcend the whole Universe at once, to live a great and valuable life in the house of the Buddhist patriarchs, is to sit in the full lotus posture. To tread over the heads of non-Buddhists and demons; to become, in the inner sanctum of the Buddhist patriarchs, a person in the concrete state, is to sit in the full lotus posture. To transcend the supremacy of the Buddhist patriarchs' supremacy, there is only this one method. Therefore, Buddhist patriarchs practice it solely, having no other practices at all. Remember, the Universe in sitting is far different from other universes. Clearly understanding this truth, Buddhist patriarchs pursue and realize the establishment of the will, training, the state of bodhi, and nirvāṇa. Just in the moment of sitting, investigate whether the Universe is vertical, and whether it is horizontal. Just in the moment of sitting, what is the sitting itself? Is it a somersault? Is it a state of vigorous activity? Is it thinking? Is it beyond thinking? Is it doing something? Is it not doing anything? Is it sitting inside of sitting? Is it sitting inside of the body-mind? Is it sitting that is free of "the inside of sitting," "the inside of the body-mind," and so on? There should be investigation of thousands and tens of thousands of points like these. Sit in the full lotus posture with the body. Sit in the full lotus posture with the mind. Sit in the full lotus posture being free of body and mind.

My late Master, the eternal Buddha, says, *"To practice [Za]zen is to get free of body and mind. Just to sit is to have attainment from the beginning. It is not necessary to burn incense, to do prostrations, to recite the Buddha's name, to confess, or to read sutras."*

Clearly, in the last four or five hundred years, only one person, my late Master, has scooped out the Eye of the Buddhist Patriarch and sat inside the Eye of the Buddhist Patriarch; few people have equaled him, even in China. Very few people realize that the act of sitting is the Buddha-Dharma and that the Buddha-Dharma is the act of sitting. Even if some physically understand sitting to be the Buddha-Dharma, none has realized sitting as sitting. How then can any be maintaining and relying upon the Buddha-Dharma as the Buddha-Dharma? This being so, there is sitting with the mind, which is not the same as sitting with the body. There is sitting with the body, which is not the same as sitting with the mind. And there is sitting that is free of body and mind, which is not the same as "sitting that is free of body and mind." Already to have attained the state like this is the Buddhist patriarchs' state in which practice and understanding are in mutual accord. Maintain and rely upon this awareness, thought, reflection. Investigate this mind, will, consciousness.

[235] *Śākyamuni Buddha addresses a large assembly: "If we sit in the full lotus posture, the body-mind will experience samādhi, and many people will revere the dignity and virtue of the state. Like the sun lighting up the world, it clears away sleepy, lazy, and melancholy mind. The body is light and tireless. Perception and consciousness are also light and responsive. We should sit like coiled dragons.[1] On seeing just a picture of the lotus posture, even the king of demons is afraid. How much more so if he sees a person really experiencing the state of truth, sitting without inclination or agitation?"[2]*

Thus, on seeing a picture of the lotus posture, even the king of demons is surprised, worried, and afraid. Still more, when we really sit in the lotus posture, the virtue is beyond imagination. In short, the happiness and virtue of everyday sitting are limitless.

[236] *Śākyamuni Buddha addresses a large assembly: "This is why we sit in the full lotus posture." Then the Tathāgata, the World-honored One, teaches his disciples that they should sit like this. Sometimes non-Buddhists pursue the truth by continuously standing on tiptoes, sometimes they pursue the truth by continuously standing up, and sometimes they pursue the truth by carrying the legs on the shoulders. Mad and obstinate mind like this sinks into the sea of wrongness, and the body is not peaceful. For this reason, the Buddha teaches his disciples to sit in the full lotus posture, sitting with the mind upright. Why? [Because] if the body is upright, the mind is easily set right. When the body sits upright, the mind is not weary, the mind is regulated, the intention is right, and the attention is bound to what is immediately present. If the mind races or becomes distracted and if the body leans or becomes agitated, [sitting upright] regulates them and causes them to recover. When we want*

1. 如龍蟠 (*ryu [no] wadakama[ru ga] goto[ku seyo]*), "like a dragon in its coil," suggests a sitting posture in which there is stability and power without undue rigidity or exertion.

2. Quoted from vol. 7 of *Daichido-ron,* the Chinese translation of the Mahā-prajñā-pāramitopadeśa.

to experience samādhi and want to enter samādhi, even if the mind is chasing various images and is variously distracted, [sitting upright] completely regulates all such states. Practicing like this, we experience and enter the samādhi that is king of samādhis.[3]

7] Evidently, sitting in the full lotus posture is just the samādhi that is king of samādhis, and is just experience and entry. All samādhis are the followers[4] of this, the king of samādhis. To sit in the full lotus posture is to set the body straight,[5] to set the mind straight, to set the body-mind straight, to set Buddhist patriarchs straight, to set practice-and-experience straight, to set the brain straight, and to set the life-blood straight. Now, sitting our human skin, flesh, bones, and marrow in the full lotus posture, we sit the samādhi that is king among samādhis in the full lotus posture. The World-honored One is constantly maintaining and relying upon the practice of sitting in the full lotus posture. He authentically transmits the practice of sitting in the full lotus posture to his disciples, and he teaches human beings and gods to sit in the full lotus posture. The mind-seal authentically transmitted by the Seven Buddhas is just this. Under the Bodhi tree Śākyamuni Buddha passes fifty minor kalpas, passes sixty kalpas, and passes countless kalpas, sitting in the lotus posture. Sitting in the full lotus posture for three weeks, or sitting for hours, is the turning of the splendid Dharma wheel, and is the lifelong teaching of the Buddha. It lacks nothing. It is just a yellow scroll on a red stick.[6] The meeting of Buddha with Buddha is this moment. This is just the time when living beings become Buddha.

] The first Patriarch,[7] the Venerable Bodhidharma, after arriving from the west, passed nine years facing the wall at Shorin-ji temple on Shoshitsu-ho peak in the Sugaku mountains, sitting in Zazen in the lotus posture. From that time through to today, brains and eyes have pervaded China. The life-blood of the first Patriarch is only the practice of sitting in the full lotus posture. Before the first Patriarch came from the west the people of eastern lands never knew sitting in the full lotus posture. Since the ancestral Master came from the west they have known it. This being so, just to sit in the lotus posture, day and night, from the beginning to the end of this life, and for tens of

3. Also quoted from vol. 7 of *Daichido-ron*.

4. 眷属 (KENZOKU), lit. "family," "household," or "kin," represents the Sanskrit *parivāra* (dependents, followers). The words are used in the Lotus Sutra to indicate the followers of a god or a king. See LS 1.14.

5. 直身 (JIKI-SHIN), 直 (JIKI, *nao[su]*) used in the previous paragraph as an adjective and as an adverb, means straight or upright. Used here as a transitive verb, 直 (JIKI, *nao[su]*) means to make upright, to set straight, to rectify, to restore to order or normality, or to cure.

6. A concrete sutra.

7. Master Bodhidharma (died c. 528), the twenty-eighth patriarch in India and the first patriarch in China.

thousands of lives, without leaving the temple grounds[8] and without having any other practices, is the samādhi that is king of samādhis.

Shobogenzo Zanmai-o-zanmai

Preached to the assembly at Kippo temple in Etsu-u,[9] on the 15th day of the 2nd lunar month in the 2nd year of Kangen.[10]

8. 不離叢林 (FURI SORIN). 叢林 (SORIN), lit. "thicket-forest," from the Sanskrit *piṇḍa-vana,* suggests a place where many practitioners are gathered for Buddhist practice; or, more widely, the state of Buddhist practice. See chap. 39, *Dotoku.*

9. Modern-day Fukui prefecture.

10. 1244.

Appendices

Chinese Masters

Japanese	Pinyin
Banzan Hoshaku	Panshan Baoji
Baso Do-itsu	Mazu Daoyi
Bokushu Domyo	Muzhou Daoming
Bussho Hotai	Foxing Fatai
Chimon Koso	Zhimen Guangzu
Chorei (Fukushu) Shutaku	Changqing Daan
Chosa Keishin	Changsha Jingcen
Dai-e Soko	Dahui Zonggao
Daibai Hojo	Damei Fachang
Daikan Eno	Dajian Huineng
Do-iku	Daoyu
Dofuku	Daofu
Dogo Enchi	Daowu Yuanjie
Enchi Dai-an	Yuanzhi Daan
Engo Kokugon	Yuanwu Keqin
Esshu Kenpo	Yuezhou Qianfeng
Fuyo Dokai	Furong Daokai
Fuyo Reikun	Furong Lingxun
Gensa Shibi	Xuansha Shibei
Goso Ho-en	Wuzu Fayan
Gutei	Juzhi
Ho-un Ihaku	Fayun Weibai
Hogen Bun-eki	Fayan Wenyi
Honei Nin-yu	Baoning Renyong
Hyakujo Ekai	Baizhang Huaihai
Isan Reiyu	Guishan Lingyou
Jinshu	Shenxiu
Joshu Jushin	Zhaozhou Congshen
Kaigen Chiso	Huiyan Zhicong
Kakuhan Eko	Jiaofan Huihong
Kazan Shujun	Heshan Shouxun
Kisu Chijo	Guizong Zhichang
Koan Daigu	Gaoan Daiyu
Koboku Hojo	Kumu Facheng
Kyogen Chikan	Xiangyan Zhixian
Kyozan Ejaku	Yangshan Huiji
Nan-yo Echu	Nanyang Huizhong
Nangaku Ejo	Nanyue Huairang
Nansen Fugan	Nanquan Puyuan

Japanese	Pinyin
O-an Donge	Yingan Tanhua
Obaku Ki-un	Huangbo Xiyun
Oryu Enan	Huanglong Huinan
Rakan Keichin	Luohan Guichen
Rinzai Gigen	Linji Yixuan
Roya Ekaku	Langye Huijiao
Sansho Enen	Sansheng Huiran
Seccho Chikan	Xuedou Zhijian
Seccho Juken	Xuedou Chongxian
Seigen Gyoshi	Qingyuan Xingsi
Sekimon Etetsu	Shimen Huiche
Sekiso Keisho	Shishuang Qingzhu
Sekito Kisen	Shitou Xiqian
Sempuku Shoko	Jianfu Chenggu
Seppo Gison	Xuefeng Yicun
Shinzan Somitsu	Shenshan Zongmi
Soji	Zongchi
Sozan Honjaku	Caoshan Benji
Sozan Konin	Shushan Guangren
Taigen Fu	Taiyuan Fu
Taiso Eka	Dazu Huike
Tando Bunjun	Zhantang Wenzhun
Tanka Shijun	Danxia Zichun
Tendo Nyojo	Tiantong Rujing
Tenryu	Tianlong
Tokuzan Senkan	Deshan Xuanjian
Tosu Daido	Touzi Datong
Tosu Gisei	Touzi Yiqing
Tozan Ryokai	Dongshan Liangjie
Ungan Donjo	Yunyan Tansheng
Ungo Doyo	Yunju Daoying
Unmon Bun-en	Yunmen Wenyan
Wanshi Shokaku	Hongzhi Zhengjue
Yakusan Igen	Yueshan Weiyan
Zengen Chuko	Jianyuan Zhongxing

Glossary of Sanskrit Terms

This glossary contains Sanskrit terms appearing in Book 3 that are not already covered in the Sanskrit Glossaries of Book 1 and Book 2. Definitions are drawn in general from *A Sanskrit-English Dictionary* by Sir Monier Monier-Williams [MW], (Oxford University Press, 1333 pp.)

Chapter references, unless otherwise stated, refer to chapters of Shobogenzo. Arrangement is according to the English alphabet.

abhaya-dāna (giving of fearlessness)
Represented by 無畏施 (MUI-SE), "giving of fearlessness."
[MW] giving assurance of safety
abhaya: unfearful, not dangerous, secure; fearless, undaunted; absence or removal of fear, peace, safety, security.
dāna: giving.
Ref. ch. 45 [72]; Lotus Sutra ch. 25.

adhipati-pratyaya (overarching circumstances)
Represented by 增上緣 (ZOJO-EN), "circumstances over and above; promoting circumstances."
[MW] *adhi:* as a prefix to verbs and nouns, expresses above, over and above, besides.
adhipati: a ruler, commander, regent, king.
pratyaya: a co-operating cause, a circumstance.
One of the four types of circumstance (see **catvāraḥ pratyayāh**).
Ref. ch. 70 [201].

āhrīkya (shamelessness)
[MW] *ahri:* shameless (as a beggar), shamelessness.
ahrīka: 'shameless beggar,' a Buddhist mendicant.
[JEBD] *āhrīkya:* shamelessness
One of the upakleśa, or secondary hindrances.
Ref. ch. 70 [216].

Ājñāta-kauṇḍinya (name; "Kauṇḍinya, He Who Has Known")
Represented phonetically.
[MW] name of one of the first five pupils of Śākyamuni.
ājñāta: see *an-ājñāta.*
an-ājñāta: unknown.
Ref. ch. 55 [112]; ch. 79.

ālambana-pratyaya (a connected circumstance)
Represented by 所緣緣 (SHO-EN-EN), "a connected circumstance."
[MW] *ālambana:* depending on or resting upon; hanging from; supporting, sustaining; foundation, base; reason, cause; (in rhetoric) the natural and necessary connection of a sensation with the cause that excites it; (with Buddhists) the five attributes of things (apprehended by or connected with the five senses).
pratyaya: a co-operating cause, a circumstance.
One of the four types of circumstance (see **catvāraḥ pratyayāh**).
Ref. ch. 70 [201].

ālaya-vijñāna (store-consciousness)
Represented phonetically.
[MW] *ālaya:* a house, dwelling; a receptacle, asylum; (often at the end of a compound; e.g. *himālaya,* 'the abode of snow').
vijñāna: consciousness (see Book 1).
Ref. ch. 70 [216].

amisa-dāna (giving of material objects)
Represented by 財施 (ZAISE), "giving of goods."
[MW] *amisa:* flesh; food, meat, prey; an object of enjoyment, a pleasing or beautiful object; a gift, boon, fee.
dāna: giving.
Ref. ch. 45 [72].

āmra (mango)
Represented phonetically.
[MW] the mango tree, the fruit of the mango tree.
Ref. ch. 45 [72]; ch. 70 [213].

anapatrāpya (lack of reserve)
[MW] *apatrap:* to be ashamed or bashful, turn away the face.
anapatra: shameless.
[JEBD] *anapatrāpya:* non-bashfulness.
One of the upakleśa, or secondary hindrances.
Ref. ch. 70 [216].

an-ātman (not self, not spiritual)
Represented by 無我 (MUGA), "no self; without self."
[MW] not self, another; something different from spirit or soul; not spiritual, corporeal; destitute of spirit or mind.
Ref. ch. 49 [158]; ch. 73 [12].

anuttara-pūja (highest worship)
Represented by 最上礼拝 (SAIJO-RAIHAI), "highest worship; highest prostration."
[MW] *anuttara:* chief, principal, best, excellent.
pūja: honour, worship, respect, reverence, veneration, homage to superiors or adoration of the gods.
Ref. ch. 55 [110].

artha-carya (useful conduct)
Represented by 利行 (RIGYO), "beneficial conduct."
[MW] *artha:* aim, purpose; cause, motive, reason; advantage, use, utility; substance, wealth, property.
carya: conduct (see Book 1, **brahma-carya**).
Ref. ch. 45 [80].

āśraddha (unbelief)
[MW] want of trust, unbelief.
One of the upakleśa, or secondary hindrances.
Ref. ch. 70 [216].

aṣṭākṣaṇāh (eight inopportune situations)
Represented by 八難処 (HACHI-NAN-SHO), "eight places of difficulty."
[MW] *aṣṭa:* eight.
ākṣaṇa: inopportune.
Ref. ch. 70 [196].

auddhatya (disdain)
[MW] arrogance, insolence, overbearing manner, disdain.
[JEBD] restlessness.
One of the upakleśa, or secondary hindrances.
Ref. ch. 70 [216].

bhūta (actually happened)
Represented by 誠諦 (JOTAI), "true, real."
[MW] become, been, gone, past; actually happened, true, real; existing, present.
Ref. ch. 61 [39].

Buddhānusmṛti (mindfulness of the Buddha)
Represented by 念仏 (NENBUTSU), "mindfulness of the Buddha."
[MW] continual meditation on Buddha; name of a Buddhist Sūtra.
Ref. ch. 69 [175].

Candra-sūrya-pradīpa (Sun Moon Light; name of a buddha)
Represented by 日月燈明 (JITSU-GETSU-TOMYO), "Sun Moon Torchlight."
[MW] *candra:* glittering, shining (as gold); having the brilliancy or hue of light (said of gods, of water); the moon (also personified as a deity); 'the moon of' i.e. the most excellent among.
sūrya: the sun or its deity.
pradīpa: a light, lamp, lantern; also in titles of explanatory works = elucidation, explanation.
Ref. ch. 50 [214]; Lotus Sutra ch. 1.

caturmahārāja-kāyika (deities serving the Four Quarter Kings)
Represented by 四王天 (SHI-O-DEN), "gods of the four kings."
[MW] 'belonging to the attendance of those 4 great kings,' name of a class of deities.
catur: four.
mahārāja: great king; (with Buddhists) a particular class of divine beings (the guardians of the earth and heavens against the demons).
kāyika: performed with the body; corporeal; (at the end of compounds) belonging to an assemblage or multitude.
Ref. ch. 70 [210].

catvāraḥ pratyayāḥ (four classes of cooperating cause, four types of circumstance)

Represented by 四縁 (SHI-EN), "four circumstances; four types of connection."

[MW] *catur:* four.
pratyaya: ground, basis, motive, or cause of anything; a co-operating cause; the concurrent occasion of an event as distinguished from its approximate cause (see also Book 1).

The four are *hetu-pratyaya, samanantara-p., ālambana-p.,* and *adhipati-p.*(q.v.).
Ref. ch. 70 [201].

Daśabala-kāśyapa (name; "Kāśyapa, Possessor of Ten Powers.")

Represented by 十力迦葉 (JURIKI-KASHO), "Ten-Powers Kāśyapa."

[MW] name of one of the first five pupils of Śākyamuni.
daśabala: 'possessing ten powers,' name of a Buddha.
Ref. ch. 55 [112].

devaputra-māra (celestial demons)

Represented by 天子魔 (TENSHI-MA), "demons who are sons of gods."

[MW] name of one of the 4 Māras, Buddhist literature.
deva: heavenly, divine; a deity god; (rarely applied to) evil demons.
putra: a son, child.
māra: [q.v.] demons.
Ref. ch. 70 [216].

dharmoddāna (that which fastens the dharma together)

Represented by 法印 (HO-IN), "the Dharma-seal."

[MW] *dharma:* the teaching of the Buddha.
uddāna: the act of binding on, fastening together, stringing.
Ref. ch. 49 [158].

Dharmasaṃgraha (name of a Buddhist glossary)

[MW] name of a collection of Buddhist technical terms.

Note: Dharmasaṃgraha is attributed to Master Nāgārjuna.
Ref. ch. 70 [216].

dharma-svabhāva-mudrā (the seal of reality itself)

Represented by 実相印 (JISSO-IN), "the seal of real form."

[MW] *dharma:* reality.
svabhāva: native place; own condition or state of being, natural state or constitution, innate or inherent disposition, nature.
mudrā: seal.
Ref. ch. 50 [213]; Lotus Sutra ch. 2.

dīrghāyur-deva (gods of long life)

Represented by 長寿天 (CHOJU-TEN), "gods of long life."

[MW] *dīrghāyu:* long-lived.
deva: god, deity.

One of the eight inopportune situations (*aṣṭākṣaṇāh*).
Ref. ch. 70 [196].

dvāra-bhūtāni (the gate of actual occurrences)

Represented by 方便門 (HOBEN-MON), "the gate of expedient means"

[MW] *dvāra:* door, gate, passage, entrance.
bhūta: [q.v.] an actual occurrence, fact, matter of fact, reality.
Ref. ch. 50 [215]; Lotus Sutra ch. 10.

dveṣa (hatred)

[MW] hatred, dislike, repugnance, enmity to. *Ref. ch. 56 [124].*

hetu-pratyaya (a directly responsible circumstance)

Represented by 因縁 (INNEN), "a causal connection; a circumstance that is a direct cause."

[MW] *hetu:* 'impulse,' motive, cause, cause of, reason for.
pratyaya: a co-operating cause, a circumstance.

One of the four types of circumstance (see **catvāraḥ pratyayāḥ**).
Ref. ch. 70 [201].

indriyavaikalya (impairment of the senses)

Represented by 盲聾唖 (MO-RO-A), "blindness, deafness, muteness."

[MW] *indriya:* power, force, the quality of which belongs especially to the mighty Indra; bodily power,

power of the senses; faculty of sense, sense, organ of sense.
vaikalya: imperfection, weakness, defectiveness, incompetency, insufficiency; confusion, flurry.
One of the eight inopportune situations (*aṣṭākṣaṇāḥ*).
Ref. ch. 70 [196].

īrṣyā (envy)
[MW] envy or impatience of another's success; spite, malice; jealousy.
One of the upakleśa, or secondary hindrances.
Ref. ch. 70 [216].

kāma-dhātu (the world of volition)
Represented by 欲界 (YOKKAI), "the world of desire."
[MW] the region of the wishes, seat of the Kāmavacara (q.v.).
kāma: wish, desire, longing.
dhātu: layer, constituent part; element (see Book 1).
Ref. ch. 47 [107]; ch. 70 [216].

kāmavacara (the worlds of desire; the gods or inhabitants thereof)
Represented by 六欲天 (ROKU-YOKU-TEN), "six heavens of desire."
[MW] the spheres or worlds of desire (six in number, also called *deva-loka*), Buddhist; the gods or inhabitants of the worlds of desire:
1) *caturmahārāja-kāyikās;*
2) *trāyastriṃśās;* 3) *tuṣitās;*
4) *yāmās;* 5) *nirmāṇa-ratayas;*
6) *paranirmitavaśa-vartinas.*
Ref. ch. 70 [216].

Kanyākubja (name of ancient city)
Represented phonetically.
[MW] name of an ancient city of great note (in the north-western provinces of India, situated on the Kālī nadī, a branch of the Gangā, in the modern district of Farrukhabad… the ruins of the ancient city are said to occupy a site larger than that of London).
Ref. ch. 57 [170].

kaukṛtya (remorse)
[MW] evil doing, wickedness, repentance.
One of the upakleśa, or secondary hindrances.
Ref. ch. 70 [216].

kausīdya (indolence)
[MW] sloth, indolence; the practice of usury.
One of the upakleśa, or secondary hindrances.
Ref. ch. 70 [216].

kleśa (affliction, trouble)
Represented by 煩悩 (BONNO), "affliction, trouble, hindrance."
[MW] pain, affliction, distress, pain from disease, anguish; (in Yoga philosophy five kleśas are named, viz *a-vidyā*, 'ignorance,' *asmi-tā*, 'egotism,' *rāga*, 'desire,' *dvesha*, 'aversion,' and *abhiniveśa*, 'tenacity of mundane existence'; the Buddhists reckon ten, viz three of the body [murder, theft, adultery], four of speech [lying, slander, abuse, unprofitable conversation], three of the mind [covetousness, malice, skepticism]); wrath, anger; worldly occupation, care, trouble.
Ref. ch. 57 [170]; ch. 70 [216].

kleśāvaraṇa (the obstacle of delusion, layers of interference)
Represented by 煩悩障 (BONNO-SHO), "anguish-obstacle" or 惑障 (WAKU-SHO), "delusion-obstacle."
[MW] *kleśa:* [q.v.] affliction, trouble.
āvaraṇa: hiding, concealing; shutting, enclosing; an obstruction, interruption; a covering, garment, cloth; anything that protects, an outer bar or fence; a wall, a shield; (in philosophy) mental blindness.
śakti: the power of illusion (that which veils the real nature of things).
Ref. ch. 57 [170].

krodha (wrath)
[MW] anger, wrath, passion.
One of the upakleśa, or secondary hindrances.
Ref. ch. 70 [216].

mada (presumption)
[MW] hilarity, rapture, excitement, inspiration, intoxication; ardent passion for; sexual desire or enjoyment, wanton lust, ruttishness; pride, arrogance, presumption, conceit of or about.
One of the upakleśa, or secondary hindrances.
Ref. ch. 70 [216].

Malaya (name of a mountain range)
Represented phonetically.
[MW] name of a mountain range on the west of Malabar, the western Ghāts (abounding in sandal trees).
Ref. ch. 56 [130].

māna (arrogance)
[MW] opinion, notion, conception, idea; purpose, wish, design; self-conceit; arrogance, pride; (with Buddhists, one of the 6 evil feelings; or one of the 10 fetters to be got rid of).
One of the mūla-kleśa, or root causes of suffering.
Ref. ch. 70 [216].

mañjūṣaka (name of a celestial flower)
Represented phonetically.
[MW] name of a species of celestial flower.
Ref. ch. 59 [204].

māra (death, the Evil One, demons)
Represented by 魔 (MA), "demon, devil, evil spirit."
[MW] killing, destroying; death, pestilence; slaying, killing; an obstacle, hindrance; the passion of love, god of love; (with Buddhists) the Destroyer, Evil One (who tempts men to indulge their passions and is the great enemy of the Buddha and his religion; four Māras are enumerated in Dharmasaṃgraha 80, viz. *skandha-māra, kleśa-māra, devaputra-māra,* and *mṛityu-māra;* but the later Buddhist theory of races of gods led to the figment of millions of Māras ruled over by a chief Māra).
Ref. ch. 70 [216].

mātsarya (meanness)
[MW] envy, jealousy.
[JEBD] parsimony.
One of the upakleśa, or secondary hindrances.
Ref. ch. 70 [216].

māya (duplicity)
[MW] wisdom, extraordinary or supernatural power (only in the earlier language); illusion, unreality, deception, fraud, trick, sorcery, witchcraft, magic; duplicity (with Buddhists one of the 24 minor evil passions), Dharmasaṃgraha 69.
One of the upakleśa, or secondary hindrances.
Ref. ch. 70 [216].

middha (indolence, drowsiness)
[MW] sloth, indolence (one of the 24 minor evil passions, Dharmasaṃgraha 69).
[JEBD] drowsiness.
One of the *upakleśa*, or secondary hindrances.
Ref. ch. 70 [216].

mithyādarśana (pretensiousness; making a false show)
Represented by 世智弁聡 (SECHI-BENSO), "worldly wise and fast-talking."
[MW] a false appearance.
mithyā: invertedly, contrarily, incorrectly, wrongly, improperly.
darśana: showing; exhibiting, teaching; seeing, observing, looking, noticing, observation, perception; audience, meeting; experiencing; judgement; discernment, understanding, intellect; opinion; intention; view, doctrine, philosophical system; appearance (before the judge); appearance, aspect, semblance; colour.
One of the eight inopportune situations (*aṣṭākṣaṇāḥ*).
Ref. ch. 70 [196].

mrakṣa (hypocrisy)
[MW] concealment of one's vices, hypocrisy (with Buddhists, one of the 24 minor evil qualities), Dharmasaṃgraha 69.

One of the upakleśa, or secondary hindrances.
Ref. ch. 70 [216].

mṛtyu-māra (demons of death)
Represented by 死魔 (SHIMA), "demons of death."
[MW] (with Buddhists) name of one of the 4 Māras.
mṛtyu: death, dying.
māra: [q.v.] demons.
Ref. ch. 70 [216].

mūḍha (ignorance)
[MW] stupified, bewildered, perplexed, confused, uncertain or at a loss about; stupid, foolish, dull, silly, simple; swooned, indolent; gone astray or adrift; driven out of its course (as a ship); wrong, out of the right place (as the fetus in delivery); not to be ascertained, not clear, indistinct; confusion of mind.
One of the mūla-kleśa, or root causes of suffering.
Ref. ch. 70 [216].

namas (obeisance, reverential salutation)
Represented phonetically.
[MW] bow, obeisance, reverential salutation, adoration (by gesture or word).
Ref. ch. 69 [175]; ch. 87 [152]; ch. 88; ch.93.

nikāya (school, collection)
Represented by 部 (BU), "part."
[MW] a heap, an assemblage, a group, class, association (especially of persons who perform the same duties); congregation, school; collection (of Buddhist Sutras).
Ref. ch. 56 [132].

nirmāṇa-kāya (the body of transformation)
Represented by 応身 (OJIN), "the befitting body."
[MW] the body of transformation.
nirmāṇa: measuring, measure, reach, extent; forming, making, creating, creation, building, composition, work; (with Buddhists) transformation.
kāya: body.
One of the three bodies, the other two being the dharma-kāya and the saṃbhoga-kāya.
Ref. ch. 23 [99]; ch. 42 [3]; Lotus Sutra ch. 25.

nirmāṇarati-deva (name of inhabitants of the 5th heaven in the world of desire)
Represented by 化楽天 (KERAKU-TEN), "gods who create pleasure."
[MW] "enjoying pleasures provided by themselves," a class of beings inhabiting the fifth heaven.
nirmā: to build, make out of, form, fabricate, produce, create.
rati: pleasure, enjoyment, delight in, fondness for; the pleasure of love, sexual passion or union, amorous enjoyment.
deva: a deity, god.
Ref. ch. 70 [210].

nivāsana ([garment for] everyday living)
Represented by 裙 (KUN) or 裙子 (KUNZU) "skirt."
[MW] living, residing, sojourn, abode; passing or spending time.
Ref. ch. 7; ch. 56 [132].

om ("Truly!")
Represented phonetically.
[MW] a word of solemn affirmation and respectful assent, sometimes translated by 'yes, verily, so be it' (and in this sense compared with Amen; it is placed at the commencement of most Hindu works, and as a sacred exclamation may be uttered at the beginning and end of a reading of the Vedas or previously to any prayer; it is also regarded as a particle of auspicious salutation [Hail]). Buddhists place *om* at the beginning of their *vidyā shadaksharī* or mystical formulary in six syllables [viz, *om maṇi padme hūṃ*].
Ref. ch. 61 [54].

pāpīyas (most wicked ones, evil spirits, the devil)
Represented phonetically.
[MW] worse, worse off, lower, poorer, more or most wicked or miserable; a villain, a rascal; (with

Buddhists) *mārah-pāpīyān* the evil spirit, the devil.
Ref. ch. 70.

paranirmita-vaśa-vartin (name of deities
in the 6th heaven in the world of desire)
Represented by 他化自在天 (TAKE-JIZAI-TEN), "gods who transform others and do as they please."
[MW] 'constantly enjoying pleasures provided by others,' name of a class of Buddhist deities.
Ref. ch. 70.

parivrājaka (a wandering religious mendicant)
[MW] a wandering religious mendicant.
Ref. ch. 56 [142].

pitṛs (deceased ancestors)
[MW] deceased ancestors (they are of 2 classes, viz. the deceased father, grandfathers and great-grandfathers of any particular person, and the progenitors of mankind generally; they inhabit a peculiar region, which, according to some, is the Bhuvas or region of the air, according to others, the orbit of the moon.)
See under **Yama-rāja.**

pradāsa (devil) [MW] *pra:* as prefix to substantive; in nouns of relationship = great-.
dāsa: fiend, demon.
[JEBD] affliction.
One of the upakleśa, or secondary hindrances.
Ref. ch. 70 [216].

pramāda (negligence)
[MW] intoxication, insanity; negligence, carelessness about.
One of the upakleśa, or secondary hindrances.
Ref. ch. 70 [216].

pratigha (anger)
[MW] hindrance, obstruction, resistance, opposition; struggling against; anger, wrath, enmity (one of the 6 evil passions).
One of the mūla-kleśa, or root causes of suffering.
Ref. ch. 70 [216].

prati-pādana (accomplishing, action)
Represented by 趣向 (SHUKO), "plan, device, scheme."
[MW] causing to attain, giving, granting; putting in, appointing to; inauguration; producing, causing, effecting, accomplishing; stating, setting forth; explaining; beginning, commencement; action, wordly conduct.
Ref. ch. 61 [54].

prati-sammodana (salutation)
Represented by 問訊 (MONJIN), "inquiring after [a person's health]."
[MW] greeting, salutation.
Ref. ch. 55 [106].

pratyantajanapada (a bordering country)
Represented by 辺地 (HENCHI), "a remote place."
[MW] a bordering country.
pratyanta: bordering on, adjacent or contiguous to, skirting; a bordering country; i.e. a country occupied by barbarians; barbarous tribes.
janapada: a community, nation, people (as opposed to the sovereign); an empire, inhabited country.
One of the eight inopportune situations (*aṣṭākṣaṇāh*).
Ref. ch. 70 [196].

priyākhyāna (kind communication)
Represented by 愛語 (AIGO), "loving words."
[MW] *priya:* beloved, dear to, liked, favourite; dear, expensive; pleasant, agreeable; love, kindness.
ākhyāna: telling, communication.
Ref. ch. 45.

rāja-samādhi (king of samādhis)
Represented by 王三昧 (O-ZANMAI), "king of samādhis."
[MW] *rāja:* a king, sovereign, chief or best of its kind.
samādhi: putting together, joining or combining with; a joint or a particular position of the neck; union, a whole, aggregate, set; completion, accomplishment,

conclusion; setting to rights, adjustment, settlement; justification of a statement, proof; bringing into harmony, agreement, assent; intense application or fixing the mind on, intentness, attention; concentration of the thoughts, profound or abstract meditation, intense contemplation of any particular object (so as to identifty the contemplator with the object meditated upon; this is the eighth and last stage of Yoga; with Buddhists Samādhi is the fourth and last stage of Dhyāna or intense abstract meditation); intense absorption or a kind of trance.

Note: among these definitions, "union," "setting to rights," and "bringing into harmony," are most relevant to the meaning of samādhi as described in Shobogenzo. Also instructive is the definition of *samādheya:* to be put in order or set right; to be directed or informed or instructed.

Ref. ch. 72.

rūpa-dhātu (the world of form)

Represented by 色界 (SHIKIKAI), "the world of form."

[MW] the element of form, original seat or region of form (with Buddhists; the other two elements being *kāma-dhātu* q.v., and *arūpa-dhātu* 'the element of formlessness'). *rūpa:* any outward appearance or phenomenon or colour, form, shape, figure; (with Buddhists) material form. *dhātu:* layer, constituent part; element (see Book 1).

Ref. ch. 47.

samanantara-pratyaya (immediately contiguous circumstance)

Represented by 等無間縁 (TOMUKAN-EN), "an immediate circumstance."

[MW] *samanantara:* immediately contiguous to or following; immediately behind or after. *pratyaya:* a co-operating cause, a circumstance.

One of the four types of circumstance (see **catvāraḥ pratyayāḥ**).

Ref. ch. 70 [201].

samāna-arthatā (sharing the same aim)

Represented by 同事 (DOJI), "identity of task; cooperation."

[MW] equivalence; having the same object or end; identity of meaning. *samāna:* same, identical, uniform, one; alike, similar, equal; holding the middle between two extremes, middling, moderate; common, general, universal. *artha:* aim, purpose.

Ref. ch. 45.

saṃgraha-vastūni (elements of sociability)

Represented by 摂法 (SHOBO), "elements of social relations; methods for social relations."

[MW] elements of popularity. *saṃgraha:* holding together, seizing, grasping, taking, reception, obtainment; bringing together, assembling (of men); collecting, gathering; inclusion; check, restraint, control; attracting, kind treatment, propiation, entertaining. *vastu:* the seat or place of; any really existing or abiding substance or essence, thing, object, article; the pith or substance of anything.

Ref. ch. 45.

saṃjñā (thought)

Represented by 想 (SO), "idea, thought, conception."

[MW] agreement, mutual understanding, harmony; consciousness, clear knowledge or understanding or notion or conception; a sign, token, signal, gesture (with the hand, eyes, etc.); direction; a track; a name, appellation; (with Buddhists) perception (one of the 5 skandhas).

Ref. ch. 70 [216].

śāṭhya (roguery)

[MW] wickedness, deceit, guile, roguery, dishonesty.

One of the upakleśa, or secondary hindrances.
Ref. ch. 70 [216].

śrī (to diffuse light)
Represented phonetically.
[MW] to burn, flame, diffuse light.
Ref. ch. 61 [54].

styāna (sloth)
[MW] idleness, sloth, apathy (see Book 1)
[JEBD] low spirits.
One of the upakleśa, or secondary hindrances.
Ref. ch. 70 [216].

Śubha-vyūha-rāja (name of a legendary king)
Represented by 妙荘厳王 (MYO-SHOGON-O), "King Wonderfully Adorned," "King Resplendent."
[MW] name of a king, Buddhist literature.
śubha: splendid, bright, beautiful; pleasant, good; auspicuous; good (in moral sense), righteous, virtuous.
vyūha: placing apart, distribution, arrangement; orderly arrangement of the parts of the whole; military array; form, manifestation, appearance.
rāja: king.
Ref. ch. 61 [47]; Lotus Sutra ch. 27.

sūrya (the sun)
Represented phonetically.
[MW] the sun or its deity.
Ref. ch. 61 [54].

tathāgatānām-anutpāda (absence of the Tathāgata)
Represented by 仏前仏後 (BUTSU-ZEN-BUTSU-GO), "periods before and after the Buddha."
[MW] *tathāgata:* 'being in such a state' [epithet of the Buddha].
anutpāda: non-production; not coming into existence; not taking effect.
One of the eight inopportune situations (*aṣṭākṣaṇāh*).
Ref. ch. 70 [196].

tatkṣaṇa ('that moment'; a measure of time)
Represented phonetically.
[MW] the same moment; at the same moment, directly, immediately.
tat: (in compounds for *tad*) he, she, it, that, this.
kṣaṇa: any instantaneous point of time, instant, twinkling of an eye, moment; a moment regarded as a measure of time.
Ref. ch. 70 [196].

tiryañc (animals)
Represented by 畜生 (CHIKUSHO), "animals."
[MW] 'going horizontally," an animal (amphibious, animal, bird, etc.).
One of the eight inopportune situations (*aṣṭākṣaṇāh*).
Ref. ch. 70 [196].

Trāyastriṃśa (numbering 33; name of a heaven)
Represented by 三十三天 (SANJUSAN-TEN), "thirty-three gods."
[MW] the 33rd; consisting of 33 parts; numbering 33 (the gods).
Ref. ch. 70.

trayo dhātavaḥ (the triple world)
Represented by 三界 (SANGAI), "the three worlds, the triple world."
[MW] *traya:* triple, threefold, consisting of 3, of 3 kinds.
dhā: putting, placing, holding, having.
tavas: strong, energetic; strength, power.
Ref. ch. 47.

upakleśa (secondary hindrances)
Represented by 随煩悩 (ZUI-BONNO), "secondary hindrances."
[MW] (with Buddhists) a lesser kleśa or cause of misery (as conceit, pride, etc.).
upa: (prefixed to nouns *upa* expresses) direction towards, nearness, contiguity in space, time, number, degree, resemblance, and relationship, but with the idea of subordination and inferiority.
kleśa: (q.v.) affliction, pain from disease, trouble.
Ref. ch. 70 [216].

upanāha (continual enmity)
[MW] bundle, a plaster, unguent; inflammation of the ciliary glands, stye; the tie of a lute (the lower part of the tail piece where the wires are fixed); continual enmity.
One of the upakleśa, or secondary hindrances.
Ref. ch. 70 [216].

vaiḍūrya (a cat's eye gem; lapis lazuli)
Represented phonetically.
[MW] a cat's eye gem (at the end of a compound: 'a jewel' = 'anything excellent of its kind').
Ref. ch. 61 [39].

Vajragarbha (Diamond-Treasury; name of a bodhisattva)
Represented by 金剛蔵 (KONGOZO), "Diamond-Treasury."
[MW] name of a Bodhisattva.
Vajra: a diamond (see Book 1 **Vajra-sattva**).
garbha: the womb; the inside, middle, interior of anything, calyx (as of a lotus); (at the end of a compound 'having in the interior, containing, filled with').
Ref. ch. 42 [12].

vicikitsā (doubt)
[MW] doubt, uncertainty, question, inquiry; error, mistake.
One of the mūla-kleśa, or root causes of suffering.
Ref. ch. 70 [216].

vidyā ṣaḍakṣarī ('six-syllable philosophy')
[MW] *vidyā:* knowledge, learning, scholarship, philosophy (see Book 1).
ṣaḍakṣarī: consisting of six syllables.
Ref. ch. 61 [54].

vihiṃsā (harming)
[MW] the act of harming or injuring.
One of the upakleśa, or secondary hindrances.
Ref. ch. 70 [216].

vijñāna-mātratā (consciousness as no more or less than it is) Represented by 唯識 (YUISHIKI), "consciousness alone."
[MW] *vijñāna:* consciousness (see below).
mātra: an element, elementary matter; (at the end of compounds) measure, quantity, sum, size, duration, measure of any kind; the full or simple measure of anything; the whole or totality, the one thing and no more.
mātratā: (at the end of compounds) the being as much as, no more nor less than anything.
Ref. ch. 70 [216].

Vijñānavāda (the doctrine of consciousness)
[MW] the doctrine (of the Yogācāras) that only intelligence has reality (not the objects exterior to us).
vijñāna: (with Buddhists) consciousness or thought-faculty (one of the 5 constituent elements or Skandhas, also considered as one of the 6 elements or Dhātus, and as one of the 12 links in the chain of causation.
vāda: thesis, proposition, argument, doctrine.
Note: in spite of MW's interpretation here, the Vijñānavāda teaching does not deny the reality of external objects; it affirms the reality of consciousness. Vijñānavāda should not be confused with idealism.
Ref. ch. 43; ch. 70 [216].

Yama-rāja (King Yama, ruler of the spirits of the dead)
Represented phonetically.
[MW] king Yama.
yama: a rein, curb, bridle; a driver, charioteer; the act of checking or curbing, suppression, restraint; name of the god who presides over the Pitṛis (q.v.) and rules the spirits of the dead; in post-vedic mythology he is the appointed Judge and 'Restrainer' or 'Punisher' of the dead; his abode is in some region of the lower world called Yama-pura.
rāja: a king, sovereign, chief or best of its kind.
Ref. ch. 52 [49]; ch. 70; ch. 86 [88].

Bibliographies

Bibliography One: Main Chinese Sources Quoted by Master Dogen in Shobogenzo

A. Sutras

Attempts at English translations of sutra titles are provisional, and provided only for reference.

Agon-kyo 阿含経 (Āgama Sutras).

In Chinese translation, there are four:

Cho-agon-kyo 長阿含経 (Long Āgama Sutra—in Pali, Digha-nikāya);
Chu-agon-kyo 中阿含経 (Middle Āgama Sutra—in Sanskrit, Madhyamāgama; in Pali, Majjhima-nikāya);
Zo-agon-kyo 雑阿含経 (Miscellaneous Āgama Sutra—in Sanskrit, Saṃyuktāgama; in Pali, Samyutta-nikāya);
Zo-itsu-agon-gyo 増一阿含経 (Āgama Sutras Increased by One—in Sanskrit, Ekottarāgama; in Pali, Aṅguttara-nikāya)

These are supplemented by the **Sho-agon-kyo** 小阿含経 (Small Āgama Sutras—in Sanskrit, Kṣudrakāgama; in Pali, Khuddaka-nikāya), a collection of all the āgamas beside the four āgamas. In the Pali canon, Khuddaka-nikāya is the fifth of the five nikāyas and comprises fifteen short books.

Aiku-o-kyo 阿育王経 (Aśoka Sutra)

Butsu-hongyo-jikkyo 佛本行集経 (Sutra of Collected Past Deeds of the Buddha)

Daibonten-o-monbutsu-ketsugi-kyo 大梵天王問佛決疑経 (Sutra of Questions and Answers between Mahābrahman and the Buddha)

Dai-hannya-kyo 大般若波羅密多経 (Great Prajñā Sutra), short for **Dai-hannya-haramitta-kyo** (Sutra of the Great Prajñā-pāramitā—in Sanskrit, Mahā-prajñā-pāramitā-sūtra)

Daihatsu-nehan-kyo 大般涅槃経 (Sutra of the Great Demise—in Sanskrit, Mahāparinirvāṇa-sūtra)

Dai-hoko-hokyo-gyo 大方廣寶篋経 (The Mahāvaipulya Treasure Chest Sutra)

Dai-hoko-engaku-shutara-ryogi-kyo 大方廣円覚修多羅了義 経 (The Mahāvaipulya Round Realization Sutra)

Dai-ho-shak-kyo 大寶積経 (Great Treasure Accumulation Sutra—in Sanskrit, Mahāratnakūta-sūtra)

Daijo-honsho-shinchi-kan-kyo 大乗本生心地観経 (The Mahāyāna Sutra of Reflection on the Mental State in Past Lives)

Daishu-kyo 大集経 (Great Collection Sutra—in Sanskrit, Mahā-saṃnipāta-sūtra)

Engaku-kyo 円覚経 (Sutra of Round Realization)

Fuyo-kyo 普曜経 (Sutra of Diffusion of Shining Artlessness—in Sanskrit, Lalita-vistara-sūtra)

Hige-kyo 悲華経 (Flower of Compassion Sutra—in Sanskrit, Karuṇā-puṇḍarīka-sūtra)

Hokke-kyo 法華経 (Lotus Sutra, Sutra of the Flower of Dharma), short for **Myoho-renge-kyo** (Sutra of the Lotus Flower of the Wonderful Dharma—in Sanskrit, Saddharma-puṇḍarika-sūtra)

Hoku-kyo 法句経 (Sutra of Dharma-phrases—in Pali, Dhammapada)

Honsho-kyo 本生経 (Past Lives Sutra—in Sanskrit, Jātaka)

Ju-o-kyo 十王経 (Ten Kings Sutra).

Kan-fugen-bosatsu-gyobo-kyo 観普賢菩薩行法経 (Sutra of Reflection on the Practice of Dharma by Bodhisattva Universal Virtue)

Kegon-kyo 華厳経 (Garland Sutra—in Sanskrit, Avataṇsaka-sūtra)

Kengu-kyo 賢愚経 (Sutra of the Wise and the Stupid)

Ke-u-koryo-kudoku-kyo 希有校量功徳経 (Sutra of Comparison of the Merits of Rare Occurrences)

Konkomyo-kyo 金光明経 (Golden Light Sutra), short for **Konkomyo-saisho-o-kyo** (Golden Light Sutra of the Supreme King—in Sanskrit, Suvarṇa-prabhāsottama-rāja-sūtra)

Kongo-kyo 金剛般若波羅密経 (Diamond Sutra), short for **Kongo-hannya-haramitsu-kyo** (Sutra of the Diamond-Prajñā-Pāramitā—in Sanskrit, Vajraccedikā-prajñā-pāramitā-sūtra)

Miroku-josho-kyo 弥勒上生経 (Sutra of Maitreya's Ascent and Birth [in Tuṣita Heaven])

Mizo-u-innen-kyo 未曾有因縁経 (Sutra of Unprecedented Episodes)

Ninno-gyo 仁王般若波羅密経 (Benevolent King Sutra), short for **Ninno-hannya-haramitsu-gyo** (Prajñā-pāramitā Sutra of the Benevolent King)

Senju-hyaku-en-kyo 撰集百縁経 (Sutra of a Hundred Collected Stories)

Shobutsu-yoshu-kyo 諸佛要集経 (Sutra of the Collected Essentials of the Buddhas)

Shuryogon-kyo 首楞厳経 (Śūraṃgama Sutra—in Sanskrit, Śūraṃgama-samādhi-nirdeśa)

Shakubuku-rakan-kyo 折伏羅漢経 (Sutra of the Defeat of the Arhat)

Shugyo-hongi-kyo 修行本起経 (Sutra of Past Occurences of Practice)

Yoraku-hongyo-kyo 瓔珞本起経 (Sutra of Past Deeds as a String of Pearls)

Yuima-gyo 維摩経 (Vimalakīrti Sutra—in Sanskrit, Vimalakīrti-nīrdeśa)

Zuio-hongi-kyo 瑞應本起経 (Sutra of Auspicious Past Occurrences)

B. Precepts

Bonmo-kyo 梵網経 (Pure Net Sutra)

Daibiku-sanzen-yuigi-kyo 大比丘三千威儀経 (Sutra of Three Thousand Dignified Forms for Ordained Monks)

Juju-ritsu 十誦律 (Precepts in Ten Parts), a 61-fascicle translation of the vinaya of the Sarvāstivādin School

Konpon-issai-u-bu-hyaku-ichi-katsuma 根本説一切有部百一羯磨 (101 Customs of the Mūla-sarvāstivādin School)

Makasogi-ritsu 摩訶僧祇律 (Precepts for the Great Saṃgha), a 40-fascicle translation of the vinaya of the Mahāsaṃghika School of Hīnayāna Buddhism

Shibun-ritsu 四分律 (Precepts in Four Divisions), a 60-fascicle translation of the vinaya of the Dharmagupta School

Zen-en-shingi 禪苑清規 (Pure Criteria for Zen Monasteries)

C. Commentaries

Bosatsuchi-ji-kyo 菩薩地持経 (Sutra of Maintaining the Bodhisattva-State)

Daibibasha-ron 大毘婆沙論 (Abhidharma-mahāvibhāṣa-śāstra)

Daichido-ron 大智度論 (Commentary on the Accomplishment which is Great Wisdom—in Sanskrit, Mahā-prajñā-pāramitopadeśa)

Daijogi-sho 大乗義章 (Writings on the Mahāyāna Teachings)

Hokke-zanmai-sengi 法華三昧懺儀 (A Humble Expression of the Form of the Samādhi of the Flower of Dharma)

Kusha-ron 倶舎論 (Abhidharma-kośa-śāstra)

Maka-shikan 摩訶止観 (Great Quietness and Reflection), a record of the lectures of Master Tendai Chigi, founder of the Tendai Sect

Maka-shikan-hogyo-den-guketsu 摩訶止観輔行伝弘決 (Extensive Decisions Transmitted in Support of Great Quietness and Reflection), a Chinese commentary on **Maka-shikan** by Master Keikei Tannen

D. General Chinese Buddhist Records

Daito-sai-iki-ki 大唐西域記 (Great Tang Records of Western Lands)

Go-to-roku 五燈録 (The Five Records of the Torch), five independent but complimentary collections compiled during the Sung era (960–1279). They are represented in summary form in **Go-to-egen** 五燈会元 (Collection of the Fundamentals of the Five Torches). Namely, the five records are:

Keitoku-dento-roku 景徳伝燈録 (Keitoku Era Record of the Transmission of the Torch)

Tensho-koto-roku 天聖廣燈録 (Tensho Era Record of the Widely Extending Torch)

Zokuto-roku 続燈録 (Supplementary Record of the Torch)

Rento-eyo 聯燈會要 (Collection of Essentials for Continuation of the Torch)
Katai-futo-roku 嘉泰普燈録 (Katai Era Record of the Universal Torch)

Hekigan-roku 碧巌録 (Blue Cliff Record)

Ho-en-shu-rin 法苑珠林 (A Forest of Pearls in the Garden of Dharma), a kind of Buddhist encyclopedia in 100 volumes

Kaigen-shakkyo-roku 開元釈教録 (Kaigen-era Records of Śākyamuni's Teaching)

Kosonshuku-goroku 古尊宿語録 (Record of the Words of the Venerable Patriarchs of the Past)

Rinkan-roku 石門林間録 (Forest Record), or **Sekimon-rinkan-roku** (Sekimon's Forest Record)

So-koso-den 宋高僧伝(Biographies of Noble Monks of the Sung-era)

Zenmon-shososhi-geju 禪門諸祖師偈頌 (Verses and Eulogies of Ancestral Masters of the Zen Lineages)

Zenrin-hokun 禪林寳訓 (Treasure-Instruction from the Zen Forest)

Zenshu-juko-renju-tsushu 禪宗頌古聯珠通集 (Complete String-of-Pearls Collection of Eulogies to Past Masters of the Zen Sect)

Zoku-dento-roku 続伝燈録 (Continuation of the Record of the Transmission of the Torch), published in China in 1635; sequel to Keitoku-dento-roku

Zokukan-kosonshuku-goyo 続刊古尊宿語要 (Summarized Collection of the Words of the Venerable Patriarchs of the Past)

E. RECORDS OF, AND INDEPENDENT WORKS BY, CHINESE MASTERS

Baso-Do-itsu-zenji-goroku 馬祖道一禪師語録 (Record of the Words of Zen Master Baso Do-itsu)

Bukka-geki-setsu-roku 佛果擊節録 (Record of Bukka's Attacks on Knotty Problems); Bukka is an alias of Master Seccho Juken

Chorei-Shutaku-zenji-goroku 長霊守卓禪師語録 (Record of the Words of Zen Master Chorei Shutaku)

Dai-e-Fugaku-zenji-shumon-buko 大慧普覚禪師宗門武庫 (The War Chest of the School of Zen Master Dai-e Fugaku [Dai-e Soko])

Dai-e-goroku 大慧語録 (Record of the Words of Dai-e [Soko])

Dai-e-zenji-tomei 大慧禪師塔銘 (Inscriptions on the Stūpa of Zen Master Dai-e [Soko])

Engo-zenji-goroku 圜悟禪師語録 (Record of the Words of Zen Master Engo [Kokugon])

Joshu-roku 趙州録 (Records of Joshu [Jushin])

Jugendan 十玄談 (Discussion of the Ten Kinds of Profundity), by Master Do-an Josatsu

Ho-en-zenji-goroku 法演禪師語録 (Record of the Words of Zen Master [Yogi] Ho-en)

Hokyo-zanmai 寶鏡三昧 (Samadhi, the State of a Jewel-Mirror), by Master Tozan Ryokai

Honei-Nin-yu-zenji-goroku 法寧仁勇禪師語録 (Record of the Words of Zen Master Honei Nin-yu)

Hyakujo-roku 百丈録・百丈懐海禪師語録 (Record of Hyakujo [Ekai])

Koke-zenji-goroku 興化禪師語録 (Record of the Words of Zen Master Koke [Sonsho])

Kido-shu 虚堂集 (The Kido Collection), a collection of the words of Master Tanka Shijun, compiled by Rinsen Jurin

Nyojo-osho-goroku 如浄和尚語録 (Record of the Words of Master [Tendo] Nyojo)

O-an-Donge-zenji-goroku 応菴曇華禪師語録(Record of the Words of Zen Master O-an Donge)

Rinzai-zenji-goroku 臨済禪師語録 (Record of the Words of Zen Master Rinzai [Gigen])

Rokuso-dankyo 六祖壇経 (The Sixth Patriarch's Platform Sutra), attributed to Master Daikan Eno

Sandokai 参同契 (Experiencing the State), by Master Sekito Kisen

Seccho-Myokaku-zenji-goroku 雪竇明覚禪師語録 (Record of the Words of Zen Master Seccho Myokaku [Seccho Juken])

Sekito-so-an no Uta 石頭草庵歌 (Songs from Sekito's Thatched Hut), by Master Sekito Kisen

Shodoka 証道歌 (Song of Experiencing the Truth), by Master Yoka Genkaku

Shinjinmei 信心銘 (Inscription on Believing Mind), by Master Kanchi Sosan

Sotai-roku 奏対録 (Record of Answers to an Emperor), by Master Bussho Tokko

Tozan-goroku 洞山語録 (Record of the Words of Tozan [Ryokai])

Unmon-koroku 雲門語録(Broad Record of Unmon [Bun-en])

Wanshi-zenji-goroku 宏智禅師語録 (Record of the Words of Wanshi [Shokaku])

Wanshi-koroku 宏智廣録 (Broad Record of Wanshi [Shokaku])

Wanshi-juko 宏智頌古 (Wanshi's Eulogies to Past Masters), also known as **Shoyo-roku** 従容録 (The Relaxation Record)

Yafu-Dosen-kongo-kyo 冶父道川金剛経 (Yafu Dosen's Diamond Sutra)

F. CHINESE SECULAR BOOKS ETC.

Confucianist:

Kokyo 孝経 (The Book of Filial Piety)

Rongo 論語 (The Discourses [of Confucius])

Taoist:

Bunshi 文子 from the Chinese *Wen-tzu*, the name of the author to whom the text is ascribed

Kanshi 管子 from the Chinese *Guan-tzu*, the name of the supposed author

Shishi 尸子 from the Chinese *Shi-tzu*, the name of the supposed author

Soji 荘子 from the Chinese *Chuang-tzu*, the name of a disciple of Lao-tzu (the ancient Chinese philosopher regarded as the founder of Taoism)

Inzui 韻瑞 (Rhymes of Good Fortune)

Rikuto 六韜 (Six Strategies)

Sango-ryaku-ki 三五暦記 (History of the Three [Elements] and Five [Elements])

Miscellaneous

Jirui-senshu 事類撰集 (Collection of Matters and Examples)

Jibutsu-gen-ki 事物原記 (Record of the Origin of Things)

Jokan-seiyo 貞観政要 (Jokan Era {Treatise] on the Essence of Government)

Mei-hoki 冥報記 (Chronicles of the Underworld)

Taihei-koki 太平弘記 (Widely Extending Record of the Taihei Era)

Bibliography Two: Other Works by Master Dogen

Fukan-zazengi 普勧坐禅儀 (Universal Guide to the Standard Method of Zazen)

Gakudo-yojin-shu 學道用心集 (Collection of Concerns in Learning the Truth)

Hogyo-ki 寳慶記 (Hogyo Era Record)

Shinji-shobogenzo 真字正法眼蔵 (Right-Dharma-Eye Treasury, in Original [Chinese] Characters)

Eihei-koroku 永平廣録 (Broad Record of Eihei)

Eihei-shingi 永平清規 (Pure Criteria of Eihei), including:
- **Tenzo-kyokun** 典座教訓 (Instructions for the Cook)
- **Bendo-ho** 辨道法 (Methods of Pursuing the Truth)
- **Fu-shuku-han-ho** 赴粥飯法 (The Method of Taking Meals)
- et cetera

Bibliography Three: Main Japanese References

Bukkyo-jiten:	edited by Ui Hakuju
Bukkyogo-daijiten:	3 volumes edited by Hajime Nakamura
Dai-kanwa-jiten:	13 volumes by Tetsuji Morohashi
Dogen-no-kenkyu:	by Hanji Akiyama

Dogen-zenji-den-no-kenkyu:	by Doshu Ohkubo
Dogen-zenji-no-hanashi:	by Ton Satomi
Hokke-kyo:	published by Iwanami Shoten
Jikai:	edited by Kyosuke Kinta-ichi
Sawaki-Kodo-zenshu:	19 volumes by Master Kodo Sawaki
Shin-bukkyo-jiten:	edited by Hajime Nakamura
Shinshu-kanwa-daijiten:	by Shikita Koyanagi
Shinshu-taisho-daizokyo:	by Daizo Shuppansha
Shobogenzo-chukai-zensho:	10 volumes by Nyoten Jinbo & Bun-ei Ando
Shobogenzo-ji-i:	by Soku-o Eto
Shobogenzo-keiteki:	by Bokuzan Nishi-ari
Shobogenzo-shaku-i:	4 volumes by Kunihiko Hashida
Shobogenzo:	published by Iwanami Shoten, commentary by Nishi-o, Kagamishima, Sakai, and Mizuno
Shoten-zoku-cho:	by Master Osen Mujaku
Sogo-rekishi-nenpyo:	edited by Kenzo Nakajima
Tetsugaku-jiten:	published by Heibon Sha
Tetsugaku-shojiten:	published by Iwanami Shoten
Watsuji-tetsuro-zenshu (vols. 4,5):	by Tetsuro Watsuji
Zengaku-daijiten:	edited by scholars of Komazawa University
Zengaku-jiten:	by Nyoten Jinbo & Bun-ei Ando

(Texts printed in Taiwan)

Keitoku-dento-roku:	Shin Zen Bi Shuppansha
Zoku-zokyo:	Collection of Buddhist Sutras not included in Shinshu-taisho-daizokyo

Shobogenzo in Modern Japanese:

Gendaigo-yaku-shobogenzo 現代語訳正法眼蔵 (Shobogenzo in Modern Japanese) by Nishijima Roshi, twelve volumes plus a one-volume appendix

Shobogenzo-teisho-roku 正法眼蔵提唱録 (Record of Lectures on Shobogenzo), by Nishijima Roshi, thirty-four volumes

These volumes are obtainable from the publisher, whose name and address is as follows:

Kanazawa Bunko Co. Ltd., Sumitomo Ichigaya Bldg., Honmura-cho 1-1, Ichigaya, Shinjuku-ku, Tokyo
Tel: (03) 3235-7060
Fax: (03) 3235-7135

Bibliography Four: Main English References:

Kenkyusha's New Japanese-English Dictionary: editor in chief, Koh Masuda

Japanese Character Dictionary: Andrew Nelson, published by Charles Tuttle

Japanese Character Dictionary: Mark Spahn/Wolfgang Hadamitzky, published by Nichigai Asssociates

Japanese English Buddhist Dictionary [JEBD]: published by Daito Shuppansha

A Sanskrit-English Dictionary [MW]: Sir Monier Monier-Williams, Oxford University Press

The Threefold Lotus Sutra [LSW]: Kato and Soothill, published by Weatherhill

The Historical Buddha [HB]: H.W. Schumann, published by Arkana

PRODUCTION NOTES:

This book was designed by Michael Luetchford and produced by Michael Luetchford and Jeremy Pearson. Typesetting was done entirely on an Apple Macintosh system using Microsoft Word, and output to a Fuji-Xerox Laserwind 1040PS laser printer.

New kanji Postscript characters were created using the Gaiji Edit Kit from Enfour Media Laboratory, Tokyo. Sanskrit fonts were created and supplied by Lew Mark-Andrews of Image Arts Inc., Tokyo.

The text and display typeface is Palatino.

Front cover: Portrait of Master Dogen Viewing the Moon, reproduced courtesy of Hokyo-ji, Fukui Prefecture.

Back cover: Portion of a scroll of *Fukan-zazengi,* believed to be in Master Dogen's own hand.